Practical Predictive Analytics

Back to the future with R, Spark, and more!

Ralph Winters

BIRMINGHAM - MUMBAI

Practical Predictive Analytics

First published: June 2017

Production reference: 1300617

Published by Packt Publishing Ltd.
Livery Place
35 Livery Street
Birmingham
B3 2PB, UK.
ISBN 978-1-78588-618-8

www.packtpub.com

Credits

Author
Ralph Winters

Reviewers
Alberto Boschetti
Armando Fandango

Commissioning Editor
Veena Pagare

Acquisition Editor
Chandan Kumar

Content Development Editor
Amrita Noronha

Technical Editor
Sneha Hanchate

Copy Editor
Saafis Editing

Project Coordinator
Shweta H Birwatkar

Proofreader
Safis Editing

Indexer
Mariammal Chettiyar

Graphics
Tania Dutta

Production Coordinator
Melwyn Dsa

About the Author

Ralph Winters started his career as a database researcher for a music performing rights organization (he composed as well!), and then branched out into healthcare survey research, finally landing in the Analytics and Information technology world. He has provided his statistical and analytics expertise to many large fortune 500 companies in the financial, direct marketing, insurance, healthcare, and pharmaceutical industries. He has worked on many diverse types of predictive analytics projects involving customer retention, anti-money laundering, voice of the customer text mining analytics, and health care risk and customer choice models.

He is currently data architect for a healthcare services company working in the data and advanced analytics group. He enjoys working collaboratively with a smart team of business analysts, technologists, actuaries as well as with other data scientists.

Ralph considered himself a practical person. In addition to authoring *Practical Predictive Analytics* for Packt Publishing, he has also contributed two tutorials illustrating the use of predictive analytics in Medicine and Healthcare in *Practical Predictive Analytics and Decisioning Systems for Medicine: Miner et al., Elsevier September, 2014*, and also presented *Practical Text Mining with SQL using Relational Databases*, at the 2013 11th Annual Text and Social Analytics Summit in Cambridge, MA.

Ralph resides in New Jersey with his loving wife Katherine, amazing daughters Claire and Anna, and his four-legged friends, Bubba and Phoebe, who can be unpredictable.

Ralph's web site can be found at `ralphwinters.com`.

About the Reviewers

Armando Fandango serves as chief technology officer of REAL Inc., building AI-based products and platforms for making smart connections between brands, agencies, publishers, and audiences. Armando founded NeuraSights with the goal of creating insights from small and big data using neural networks and machine learning. Previously, as chief data scientist and chief technology officer (CTO) for Epic Engineering and Consulting Group LLC, Armando worked with government agencies and large private organizations to build smart products by incorporating machine learning, big data engineering, enterprise data repositories, and enterprise dashboards. Armando has led data science and engineering teams as head of data for Sonobi Inc., driving big data and predictive analytics technology and strategy for JetStream, Sonobi's AdTech platform. Armando has managed high-performance computing (HPC) consulting and infrastructure for the Advanced Research Computing Centre at UCF. Armando has also been advising high-tech startups Quantfarm, Cortxia Foundation, and Studyrite as an advisory board member and AI expert. Armando has authored a book titled *Python Data Analysis - Second Edition* and has published research in international journals and conferences.

Alberto Boschetti is a data scientist, with strong expertise in signal processing and statistics. He holds a Ph.D. in telecommunication engineering and currently lives and works in London. In his work projects, he daily faces challenges spanning among natural language processing (NLP), machine learning, and distributed processing. He is very passionate about his job and he always tries to be updated on the latest developments in data science technologies, attending meetups, conferences, and other events. He is the author of *Python Data Science Essentials*, *Regression Analysis with Python* and *Large Scale Machine Learning with Python*, all published by Packt.

www.PacktPub.com

https://www.packtpub.com/mapt

Get the most in-demand software skills with Mapt. Mapt gives you full access to all Packt books and video courses, as well as industry-leading tools to help you plan your personal development and advance your career.

Why subscribe?

- Fully searchable across every book published by Packt
- Copy and paste, print, and bookmark content
- On demand and accessible via a web browser

Customer Feedback

Thanks for purchasing this Packt book. At Packt, quality is at the heart of our editorial process. To help us improve, please leave us an honest review on this book's Amazon page at https://www.amazon.com/dp/1785886185.

If you'd like to join our team of regular reviewers, you can e-mail us at customerreviews@packtpub.com. We award our regular reviewers with free eBooks and videos in exchange for their valuable feedback. Help us be relentless in improving our products!

Table of Contents

Preface

This is a different kind of predictive analytics book. My original intention was to introduce predictive analytics techniques targeted towards legacy analytics folks, using open source tools.

However, I soon realized that they were certain aspects of legacy analytics tools that could benefit the new generation of data scientists. Having worked a large part of my career in enterprise data solutions, I was interested in writing about some different kinds of topics, such as analytics methodologies, agile, metadata, SQL analytics, and reproducible research, which are often neglected in some data science/predictive analytics books, but still critical to the success of analytics project.

I also wanted to write about some underrepresented analytics techniques that extend beyond standard regression and classification tasks, such as using survival analysis to predict customer churn, and using market basket analysis as a recommendation engine.

Since there is a lot of movement towards cloud-based solutions, I thought it was important to include some chapters on cloud based analytics (big data), so I included several chapters on developing predictive analytics solutions within a Spark environment.

Whatever your orientation is, a key point of this book is collaboration, and I hope that regardless of your definition of data science, predictive analytics, big data, or even a benign term such as forecasting, you will find something here that suits your needs.

Furthermore, I wanted to pay homage to the domain expert as part of the data science team. Often, these analysts are not given fancy titles, but business analysts, can make the difference between a successful analytics project and one that falls flat on its face. Hopefully, some of the topics I discuss will strike a chord with them, and get them more interested in some of the technical concepts of predictive analytics.

When I was asked by Packt to write a book about predictive analytics, I first wondered what would be a good open source language to bridge the gap between legacy analytics and today's data scientist world. I thought about this considerably, since each language brings its own nuances in terms of how solutions to problems are expressed. However, I decided ultimately not to sweat the details, since predictive analytics concepts are not language-dependent, and the choice of language often is determined by personal preference as well as what is in use within the company in which you work.

I chose the R language because my background is in statistics, and I felt that R had good statistical rigor and now has reasonable integration with propriety software such as SAS, and also has good integration with relational database systems, as well as web protocols. It also has an excellent plotting and visualization system, and along with its many good user contributed packages, covers most statistical and predictive analytics tasks.

Regarding statistics, I suggest that you learn as much statistics as you can. Knowing statistics can help you separate good models from bad, and help you identify many problems in bad data just by understanding basic concepts such as measures of central tendencies (mean, median, mode), hypothesis testing, p-values, and effect sizes. It will also help you shy away from merely running a package in an automated way, and help you look a little at what is under the hood.

One downside to R is that it processes data in memory, so the software can limit the size of potentially larger datasets when used on a single PC. For the datasets we use in this book, there should be no problems running R on a single PC. If you are interested in analyzing big data, I do spend several chapters discussing R and Spark within a cloud environment, in which you can processes very large datasets that are distributed between many different computers.

Speaking of the datasets used in this book, I did not want to use the same datasets that you see analyzed repeatedly. Some of these are datasets are excellent for demonstrating techniques, but I wanted some alternatives. However, I did not see a whole lot of them that I thought would be useful for this book. Some were from unknown sources, some needed formal permission to use, some lacked a good data dictionary. So, for many chapters, I ended up generating my own data using simulation techniques in R. I believe that was a good choice, since it enabled me to introduce some data generating techniques that you can use in your own work.

The data I used covers a good spectrum of marketing, retail and healthcare applications. I also would have liked to include some financial predictive analytics use cases but ran out of time. Maybe I will leave that for another book!

What this book covers

Chapter 1, *Getting Started with Predictive Analytics*, begins with a little bit of history of how predictive analytics developed. We then discuss some different roles of predictive analytics practitioners, and describe the industries in which they work. Ways to organize predictive analytic projects on a PC is discussed next, the R language is introduced, and we end the chapter with a short example of a predictive model.

Chapter 2, *The Modeling Process,* discusses how the development of predictive models can be organized into a series of stages, each with different goals, such as exploration and problem definition, leading to the actual development of a predictive model. We discuss two important analytics methodologies, CRISP-DM and SEMMA. Code examples are sprinkled through the chapter to demonstrate some of the ideas central to the methodologies, so you will hopefully, never be bored...

Chapter 3, *Inputting and Exploring Data,* introduces various ways that you can bring your own input data into R. We also discuss various data preparation techniques using standard SQL functions as well as analogous methods using the R dplyr package. Have no data to input? No problem. We will show you how to generate your own human-like data using the R package wakefield.

Chapter 4, *Introduction to Regression Algorithms,* begins with a discussion of supervised versus unsupervised algorithms. The rest of the chapter concentrates on regression algorithms, which represent the supervised algorithm category. You will learn about interpreting regression output such as model coefficients and residual plots. There is even an interactive game that supplies an interact test to see if you can determine if a series of residuals are random or not.

Chapter 5, *Introduction to Decision trees, Clustering, and SVM,* concentrates on three other core predictive algorithms that have widespread use, and, along with regression, can be used to solve many, if not most, of your predictive analytics problems. The last algorithm discussed, Support Vector Machines (SVMs), are often used with high-dimensional data, such as unstructured text, so we will accompany this example with some text mining techniques using some customer complaint comments.

Chapter 6, *Using Survival Analysis to Predict and Analyze Customer Churn,* discusses a specific modeling technique known as survival analysis and follows a hypothetical customer marketing satisfaction and retention example. We will also delve more deeply into simulating customer choice using some sampling functions available in R.

Chapter 7, *Using Market Basket Analysis as a Recommender Engine,* introduces the concept of association rules and market basket analysis, and steps you through some techniques that can predict future purchases based upon various combinations of previous purchases from an online retail store. It also introduces some text analytics techniques coupled with some cluster analysis that places various customers into different segments. You will learn some additional data cleaning techniques, and learn how to generate some interesting association plots.

Chapter 8, *Exploring Health Care Enrollment Data as a Time Series*, introduces time series analytics. Healthcare enrollment data from the CMS website is first explored. Then we move on to defining some basic time series concepts such as simple and exponential moving averages. Finally, we work with the R forecast package which, as its name implies, helps you to perform some time series forecasting.

Chapter 9, *Introduction to Spark Using R*, introduces RSpark, which is an environment for accessing large Spark clusters using R. No local version of R needs to be installed. It also introduces Databricks, which is a cloud-based environment for running R (as well as Python, SQL, and other language), against Spark-based big data. This chapter also demonstrates techniques for transforming small datasets into larger Spark clusters using the Pima Indians Diabetes database as reference.

Chapter 10, *Exploring Large Datasets Using Spark*, shows how to perform some exploratory data analysis using a combination of RSpark and Spark SQL using the Pima Indians Diabetes data loaded into Spark. We will learn the basics of exploring Spark data using some Spark-specific commands that allow us to filter, group and summarize, and visualize our Spark data.

Chapter 11, *Spark Machine Learning – Regression and Cluster Models*, covers machine learning by first illustrating a logistic regression model that has been built using a Spark cluster. We will learn how to split Spark data into training and test data in Spark, run a logistic regression model, and then evaluate its performance.

Chapter 12, *Spark Models - Rules-Based Learning*, teaches you how to run decision tree models in Spark using the Stop and Frisk dataset. You will learn how to overcome some of the algorithmic limitations of the Spark MLlib environment by extracting some cluster samples to your local machine and then run some non-Spark algorithms that you are already familiar with. This chapter will also introduce you to a new rule-based algorithm, OneR, and will also demonstrate how you can mix different languages together in Spark, such as mixing R, SQL, and even Python code together in the same notebook using the %magic directive.

What you need for this book

This is neither an introductory predictive analytics book, not an introductory book for learning R or Spark. Some knowledge of base R data manipulation techniques is expected. Some prior knowledge of predictive analytics is useful. As mentioned earlier, knowledge of basic statistical concepts such as hypothesis testing, correlation, means, standard deviations, and p-values will also help you navigate this book.

Who this book is for

This book is for those who have already had an introduction to R, and are looking to learn how to develop enterprise predictive analytics solutions. Additionally, traditional business analysts and managers who wish to extend their skills into predictive analytics using open source R may find the book useful. Existing predictive analytic practitioners who know another language, or those who wish to learn about analytics using Spark, will also find the chapters on Spark and R beneficial.

Conventions

In this book, you will find a number of styles of text that distinguish between different kinds of information. Here are some examples of these styles, and an explanation of their meaning.

Code words in text, database table names, folder names, filenames, file extensions, pathnames, dummy URLs, user input, and Twitter handles are shown as follows:

"Save all output to the /PracticalPredictiveAnalytics/Outputs directory."

A block of code is set as follows:

```
#run the model
model <- OneR(train_data, frisked ~ ., verbose = TRUE)
#summarize the model
summary(model)
#run the sql function from the SparkR package
SparkR::sql("SELECT sample_bin , count(*)
\FROM out_tbl group by sample_bin")
```

When we wish to draw your attention to a particular part of a code block, the relevant lines or items are set in bold:

```
#note we are specifing the SparkR filter, not the dplyr filer
head(SparkR::filter(out_sd1,out_sd1$sample_bin==1),1000)
```

Any command-line, (including commands at the R console) input or output is written as follows:

```
> summary(xchurn)
```

New terms and **important words** are shown in bold. Words that you see on the screen, in menus or dialog boxes for example, appear in the text like this: "Clicking the **Next** button moves you to the next screen."

Warnings or important notes appear in a box like this.

Tips and tricks appear like this.

Reader feedback

Feedback from our readers is always welcome. Let us know what you think about this book-what you liked or disliked. Reader feedback is important for us as it helps us develop titles that you will really get the most out of. To send us general feedback, simply e-mail feedback@packtpub.com, and mention the book's title in the subject of your message. If there is a topic that you have expertise in and you are interested in either writing or contributing to a book, see our author guide at www.packtpub.com/authors.

Customer support

Now that you are the proud owner of a Packt book, we have a number of things to help you to get the most from your purchase.

Downloading the example code

You can download the example code files for this book from your account at http://www.packtpub.com. If you purchased this book elsewhere, you can visit http://www.packtpub.com/support and register to have the files e-mailed directly to you.

You can download the code files by following these steps:

1. Log in or register to our website using your e-mail address and password.
2. Hover the mouse pointer on the **SUPPORT** tab at the top.
3. Click on **Code Downloads & Errata**.
4. Enter the name of the book in the **Search** box.

5. Select the book for which you're looking to download the code files.
6. Choose from the drop-down menu where you purchased this book from.
7. Click on **Code Download**.

Once the file is downloaded, please make sure that you unzip or extract the folder using the latest version of:

- WinRAR / 7-Zip for Windows
- Zipeg / iZip / UnRarX for Mac
- 7-Zip / PeaZip for Linux

The code bundle for the book is also hosted on GitHub at `https://github.com/PacktPubl ishing/Practical-Predictive-Analytics`. We also have other code bundles from our rich catalog of books and videos available at `https://github.com/PacktPublishing/`. Check them out!

Downloading the color images of this book

We also provide you with a PDF file that has color images of the screenshots/diagrams used in this book. The color images will help you better understand the changes in the output. You can download this file from `https://www.packtpub.com/sites/default/files/down loads/PracticalPredictiveAnalytics_ColorImages.pdf`.

Errata

Although we have taken every care to ensure the accuracy of our content, mistakes do happen. If you find a mistake in one of our books-maybe a mistake in the text or the code-we would be grateful if you could report this to us. By doing so, you can save other readers from frustration and help us improve subsequent versions of this book. If you find any errata, please report them by visiting `http://www.packtpub.com/submit-errata`, selecting your book, clicking on the **Errata Submission Form** link, and entering the details of your errata. Once your errata are verified, your submission will be accepted and the errata will be uploaded to our website or added to any list of existing errata under the Errata section of that title.

To view the previously submitted errata, go to `https://www.packtpub.com/books/conten t/support` and enter the name of the book in the search field. The required information will appear under the **Errata** section.

Piracy

Piracy of copyrighted material on the Internet is an ongoing problem across all media. At Packt, we take the protection of our copyright and licenses very seriously. If you come across any illegal copies of our works in any form on the Internet, please provide us with the location address or website name immediately so that we can pursue a remedy.

Please contact us at `copyright@packtpub.com` with a link to the suspected pirated material.

We appreciate your help in protecting our authors and our ability to bring you valuable content.

Questions

If you have a problem with any aspect of this book, you can contact us at `questions@packtpub.com`, and we will do our best to address the problem.

1
Getting Started with Predictive Analytics

"In God we trust, all others must bring Data"

- Deming

I enjoy working and explaining predictive analytics to people because it is based upon a simple concept: predicting the probability of future events based upon historical data. Its history may date back to at least 650 BC. Some early examples include the Babylonians, who tried to predict short-term weather changes based on cloud appearances and halos: *Weather Forecasting through the Ages, NASA*.

Medicine also has a long history of needing to classify diseases. The Babylonian king Adad-apla-iddina decreed that medical records be collected to form the *Diagnostic Handbook*. Some predictions in this corpus list treatments based on the number of days the patient had been sick, and their pulse rate (Linda Miner et al., 2014). One of the first instances of bioinformatics!

In later times, specialized predictive analytics was developed at the onset of the insurance underwriting industries. This was used as a way to predict the risk associated with insuring marine vessels (https://www.lloyds.com/lloyds/about-us/history/corporate-history). At about the same time, life insurance companies began predicting the age that a person would live to in order to set the most appropriate premium rates.

Although the idea of prediction always seemed to be rooted early in the human need to understand and classify, it was not until the 20th century, and the advent of modern computing, that it really took hold.

In addition to helping the US government in the 1940s break code, Alan Turing also worked on the initial computer chess algorithms that pitted man against machine. Monte Carlo simulation methods originated as part of the Manhattan project, where mainframe computers crunched numbers for days in order to determine the probability of nuclear attacks (Computing and the Manhattan Project, n.d).

In the 1950s, **Operations Research** (**OR**) theory developed, in which one could optimize the shortest distance between two points. To this day, these techniques are used in logistics by companies such as UPS and Amazon.

Non-mathematicians have also gotten in on the act. In the 1970s, cardiologist Lee Goldman (who worked aboard a submarine) spend years developing a decision tree that did this efficiently. This helped the staff determine whether or not the submarine needed to resurface in order to help the chest pain sufferers (Gladwell, 2005)!

What many of these examples had in common was that people first made observations about events which had already occurred, and then used this information to generalize and then make decisions about might occur in the future. Along with prediction, came further understanding of cause and effect and how the various parts of the problem were interrelated. Discovery and insight came about through methodology and adhering to the scientific method.

Most importantly, they came about in order to find solutions to important, and often practical, problems of the times. That is what made them unique.

Predictive analytics are in so many industries

We have come a long way since then, and practical analytics solutions have furthered growth in so many different industries. The internet has had a profound effect on this; it has enabled every click to be stored and analyzed. More data is being collected and stored, some with very little effort, than ever before. That in itself has enabled more industries to enter predictive analytics.

Predictive Analytics in marketing

One industry that has embraced PA for quite a long time is marketing. Marketing has always been concerned with customer acquisition and retention, and has developed predictive models involving various promotional offers and customer touch points, all geared to keeping customers and acquiring new ones. This is very pronounced in certain segments of marking, such as wireless and online shopping cards, in which customers are always searching for the best deal.

Specifically, advanced analytics can help answer questions such as, *If I offer a customer 10% off with free shipping, will that yield more revenue than 15% off with no free shipping?* The 360-degree view of the customer has expanded the number of ways one can engage with the customer, therefore enabling marketing mix and attribution modeling to become increasingly important. Location-based devices have enabled marketing predictive applications to incorporate real-time data to issue recommendation to the customer while in the store.

Predictive Analytics in healthcare

Predictive analytics in healthcare has its roots in clinical trials, which use carefully selected samples to test the efficacy of drugs and treatments. However, healthcare has been going beyond this. With the advent of sensors, data can be incorporated into predictive analytics to monitor patients with critical illness, and to send alerts to the patient when he is at risk. Healthcare companies can now predict which individual patients will comply with courses of treatment advocated by health providers. This will send early warning signs to all parties, which will prevent future complications, as well as lower the total cost of treatment.

Predictive Analytics in other industries

Other examples can be found in just about every other industry. Here are just a few:

- Finance:
    - Fraud detection is a huge area. Financial institutions are able to monitor client's internal and external transactions for fraud, through pattern recognition and other machine learning algorithms, and then alert a customer concerning suspicious activity. Analytics are often performed in real time. This is a big advantage, as criminals can be very sophisticated and be one step ahead of the previous analysis.

- Wall street program trading. Trading algorithms will predict intraday highs and lows, and will decide when to buy and sell securities.
- Sports management:
    - Sports management analytics is able to predict which sports events will yield the greatest attendance and institute variable ticket pricing based upon audience interest.
    - In baseball, a pitcher's entire game can be recorded and then digitally analyzed. Sensors can also be attached to their arm, to alert when future injury might occur .
- Higher education:
    - Colleges can predict how many, and which kind of, students are likely to attend the next semester, and be able to plan resources accordingly. This is a challenge which is beginning to surface now, many schools may be looking at how scoring changes made to the SAT in 2016 are affecting admissions.
    - Time-based assessments of online modules can enable professors to identify students' potential problems areas, and tailor individual instruction.
- Government:
    - Federal and State Governments have embraced the open data concept and have made more data available to the public, which has empowered *Citizen Data Scientists* to help solve critical social and governmental problems.
    - The potential use of data for the purpose of emergency services, traffic safety, and healthcare use is overwhelmingly positive.

Although these industries can be quite different, the goals of predictive analytics are typically implemented to increase revenue, decrease costs, or alter outcomes for the better.

Skills and roles that are important in Predictive Analytics

So what skills do you need to be successful in predictive analytics? I believe that there are three basic skills that are needed:

- **Algorithmic/statistical/programming skills**: These are the actual technical skills needed to implement a technical solution to a problem. I bundle these all together since these skills are typically used in tandem. Will it be a purely statistical solution, or will there need to be a bit of programming thrown in to customize an algorithm, and clean the data? There are always multiple ways of doing the same task and it will be up to you, the predictive modeler, to determine how it is to be done.

- **Business skills**: These are the skills needed for communicating thoughts and ideas among groups of the interested parties. Business and data analysts who have worked in certain industries for long periods of time, and know their business very well, are increasingly being called upon to participate in predictive analytics projects. Data science is becoming a team sport and most projects include working with others in the organization, summarizing findings, and having good presentation and documentation skills are important. You will often hear the term domain knowledge associated with this. Domain knowledge is important since it allows you to apply your particular analytics skills to the particular analytic problems of whatever business you are (or wish to) work within. Everyone business has its own nuances when it comes to solving analytic problems. If you do not have the time or inclination to learn all about the inner workings of the problem at hand yourself, partner with someone who does. That will be the start of a great team!

- **Data storage/Extract Transform and Load (ETL) skills**: This can refer to specialized knowledge regarding extracting data, and storing it in a relational or non-relational NoSQL data store. Historically, these tasks were handled exclusively within a data warehouse. But now that the age of big data is upon us, specialists have emerged who understand the intricacies of data storage, and the best way to organize it.

Related job skills and terms

Along with the term predictive analytics, here are some terms that are very much related:

- **Predictive modeling**: This specifically means using a mathematical/statistical model to predict the likelihood of a dependent or target variable. You may still be able to predict; however, if there is no underlying model, it is not a predictive model.
- **Artificial intelligence (AI)**: A broader term for how machines are able to rationalize and solve problems. AI's early days were rooted in neural networks.
- **Machine learning**: A subset of AI. Specifically deals with how a machine learns automatically from data, usually to try to replicate human decision-making or to best it. At this point, everyone knows about Watson, who beat two human opponents in Jeopardy.
- **Data science**: Data science encompasses predictive analytics but also adds algorithmic development via coding, and good presentation skills via visualization.
- **Data engineering**: Data engineering concentrates on data extraction and data preparation processes, which allow raw data to be transformed into a form suitable for analytics. A knowledge of system architecture is important. The data engineer will typically produce the data to be used by the predictive analysts (or data scientists).
- **Data analyst/business analyst/domain expert**: This is an umbrella term for someone who is well versed in the way the business at hand works, and is an invaluable person to learn from in terms of what may have meaning, and what may not.
- **Statistics**: The classical form of inference, typically done via hypothesis testing. Statistics also forms the basis for the probability distributions used in machine learning, and is closely tied with predictive analytics and data science.

Predictive analytics software

Originally, predictive analytics was performed by hand, by statisticians on mainframe computers using a progression of various language such as FORTRAN. Some of these languages are still very much in use today. FORTRAN, for example, is still one of the fastest-performing languages around, and operates with very little memory. So, although it may no longer be as widespread in predictive model development as other languages, it certain can be used to implement models in a production environment.

Nowadays, there are many choices about which software to use, and many loyalists remain true to their chosen software. The reality is that for solving a specific type of predictive analytics problem, there exists a certain amount of overlap, and certainly the goal is the same. Once you get the hang of the methodologies used for predictive analytics in one software package, it should be fairly easy to translate your skills to another package.

Open source software

Open source emphasizes agile development and community sharing. Of course, open source software is free, but free must also be balanced in the context of **Total Cost Of Ownership** (**TCO**). TCO costs include everything that is factored into a software's cost over a period of time: that not only includes the cost of the software itself, but includes training, infrastructure setup, maintenance, people costs, as well as other expenses associated with the quick upgrade and development cycles which exist in some products.

Closed source software

Closed source (or proprietary) software such as SAS and SPSS was at the forefront of predictive analytics, and has continued to this day to extend its reach beyond the traditional realm of statistics and machine learning. Closed source software emphasizes stability, better support, and security, with better memory management, which are important factors for some companies.

Peaceful coexistence

There is much debate nowadays regarding which one is better. My prediction is that they both will coexist peacefully, with one not replacing the other. Data sharing and common APIs will become more common. Each has its place within the data architecture and ecosystem that are deemed correct for a company. Each company will emphasize certain factors, and both open and closed software systems are constantly improving themselves. So, in terms of learning one or the other, it is not an either/or decision. Predictive analytics, per second does not care what software you use. Please be open to the advantages offered by both open and closed software. If you do, that will certainly open up possibilities for working for different kinds of companies and technologies

Other helpful tools

Man does not live by bread alone, so it would behave you to learn additional tools in addition to R, so as to advance your analytic skills:

- **SQL**: SQL is a valuable tool to know, regardless of which language/package/environment you choose to work in. Virtually every analytics tool will have a SQL interface, and knowledge of how to optimize SQL queries will definitely speed up your productivity, especially if you are doing a lot of data extraction directly from a SQL database. Today's common thought is to do as much pre-processing as possible within the database, so if you will be doing a lot of extracting from databases such as MySQL, PostgreSQL, Oracle, or Teradata, it will be a good thing to learn how queries are optimized within their native framework.
  In the R language, there are several SQL packages that are useful for interfacing with various external databases. We will be using `sqldf`, which is a popular R package for interfacing with R dataframes. There are other packages that are specifically tailored for the specific database you will be working with.
- **Web extraction tools**: Not every data source will originate from a data warehouse. Knowledge of APIs that extract data from the internet will be valuable to know. Some popular tools include Curl and Jsonlite.
- **Spreadsheets**: Despite their problems, spreadsheets are often the fastest way to do quick data analysis and, more importantly, enable you to share your results with others! R offers several interfaces to spreadsheets but, again, learning standalone spreadsheet skills such as pivot tables and Virtual Basic for applications will give you an advantage if you work for corporations in which these skills are heavily used.
- **Data visualization tools**: Data visualization tools are great for adding impact to an analysis, and for concisely encapsulating complex information. Native R visualization tools are great, but not every company will be using R. Learn some third-party visualization tools such as D3.js, Google Charts, Qlikview, or Tableau.
- **Big data, Spark, Hadoop, NoSQL database**: It is becoming increasingly important to know a little bit about these technologies, at least from the viewpoint of having to extract and analyze data that resides within these frameworks. Many software packages have APIs that talk directly to Hadoop and can run predictive analytics directly within the native environment, or extract data and perform the analytics locally.

Past the basics

Given that the predictive analytics space is so huge, once you are past the basics, ask yourself what area of predictive analytics really interests you, and what you would like to specialize in. Learning all you can about everything concerning predictive analytics is good at the beginning, but ultimately you will be called upon because you are an expert in certain industries or techniques. This could be research, algorithmic development, or even managing analytics teams.

Data analytics/research

But, as general guidance, if you are involved in, or are oriented toward, data, the analytics or research portion of data science, I would suggest that you concentrate on data mining methodologies and specific data modeling techniques that are heavily prevalent in the specific industries that interest you.

For example, logistic regression is heavily used in the insurance industry, but social network analysis is not. Economic research is geared toward time series analysis, but not so much cluster analysis. Recommender engines are prevalent in online retail.

Data engineering

If you are involved more on the data engineering side, concentrate more on data cleaning, being able to integrate various data sources, and the tools needed to accomplish this.

Management

If you are a manager, concentrate on model development, testing and control, metadata, and presenting results to upper management in order to demonstrate value or return on investment.

Team data science

Of course, predictive analytics is becoming more of a team sport, rather than a solo endeavor, and the data science team is very much alive. There is a lot that has been written about the components of a data science team, much of which can be reduced to the three basic skills that I outlined earlier.

Two different ways to look at predictive analytics

Various industries interpret the goals of predictive analytics differently. For example, social science and marketing like to understand the factors which go into a model, and can sacrifice a bit of accuracy if a model can be explained well enough. On the other hand, a black box stock trading model is more interested in minimizing the number of bad trades, and at the end of the day tallies up the gains and losses, not really caring which parts of the trading algorithm worked. Accuracy is more important in the end.

Depending upon how you intend to approach a particular problem, look at how two different analytical mindsets can affect the predictive analytics process:

1. **Minimize prediction error goal**: This is a very common use case for machine learning. The initial goal is to predict using the appropriate algorithms in order to minimize the prediction error. If done incorrectly, an algorithm will ultimately fail and it will need to be continually optimized to come up with the *new* best algorithm. If this is performed mechanically without regard to understanding the model, this will certainly result in failed outcomes. Certain models, especially over optimized ones with many variables, can have a very high prediction rate, but be unstable in a variety of ways. If one does not have an understanding of the model, it can be difficult to react to changes in the data input.

2. **Understanding model goal**: This came out of the scientific method and is tied closely to the concept of hypothesis testing. This can be done in certain kinds of models, such as regression and decision trees, and is more difficult in other kinds of models such as **Support Vector Machine** (**SVM**) and **neural networks**. In the understanding model paradigm, understanding causation or impact becomes more important than optimizing correlations. Typically, understanding models has a lower prediction rate, but has the advantage of knowing more about the causations of the individual parts of the model, and how they are related. For example, industries that rely on understanding human behavior emphasize understanding model goals. A limitation to this orientation is that we might tend to discard results that are not immediately understood. It takes discipline to accept a model with lower prediction ability. However, you can also gain model stability

Of course, the previous examples illustrate two disparate approaches. Combination models, which use the best of both worlds, should be the ones we should strive for. Therefore, one goal for a final model is one which:

- Has an acceptable prediction error
- Is stable over time

- Needs a minimum of maintenance
- Is simple enough to understand and explain.

You will learn later that is this related to Bias/Variance tradeoff.

R

Most of the code examples in this book are written in R. As a prerequisite to this book, it is presumed that you will have some basic R knowledge, as well as some exposure to statistics. If you already know about R, you may skip this section, but I wanted to discuss it a little bit for completeness.

The R language is derived from the S language which was developed in the 1970s. However, the R language has grown beyond the original core packages to become an extremely viable environment for predictive analytics.

Although R was developed by statisticians for statisticians, it has come a long way since its early days. The strength of R comes from its *package* system, which allows specialized or enhanced functionality to be developed and linked to the core system.

Although the original R system was sufficient for statistics and data mining, an important goal of R was to have its system enhanced via user-written contributed packages. At the time of writing, the R system contains more than 10,000 packages. Some are of excellent quality, and some are of dubious quality. Therefore, the goal is to find the truly useful packages that add the most value.

Most, if not all, R packages in use address most common predictive analytics tasks that you will encounter. If you come across a task that does not fit into any category, the chances are good that someone in the R community has done something similar. And of course, there is always a chance that someone is developing a package to do exactly what you want it to do. That person could be eventually be you!

CRAN

The **Comprehensive R Archive Network** (**CRAN**) is a go-to site which aggregates R distributions, binaries, documentation, and packages. To get a sense of the kind of packages that could be valuable to you, check out the **Task Views** section maintained by CRAN here:

```
https://cran.r-project.org/web/views/
```

R installation

R installation is typically done by downloading the software directly from the **Comprehensive R Archive Network (CRAN)** site:

1. Navigate to `https://cran.r-project.org/`.
2. Install the version of R appropriate for your operating system. Please read any notes regarding downloading specific versions. For example, if you are a Mac user may need to have XQuartz installed in addition to R, so that some graphics can render correctly.

Alternate ways of exploring R

Although installing R directly from the CRAN site is the way most people will proceed, I wanted to mention some alternative R installation methods. These methods are often good in instances when you are not always at your computer:

- **Virtual environment**: Here are a few ways to install R in the virtual environment:
  - VirtualBox or VMware: Virtual environments are good for setting up protected environments and loading preinstalled operating systems and packages. Some advantages are that they are good for isolating testing areas, and when you do not wish to take up additional space on your own machine.
  - Docker: Docker resembles a virtual machine, but is a bit more lightweight since it does not emulate an entire operating system, but emulates only the needed processes.
- **Cloud-based**: Here are a few methods to install R in the cloud-based environment. Cloud based environments as perfect for working in situations when you are not working directly on your computer:
  - AWS/Azure: These are three environments which are very popular. Reasons for using cloud based environments are similar to the reasons given for virtual environment, but also have some additional advantages: such as the additional capability to run with very large datasets and with more memory. All of the previously mentioned require a subscription service to use, however free tiers are offered to get started. We will explore Databricks in depth in later chapters, when we learn about predictive analytics using R and SparkR

- **Web-based**: Web-based platforms are good for learning R and for trying out quick programs and analysis. R-Fiddle is a good choice, however there are other including: R-Web, Jupyter, Tutorialspoint, and Anaconda Cloud.
- **Command line**: R can be run purely from a command line. When R is run this way, it is usually coupled with other Linux tools such as `curl`, `grep`, `awk`, and various customized text editors, such as **Emacs Speaks Statistics (ESS)**. Often R is run this way in production mode, when processes need to be automated and scheduled directly via the operating system

How is a predictive analytics project organized?

After you install R on your own machine, I would give some thought to how you want to organize your data, code, documentation, and so on. There will probably be many different kinds of projects that you will need to set up, ranging from exploratory analysis to full production-grade implementations. However, most projects will be somewhere in the middle, that is, those projects that ask a specific question or a series of related questions. Whatever their purpose, each project you will work on will deserve its own project folder or directory.

Some important points to remember about constructing projects:

- It is never a good idea to boil the ocean, or try to answer too many questions at once. Remember, predictive analytics is an iterative process.
- Another trap that people fall into is not having their project reproducible. Nothing is worse than to develop some analytics on a set of data, and then backtrack, and oops! different results.
- When organizing code, try to write code as building block, which can be reusable. For R, write code liberally as functions.
- Assume that anything concerning requirements, data, and outputs will change, and be prepared.
- Considering the dynamic nature of the R language. Changes in versions, and packages could all change your analysis in various ways, so it is important to keep code and data in sync, by using separate folders for the different levels of code, data, and so on or by using version management packages such as `subversion`, `git`, or `cvs`.

Once you have considered all of the preceding points, physically set up your folder environment.

Setting up your project and subfolders

We will start by creating folders for our environment. Often projects start with three subfolders which roughly correspond to:

- Data source
- Code-generated outputs
- The code itself (in this case, R)

There may be more in certain cases, but let's keep it simple:

- First, decide where you will be housing your projects. Then create a sub-directory and name it `PracticalPredictiveAnalytics`. For this example, we will create the directory under Windows drive C.
- Create three subdirectories under this project: `Data`, `Outputs`, and `R`:
    - The `R` directory will hold all of our data prep code, algorithms, and so on.
    - The `Data` directory will contain our raw data sources that will typically be read in by our programs.
    - The `Outputs` directory will contain anything generated by the code. That can include plots, tables, listings, and output from the log.

Here is an example of how the structure will look after you have created the folders:

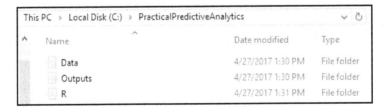

GUIs

R, like many languages and knowledge discovery systems, started from the command line. However, predictive analysts tend to prefer **Graphic User Interfaces (GUIs)**, and there are many choices available for each of the three different operating systems (Mac, Windows, and Linux). Each of them has its strengths and weaknesses, and of course there is always the question of preference.

Memory is always a consideration with R, and if that is of critical concern to you, you might want to go with a simpler GUI, such as the one built in with R.

If you want full control, and you want to add some productive tools, you could choose RStudio, which is a full-blown GUI and allows you to implement version control repositories, and has nice features such as code completion.

R Commander (Rcmdr), and **Rattle** unique features are that they offer menus that allow guided point and click commands for common statistical and data mining tasks. They are always both code generators. This is a way to start when learning R, since you can use the menus to accomplish the tasks, and then by looking at the way the code was generated for each particular task. If you are interested in predictive analytics using `Rattle`, I have written a nice tutorial on using R with `Rattle` which can be found in the tutorial section of *Practical Predictive Analytics and Decisioning Systems for Medicine*, which is referenced at the end of this chapter.

Both RCmdr and RStudio offer GUIs that are compatible with the Windows, Apple, and Linux operator systems, so those are the ones I will use to demonstrate examples in this book. But bear in mind that they are only user interfaces, and not R proper, so it should be easy enough to paste code examples into other GUIs and decide for yourself which ones you like.

Getting started with RStudio

After R installation has completed, point your browser to the download section found through the RStudio web site (`https://www.rstudio.com/`) and install the RStudio executable appropriate for your operating system:

- Click the **RStudio** icon to bring up the program.

- The program initially starts with three tiled window panes, as shown in the following screenshot. If the layout does not correspond exactly to what is shown, the next section will show you how to rearrange the layout to correspond with the examples shown in this chapter:

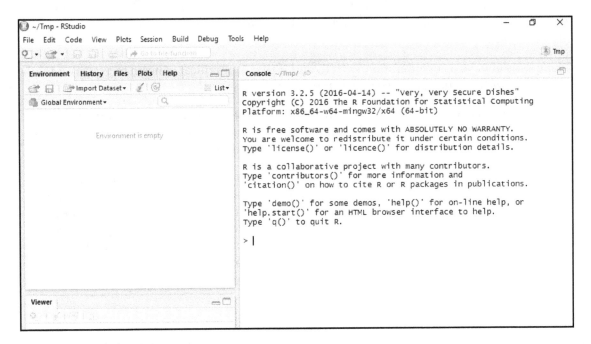

Rearranging the layout to correspond with the examples

To rearrange the layout, see the following steps:

1. Select **Tools | Global Options | Pane Layout** from the top navigation bar.
2. Select the drop-down arrow in each of the four quadrants, and change the title of each pane to what is shown in the following diagram.
    - Make sure that **Environment | History | Files | Plots** and **Help** are selected for the upper left pane
    - Make sure that **Viewer** is selected for the bottom left pane.
    - Select **Console** for the bottom right pane
    - Select **Source** for the upper right pane
3. Click **OK**.

After the changes are applied the layout should more closely match the layout previously shown . However, it may not match exactly. A lot will depend upon the version of RStudio that you are using as well as the packages you may have already installed.

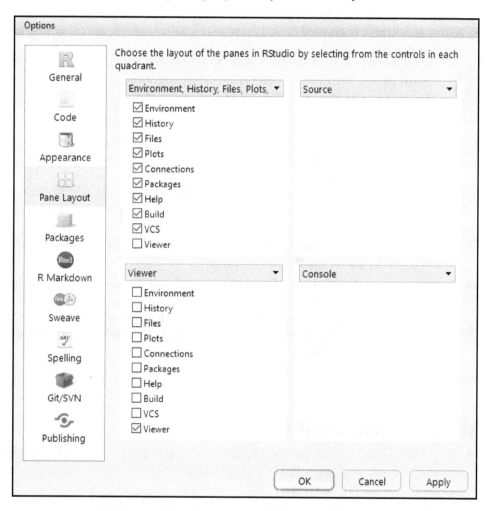

Brief description of some important panes

- The **Source** pane will be used to code and save your programs. Once code is created you can use **File | Save** to save your work to an external file, and **File | Open** to retrieve the saved code.

 If you are installing RStudio for the first time nothing may be shown as the fourth pane. However, as you create new programs (as we will later in this chapter), it will appear in the upper right quadrant.

- The **Console** pane provides important feedback and information about your program after it has been run. It will show you any syntax or error messages that have occurred. It is always a best practice to examine the console to make sure you are getting the results you expect, and make sure the console is clear of errors. The console is also the place that you will see a lots of output which has been created from your programs.
- We will rely heavily on the **View** pane. This pane displays formatted output which is run by using the R `View` command.
- The **Environment | History | Plots** pane is sort of a catch-all pane which changes functions depending upon what which tabs have been selected via the pane layout dialogue. For example, all plots issued by R command are displayed under the **Plots** tab. Help is always a click away by selecting the **Help** tab. There is also a useful tab called **Packages** which will automatically load a package, when a particular package is checked.

Creating a new project

Once you are set with your layout, proceed to create a new project by following these steps:

Create a new project by following these steps:

1. Identify the menu bar, above the icons at the top left of the screen.
2. Click **File** and then **New Project**
3. At the next screen select **Existing Directory**:

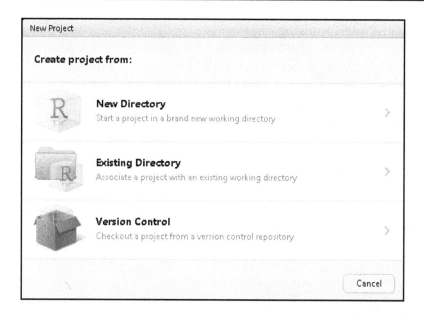

4. The following screen will appear:

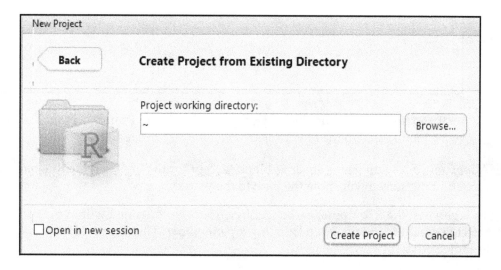

5. The **Project working directory** is initial populated with a tilde (~). This means that the project will be created in the directory you are currently in.
6. To specify the directory first select **Browse**, and then navigate to the `PracticalPredictiveAnalytics` folder you created in the previous steps.
7. When the **Choose Directory** dialog box appear, select this directory using the **Select Folder** button.
8. After selecting the directory, the following should appear (Windows only):

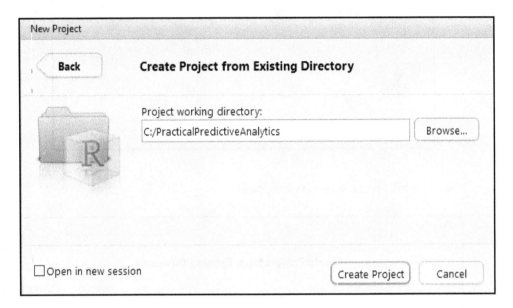

9. To finalize creating the project, Select the **Create Project** button. Rstudio will then switch to the new project you have just created.

All screen panes will then appear as blank (except for the log), and the title bar at the top left of the screen will show the path to the project.

To verify that the R, outputs, and data directories are contained within the project, select **File**, and then **File Open** from the top menu bar. The three folders should appear, as indicated as follows:

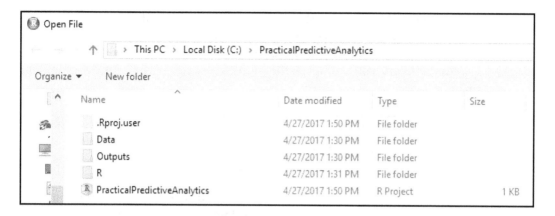

Once you have verified this, cancel the **Open File** dialogue, and return to RStudio main screen.

The R console

Now that we have created a project, let us take a look at the R Console window. Click on the window marked **Console**. All console commands are issued by typing your command following the command prompt >, and then pressing *Enter*. I will just illustrate three commands that will help you answer the questions "Which project am I on?", and "What files do I have in my folders?"

1. getwd(): The getwd() command is very important since it will always tell you which directory you are in. Since we just created a new project, we expect that we will be pointing to the directory we just created, right?
    To double check, switch over to the console, issue the getwd() command, and then press *Enter*. That should echo back the current working directory:

    ```
    > getwd()
    [1] "C:/PracticalPredictiveAnalytics"
    >
    ```

2. `dir()`: The `dir()` command will give you a list of all files in the current working directory. In our case, it is simply the names of the three directories you have just created. However, typically may see many files, usually corresponding to the type of directory you are in (`.R` for source files, `.dat`, `.csv` for data files, and so on):

```
> dir()
[1] "Data"                              "Outputs"
[3] "PracticalPredictiveAnalytics.Rproj" "R"
>
```

3. `setwd()`: Sometimes you will need to switch directories within the same project or even to another project. The command you will use is `setwd()`. You will supply the directory that you want to switch to, all contained within the parentheses.
Here is an example which will switch to the sub-directory which will house the R code. This particular example supplies the entire path as the directory destination. Since you are already in the `PracticalPredictiveAnalytics` directory, you can also use `setwd("R")` which accomplishes the same thing:

```
> setwd("C:/PracticalPredictiveAnalytics/R")
```

To verify that it has changed, issue the `getwd()` command again:

```
> getwd()
[1] "C:/PracticalPredictiveAnalytics/R"
```

I suggest using `getwd()` and `setwd()` liberally, especially if you are working on multiple projects, and want to avoid reading or writing the wrong files.

The source window

The **Source** window is where all of your R code appears. It is also where you will be probably spending most of your time. You can have several script windows open, all at once.

Creating a new script

To create a new script select **File | New File | R Script** from the top navigation bar. A new blank script window will appear with the name Untitled1.

Once it appears you can start entering code!

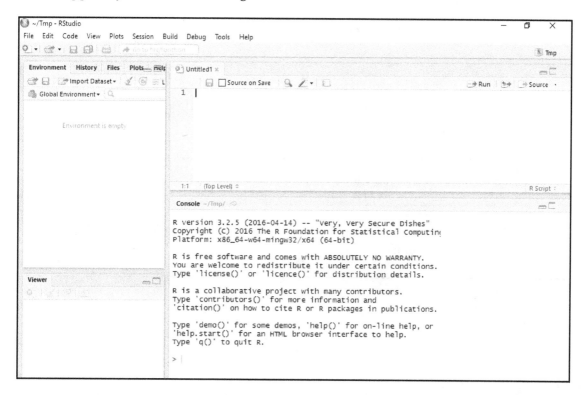

Our first predictive model

Now that all of the preliminary things are out of the way, we will code our first extremely simple predictive model. There will be two scripts written to accomplish this.

Our first R script is not a predictive model (yet), but it is a preliminary program which will view and plot some data. The dataset we will use is already built into the R package system, and is not necessary to load externally. For quickly illustrating techniques, I will sometimes use sample data contained within specific R packages themselves in order to demonstrate ideas, rather than pulling data in from an external file.

In this case our data will be pulled from the `datasets` package, which is loaded by default at startup.

- Paste the following code into the `Untitled1` scripts that was just created. Don't worry about what each line means yet. I will cover the specific lines after the code is executed:

```
require(graphics)
data(women)
head(women)
View(women)
plot(women$height,women$weight)
```

- Within the code pane, you will see a menu bar right beneath the **Untitled1** tab. It should look something like this:

- To execute the code, Click the **Source** icon. The display should then change to the following diagram:

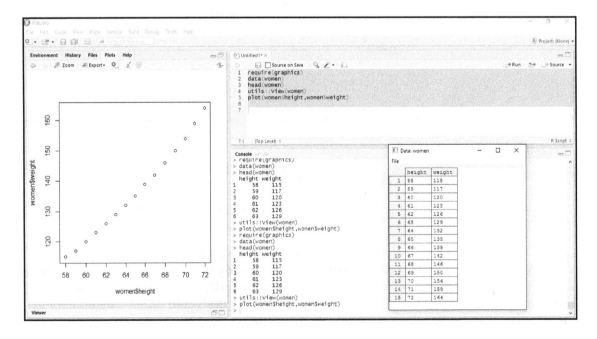

Notice from the preceding picture that three things have changed:

1. Output has been written to the **Console** pane.
2. The **View** pane has popped up which contains a two column table.
3. Additionally, a plot will appear in the **Plot** pane.

Code description

Here are some more details on what the code has accomplished:

- Line 1 of the code contains the function `require`, which is just a way of saying that R needs a specific package to run. In this case `require(graphics)` specifies that the `graphics` package is needed for the analysis, and it will load it into memory. If it is not available, you will get an error message. However, `graphics` is a base package and should be available.
- Line 2 of the code loads the `Women` data object into memory using the `data(women)` function.
- Lines 3-5 of the code display the raw data in three different ways:
    - `View(women)`: This will visually display the DataFrame. Although this is part of the actual R script, viewing a DataFrame is a very common task, and is often issued directly as a command via the R Console. As you can see in the previous figure , the `Women` dataframe has 15 rows, and 2 columns named **height** and **weight**.
    - `plot(women$height, women$weight)`: This uses the native R `plot` function, which plots the values of the two variables against each other. It is usually the first step one does to begin to understand the relationship between two variables. As you can see, the relationship is very linear.
    - `head(women)`: This displays the first *N* rows of the `Women` dataframe to the console. If you want no more than a certain number of rows, add that as a second argument of the function. For example, `Head(women, 99)` will display up to 99 rows in the console. The `tail()` function works similarly, but displays the last rows of data.

The `utils:View(women)` function can also be shortened to just `View(women)`. I have added the prefix `utils::` to indicate that the `View()` function is part of the `utils` package. There is generally no reason to add the prefix unless there is a function name conflict. This can happen when you have identically named functions sourced from two different packages which are loaded in memory. We will see these kind of function name conflicts in later chapters. But it is always safe to prefix a function name with the name of the package that it comes from.

Saving the script

To save this script, navigate to the top navigation menu bar and select **File | Save**. When the file selector appears navigate to the `PracticalPredictiveAnalytics/R` folder that was created, and name the file `Chapter1_DataSource`. Then select **Save**.

Your second script

Our second R script is a simple two variable regression model which predicts women's height based upon weight.

Begin by creating another R script by selecting **File | New File | R Script** from the top navigation bar. If you create new scripts via **File | New File | R Script** often enough you might get **Click Fatigue** (uses three clicks), so you can also save a click by selecting the icon in the top left with the **+** sign:

Whichever way you choose , a new blank script window will appear with the name
`Untitled2`.

Now paste the following code into the new script window:

```
require(graphics)
data(women)
lm_output <- lm(women$height ~ women$weight)
summary(lm_output)
prediction <- predict(lm_output)
error <- women$height-prediction
plot(women$height,error)
```

Press the **Source** icon to run the entire code. The display will change to something similar to
what is displayed as follows:

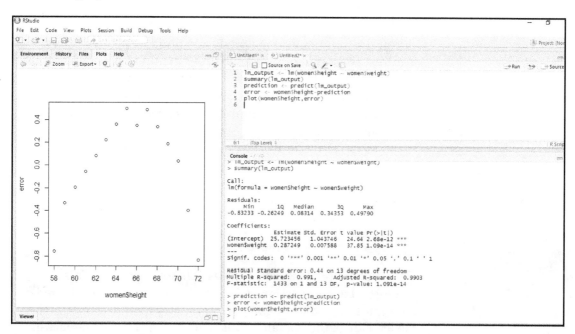

Code description

Here are some notes and explanations for the script code that you have just run:

- `lm()` function: This function runs a simple linear regression using the `lm()` function. This function predicts women's height based upon the value of their weight. In statistical parlance, you will be *regressing* height on weight. The line of code which accomplishes this is:

```
lm_output <- lm(women$height ~ women$weight)
```

- There are two operations that you will become very familiar with when running predictive models in R:
  - The ~ operator: Also called the tilde, this is a shorthand way for separating what you want to predict, with what you are using to predict. This is an expression in formula syntax. What you are predicting (the dependent or target variable) is usually on the left side of the formula, and the predictors (independent variables, features) are on the right side. In order to improve readability, the independent variable (`weight`) and dependent variable (`height`) are specified using `$` notation which specifies the object name, `$`, and then the dataframe column. So women's height is referenced as `women$height` and women's weight is referenced as `women$weight`. Alternatively, you can use the `attach` command, and then refer to these columns only by specifying the names `height` and `weight`. For example, the following code would achieve the same results:

```
attach(women)
lm_output <- lm(height ~ weight)
```

  - The <- operator: Also called the assignment operator. This common statement assigns whatever expressions are evaluated on the right side of the assignment operator to the object specified on the left side of the operator. This will always create or replace a new object that you can further display or manipulate. In this case, we will be creating a new object called `lm_output`, which is created using the function `lm()`, which creates a linear model based on the formula contained within the parentheses.

Note that the execution of this line does not produce any displayed output. You can see whether the line was executed by checking the console. If there is any problem with running the line (or any line for that matter), you will see an error message in the console.

- `summary(lm_output)`: The following statement displays some important summary information about the object `lm_output` and writes to output to the R Console as pictured previously:

    ```
    summary(lm_output)
    ```

- The results will appear in the **Console** window as pictured in the previous figure. Just to keep thing a little bit simpler for now, I will just show the first few lines of the output, and underline what you should be looking at. Do not be discouraged by the amount of output produced.

- Look at the lines marked `Intercept` and `women$weight` which appear under the coefficients line in the console.

    ```
    Coefficients:
                  Estimate Std. Error t value Pr(>|t|)
    (Intercept)   25.723456   1.043746    24.64 2.68e-12 ***
    women$weight   0.287249   0.007588    37.85 1.09e-14 ***
    ```

- The `Estimate` column illustrates the linear regression formula needed to derive height from weight. We can actually use these numbers along with a calculator to determine the prediction ourselves. For our example the output tells us that we should perform the following steps for all of the observations in our dataframe in order to obtain the prediction for height. We will obviously not want to do all of the observations (R will do that via the following `predict()` function), but we will illustrate the calculation for 1 data point:

    - Take the weight value for each observation. Let's take the weight of the first woman which is 115 lbs.
    - Then,multiply weight by 0.2872 . That is the number that is listed under Estimate for womens$weight. Multiplying 115 lbs. by 0.2872 yield 33.028
    - Then add 25.7235 which is the estimate of the (intercept) row. That will yield a prediction of 58.75 inches.

- If you do not have a calculator handy, the calculation is easily done in calculator mode via the R Console, by typing the following:

```
> 115 * .2872 +  25.7235
[1] 58.7515
```

The predict function

To predict the value for all of the values we will use a function called `predict()`. This function reads each input (independent) variable and then predicts a target (dependent) variable based on the linear regression equation. In the code we have assigned the output of this function to a new object named `prediction`.

Switch over to the console area, and type `prediction`, then *Enter*, to see the predicted values for the 15 women. The following should appear in the console.

```
> prediction
        1        2        3        4        5        6        7
58.75712 59.33162 60.19336 61.05511 61.91686 62.77861 63.64035
        8        9       10       11       12       13       14
64.50210 65.65110 66.51285 67.66184 68.81084 69.95984 71.39608
       15
72.83233
```

Notice that the value of the first prediction is very close to what you just calculated by hand. The difference is due to rounding error.

Examining the prediction errors

Another R object produced by our linear regression is the `error` object. The `error` object is a vector that was computed by taking the difference between the predicted value of height and the actual height. These values are also known as the residual errors, or just residuals.

```
error <- women$height-prediction
```

Since the `error` object is a vector, you cannot use the `nrow()` function to get its size. But you can use the `length()` function:

```
>length(error)
[1] 15
```

In all of the previous cases, the counts all total 15, so all is good. If we want to see the raw data, predictions, and the prediction errors for all of the data, we can use the `cbind()` function (Column bind) to concatenate all three of those values, and display as a simple table.

At the console enter the follow `cbind` command:

```
>
cbind(height=women$height,PredictedHeight=prediction,ErrorInPrediction=erro
r)
      height PredictedHeight ErrorInPrediction
1        58         58.75712       -0.75711680
2        59         59.33162       -0.33161526
3        60         60.19336       -0.19336294
4        61         61.05511       -0.05511062
5        62         61.91686        0.08314170
6        63         62.77861        0.22139402
7        64         63.64035        0.35964634
8        65         64.50210        0.49789866
9        66         65.65110        0.34890175
10       67         66.51285        0.48715407
11       68         67.66184        0.33815716
12       69         68.81084        0.18916026
13       70         69.95984        0.04016335
14       71         71.39608       -0.39608278
15       72         72.83233       -0.83232892
```

From the preceding output, we can see that there are a total 15 predictions. If you compare the `ErrorInPrediction` with the error plot shown previously, you can see that for this very simple model, the prediction errors are much larger for extreme values in height (shaded values).

Just to verify that we have one for each of our original observations we will use the `nrow()` function to count the number of rows.

At the command prompt in the console area, enter the command:

```
nrow(women)
```

The following should appear:

```
>nrow(women)
[1] 15
```

Refer back to the seventh line of code in the original script: `plot(women$height,error)` plots the predicted height versus the errors. It shows how much the prediction was off from the original value. You can see that the errors show a non-random pattern.

After you are done, save the file using **File** | **File Save**, navigate to the `PracticalPredictiveAnalytics/R` folder that was created, and name it `Chapter1_LinearRegression`.

R packages

An R package extends the functionality of basic R. Base R, by itself, is very capable, and you can do an incredible amount of analytics without adding any additional packages. However adding a package may be beneficial if it adds a functionality which does not exist in base R, improves or builds upon an existing functionality, or just makes something that you can already do easier.

For example, there are no built in packages in base R which enable you to perform certain types of machine learning (such as Random Forests). As a result, you need to search for an add on package which performs this functionality. Fortunately you are covered. There are many packages available which implement this algorithm.

Bear in mind that there are always new packages coming out. I tend to favor packages which have been on CRAN for a long time and have large user base. When installing something new, I will try to reference the results against other packages which do similar things. Speed is another reason to consider adopting a new package.

The stargazer package

For an example of a package which can just make life easier, first let's consider the output produced by running a summary function on the regression results, as we did previously. You can run it again if you wish.

```
summary(lm_output)
```

The amount of statistical information output by the `summary()` function can be overwhelming to the initiated. This is not only related to the amount of output, but the formatting. That is why I did not show the entire output in the previous example.

One way to make output easier to look at is to first reduce the amount of output that is presented, and then reformat it so it is easier on the eyes.

To accomplish this, we can utilize a package called `stargazer`, which will reformat the large volume of output produced by `summary()` function and simplify the presentations. Stargazer excels at reformatting the output of many regression models, and displaying the results as HTML, PDF, Latex, or as simple formatted text. By default, it will show you the most important statistical output for various models, and you can always specify the types of statistical output that you want to see.

To obtain more information on the `stargazer` package you can first go to CRAN, and search for documentation about `stargazer` package, and/or you can use the R help system:

IF you already have installed stargazer you can use the following command:

```
packageDescription("stargazer")
```

If you haven't installed the package, information about `stargazer`, (or other packages) can also be found using R specific internet searches:

```
RSiteSearch("stargazer")
```

If you like searching for documentation within R, you can obtain more information about the R help system at:

```
https://www.r-project.org/help.html
```

Installing stargazer package

Now, on to installing stargazer:

- First create a new R script (**File** | **New File** | **R Script**).
- Enter the following lines and then select **Source** from the menu bar in the code pane, which will submit the entire script:

```
install.packages("stargazer")
library(stargazer)
stargazer(lm_output, , type="text")
```

After the script has been run, the following should appear in the **Console**:

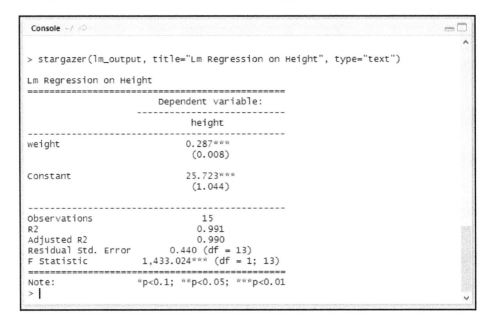

```
Console ~/
> stargazer(lm_output, title="Lm Regression on Height", type="text")

Lm Regression on Height
===============================================
                         Dependent variable:
                         --------------------------
                                height
-----------------------------------------------
weight                         0.287***
                               (0.008)

Constant                       25.723***
                               (1.044)

-----------------------------------------------
Observations                      15
R2                               0.991
Adjusted R2                      0.990
Residual Std. Error       0.440 (df = 13)
F Statistic         1,433.024*** (df = 1; 13)
===============================================
Note:              *p<0.1; **p<0.05; ***p<0.01
>
```

Code description

Here is a line by line description of the code which you have just run:

- `install.packages("stargazer")`: The line will install the package to the default package directory on your machine. If you will be rerunning this code again, you can comment out this line, since the package will have already be installed in your R repository.
- `library(stargazer)`: Installing a package does not make the package automatically available. You need to run a library (or `require()`) function in order to actually load the `stargazer` package.

- `stargazer(lm_output, , type="text")`: This line will take the output object `lm_output`, that was created in the first script, condense the output, and write it out to the console in a simpler, more readable format. There are many other options in the `stargazer` library, which will format the output as HTML, or Latex.

Please refer to the reference manual at `https://cran.r-project.org/web/packages/stargazer/index.html` for more information.

The reformatted results will appear in the R Console. As you can see, the output written to the console is much cleaner and easier to read.

Saving your work

After you are done, select **File** | **File Save** from the menu bar.

Then navigate to the `PracticalPredictiveAnalytics/Outputs` folder that was created, and name it `Chapter1_LinearRegressionOutput`. Press **Save**.

References

- *Computing and the Manhattan Project* retrieved from `http://www.atomicheritage.org/history/computing-and-manhattan-project`
- Gladwell, M. (2005). *Blink : The Power of Thinking Without Thinking*. New York: Little, Brown and Co.
- *Linda Miner et al. (2014). Practical Predictive Analytics and Decisioning Systems for Medicine. Elsevier.*
- *Watson (Computer)* retrieved from Wikipedia: `https://en.wikipedia.org/wiki/Watson_(computer).`
- *WEATHER FORECASTING THROUGH THE AGES* retrieved from `http://earthobservatory.nasa.gov/Features/WxForecasting/wx2.php.`

Summary

In this chapter, we have learned a little about what predictive analytics is and how they can be used in various industries. We learned some things about data, and how they can be organized in projects. Finally, we installed RStudio, ran a simple linear regression, and installed and ran our first package. We learned that it is always good practice to examine data after it has been loaded into memory, and a lot can be learned from simply displaying and plotting the data.

In the next chapter, we will discuss the overall predictive modeling process itself, introduce some key model packages using R, and provide some guidance on avoiding some predictive modeling pitfalls.

2
The Modeling Process

Remember that all models are wrong; the practical question is how wrong do they have to be to not be useful.

-George Edward Pelham Box

Today, we are at a juncture in which many different types of skill sets are needed to participate in predictive analytics projects. Once, this was the pure domain of statisticians, programmers, and business analysts. Now, the roles have expanded to include visualization experts, data storage experts, and other types of specialists. Yet, so many are unfamiliar with an understanding of how predictive analytics projects can be structured. This lack of structure can be inhibited by several factors. Often there is a lack of understanding of the critical parts of a business problem, and a model is developed much too early. Alternatively, a formal methodology may be put off to the future, in favor of a quick solution.

In this chapter, we will start by discussing the advantages of using structured analytics methodologies. Methodologies are a great way to demonstrate a value to the upper management, and groups or individuals advocating for a structured approach is one way to obtain buy-in from the management. If the project gains acceptance using a methodology, there is a strong possibility that future projects will have support.

We will cover the following points in this chapter:

- Advantages of a structured approach
- Analytic process methodologies
- An outline of the specific steps used within an analytics process methodology
- Short descriptions of specific analytic techniques, with code examples

Advantages of a structured approach

Analytic projects have many components. That is where a structured methodology can help. Many benefits can be gained if there is a structure which is placed upon discovery and analysis, rather than only on pure model building. The discovery and insight gained will certainly be utilized past the original intent of the problem.

> *We assume that the quick-thinking "hare brain" will beat out the slower Intuition of the "tortoise mind." However, now research in cognitive science is changing this understanding of the human mind. It suggests that patience and confusion--rather than rigor and certainty--are the essential precursors of wisdom.*
> *-Guy Claxton*

Ways in which structured methodologies can help

Here are several points to bear in mind concerning the advantages of structured methodologies:

- Data is coming at us fast and furious. We need to keep track of the many data sources, evaluate which ones are the best ones to use at any given time and continually monitor them for data accuracy. Expect changes to come quicker than expected. Predictive modelers need a structured methodology to be able to keep track of things; changes can be disruptive at whatever stage of the modeling process they are in.
- The difference between useful data and data masquerading as useful data is increasing. Structured methodologies help with maintaining metadata repositories for information, which can help in determining what data is useful and what is not.
- The number of data analysis techniques are increasing. Knowing which analytical techniques to choose can be a daunting task. Dedicating projects purely for evaluating which data techniques are more useful than others for a particular business problem is a laudable goal.
- Structured methodologies help with objectivity. Everyone has their own subjective technical biases that they bring to the table. Creating a structured way for sharing code and results can encourage out-of-the-box thinking.
- Incremental Improvement: Often projects are too large or ambitious. Projects can be organized in a way which offers small ways to provide value. This is easier to attain when projects are encapsulated within a structured methodology.

- Iterative analytics development uses structured techniques that enforce good data analytics practice such as being able to iterate in small steps. If any discrepancies are found later on, it is relatively easy to backtrack through the incremental updates.
- Divide and conquer helps to organize projects involving multiple team members who work on different parts of project
- Reproducibility helps analytic teams reproduce the same results again and again. This has always been important in research, but also has implications for any large-scale data project, in which you can be dealing with a multitude of data raw sources. Often, one needs help with understanding transformed data sources in which business rule transformations are unclear and can be changed without your knowledge. Certainly, this is also important when implementing version control, but this is also important when you are upgrading packages and need to recreate results. When data sampling is involved, it might also be possible that the original selection criteria which produced the sample is no longer available, and that reproducibility may be lost. Therefore, it is important to develop sample strategies in a structured way, which are robust and can be reproduced with future analyses.

Analytic process methodologies

There are several analytic process methodologies which are currently practiced; however, I will be discussing only two longstanding methodologies that have been in existence for a while, CRISP-DM and SEMMA, which can help you organize your journey from problem definition to insight.

CRISP-DM and SEMMA

Cross-Industry Standard process for Data Mining (CRISP-DM) and **Sample, Explore, Modify, Model, and Assess (SEMMA)** are two standard data mining methodologies that have been utilized for many years and describe a general methodology for implementing analytical projects. There is a good deal of overlap between the methodologies, even though the names for each step are different. All of the listed steps are important to the success of a predictive analytics project. However, it is not necessary that these steps be followed exactly in order. The concepts outlined are more or less an outline of best practices. It helps to be aware of the importance of each of these steps, and understand how each step is built upon the knowledge of the previous ones.

Although these steps are listed in sequence for reference, you will discover that in practice, they are more iterative and that you will often be cycling back to a previous step. This often happens when you discover information, which is in conflict with what you have previously discovered.

As an example, many times you believe that you are finished with the data preparation stage, only to find during the modeling stage that you have discovered a glitch in the data collection, and that you need to perform more data prep to accommodate certain conditions. One solution might be to cycle back, try to remedy the data situation, while at the same time see how you can continue with your modeling. This often entails 'coding around' the problem by setting flags, or maintaining different include files, versions, and so on. It always pays to code defensively when dealing with data.

CRISP-DM and SEMMA chart

If you examine the differences between SEMMA and CRISP-DM in the following chart, you will notice that steps 2-5 are similar in approach.

 Note that SEMMA adds sampling as an initial phase and CRISP-DM begins with business understanding and ends with model deployment.

Step #	CRISP-DM	SEMMA
1	Business understanding	Sample
2	Data understanding	Explore
3	Data preparation	Modify
4	Modeling	Model
5	Evaluation	Assess
6	Deployment	

Critical to both processes is the concept of visualizing and communicating results to stakeholders. Note that visualization is not considered a separate step. Always try to include a presentation layer (plots, charts, and visualizations) within each of the steps, so that communications between all of the predictive analytical stakeholders are facilitated.

Agile processes

Since developing a predictive model is iterative, agile approaches such as Scrum and Kanban work well within a structured framework, especially when they are tied to product delivery. However, knowledge discovery, proof of concept, and model incremental change improvements also benefit from an agile approach. When used as part of the business understanding process, these techniques can also be useful in grouping lists of questions into an agile backlog, which can then be incorporated in sprints.

Six sigma and root cause

Six sigma has been around for a long time and is associated with process improvement. As a result, it has developed its own set of methodologies and techniques, which deal with examining business problems and their solutions. Knowledge of basic statistical techniques is useful. Often a root cause analysis step (which is an important part of six sigma) is followed in order to understand why a data quality issue is occurring. For example, data can be passed along through multiple internal and external systems and be subject to many manual updates and system glitches and failures. In complex systems, it is often unclear where the errors occur. Six sigma can also be used to examine some causal relationships using some very simple techniques such as the 5 Whys (*Determine the Root Cause: 5 Whys.*)

To sample or not to sample?

Sampling is specified as step 1 of the SEMMA process (but not specific to CRISP-DM), so I will cover this separately.

Traditionally, predictive analytics have started with sampling. Sampling is particularly important in certain industries (such as pharmaceutical and healthcare), which begin with experimental studies. Sampling is also important in studies which you follow groups of people over a long period of time (cohorts). However, other kinds of data projects are not research type projects, and they are more machine learning oriented. Given that, I hold the belief that many algorithms are easier to work with (and are more powerful) if the data follows certain statistical properties, such as transforming raw data into data which follows normal distributions, or constructing training data so that there are an equal number of observations for various sub segments of the population. Sampling can be critical in preparing the data for these algorithms, so that data is more representative of the larger dataset.

Here are some other advantages to sampling:

- With a smaller sample, you will have the ability to get to know all of your data. If necessary this means going down to the record level. This is something that would not be practical with very large datasets. This also enables you to ask more specific detailed level follow up questions, in addition to larger group level questions.
- Sampling allows you to contemplate potential interesting subsets of the population. You can first random sample a smaller subset of something that looks interesting, and then test to see if that group behaves heterogeneously.
- Sampling also speeds up algorithmic development. Spending a lot of time running algorithms on very large datasets is often not productive, since you can spend a lot of processing time running memory-consuming algorithms. If you anticipate a lot of future tweaking for the algorithm, I suggest testing your algorithms first on a smaller representative sample, and then scaling up to the much larger dataset.
- With sampling, you are more in control of the ultimate data quality of your samples. I say this since you would have already done your legwork by looking at the characteristics of your population first, and then designing an appropriate sampling strategy which minimizes biases.
- Performing Bootstrap (repeated) sampling can help illustrate any biases in large data samples. If you see some strange stuff appear via sampling, there is a good chance that there is a much larger problem in the larger data.

Using all of the data

However, many data scientists will choose to use the entire population as the basis of analysis, instead of a sample. I suspect one reason is that often it is difficult to obtain a reliable sample, especially when the data has many different sources, and some are of unknown data quality. Good reliable data costs money to collect. Another reason is that the data scientists may not be familiar with sampling techniques, or believe that more is always better. Therefore, it is important to understand some important points about using all of the data:

- You can use all of the data if it accurately represents the underlying population. If *all the data* is the underlying population, you can't do better than that, but proceed with caution. What you think is a population may just be a very large sample. Future data may reflect a reality that is completely different. For very large data sets, you can never be quite sure if what we are looking at IS representative, since the amount of data can simply be overwhelming, and the underlying data collection methods may be unknown or unreliable. Be particular careful for data which is collected over long periods of time. Often data collection methods change, or the way calculations are performed are altered.

- When you use an incredibly large amount of data, what you are measuring is not necessarily representative of the factors which motivate the response. For example, clickstream data and online survey data is not always representative of the why? Deeper inspection (through smaller samples) is always advisable to examine motivation.

- As mentioned earlier, processing huge amounts of data consumes a lot of computational resources. Processing accurate samples can take a fraction of that time

- With large datasets, you will just about always find correlations somewhere. Related to this is the concept of significant correlation versus effect size. This means that even if you find a statistically significant correlation, the differences can be so slight, so as to render any association meaningless or nonactionable.

So the first line of attack for this is to try to understand how the data was collected. It may be biased towards certain age groups, genders, technology users, and so on. There may be ways to fix this using a technique known as **oversampling** in which you weigh certain under-represented groups in a way which more realistically represents their frequency.

Comparing a sample to the population

To illustrate some of the benefits of sampling, and to see how you can often get close to the same results with a sample as with a larger population, copy the following code and run it within an R script. This script will generate a 15,000,000 row population and then extract a 100-row random sample. Then we will compare the results:

```
large.df <- data.frame(
gender = c(rep(c("Male", "Female", "Female"), each = 5000000)),
purchases = c(0:9, 0:5, 0:7)
)
#take a small sample
y <- large.df[sample(nrow(large.df), 100), ]
mean(large.df$purchases)
```

```
mean(y$purchases)
#Render 2 plots side-by-side by setting the plot frame to 1 by 2
par(mfrow=c(1,2))
barplot(table(y$gender)/sum(table(y$gender)))
)barplot(table(large.df$gender)/sum(table(large.df$gender)))
#Return the plot window to a 1 by 1 plot frame
par(mfrow = c(1, 1))
```

Switch over to the console and note that the sample mean is close to the population mean:

```
> mean(large.df$purchases)
[1] 3.666667
> mean(y$purchases)
[1] 3.64
```

Now, switch over to the plot area and note that the distribution of gender is also similar when comparing the sample (left plot), and the population (right plot):

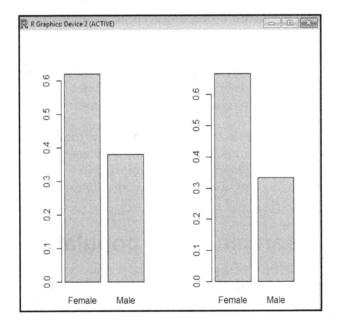

I encourage you to take some large datasets on your own, practice taking some random samples and seeing how close you get to population results. Possibly that will enable you to work faster and in a more productive manner.

An analytics methodology outline – specific steps

This section will look at each of the analytics methodology steps individually. I will use CRISP-DM as the template, because it covers model deployment, and we have already mentioned the benefits of sampling (which is the first step in SEMMA).

Step 1 business understanding

Many predictive modelers assume that the actual modeling phase is where the most insightful model development takes place. However, much of the groundwork and insight can be discovered early on, and a good understanding of business objectives can avoid pitfalls later on.

Communicating business goals – the feedback loop

I must admit, business people and technical people can be better at communicating with each other. How business goals are communicated can run the gamut. It can be anything from a business partner stating, "Tell me how sales need to be increased" or "Tell me something I don't know."

So, it really starts with understanding what the specific business objectives are. During this step, you will also get involved in breaking down the babble and buzzwords into specifics so that communication can begin using data as a common language. As exchanges begin between the domain experts and data scientists, it will become clear that business people often do know what they are looking for in terms of outcomes, but do not understand the analytic modeling process well enough to verbalize their goals. This is often the case in reverse for technical people who do not understand the nuances of the business.

The understanding phase is characterized by people asking many questions, and establishing an analytic dialogue between all parties. So, even with a more precise question like, "Who are our best customers?", the dialog can go as follows:

1. What do you mean by best?
2. Do you mean best now or best compared to what it was a year ago?
3. What metric are you using to define best? Do you mean best in terms of revenue or in terms of frequency of purchase?
4. How will we measure success? What are the key metrics? What are the possible outcomes?

The process of business understanding also involves an understanding of where, how, and when you obtain your data.

Internal data

Your own internal data is the first and best place to start. Many projects start with examining data from business operational systems, such as sales systems. You can start by analyzing transaction data, such as looking at all orders for a customer and analyzing the number of units sold, total sales price, and so on. However, transaction data by itself does not tell you anything about the customer. You need to also enrich your basic data by augmenting it with other attributes which can be obtained by matching common elements of your database transactions (such as customer ID, product keys) with valuable data which exists in other related databases. For example, a rich source of data is demographic and attitudinal data which may be stored in company customer surveys.

In addition to customer surveys, there may be other internal repositories that you can use to derive insight. Web logs may reveal more information about customer clickstream buying patterns. Data can be captured from customer call center data, HR and other administrative systems.

Finding other data sources often involves a lot of digging, since often internal data is siloed in large organizations.

External data

Data can also be augmented by integrating a company's internal data combined with data obtained from a variety of sources, including government data, social media feeds, and data purchased from vendors. Often demographic, behavioral, and risk data is purchased separately, and then merged within the data warehouse.

Beware of the daunting task of data integration. A key problem encountered in this task is being able to associate data from a variety of disparate sources with each other. This is less of a problem when dealing with internal data, but when dealing with external data you may have to use alternative methods available to perform matching, such as using fuzzy match (similarity) algorithms or performing entity extraction methods (which, for example, can extract a customer name). These are just two ways which can help you with associating data with external sources.

Tools of the trade

Defining the objectives can be tough at the beginning, and it is not advisable to start using advanced analytic tools at the business understanding stage. The best tools to use at this stage are somewhat low-tech and include important concepts such as process understanding, data dictionaries, and data linkage, and **Structured Query Language** (SQL).

Process understanding

An understanding of how data is generated in your domain as well as how it has been generated in the past is important. This means understanding how data has been transformed from its original raw state to how it is consumed by the ultimate user of the data. Understanding the imperfections of the current process will enable you to get a sense of which data can be consistently relied upon. Additionally, try to gather a history of what data changes and methodologies have been attempted in the past. This is important since the different ways that data used might have been quite different, and the goals might have been different. Knowing what has succeeded and what has failed in the past will prevent you from reinventing the wheel, keep you from replicating the very same mistakes, and help you build upon what has been attempted before.

Data lineage

Data lineage tools are helpful for documentation, and for following the changes of the nuanced meaning of data as it progresses from raw data form, to data storage, and then to the final definition. The general term for the type of data that lineage tools deal with is known as **metadata** (data about data).

Data dictionaries

Data dictionaries can be valuable as a source for understanding the types of variables under analysis and how they are measured. Here are some useful metadata items to keep in a data dictionary:

- **Name of the variable**: Consistency in naming conventions helps in understanding and readability. Some analysts like to use CamelCase, others like to use punctuation for an object, as in `Variable.data.frame`, and others will insist on only having lowercase letters.
- **Measurement data**: This answers questions such as, "Is the data numeric or categorical?", "How many levels are contained in each category?", and "What is the length of each variable?"
- **Sources of the data**: This covers, "Where did the data originally came from?"

- **Transformations**: This answers, "How was the data manipulated from its original form to what it is now?"
- **Data quality items**: Attaching frequency distributions and summary statistics to each variable will be helpful, along with any comments regarding any questionable data quality.

It is important to keep a data dictionary up to date, because variables or their values can change meaning over time. For example, a marketing offer with the value of A100 could mean we give a 15% discount to the customer now, but upon closer inspection, the same A100 code happened to be used five years ago in a different marketing application where it meant 10% discount to the customer.

Here is an example of a simple data dictionary:

Variable name	This is the name of the data element used in your program.
Business source element	This is the mapping of the variable to a business element. If the variable is a new or transformed variable, list the logic that is used to create or transform the variable.
Type of variable	This indicates the type of variable: nominal, interval, binary, continuous, and so on.
Variable role	This indicates whether it is a potentially dependent, independent, or informational variable.
Additional metadata	The total sales include Widget1 up until 2016. 10% missing values in sales for Northeast due to system glitch in February 2016.

As you begin to explore your dataset, you can also add additional columns, such as the percentage of missing values, variable means, extreme values, and so on.

SQL

SQL has been referred to as a universal query language. One of the reasons to learn SQL is that it has a relatively common syntax that runs on a variety of operating systems. Most importantly, knowledge of SQL is paramount for communicating ideas with managers who are familiar with it. While queries can also be done natively in R via native tools and packages, I prefer SQL as a first query language since work performed using SQL in R can then be modified to run natively within other systems, where the code can be optimized in its native environment, in order to make it run faster.

Example – Using SQL to get sales by region

In this example, we will use the R package `sqldf` to show the difference in sales and units in four sales regions. Note that this is an artificial example since we will first generate separate data for the `West` region with sales figures that are higher than the other three regions:

```
install.packages("sqldf")
library(sqldf)
set.seed(10)
rows=100
y <- rbind(
data.frame(indv=factor(paste("TransId-", 1:100, sep = "")),
           Sales=rnorm(rows, mean=1500000,sd=100000),
           Units=round(rnorm(rows,mean=10, sd=3)),
           Region=sample(c("North","East","South"),rows,
replace=TRUE)),
data.frame(indv=factor(paste("TransId-", 101:200, sep = "")),
           Sales=rnorm(rows, mean=2000000,sd=100000),
           Units=round(rnorm(rows,mean=10, sd=3)),
           Region=sample(c("West"),rows, replace=TRUE))
)
query <- "select Region,avg(Sales),avg(Units) from y group by Region"
results <- sqldf(query,stringsAsFactors = FALSE)
results
```

The results will appear in the console window:

```
> results
  Region avg(Sales) avg(Units)
1   East    1493504   9.333333
2  North    1487338  10.457143
3  South    1477877   9.250000
4   West    2016626  10.270000
>
```

This is randomly generated data. The functions `rnorm()` and `sample()` in the written code are giveaways. Generating random data is a great way to begin to test code and algorithms since you will always have a better idea of what kind of results to expect, given the assumptions.

Charts and plots

At the business understanding phase, it is not necessary to get too complex with visualizations. The reason I say this is that in some instances complex visualization can influence interpretation, rather than provide objective data. Basic charts and plots, which indicate the relationship between the variables are more than adequate for communicating ideas.

When passing charts and plots back and forth during this phase, it is a good idea to include basic statistical measures of distribution and association—this will give management a rough idea of how significant the relationships are, rather than having them rely purely on the visual representation.

Spreadsheets

Sending the data to spreadsheets and creating pivot tables is another way to get management involved in the process. Spreadsheets have definite disadvantages, but they are heavily used in the industry and knowing how to manipulate spreadsheets will be another way that you can communicate with managers.

Simulation

Simulation is a tool which can demonstrate what-ifs. This technique is very useful if there is not a lot of historical data to go by, and you need to make assumptions about the behavior of some of your variables. Typically, you do not have a lot of data at this point, so you are really constructing your own data, based upon how you think it will behave.

In the later sections of the book, I will use simulation techniques heavily to illustrate this.

Example – simulating if a customer contact will yield a sale

Here is an example that is based upon a business estimate that one of three customer contacts will result in a sale. Another assumption is that if a sale is made, it will result in an average of $100 each with a standard deviation of $5.

`ExpectedPayoff` either produces 0 revenue or a figure that hovers around $100, as specified in line 5 of the following code:

```
library(ggplot2)
set.seed(123)
CustomerAcquired.Flag <- sample(c(0,0,1), 100, replace = TRUE)
Revenue <- sample(rnorm(100,100,5))
```

```
ExpectedPayoff <- CustomerAcquired.Flag*Revenue
head(ExpectedPayoff)
PayoffCompare = ggplot(data.frame(ExpectedPayoff), aes(x=ExpectedPayoff)) +
stat_bin(binwidth=5, position="identity")
PayoffCompare
```

```
> head(ExpectedPayoff)
[1]    0.00000 101.26659   0.00000 100.58823  97.12327   0.00000
```

We can view this conditional customer acquisition problem as two separate charts contained within one visualization. The left side of the visualization is the count of customer contacts which result in no revenue, and the right side shows the histogram of binned sales when they occur:

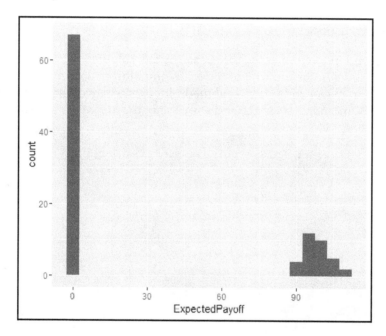

Example – simulating customer service calls

In this example, we can simulate calls to the customer service which might occur at the beginning and at the end of the week. Management projects that weekend volume will be heavy, with an average of 1500000 calls and an average turnaround time of 4 minutes. Customer service call volume for Monday-Thursday is estimated as handling 1000000 calls with an average turnaround time of 1 minute. We could use this simulation to build a model to include weekends versus nonweekends as new variables in a predictive model:

```
library(ggplot2)
library(grid)
library(gridExtra)
set.seed(123)
MonTuesWedThurs=rnorm(1000000,1,1)
FriSatSun=rnorm(1500000,4,1)
weekly = c(MonTuesWedThurs,FriSatSun)
```

If we were interested in looking at the difference in call volumes, we could look at them individually (as shown in the top row of the following plot) or as a combined distribution for weekends and nonweekends. The combined plot is one way of illustrating the difference between weekends and nonweekends, and shows that they have similar shapes, but different mean values:

```
p1 = ggplot(data.frame(FriSatSun), aes(x=FriSatSun)) +
stat_bin(binwidth=0.25, position="identity")

p2 = ggplot(data.frame(MonTuesWedThurs), aes(x=MonTuesWedThurs)) +
stat_bin(binwidth=0.25, position="identity")

p3 = ggplot(data.frame(weekly), aes(x=weekly)) + stat_bin(binwidth=0.25,
position="identity")

grid.arrange(p1, p2, p3, ncol = 2)
```

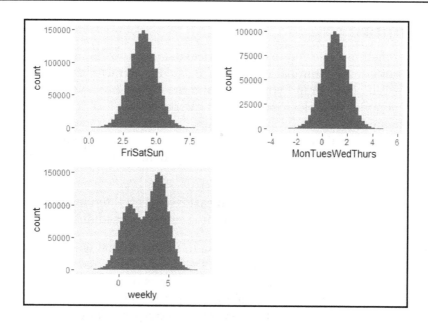

Step 2 data understanding

Once an objective is established and data sources have been identified, you can begin looking at the data in order to understand how each data element behaves individually, as well as how it interacts in combination with other variables. But even before you start looking at the values of variables, it is important to understand the different types of data levels of measurement and the kind of analyses you can perform with them.

Levels of measurement

Levels of measurement is a classification system for classifying data into 4 different categories which is discussed as follows (ratio, ordinal, interval, and nominal). It is an important aspect of the project or studies metadata.

Levels of measurement is important in the world of predictive analytics since the specific measurements will often dictate which algorithm or techniques can be applied. For example k-means clustering does work if you want to incorporate nominal data, and logistic regression can not use ratio data as a dependent variable (although you can transform variables to a lower scale).

Nominal data

Nominal data, sometimes referred to as categorical data, simply defines a class or group without any natural order. Nominal variables are usually character data, but not always. Your gender, the cell phone brand you prefer, and the type of book you are reading now are all examples of nominal variables. Sometimes it can be tricky, since the number 1 and 2 written on a sign are also nominal variables when they are used to designate two possible waiting lines you may need to visit at the motor vehicle bureau. Nominal data only designates classes and you cannot perform any mathematical operations on them, such as addition or subtraction.

When characterizing nominal data, the only measure of central tendency is the *mode*, which is the most frequently occurring value. Computing means or medians cannot be performed.

In the R language, we can convert character data to factors so that we can analyze them as nominal data. That will be an important part of the cleaning process, which we will learn about later on. When analyzing nominal data, frequencies of occurrence (counts) are a good starting point. Alternatively, you can begin by grouping calculations with other nominal variables, in order to determine counts, or averages of other numeric variables.

Ordinal data

Ordinal data only has rank order. Statements can be made such as $A>B$ and $B < C$, but you cannot compute the numeric differences between any of the groups. A top ten list is an example of the presentation of ordinal data. Often categorical data can be classified as ordinal data if they have an implied order, such as two categories labeled *Better*, and *Best*. One problem with ordinal data is we never know what is the exact difference between each of the ranked data points.

Interval data

This is numeric data in which you can measure distances but cannot take ratios. Temperature data and calendar data are two examples of interval data. All of the arithmetic differences between two consecutive data points on the numeric scale are measured exactly the same way, so you can take meaningful differences.

Often, interval data is treated as ratio data. This is often seen when performing calculations such as averages on likert scales (even though this is not technically correct). With ordinal data, you can compute frequencies, calculate the median, and compute percentiles but you cannot do any arithmetic or calculate a mean.

Ratio data

The highest level of numeric data is ratio scale. With ratio data, you can make meaningful comparisons using division and subtraction. It is meaningful to say that you have acquired twice as many customers when you went from 50 to 100 customers in one month. Ratio data also adds 0 to the domain of numbers (which interval data does not contain), so it is meaningful to say that you have 0 customers (although not desireable). Weight and income are other examples of ratio data. however, the fahrenheit and celsius temperature scale do not have a 0 meaning *no temperature*. That creates some interesting comparisons if you would try to make temperature comparisons. For example, in fahrenheit, a temperature of 36/18 equals 2, but the equivalent celsius is 2.22/-7.78 which equals 0.28 which suggests that ration comparisons are meaningless, and that both sides should be treated as interval.

To learn more about the theory of scales and measurement refer to *On the Theory of Scales and of Measurement (Stevens, 1946)*.

Converting from the different levels of measurement

As a general rule, you can always transform a higher level of measurement to a lower level of measurement, but not the reverse. Often this is done via a technique known as **binning** in which you place all values with a certain range into a bin. You may want to take various ranges of height and bin them into *tall, short*, or *medium* based upon predefined ranges. However, you would generally not take a categorical variable and map it to a numeric variable, unless you knew a lot about how that category was measured and you were willing to make a lot of assumptions.

Dependent and independent variables

The **dependent variable** is the variable that you are predicting. It can also be referred to as a target variable, response variable, or outcome variable. One goal of predictive modeling is to derive a prediction for the dependent variable based upon some function of the independent variables. A dependent variable is typically fixed and you cannot manipulate it. **Independent variables** are variables that you choose in the belief that they are important in determining the outcome of the dependent variable, also based upon some function. This function is typically applied using an algorithm.

Transformed variables

Transformed variables are variables that you create which did not exist in the raw data. Here are some examples of how you can create transformed variables:

- You can bin a numeric variable into several distinct categories such as High (all numeric values greater than 10) or low or any value less than 10. Notice that binning results in losing information, but allows you some flexibility by being able to name things and promote understandability
- Transforming count data into percentages by dividing a cell count by the total population.
- Standardizing the data in the modeling phase; it is often useful to work with standardized variables, as opposed to using the raw data itself. A standardized variable is a transformation which forces a mean of 0, and a standard deviation of 1. This transformation preserves the distribution and structure of the original values, but makes it easier to compare one set of variables with another variable with a different scale.
- In regression modeling, it is common to replace or add another variable with a transformation such as `log()` or `exp()` so that the resultant model has a better linear fit.

Single variable analysis

After taking inventory of all your potential candidate variables, it makes sense to start with single variable analysis. Why complicate things by looking all at multiple variables at once when you can start looking at them one at a time? Often, the results of modeling will suggest immediate elimination of a variable for inclusion in a model, such as one with a high percentage of missing values, or one with data quality issues. Eliminating variables early is often the best course, rather than carrying them through an analysis only to discard them later on. This is especially true if you find two variables which measure the same thing.

Summary statistics

It is usually a good idea to begin analysis with look at summary statistics for every candidate variable which might appear in a model. Means, standard deviations, frequencies, and skewness allow quick generalization about how you expect a variable to behave. Special consideration should also be given when examining any variable deemed to be a target variable.

To display basic summary statistics about a single variable, use the R `Summary()` function. This can be issued as part of an R scripts or directly from the command line. The general form of the `Summary()` function is:

```
#for a single variable
Summary(dataframe$variable)
#for all of the variables
Summary(dataframe)
```

Two other typical single variable analysis summary techniques to use are:

- **Distributions**: A distribution plot (histogram, probability density plot, and so on) will give you an idea of what a variable looks like versus a theoretical statistical distribution. Some modeling techniques will require some assumptions regarding distributions and others will not. If you find that a variable follows a particular distribution, you will be lucky. That will make modeling easier later on. In R, you can use the `hist()` function.

- **Boxplots**: A boxplot is a simple graphic representation of a distribution, which always includes five key elements of a distribution minimum, first quartile, median, third quartile, and maximum. (Refer to *Comparing treatments* in the next section for an example the R function `boxplot()`, which produces these five key elements.)

  - The box has the upper and lower lines of the box representing the third and first quartile, with the median line in between.
  - The whiskers has the top line representing the maximum and the bottom line representing the minimum.

Bivariate analysis

Bivariate analysis is typically the next step you would take after single variable analysis. Bivariate analysis is used to show the relationship between any two variables. You are performing bivariate analysis for two reasons:

- In a modeling framework, one key outcome we are looking for would be any association between the target variable and any one of the independent variables.
- Another, equally important outcome we are looking for is any possible associations between any two of the independent variables. That will help us understand which of the independent variables are correlated with each other, or help us understand how one variable changes the behavior of another.

Types of questions that bivariate analysis can answer

As you examine the relationship between any two variables, here are some key points to keep in mind:

- Do the two variables move in the same direction as one changes, or do they move in opposite directions? Is there one critical value in either of the variables that alters the relationship?
- Are the changes in the values dramatic, or are they slow and steady?
- Is there strength in the relationship, and is the relationship linear, or is there curvature?
- Are there specific subsets of data that have correlations that are more interesting than others?

The kinds of plots and charts one uses to display these relationships are dependent upon the variable data types. For interval and ratio scale data, we will group them together into one category and refer to them as quantitative data.

Therefore, when we look at bivariate relations between quantitative and nominal data, we can have three basic combinations:

- Quantitative with quantitative
- Nominal with nominal
- Nominal with quantitative

Quantitative with quantitative variables

Scatterplots are often used to show relationships between two quantitative variables. In the following code, we will use the R `pairs()` function to plot some associations. As you can see, `Petal.Width` has a strong relationship with `Petal.Length` (row 3, column 4), while the relationship between `Sepal.Width` and `Sepal.Length` (row 1, column 2) is not as strong.

Code example

```
pairs(iris[1:4], bg=c("green","blue","brown","yellow","black","orange"),
pch=21)
```

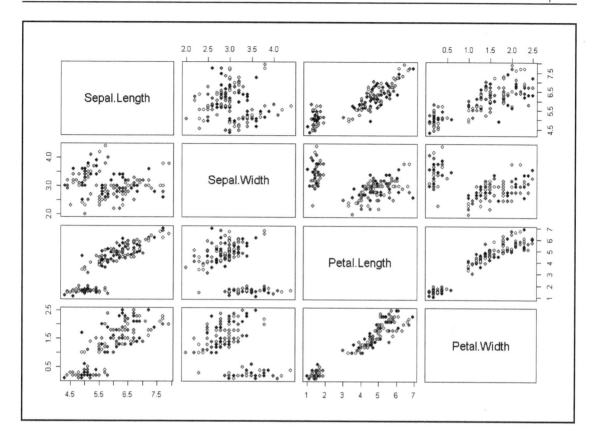

Nominal with nominal variables

We will look at versus nominal versus nominal in two different ways. One using the table style and the other using the graphic method.

Cross-tabulations

Cross-tabulations are a good starting point for examining the relationships between nominal variables. There are many ways to do this in R. I like to start off by using the `CrossTable()` function from the `gmodels` package, since it will give not only the cell counts but also the frequencies for the rows and columns totals, and supply a chi-square statistic to measure the statistical significance. It may not be pretty but it does the job well.

See the following code:

```
install.packages("gmodels")
library(gmodels)
CrossTable(mtcars$cyl, mtcars$gear, prop.t=TRUE, prop.r=TRUE, prop.c=TRUE)
```

```
> CrossTable(mtcars$cyl, mtcars$gear, prop.t=TRUE, prop.r=TRUE,
prop.c=TRUE)


   Cell Contents
|-----------------------|
|                     N |
| Chi-square contribution |
|           N / Row Total |
|           N / Col Total |
|         N / Table Total |
|-----------------------|


Total Observations in Table:  32


             | mtcars$gear
  mtcars$cyl |         3 |         4 |         5 | Row Total |
-------------|-----------|-----------|-----------|-----------|
           4 |         1 |         8 |         2 |        11 |
             |     3.350 |     3.640 |     0.046 |           |
             |     0.091 |     0.727 |     0.182 |     0.344 |
             |     0.067 |     0.667 |     0.400 |           |
             |     0.031 |     0.250 |     0.062 |           |
-------------|-----------|-----------|-----------|-----------|
           6 |         2 |         4 |         1 |         7 |
             |     0.500 |     0.720 |     0.008 |           |
             |     0.286 |     0.571 |     0.143 |     0.219 |
             |     0.133 |     0.333 |     0.200 |           |
             |     0.062 |     0.125 |     0.031 |           |
-------------|-----------|-----------|-----------|-----------|
           8 |        12 |         0 |         2 |        14 |
             |     4.505 |     5.250 |     0.016 |           |
             |     0.857 |     0.000 |     0.143 |     0.438 |
             |     0.800 |     0.000 |     0.400 |           |
             |     0.375 |     0.000 |     0.062 |           |
-------------|-----------|-----------|-----------|-----------|
Column Total |        15 |        12 |         5 |        32 |
             |     0.469 |     0.375 |     0.156 |           |
-------------|-----------|-----------|-----------|-----------|
```

Mosaic plots

Mosaic plots will also display cross-tabulations graphically. You can visually see that eight cylinders and three gears represent the largest car cylinder/gear offering (37.5% of cars shaded in the preceding contingency table), while the eight cylinder and four gear combinations seem to not exist. This is also shown in the boxed value of the preceding contingency table, along with the dotted line in the following mosaic plot:

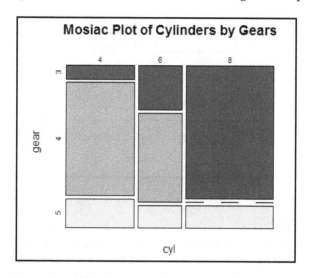

Nominal with quantitative variables

These comparisons are often examined using basic bar charts or, in the following example, using side-by-side box-plots. These boxplots give very clear comparisons.

The following code simulates two ad campaigns A, and B with two different outcomes:

```
set.seed(123)
rows=100
a <- data.frame(Sales=rnorm(rows,mean=75,sd=5),
                Treatment=factor(c("Campaign A")))
b <- data.frame(Sales=rnorm(rows,mean=80,sd=5),
                Treatment=factor(c("Campaign B")))
combined=rbind(a,b)
#Boxplots which compare treatments
boxplot(Sales~Treatment,data=combined, main="Comparing Treatments",
        xlab="Treatment", ylab="Sales")
```

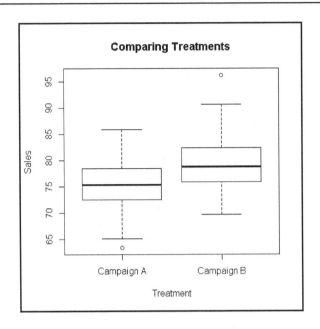

Point biserial correlation

Another basic technique that you could use if one of the categories is a nominal variable with only two classes and the other variable is quantitative would be point biserial correlation. However, since this technique uses Pearsons correlation coefficient, you need to make certain assumptions about the distributions of the data. For example, the data needs to be normally distributed and have equal variance. This assumption holds for our simulated sales example, since each category is generated using the `rnorm()` function which simulates 2 randomly distributed data frames with different means, but identical standard deviations (variances)

To show point biserial correlation, we can use our previous sales treatment. First, map each of the sales treatment to numeric variables:

```
Treatment_num <- as.integer(combined$Treatment)
```

Next, we can use the R table function simply to see how the two marketing campaigns have been mapped to numeric. Campaign A maps to number 1 and campaign B maps to number 2.

```
table(combined$Treatment,Treatment_num)
```

```
> table(combined$Treatment,Treatment_num)
            Treatment_num
              1   2
Campaign A 100   0
Campaign B   0 100
```

Now, run a biserial plot. You can restrict the *x* axis to the values 1 or 2, since you know in advance that there are only two values:

```
ggplot(combined,aes(x=as.integer(Treatment_num), y=Sales))
+ geom_point(size=1.5,shape=1)
+ geom_smooth(method=lm)
+ scale_x_continuous(breaks=c(1,2))
+ ggtitle("Point BiSerial Correlation of Campaign with Sales")
+ labs(x="Campaign Number",y="Sales")
```

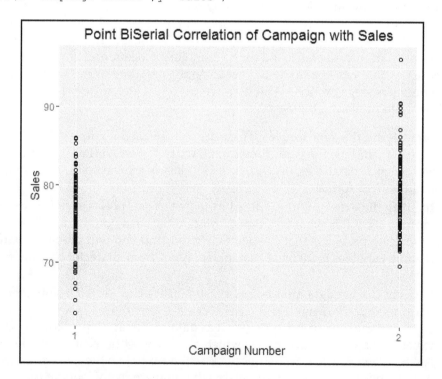

Having numeric data has its advantages. Since the data is now in numeric form, we can also run a correlation test. The output shows correlation between sales for the two campaigns is 39:

```
cor.test(Treatment_num,combined$Sales)
```

```
            Pearson's product-moment correlation

data:  Treatment_num and combined$Sales
t = 6.0315, df = 198, p-value = 7.843e-09
alternative hypothesis: true correlation is not equal to 0
95 percent confidence interval:
 0.2699868 0.5051026
sample estimates:
      cor
0.3939704
```

Step 3 data preparation

As was mentioned in `Chapter 1`, *Getting Started with Predictive Analysis*, one purpose of data preparation is preparing an input data modeling file, which can go directly into an algorithm. In theory, the input file will encompass all of the knowledge gained in steps 1 and 2. Ideally, this file will consist of a target variable, all meaningful predictor variables and other identification variables to aid in the modeling process, and any additional variables which would have been created based on the raw data sources. Data preparation, such as the previous steps outlined is an iterative process. Here are some typical steps you might follow when preparing the data:

- **Identifying the data sources**: These are the critical data inputs that you will need to read in and manipulate. They can be sourced from various data formats such as CSV files, databases, or XML or JSON files. They can be in structured format or unstructured format.
- **Identify the expected input**: Read in some test samples and closely examine the input to see if it is what you expect. More often than not, there will be some formatting problems that can be easily fixed, and you will probably want to rename variables and change some data types from character to numeric and vice versa.
- **Perform further data quality and reasonability checks**: After you have performed your own internal checks, cross-reference the data you observe with existing metadata information (such as data dictionaries, if available), domain experts, and other data artifacts which already exist to see if what you are reading is what you expected. Sometimes you will need to join the data with other lookup or reference tables in order to obtain what you are really looking for.

- **Expanding the number of input records**: After reading in and getting a test sample, you will probably want to read in a much larger sample of records and variables beyond what you read in the initial stage. Determining how much data to read in at this stage is a decision you will need to make. If you read in all of the variables, you may encounter memory problems later on, and if you read in just what you need, that may force you to go back later on and incorporate additional data or variables. Try to get a good representative sample of data at the beginning. Later on, it may make sense to rewrite your code to read in only a subset of the variables that you really need.
- **Perform some basic data cleaning**: Although cleaning the data is an important part of the modeling process, it is important not to over clean. An example of over cleaning would be attempting to fix every missing value via imputation. Models can co-exist with a reasonable amount of bad data and will perform better in the long run if some variation is included.
- **Try some aggregation**: Aggregate some of the data by some basic categories and observe the results. Consider whether using aggregated data instead of individual data will help speed model development while achieve models results than are similar to those achieved from using the individual observations.
- **Create new variables or transformations**: This is where binning and standardizing variables come into play.
- **Identify key variables**: Even though modeling has begun, you should be able to preliminarily identify which variables are important using a combination of bivariate analysis, SQL, correlations and other exploratory tools. It is not critical to identify the most important variables, but only the ones that may have some predictive power, or are already known to be relevant.
- Join any of the input files you have examined into one single analytics file. Now you are ready for the modeling phase.

Step 4 modeling

In the modeling stage, you will pick an appropriate predictive modeling technique that fits your problem and apply it to your data. There are several factors which influence the selection of a model:

1. Who will use the model?
2. How will the model be used?
3. What are the assumptions of the model?
4. How much data do I have?

5. How many variables do I need to use?
6. What is the accuracy level needed by the model?
7. Am I willing to trade some accuracy for interpretability?

Particularly related to the last point is the concept of **bias** and **variance**.

Bias is related to the ability of a model to approximate the data. Low bias algorithms are able to fit the data with little error. While this may seem to an advantage all of the time, it can result in a complex model which is unstable, and difficult to explain. On the other hand, a high bias model is relatively simple to explain (like linear regression), but may sacrifice some accuracy for explanability, and stability. You will usually start by looking at your data and matching it up with a choice of potential algorithms. A linear regression, for example, which tries to fit data which forms a U-shaped distribution would not be an appropriate algorithmic choice for that problem, regardless of the number of parameters selected or how the coefficients were adjusted. For example, 5-star ranking reviews are often skewed toward very high or very low ratings and linear regression would not be an appropriate choice.

Here is an example showing how linear regression would be a ppor choice:

```
set.seed(1010)
x <- sample(c(1,2,3,4,5),100,replace=TRUE,prob=(c(.25,.05,.05,.3,.35)))
y <- data.frame(rating=x,custid=seq(1:100))
hist(y$rating, prob=TRUE, main="Customer Ratings")
lines(density(y$rating))
```

It would be a much better fit if a regression problem involved sales prediction from inventory. Low bias models tend to result in over fitting and high bias models have lower accuracy but are simpler to explain.

Variance is related to how a model would change when supplied with different data. Low variance is also desirable.

Decision trees are an example of an algorithm, which tends to have low bias (over fits) but can come up with completely different results when given a new training sample (high variance). Even adding one additional observation to an existing decision tree model can result in a totally different tree.

To develop a good predictive model, you acknowledge that there ultimately will be a compromise or tradeoff between bias and variance. To learn more about the bias-variance trade-off, check out some of the external references in *Wikipedia*.

Description of specific models

Here are some short descriptions of some of the models that we will be covering, with some short code examples.

Poisson (counts)

A Poisson model is used to model counts of things. That could be the number of insurance claims filed in a given month, the number of calls which are received in a call center in a given minute, or the number of orders which are sold for a particular item. The Poisson distribution is the appropriate way for modeling count data since all data is positive and the range of the distribution is bound by 0 and infinity. The classic way of modeling a Poisson model is through the R glm() function using a poisson link function:

```
model.poisson <- glm(count ~ v1+v2+v3, data=inputdata, family=poisson())
```

Note that the preceding model specified merely shows the model in a generalized form. Do not try to run it since there are no variables other than the existing ones v1, v2, v3 or count. However, what the model specification says is that you will run a Poisson model via the following general steps:

- The model will be run via the glm() function with some dependent variable to the left of the ~
- The independent variable will be supplied to the right of the ~
- The Data= parameter will supply an input dataset
- The family= parameter will specify the type of general linear model that you will be running, and, in this case, it will be a Poisson model

To try a Poisson model on real data, we can use the *warpsbreaks* data, which is included with R.

- First at the console, enter help (warpbreaks) to get a description of the dataset:

[,1]	breaks	numeric	This is the number of breaks
[,2]	wool	factor	This is the type of wool (A or B)
[,3]	tension	factor	This is the level of tension (L, M, or H)

Then, set up and execute the model using the `glm()` function. We are predicting the number of breaks, using the type of wool and level of tension. Note that we need to add a `summary()` function after the `glm()` function in order to see the output, since running the `glm()` function just assigns the output to an object named the `model.poisson` model.

```
model.poisson <-glm(breaks~wool+tension, data=warpbreaks, family=poisson)
summary(model.poisson)
```

Logistic regression

Logistic regression is one of the oldest and stable techniques that one can use for classification. Logistic regression, linear regression, and Poisson regression are all considered **General Linear Models** (GLM). However, in the case of logistic regression, the predicted value can only be 0, or 1. Fortunately, this corresponds with many use cases, such as whether or not a customer will leave, or whether or not a hurricane will appear. If you are already familiar with multiple linear regressions, logistic regression should be easier to understand, since you should already be familiar with concepts such as specifying multiple independent variables, and the use of mathematical functions, such as log and exp, which can smooth the variables in the model and force it to be more linear.

Logistic regression is also useful, in that it produces an odd ratio. An odd ratio is the probability that an event will occur divided by the probability that the event will not occur.

A standard logistic regression is called in R via the `glm()` function.

The call to `glm()` contains a specification for a `link` function. The `link` function specifies which kind of model or distribution will be used for the linear model. For logistic regression, use `family=binomial()` to specify logistic regression.

The simplest general form of the `glm()` function is:

```
Model.logistic <- glm(Target~v1+v2+v3,data=sourcedata,family=binomial())
```

Support vector machines (SVM)

Support vector machines (**SVM**) can also be used to predict a binary class. SVM projects the data into a higher dimensional space so that hyperplanes can be used to separate the classifiers. SVMs can be very accurate but difficult to interpret and computationally expensive. They are a classic example of a low bias algorithm.

Here is a simple example of using an SVM to predict whether a person is satisfied based upon the day of the week and whether or not it is a payday. (The vector element is marked as 1 in the `payday` vector, which can be interpreted as Friday if you start counting from Sunday.)

```
library(e1071)
satisfied = factor(c(F,F,F,F,F,T,F))
day = c(1,2,3,4,5,6,7)
payday = c(0,0,0,0,0,1,0)
satisfaction.df = data.frame(day=day, payday=payday, satisfied=satisfied)
model.svm = svm(satisfied ~ day + payday, data = satisfaction.df)
plot(model.svm,satisfaction.df,main="",col=c('grey','black'))
```

As you can see from the following plot, the decision line is a curve near the upper-right part of the quadrant, and the area where payday is close to 1 (yes), and day of week is close to 4, 5, 6, 7 (later part of the week). So we can interpret that as saying people are satisfied on payday and at the end of the week. However, this is a very low dimension example (rendered in two axes) that we used to illustrate the concept. Higher dimensional examples are not that easy to interpret:

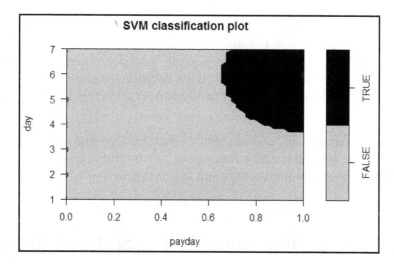

Decision trees

Decision trees are popular since they can roughly be equated with *If/Then/Else* rules used in some business contexts and are relatively easy to explain to managers. Decision trees are not only used for classification. When they are used to predict numeric outcomes, they are referred to as regression trees. The basic concept that decision trees use is that each node of the tree is split into two parts based upon an optimal split point. The tree continues to grow by adding more leafs until it is not able to make any additional splits, which improve the ability to distinguish between any of the decisions.

Random forests

Note that Random Forests (tm) is a trademark of Leo Breiman and Adele Cutler and is licensed exclusively to Salford Systems for the commercial release of the software.

One problem with decision trees is that they are highly dependent on the specific variables that are initially chosen. One could generate a slightly different set of initial variables and end up with an equally valid solution, although different.

Random forest algorithms (which are known by several different names refer to the note at end of the chapter) are an attempt to improve decision trees in that random forests randomize the selection of variables and subsamples in order to generate multiple (even thousands of) separate decision trees. After all the decision trees are generated, a consensus prediction is determined which averages the effects over all of the different trees that have been generated.

In order to determine consensus, you can specify that the algorithm implements a simple majority vote scheme. We will see how this works by running two simple decision trees on the titanic dataset first, and then comparing the results to that which is obtained using a random forest.

Example - comparing single decision trees to a random forest

First, install the titanic package and assign the training dataset to a dataframe:

```
install.packages("titanic")
library(titanic)
titanic <- titanic_train[complete.cases(titanic_train), ]
```

An age decision tree

Grow a simple decision tree to predict whether a passenger survived using `Age` as an independent variable and then plot the tree:

```
library(rpart)
library(rpart.plot)
set.seed(123)
fit <- rpart(as.factor(Survived) ~ Age,   data=titanic,   method="class")
rpart.plot(fit,extra=102)
```

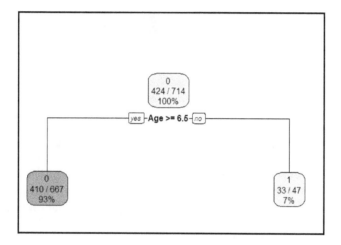

How accurate was this simple tree? Just to flex our brain, we will compute this manually.

At the console, compute the correct classification percentages. The correct number of predictions for each class is shown as the first number in each node in the preceding plot. The second number is the total number assigned to that class.

By adding up the total of the correct predictions and dividing it by the total number of predictions, the math computed via the console shows that this simple model is correct 62% of the time. however, you may ask what is the 93 % given in the lefthand node of the tree. This would be the correct classification for that node given that the passengers age was less than 6.5:

```
> (410+33) / nrow(titanic)
```

This is the following output:

```
[1] 0.6204482
```

An alternative decision tree

Let's say we arbitrarily selected another simple decision tree model; this time we will predict whether or not a passenger survived based upon the passenger class variable:

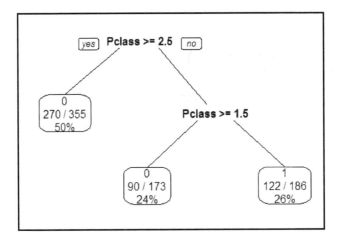

This is a slightly more complex tree, since it has four branches and three terminal nodes. Now, let's calculate the correct classification rate for the model by adding up the correct classification numbers for the three nodes and dividing this by the total number of rows, as we did before:

```
> (270+90+122) / nrow(titanic)
```

This is the following output:

```
[1] 0.67507
>
```

This simple model is even better, with a 67% correct classification.

The random forest model

Now, let's run a random forest model. We will grow 2,000 trees and just for illustration include `Age`, `Pclass` (Passenger Class), and `Fare` as the independent variables. Random forest randomizes both the observations selected as well as a sample number of observations selected, so you are never certain which specific trees you will get. You might even get one of the trees just generated in the previous example!

```
library(randomForest)
set.seed(123)
fit <- randomForest(as.factor(Survived) ~ Age + Pclass + Fare,
```

```
data=titanic,
importance=TRUE,
ntree=2000)
```

Random forest also has a predict function, with a similar syntax to the predict function we used in Chapter 1, *Getting Started with Predictive Analytics*. We will use this function to generate the predictions:

```
prediction.rf <- predict(fit, titanic)
```

Once the predictions are generated, we can construct a dataframe consisting of the predictions along with the actual survival outcomes obtained from the raw data:

```
x<-
data.frame(predict.rf=as.factor(prediction.rf),survived=titanic$Survived)
```

Now we can run a simple table() function which will count the number of actual outcomes classified by their predicted values.

```
table(x$predict.rf,x$survived)
```

This is the following output:

```
     0   1
0  384 118
1   40 172
```

The numbers in the table reflect the following predictions:

```
(Row 1,Column 1) Passenger predicted NOT to survive & DID NOT survive
(Row 1,Column 2) Passenger predicted NOT to survive DID survive
(Row 2,Column 1) Passenger predicted to survive and DID NOT survive
(Row 2,Column 2) Passenger predicted to survive and DID survive
```

Based on that, we can see that we have made correct predictions for the counts contained in (Row 1,Column 1) and (Row 2,Column 2), since our predictions agree with the outcomes.

To get the total number of predictions, we will add up the total number of correct counts, and then divide it by the number of rows. We can do the math at the console:

```
(384+172) / nrow(titanic)
```

This is the following output:

```
[1] 0.7787115
```

Using a random forest, the correct predictions rate has been raised to 77%.

Random forest versus decision trees

Even though random forests can be better predictors than singly partitioned trees, the issue of interpretability comes into play. Random forests do not generate visual decision trees, and computationally random forests can take quite a long time to run as they work to grow and optimize multiple trees from many variables. Some feel that they act as a black box since there are so many ways to optimize and the underlying methods are not readily transparent. However, it is an optimization method and can be very accurate, if extreme accuracy is your goal.

Variable importance plots

Aside from the prediction accuracy, another popular use for random forests is variable selection, using the `varImp()` function. A variable importance plot can be useful in situations in which there are <u>many</u> input variables, but I have found it to be of limited value for a manageable number of variables.

Just to illustrate on our example data, here is the `varImp()` function showing `Fare`, `Age`, and `Pclass` in the order of importance. There are a couple of ways it can do this, but I will be showing it as determined via statistics referred to as **MeanDecreaseGini**. It is not critical to understand how this statistic is computed, but it is sufficient to say at this point that the importance is related to how many different trees the variable appears in, and the part it played in deciding how well it was able to discern one outcome of a tree branch from another. We will discuss decision trees and Gini in the later chapters.

```
varImpPlot(fit,type=2)
```

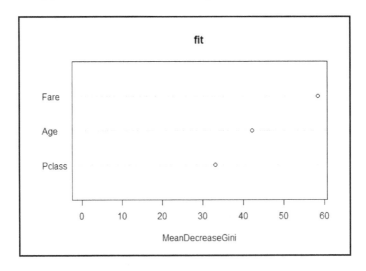

Dimension reduction techniques

You will often be examining hundreds or even thousands of variables, and dimension reduction is a technique that you can use to drastically reduce the number of rows or variables that you need to examine. The premise behind dimension reduction is duplication, that is, many variables which are measuring the same thing. For example, reading, writing, math, and musical aptitude scores are all important in predicting a college GPA, but it is possible that if you only used a musical aptitude score in combination with a writing score, you could achieve the same prediction accuracy as compared to using all four measures. It might also be easier to explain as well, that is one example of why you would use a dimension reduction technique.

When you are looking at reducing the actual number of *variables*, consider principal components. You will end up with the same number of observations but will limit the number of variables you look at (the *Principal Components* section).

When you are considering reducing the dimensionality of *rows*, use clustering methods.

Principal components

Principal Component Analysis (PCA) is useful in cases in which you have too many variables and you wish to capture all of the variation of data into one or two variables. Principal component does this using matrix algebra to create linear combinations of all of the variables.

PCA is also used to see which variables have the most influence within each of the principal components, so often it is a way to discard certain variables when a PCA analysis indicates certain variables have little effect on the outcome.

An example using the variables of height and weight is a good one. Since height and weight are positively correlated, choosing to use only height or only weight as an independent variable to predict body mass might not make much of a difference. So, we can create a new variable which is a linear combination of height and weight and use that as a variable instead.

Clustering

Clustering is a method which groups data into different classes, so that each class is similar to each other. There are various methods that can be used to define similarity. K-Means clustering is probably the most popular method of clustering. This method uses distances measured to assign data observations to the closest class. Clustering is often used in marketing in order to develop different customer segments.

Clustering is an unsupervised algorithm and is subjective. You can specify beforehand how many groups you wish to cluster into. This number is somewhat arbitrary, and if the goal is interpretability, it can yield to different interpretations.

Scatterplots are often used to show data clusters using only two variables (one is on the x axis and the other on the y axis).

Here is an example of some scatterplots which can be used to pick out clusters by seeing which data points *congregate* together.

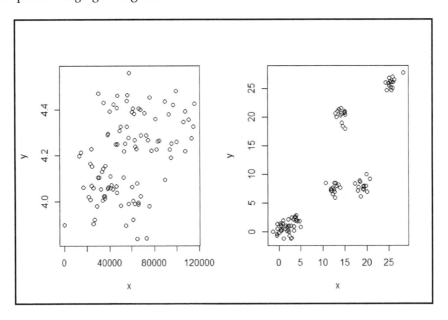

The plot on the right shows five distinct clusters. You can see that very low values of variable x tend to go with very low values of variable y. However, it is a bit unclear what the clusters should be for the plot on the left. Sometimes low values of x go with low values of y, but sometimes they are associated with high values of y. There is no apparent distinct grouping. What do you see? Do you see two clusters, three or more, or no clustering? It is really impossible to tell and that is where subjectivity creeps in.

Time series models

Problems containing data observations which are not independent of one another, such as time-based data, deserve special treatment since events which occur in time exhibit a property known as **autocorrelation**. What that means is that the independent variables are all dependent upon the previous values of that variable. Many data techniques assume that all values occur independently of each other, so special techniques were developed to deal with time-based data.

Exponential smoothing is based upon the simple concept that the most recent data is the best predictor of the future. Exponential smoothing techniques allow you to tweak the parameters so that you can decide how much weight is given to the recent data versus the older data. It is suitable for many time-series problems.

Time-series models can also be based upon cyclical, trend, seasonal, one-time occurrence, or causal factors. One of the more advanced time-series methods is known as **ARIMA** or **Box-Jenkins** models which incorporate elements of time-series and regression models.

Naive Bayes classifier

Naive Bayes originally became popular as a method for spam detection. It is quick and fast. Naive Bayes assumes that the variables are all independent and not related to each other (a bad assumption, but that is what makes it Naive!). It also has the advantage that it does not need to be retrained when adding new data. Naive Bayes has its roots in Bayes theorem.

This simple example shows Naive Bayes in action. Using the Iris dataset, Naive Bayes will make a prediction for the fifth column using the first four columns as independent variables:

```
#use 1st 4 columns to predict the fifth
library(e1071)
iris.nb<-naiveBayes(iris[,1:4], iris[,5])
table(predict(iris.nb, iris[,1:4]), iris[,5])
```

The results of the `table()` function will go to the console. This output is the confusion matrix which is as follows:

```
           setosa versicolor virginica
setosa         50          0         0
versicolor      0         47         3
virginica       0          3        47
```

The correct classification rate for the problem is 96%. This can be easily verified at the console by summing up the values corresponding with the correct classification counts (that is, row 1/column 1, row 2/column 2, and row 3/column 3) and then dividing by the total number of rows.

Here is how you would do it in the console using the R calculator:

```
> nrow(iris)
[1] 150
> (50+47+47)/nrow(iris)
[1] 0.96
```

The confusion matrix also tells you which classifications did not perform well. For example, if you sum the values of column 2, you can see that there is a total of 50 versicolor species. However, there were a total of three misclassifications for the versicolor/virginia combination (following bold underlined):

```
            setosa versicolor virginica
setosa        50         0         0
versicolor     0        47         3
virginica      0         3        47
```

To identify which combinations were misclassified, we can write a little bit of code and examine the incorrect classification rows using a DataTable object. Using a DataTable object allows you to sort, search, and filter the data.

Merge the predictions with the original data. Then, assign a Correct or Wrong flag to the dataframe to designate whether the prediction was correct or not.

```
mrg <- cbind(pred,iris)
mrg$correct <- ifelse(mrg$pred==mrg$Species,"Correct","Wrong")
```

Load the DT library and specify that you want an interactive datatable on the merged data. You will also want some interactive filtering capabilities, so specify filter='top' as a parameter.

```
library(DT)
datatable(mrg,filter='top')
```

The interactive data table will open in the RStudio viewer:

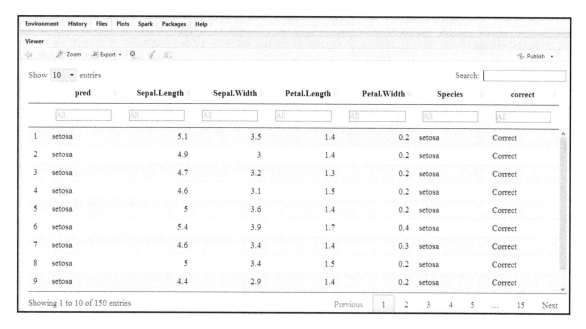

To find the misclassified species, type `Wrong`, in the search box. The display will automatically update to show the incorrect predictions:

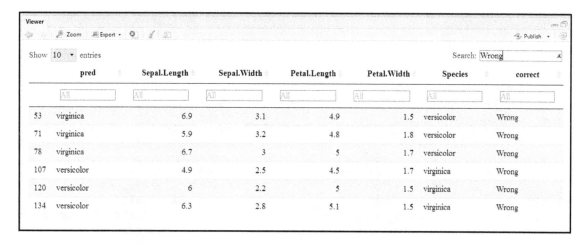

Text mining techniques

Most legacy predictive analytics techniques were originally designed to work with structured data. However, that has changed with the advent of text mining techniques, which are able to process and visualize unstructured data. Some of the more popular tools are:

- **Word clouds**: Word clouds are graphical representations of word frequencies or concepts and would be a simple tool to present important words in a corpus (collection of text documents) to management.

  Here is an example of a word cloud produced from Lincoln's Gettysburg address (Bliss Copy) (Gettysburg Address, 1863). To limit the number of words displayed, set `min.freq=2`, so that only words which appear at least two times will be displayed. Notice that the output is also eliminating some common words (stopwords), which do not usually add to the interpretation (a, and, it, and so on).

```
install.packages("wordcloud")
install.packages("RColorBrewer")
library("wordcloud")
lincoln <- "Four score and seven years ago our fathers brought forth on
this continent, a new nation, conceived in Liberty, and dedicated to the
proposition that all men are created equal. Now we are engaged in a great
civil war, testing whether that nation, or any nation so conceived and so
dedicated, can long endure. We are met on a great battle-field of that war.
We have come to dedicate a portion of that field, as a final resting place
for those who here gave their lives that that nation might live. It is
altogether fitting and proper that we should do this. But, in a larger
sense, we can not dedicate -- we can not consecrate -- we can not hallow --
this ground. The brave men, living and dead, who struggled here, have
consecrated it, far above our poor power to add or detract. The world will
little note, nor long remember what we say here, but it can never forget
what they did here. It is for us the living, rather, to be dedicated here
to the unfinished work which they who fought here have thus far so nobly
advanced. It is rather for us to be here dedicated to the great task
remaining before us -- that from these honored dead we take increased
devotion to that cause for which they gave the last full measure of
devotion -- that we here highly resolve that these dead shall not have died
in vain -- that this nation, under God, shall have a new birth of freedom -
- and that government of the people, by the people, for the people, shall
not perish from the earth."
set.seed(123)
wordcloud(lincoln, min.freq=2, scale=c(3,.5), random.order = FALSE)
```

The output of the `wordcloud` uses the size of the word to represent its frequency in the text:

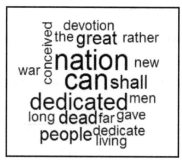

- **Bigram analysis**: Word clouds usually show the frequencies of single words in a paragraph or document. They do not usually analyze the surrounding words. Bigram, on the other hand, looks at the frequency of two consecutive words as a single pair. Often, additional insight can be derived by seeing how many times these consecutive words appear together in the various parts of the document being analyzed. This bigram concept can also be extended to three words at a time, four words at a time, and so on. In this case, they are called **ngrams**, meaning analysis of any number of consecutive words which appear together.

  For example, the following table shows four bigrams which appear twice in the preceding paragraph and one that appears three times (consecutive words). Note that this includes punctuation which is usually removed before frequency counts are determined. Punctuation, numbers, and small parts of speech such as *the*, *them*, *a*, or *an* are usually performed prior to performing text analysis. These are collectively known as **stopwords**.

	ngrams	freq
1	consecutive words	3
2	appear together	2
3	a time,	2
4	at a	2
5	words at	2
6	parts of	1
7	time, etc.	1

- Here is an example which uses the `get.phrasetable` for the `ngram` package to extract all possible ngrams. To specify a bigram we will use n=2.

```
install.packages ("ngram")
library(ngram)
df <-get.phrasetable ( ngram(lincoln, n=2) )
View(df)
```

From the output of the `View` command, we can see that **the people** occurs three times:

	ngrams	freq	prop
1	can not	3	0.010830325
2	the people,	3	0.010830325
3	to the	3	0.010830325
4	-- that	3	0.010830325
5	we can	3	0.010830325

- **Topic definitions**: With topic definition, your goal is to classify documents into a set of categories, just as we would with a nontextual problem. For example, if a customer calls and then starts complaining about the reliability of a product, we might want to direct the customer to a different call center area to that if he was calling simply to get information about a product. A key component of text mining is the ability to be able to parse unstructured data and learning how to mine this data for the important words.
- **Clustering**: Other traditional techniques, such as clustering, can also be used with free form text. However, in many cases, the text data will need to be retrofitted and will need to be preprocessed into a structured format first, before traditional predictive analytics techniques such as clustering are applied. You will learn how to convert unstructured text into a structured form called a term frequency matrix, which will allow you to perform traditional predictive analytics techniques.
- Sentiment analysis is the ability to gauge an individual's or group's opinions (whether positive or negative) about a product, service, or policy.

Here is an example which will produce a sentiment analysis prediction for various short comments made to a call center. A Naive Bayes model is used to predict the last five comments, based on the first 10 comments, which have been manually preclassified as positive or negative.

```
install.packages("RTextTools")
library(RTextTools)
library(e1071)

verbatim =
    rbind(
        c('Agent was very helpful', 'positive'),
        c('Would buy the product again', 'positive'),
        c('Satisfied with response', 'positive'),
        c('Helped me to choose between the two offers', 'positive'),
        c('Defintely would recommend to a friend', 'positive'),
        c('Terrible customer service', 'negative'),
        c('not recommended', 'negative'),
        c('Agent took too much time', 'negative'),
        c('Waiting a long time for customer service', 'negative'),
        c('Not satisfied with response', 'negative'),
        c('Not satisfied at all', 'negative'),
        c('Would not recommend', 'negative'),
        c('Helpful customer support', 'positive'),
        c('Great product support', 'positive'),
        c('excellent product', 'positive')


    )
# build Term document matrix
TDM.mat=
as.matrix(create_matrix(verbatim[,1],language="english",removeStopwords=TRU
E, removeNumbers=TRUE,stemWords=FALSE))
    classifier = naiveBayes(TDM.mat[1:10,], as.factor(verbatim[1:10,2]) )
    # test the model
    predicted = predict(classifier, TDM.mat[11:15,]);
```

The `table()` function will tell you how the predictions did for the last five customer comments. Three of the five comments were classified correctly (60%). Is 60% considered good? That depends upon what you will be doing with your model. If you are able to identify negative comments, you might want to reach out to the customer via various channels and try to win the customer back. On the other hand, positive comments imply that you are doing right by the customer and maybe you should think about offering good customer discounts.

```
table(verbatim[11:15, 2], predicted)
```

```
> table(verbatim[11:15, 2], predicted)
          predicted
           negative positive
negative       1        1
positive       1        2
```

Step 5 evaluation

Model evaluation deals with how accurate or useful the model you have just developed is or will be in the future. Model evaluation can take different forms. Some are more subjective and are domain oriented, such as placing it under the scrutiny of experts in your field, and some are more technically oriented. There are many metrics and procedures available to assess a model. At the basic level, you have many statistics (some of them with acronyms known as AIC, BIC, and AUC) which purport to convey the goodness of a model in a single metric. However, these metrics by themselves are unable to convey the purpose and application of a predictive model to a larger audience and often these metrics are in conflict. Some context is needed. Some would argue that one could also develop a perfectly good predictive model and then be unable to convey its purpose and application to a larger audience. In my opinion, that is a bad model, regardless of how well an evaluation metric fits. And then there is the performance factor. A model may work well on sample data but be too slow to become actionable in the real world. In short, there is no single metric that you should use for model evaluation. The best course is to look at it from all angles and then present the objective results.

Model validation

The basic premise of predictive analytics model validation is that you develop your model on one subset of the data (called the training dataset), and then demonstrate that your model has the capability to successfully predict similar resuls on a different set of data. Of primary importance the data set known generically as *test*. The test dataset is also known as a holdout sample. The training and test datasets are randomly determined before any model building begins, and the data is never changed. The validation data is a third dataset that is sometimes used to further test the validity of the data. It typically contains data the modeler has never seen before and is introduced after one model has been developed and determined to be the champion model.

The following code will create a simple Naive Bayes model and create a `confusionMatrix` (or classification error table), which shows how many predictions were classified correctly. For the `iris` dataset, 92% of the predictions were correct. Note that, for this example, we are using the confusion matrix, which is part of the caret package, rather than computing the accuracy manually as we did in the previous examples:

```
require(caret)
require(e1071)
data(iris)
set.seed(123)
partition.index <- createDataPartition(iris$Species, p=.5, list=FALSE)
Training <- iris[ partition.index,]
test <- iris[-partition.index,]
model <- naiveBayes(Species~.,data = Training)
predictions <- predict(model, test[,1:4])
# summarize results
% confusionMatrix(predictions, test[,5])
```

```
> confusionMatrix(predictions, test[,5])
Confusion Matrix and Statistics

            Reference
Prediction   setosa versicolor virginica
  setosa        25          0         0
  versicolor     0         22         3
  virginica      0          3        22

Overall Statistics

               Accuracy : 0.92
                 95% CI : (0.834, 0.9701)
    No Information Rate : 0.3333
    P-Value [Acc > NIR] : < 2.2e-16

                  Kappa : 0.88
 Mcnemar's Test P-Value : NA

Statistics by Class:   .

                     Class: setosa Class: versicolor Class: virginica
Sensitivity                 1.0000            0.8800           0.8800
Specificity                 1.0000            0.9400           0.9400
Pos Pred Value              1.0000            0.8800           0.8800
Neg Pred Value              1.0000            0.9400           0.9400
Prevalence                  0.3333            0.3333           0.3333
Detection Rate              0.3333            0.2933           0.2933
Detection Prevalence        0.3333            0.3333           0.3333
Balanced Accuracy           1.0000            0.9100           0.9100
>|
```

Area under the curve

Area under the curve (**AUC**) is another popular measure to assess the goodness of your model. Historically, this measurement was developed during World War II. The original terminology was **Receiver Operating Characteristic** (**ROC**) and its original purpose was to determine whether or not a blip on the radar screen was an enemy ship or just random noise.

One of the things that the AUC tells us is the ratio of the true positives to the false positives. The AUC is determined via a mathematic formula, which will be a number between 0 and 1. An AUC of 0.5 is considered a random classification. Look for points that hover near the upper-left quadrant. This would be the area where advantageous conditions converge: high true positives with low false positives.

AUC is a good measure of the tradeoffs involved in classification errors. However, it should not be considered as absolute. Costs of misclassification should be taken into account when using the AUC.

Computing an ROC curve using the titanic dataset

Here is an example of plotting an ROC curve on the titanic dataset, using a simple logistic regression model to predict survival:

```
install.packages("titanic")
install.packages("ROCR")

library(titanic)
library(ROCR)

titanic <- titanic_train[complete.cases(titanic_train), ]

 model <- glm(as.factor(Survived) ~ Sex+Age+Pclass, data=titanic,
family="binomial")
    pred <- prediction(predict(model), titanic$Survived)
    perf <- performance(pred,"tpr","fpr")
    plot(perf)
    abline(a=0,b=1)
```

The AUC curve is plotted along with the various cutoff values for the probability of the predicted outcome. The diagonal reference line represents a random model. The area under the logistic model curve looks to be about 75% of the total area:

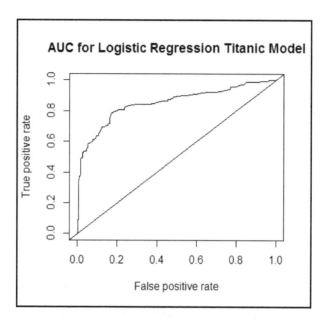

As mentioned earlier, the AUC is used for comparing models. Here is the AUC for the logistic model using only Age as a factor:

```
model2 <- glm(as.factor(Survived) ~ Age, data=titanic, family="binomial")
pred <- prediction(predict(model2), titanic$Survived)
perf <- performance(pred,"tpr","fpr")
plot(perf,main="AUC for Logistic Regression Titanic Model - Age Only")
abline(a=0,b=1)
```

We can see immediately that this single variable model has little predictive power. The AUC curve is similar to the preceding random diagonal reference line, which indicates no predictive power.

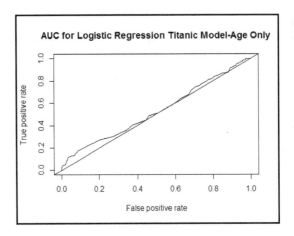

In sample/out of sample tests, walk forward tests

After a model has been developed, it is considered best practice to validate the results against other data.

Training/test/validation datasets

Training data is the data that is used to build the predictive data. Test data, also known as a hold-out sample, is the data which was not used in the training process. Test data is used to see if a trained model is able to generalize its results to another dataset which was not part of the model training.

However, even though the test dataset is not used in the training of the model, the contents are usually viewable by the modeler during model development.

A validation set is a third dataset which is sometimes used to further benchmark the model results. Validation data is also data that has never been seen before, which is incorporated after the model has passed validation against the test dataset and prior to deployment. Validation datasets are often brought from a completely different source from the original training/test data source, the goal being to provide a second corroboration, or refutation, of the model results.

Along with training, test, and validation data, you will also hear some other terms which are related:

- In-sample data refers to the data which was used to fit (model) the data and is used on the training dataset
- Out-of-sample data refers to data not used to fit the data

This means that out-of-sample data is typically used only on the test and validation datasets. Another technique to validate the data is known as **k-fold cross-validation**. This technique will use multiple folds to define different subsets of in-sample and out-of-sample datasets in order to perform multiple iterations of model testing in order to randomize the selection of training and test data.

Time series validation

Of course time series models also use this concept; however, time periods alone can be used to partition test and training data, for example, a model might be built on the previous five years of historical data (training) and then forecast on the current sixth year of data (testing or validation data).

Variations of this are common. A *walk forward* testing modeler will develop a time-series model on years 1-5, test the results on year 6, and then develop a similar model on years 2-6, and then test the results on year 7. This procedure would be repeated until there is no more data to test. In all these cases, the model is built on the *in-sample* data, and tested on out-of-sample data which is similar to k-fold validation.

Benchmark against best champion model

In champion/challenger model development, you currently have a deployed stable champion model in which you can benchmark any future results. This allows you to discard any model results which fall far below this benchmark. If you do not have a current champion, you can develop a theoretical best model using an algorithm such as random forests or SVM, and use that as a benchmark for what is achievable but (assume) is not actionable. Look at the results of the model you have just developed and see if it is close to these kinds of results. If so, the results are probably not attainable and you might want to look elsewhere.

Expert opinions: man against machine

This is often done with classification problems and it essentially pits man against machine. If an expert agrees with a lot of what your model spits out, that is another reason to deem it valid.

Meta-analysis

Much has been written about junk science and how there is always another study which produces the opposite results from a previous one. *p-value hacking* is one way to do this. We have already mentioned metadata which is data about data.

Meta-analysis is the study of studies in which a research will look at all of the previous analyses and report what they all have to say about outcomes in totality. If your analysis agrees with other similar analyses that have been performed in the past, that would be more evidence to support your model.

Dart board method

In some instances, you need not have only one model to predict the outcome. If you accept the view that *All models are useful*, why not use some of them at the same time? This is used extensively in marketing campaign management and financial portfolio management. Sometimes it pays <u>not</u> to put all of your eggs in one basket. One model can fail to work during one month but is offset with positive results from another model. Ensemble modeling, which is similar, can also incorporate several diverse models at the same time, but usually there is a single outcome and may be subject to overfitting.

Step 6 deployment

Deployment of a model is the process by which you put your models into a real-world production setting. This can depend on many factors, such as the environment in which it was developed, the algorithm that was chosen, assumptions concerning the data that was made when the model was developed, and of course, the level of the developer. Often a model is unable to scale up to the demands of a production environment and knowing your possible production environment in advance will dictate what problems or techniques are feasible.

Model scoring

Model scoring makes the model actionable. If you develop a model and you are unable to apply the results to new data, then you will be unable to do any prediction on an ongoing basis. New model scoring often involves outputing the development model outputs to a real-time scoring engine. That engine is often Java or C++. How that is performed varies vastly depending upon the modeling technique. Sometimes the scoring is performed separately, so it can be optimized for efficiency.

Regression type models are relatively easy to score, since all that is needed are the model's coefficients and intercepts. Other types of models need a little more work. For example, decision tree software should be able to output a set of decision rules which would enable production language to recode it using a series of if/then/else rules. Software packages often output the decision rules which were determined for each node.

Certain production packages will accept PMML input. PMML is a common language which is used to facilitate translation of one language's model specification into a common format.

For more complicated models, it may be necessary to have production versions of the model on a separate production machine and run the model using similar code to that used for development.

References

You can refer to the following articles:

- *Determine the Root Cause: 5 Whys*. Retrieved from
  https://www.isixsigma.com/tools-templates/cause-effect/determine-root-cause-5-whys/
- *Gettysburg Address, (1863, November 19)*. Retrieved from *Abraham Lincoln Online*:
  http://www.abrahamlincolnonline.org/lincoln/speeches/gettysburg.html
- *Stevens, S. (1946). On the Theory of Scales of Measurement. Science*
- Wikipedia. *Bias-variance tradeoff*. Retrieved from *Wikipedia*:
  https://en.wikipedia.org/wiki/Bias%E2%80%93variance_tradeoff

Notes

Random Forests (tm) is a trademark of Leo Breiman and Adele Cutler and is licensed exclusively to Salford Systems for the commercial release of the software.

Summary

In this chapter, we learned about the various structured approaches to predictive analytics and how implementing an analytics project in a methodical way can enhance the success of an analytics project through collaboration and communication. We went through the various steps of the CRISP-DM methodology and demonstrated tools that you could use to help you progress along these steps.

We discussed the benefits of sampling and how it could speed up your project. SQL was demonstrated to illustrate basic charts and plots, so that you can begin to develop insight even before you create a first model. We showed that data simulation could also be used at the data understanding phase as a preliminary modeling tool to do "what ifing", even before actual company data is obtained.

We learned about the various types of data that you will encounter, and showed some examples of independent and dependent variables and the importance of doing preliminary 1-way and 2-way variable analysis as a precursor to modeling.

Finally, we learned about some of the basic predictive models that we will be using later on, and discussed the importance of the bias/variance tradeoff when starting to examine which types of predictive models you might want to employ.

We ended with discussing some best practices for evaluating a model, and the importance of planning for the eventual deployment of models into production and how that could alter your development process.

In the next chapter, we will focus more upon getting the data into a form suitable for actual predictive modeling with a focus on data cleaning, outliers, missing values, and some data reduction and transformation techniques.

3
Inputting and Exploring Data

"On two occasions I have been asked, "Pray, Mr. Babbage, if you put into the machine wrong figures, will the right answers come out?" ... I am not able rightly to apprehend the kind of confusion of ideas that could provoke such a question."

-Charles Babbage

In this chapter, we will cover inputting and exploring data. In the first two chapters, we covered processing some datasets that already reside within R packages. We purposefully avoided reading any external data sources. However, now we will. The inputting data section will cover various mechanisms for reading your own data into R.

The exploring data section covers some techniques you can use to implement successful completion of the second and third of the data understanding and data preparation steps of the CRISP-DM process we covered in the last chapter.

The topics we will cover include the following:

- Getting data into R
- Generating your own data
- Munging and joining data
- Data cleaning techniques
- Data transformations
- Analyzing missing values and outliers
- Variable reduction techniques

Data input

Data by itself is just a pure stream of a numerical something. It is the analytics process that turns this something into knowledge, but before we start understanding it, we have to be able to obtain it. The number of ways in which we can now generate data has grown exponentially. Progressing from fixed length format, through HTML, and then to free form unstructured input, and then to today's schema on read technologies, there are so many different data formats today that there is a very good chance that you haven't, and will never work with a few of them. Reading data in and understanding the variables and what the data represents can also be incredibly frustrating. Integrating the data with other sources, both internal and external, can seem like a jigsaw puzzle at times. At times, the data will not seem to fit as nicely as you would hope.

However, with regard to raw input, most people will work with a couple of common formats in the course of their work, and it will be useful to know how to utilize them.

Text file Input

The most convenient way to read data into a predictive analytics project is via an input text file. Text files are convenient and work well for small and medium projects. You can examine text files using many different kinds of program in human readable form. However, as the data gets larger, it may be that storing data in text files becomes a bit unmanageable, and you might have to turn to retrieving directly from data warehouses, both from the SQL and NoSQL variety, and possibly incorporate ecosystems such as Spark and Hadoop, in which you will begin to use parallel processing and memory management techniques.

The read.table function

The basic function for reading text files is `read.table`. The most important information to supply to this function is a filename, a separator, and whether or not a row header is included. There are also some other important options to consider when reading in a file using `read.table` function:

- `header`: set to `header=TRUE` if the first line of the input data contains column header information.
- `col.names`: if you will be supplying your own column names, use this option to specify the columns names in a vector.

- `na.string`: The default for this is NA; however, input data contains a variety of codes that can represent NA, or can even have multiple NA values. Sometimes, the values 0, 9, or other characters such as . can be used to represent a missing value.
- `ColClasses`: use this option if you want to specifically read an input data item as a specific data type, such as string, int, or factor. Supply `ColClasses` as a vector of character types. This option is often supplied after an initial read of the data, when you discover the default data type is not what you want it to be, and you will be forcing a reading of the particular variable with the specific data type specified.
- `stringsAsFactors`: If this option is specified as TRUE, it will coerce the character input into a factor. Factors are a special representation of character categorical variables, which are represented internally as integers. Setting a character variable as a factor makes it more efficient to analyze as categorical variables, but makes it a little more difficult to perform strict text processing, for example, string manipulation. However, this are ways around these by using functions, which cast data types into alternative data types.

 Generally, it is a good idea to set `stringsasFactors` to FALSE if you will be doing a lot of string manipulations. However, factors are much more useful for analytic packages, and most of the time variables are required to be in factor format. But there are ways to convert the variables from character to factor, or vice versa, and this only becomes important when your code reaches production, or when you want to conserve memory.

- `sep:` This separator value enables the function to separate one field from another. It is typically a comma or a tab.

Along with the `read.table` function, there are also other specific functions that were developed for specialized purposes that derive from the `read.table` function:

- `read.csv`: `read.csv` is used for files that are comma delimited and that use a period in numeric values. CSV data is the most common text file format. Virtually all data applications have the ability to read or write to this format, so it is an inherent advantage to be well versed in using this format. However, CSV input can be slow, and usually works out of the box for well-behaved data. There are functions that you might want to use down the line that have better input performance (such as the `fread` or `scan` functions), but `read.csv` is a good place to start for reading csv files if you just want to get going quickly.

- `read.csv2`: this is similar to `read.csv` but uses a semicolon to separate values and uses a comma as a decimal point placeholder. For example, this is useful when reading in Euros, which uses a comma to separate the whole number from the decimal portion, as the following code illustrates.

```
#Read in a single pencil costing $1.20

cat("Product,Cost",file="outfile.txt",sep="\n")
cat("Pencil,1.20",file="outfile.txt",
sep="\n",append=TRUE)
read.csv("outfile.txt")

#Read in a single pencil costing €1,2
cat("Product,Cost",file="outfile.txt",sep="\n")
cat("Pencil;1,20",file="outfile.txt",
sep="\n",append=TRUE)
read.csv2("outfile.txt", sep=";")
```

- `read.delim`: Use this for tab delimited files with a period as the decimal placeholder.
- `read.delim2`: this is the same as `read.delim`, but uses a comma as the decimal placeholder.
- `read.fwf`: this will process data with a predetermined number of bytes per column. It is somewhat of an older and inefficient way of storing data, yet some legacy data will still be available in this format, so knowing how to use this function is still useful if you will be working with this kind of data.

Database tables

Database tables reside within an enterprise data warehouse (**EDW**) such as MySQL, SQL Server, or Oracle, or they can be housed on local PCs. This data can be accessed using R provided correct authentication credentials are supplied. Enterprise data contains some of the best data that you can get your hands on. It is usually considered an official data source that is used across a company. Additionally, in a capable enterprise data warehouse system, data is already vetted, so that saves you the work of checking for data quality. However, data extracted from a data warehouse can also be complex, and often needs a good data dictionary and metadata to accompany it.

Data warehouse tables are often optimized for speed. However, it is necessary to understand the logical and physical data structure of the warehouse, along with the column index structure. Knowing this will improve your query performance.

In an EDW, data is often organized along subject lines, with separate specialized tables for each purpose. Sometimes this leads to redundancy, but the advantage is that all the data you need may be located in just a few tables.

Reading data directly from database tables circumvents the R memory limitation, to some extent, since some of the processing is done externally to your local PC. In some instances, parallel processing can be used, which will allow you to access very large datasets.

The usual way of accessing data stored in relational databases is through SQL, ODBC, or JDBC connection. Some systems will accept a direct connection. Some specific packages used to connect to databases are listed here:

- The `RODBC` package provides an interface to SQLServer
- The `RMySQL` package is used to connect to MySQL databases
- The `ROracle`, `RJDBC`, and `RODBC` packages can be used to connect to Oracle databases

The universal connector for enterprise databases is ODBC connector. Since it is a universal and is single threaded, ODBC tends to be slow. RJDBC provides access via a JDBC interface. JDBC is faster than ODBC but will require more tweaking. Since connecting to a database is a little more involved than just reading a text file, it will take a little more time and work to get through login IDs, passwords, and optimizing queries. But once you are familiar with your environment, it will be worth the time spent to optimize access, and avoid calls from the DBA letting you know that your queries are taking too long.

Spreadsheet files

R provides direct interfaces to Excel tables via the `XLConnect` or `xlsx` packages. Excel is prevalent in the corporate world and can contain a lot of useful data and metadata. So, it pays to learn all about the tools which can access spreadsheets. It is also worth learning how to do analytics using spreadsheets, since that will give you valuable insight into the thought process that was used to create the data in the first place.

However, since Excel is a proprietary product, and has many versions on the market, it can still be tricky to use some of these packages. The most convenient way of importing Excel data is to first access it within Excel itself, and then save it as a delimited file using Excel commands, and then reading it back into R using `read.table` or `read.csv` packages. If you can't do it yourself, you can also ask the maintainer of the spreadsheet to write a CSV file for you.

XML and JSON data

XML data is used for data interchange in the financial and insurance industry so if you work in these industries, there is a good chance you will come across some format at this point. No predefined schemas are used in XML, but that also means that there is a fair amount of data parsing that needs to be performed after the data is read in order to extract the data itself. The XML() package is used to read XML data into R.

JSON is another standard derived from web technologies that was originally used to transmit sets of key pairs between different application systems. The jsonlite package can be used to parse JSON files.

> Still confused about all the different file formats? Try using the Rio package with input files. Rio is a specialized wrapper package that is able to identify the type of file that you wish to read and then call the appropriate package.

Generating your own data

Not sure which data source to use when testing a predictive model? No problem. Generate your own data with the built-in sample() function, as well as generating random observations based upon distributions such as runif (uniform), rnorm (normal), mvrnorm (multivariate normal), or rpois (poisson counts). We will also be using a specialized package called wakefield, which generates typical random values that you would find in many data sources, such as age, gender, education, and customer satisfaction scores, without having to worry about the underlying distributions.

Tips for dealing with large files

Some input files can get quite large and inefficient to read. Here are some tips to speed up the process:

- Use external Unix tools for splitting files so that they can be read in chunks. There is usually a field that you can use to split out separate files. Date fields are good ones.
- Consider using external tools to replace large character strings with numerical or shorter character strings. This will save valuable memory.
- Use parameters on input to control how much data you want to read. You may want to process your input file by starting to read your input at row 1,000,000. You don't always have to read a file from the beginning.

- Do not feel obliged to always read all of the columns. Once you have determined which columns are truly needed, read only those columns; this will speed up the processing. For example, if you are using read.table, you can specify NULL in the colClasses option to indicate that a column is to be skipped.
- Use the scan, fread, and readlines functions. They will give you a greater degree of control over the input, and can make input faster.

Data munging and wrangling

A large part of preparing the data for analysis utilizes bringing disparate information together in order to produce the final analytics dataset, which will be passed directly to the algorithm. This process is known by many different names, such as data munging, data wrangling, ETL, or simply data prep. We have already discussed some ways in which we can read data from a single source. You will be very fortunate if you are able to work with a single data file that has all of the information that you need. In fact, if you are able to utilize data that is already consolidated, go for it, since someone else has already done the work and there is no need to try to figure out how to relate them yourself. However, most of the time you will need to relate at least two different sources, and somehow relate them based upon some common data elements.

Joining data

If you need to bring together different data sources, SQL is one method for bringing data together. As mentioned, SQL syntax is common to a lot of environments, so if you learn SQL syntax in R, you have started to learn how data is processed in other environments. But do not restrict yourself to just SQL. Other options exist for joining data, such as using the merge statement. Merge is a native function that accomplishes the same objective. And some other packages handle data integration fairly well. I will also be using the dplyr package to perform some of the same tasks as could be done in SQL.

The sqldf package is a standard R package that uses standard SQL syntax to merge, or join, two tables together. For relational data, this is accomplished by associating a variable on one table (primary key) with a similar variable on another associated table. Note that I am using the term table in the context of a relational database environment. In the R environment, an SQL table is equivalent to an R dataframe. An R table is a specific R object that refers to a contingency table produced by a crosstab, or similar function.

Using the sqldf function

This example uses the `sqldf` and `RSQLite` packages to illustrate some SQL joins, and also uses it to demonstrate reading a CSV file with filters. This example also uses the `wakefield` package to generate a hypothetical membership file along with a purchase transaction file.

Housekeeping and loading of necessary packages

First, clear out the workspace (after saving any R objects you will need later):

```
rm(list = ls())
```

Then, install the required packages:

```
install.packages("dplyr")
install.packages("wakefield")
install.packages("sqldf")
install.packages("RSQLite")
```

The convention in this book will be to specify a simple
`install.packages("packagename")` instruction to install the necessary packages,
followed by a `library("packagename")` to load them into memory. Once the required
packages are installed, you can either comment them out, or replace the line with
conditional installation code:

```
try(require(dplyr) || install.packages("dplyr"))
```

But this syntax may not work on all R installations and GUIs, so we will keep it simple, and
explicitly specify `install.package()`.

Now we will load the required packages into memory:

```
library(dplyr)
library(wakefield)
library(sqldf)
library(RSQLite)
```

Generating the data

Next, generate the membership file with 1,000 members and assign it to the member
dataframe. The `wakefield` package uses specialized functions to generate typical values for
each of the specified variables:

- The `gender` function will generate M, or F with a 50% chance of any individual row being a male or female
- The `set.seed(1010)` directive guarantees that the results will be the same no matter how many times you run the code
- The `r_sample_replace()` function will generate a unique member ID with a value from 1 to 1000
- The `income`, `children`, `employment`, `level`, `grad`, `year`, `state`, and `zip_code` variables are all randomly generated without supplying any specialized parameters

Open up a new script window, and run the following code:

```
#GENERATE MEMBER
set.seed(1010)
member <- r_data_frame(
  n=1000,
  r_sample_replace(x =   1:1000,replace=FALSE,name="memberid"),
  age,
  gender(x = c("M","F"), prob = c(.5,.5),name="Gender"),
  dob,
  income,
  children,
  employment,
  level,
  grade,
  year,
  state,
  zip_code
)
```

Similarly, generate the purchases file, and assign it to the purchases dataframe. The total amount purchases will come from a normal distribution with a mean purchases amount of 20,000 and a standard deviation of 1,000. The `Product` variable is a random product name coming from the letters A-Z.

This next code snippet will generate the purchases:

```
#GENERATE PURCHASES
set.seed(1010)

purchases <- r_data_frame(
  n=1000,
  r_sample_replace(x = 1:1000,replace=TRUE,name="memberid2"),
  purch=rpois(lambda=1),
```

```
   normal(mean = 20000, sd = 1000, min = NULL, max = NULL, name =
"TotalAmount"),
   upper(x = LETTERS, k=3, prob = NULL, name = "Product")
)
purchases$purch <- purchases$purch + 1
str(purchases)
```

After generating the purchases dataframe, we will write it to an external CSV file. The reason we are doing this is to demonstrate how we can filter rows from an external file using `read.csv.sql`:

```
#WRITE PURCHASES TO FILE

write.csv(purchases, "purchases.csv", quote = FALSE, row.names = FALSE)
```

Now we will read the `purchases.csv` back into R. But instead of reading the whole file, we will only read in those records where the `TotalAmount` > 20,000:

```
#read it back in

purchases_filtered  <- read.csv.sql("purchases.csv",sql = "select * from
file where TotalAmount > 20000 ")
```

You may be asking why we did it this way instead of just reading the whole file and then filtering it later. The answer is efficiency. Let's assume that in reality, the purchases file would be much larger than the 1,000 records it really is, and would contain lots of small purchases. We wouldn't want to take up processing time by reading all of these small transactions, since we are only interested in looking at high-value members. So, you can filter the data while reading the file, and only read in those members who had purchases greater than 20,000.

Examining the metadata

After reading in any file, it is always a good practice to verify the number of rows, and look at the metadata after a dataframe is created. We can do that easily with the `str()` function. The `str()` function is an incredibly useful function that is packed with a lot of the type of metadata information that we discussed in Chapter 2, *The Modeling Process*. It is always a good idea to run the `str()` function every time you read, merge, join, or create a new file:

```
str(member)
str(purchases)
str(purchases_filtered)
```

```
> str(member)
Classes 'tbl_df', 'tbl' and 'data.frame':        1000 obs. of  12 variables:
 $ memberid  : int   553 192 185 676 909 818 659 971 384 792 ...
 $ Age       : int   30 23 29 20 31 23 26 29 28 28 ...
 $ Gender    : Factor w/ 2 levels "M","F": 2 2 1 2 2 2 1 2 2 1 ...
 $ DOB       : Date, format: "2002-04-30" "2001-12-16" "2002-08-14" "2002-09-08" ...
 $ Income    : num   52826 53330 50949 31842 47418 ...
 $ Children  : int   2 1 5 1 3 1 1 7 0 3 ...
 $ Employment: Factor w/ 5 levels "Full Time","Part Time",..: 4 5 1 1 1 1 1 1 1 4 ...
 $ Level     : int   1 4 4 4 2 3 2 3 1 3 ...
 $ Grade     : num   88.6 78.3 88.7 82.8 83.2 85.8 89.2 91.6 84.4 94.2 ...
 $ Year      : int   2009 1998 2010 2015 2013 1997 2012 1998 2015 2012 ...
 $ State     : Factor w/ 50 levels "Alabama","Alaska",..: 43 5 43 38 43 17 6 4 35 36 ...
 $ Zip       : chr   "82942" "37189" "89850" "49835" ...
> str(purchases)
Classes 'tbl_df', 'tbl' and 'data.frame':        1000 obs. of  4 variables:
 $ memberid2  : int   553 192 185 678 912 822 663 977 387 799 ...
 $ purch      : num   2 1 2 1 2 1 2 2 2 2 ...
 $ TotalAmount: num   19457 21222 19469 20331 19003 ...
 $ Product    : chr   "B" "C" "C" "C" ...
> str(purchases_filtered)
'data.frame':    489 obs. of  4 variables:
 $ memberid2  : int   192 678 822 663 387 914 830 974 549 902 ...
 $ purch      : int   1 1 1 2 2 2 1 1 3 1 ...
 $ TotalAmount: num   21222 20331 21208 21151 21869 ...
 $ Product    : chr   "C" "C" "C" "A" ...
```

If you switch over to the console, you can see that both member and purchases have 1,000 rows, and the `purchases_filtered` dataframe has 489 rows. Looking across the `TotalAmount` row in `str(purchases_filtered)` suggests that all of the purchases are all in fact > 20,000.

Always take a look at the number of missing values (NAs), and the levels specified for all of the factors. There are no missing values in the data. Look for any situations in which character variables should be treated as factors, and v.v. For example, the `Product` variable is listed as a character (`chr`), when it should probably be treated as a factor. We can always switch the type later.

If you just want to see the number of rows created, you can use the `nrow` function, instead of the `str()` function:

```
nrow(member) #1000 members
nrow(purchases_filtered) #489
```

Merging data using Inner and Outer joins

Now let's merge the membership file with the purchases. In SQL there are two kinds of merge that you can consider when associating two dataframes. An inner join will consolidate two records based on the matching of a single or multiple key that they both have in common. An outer join will also merge the two tables together by keys, but will also include any rows that are not matched. You can identify an outer join by observing the existence of NAs in any of the matching keys. Inner joins are usually more efficient, but should only be used if you expect to have matching keys of both of the joined files.

The `join2` dataframe is an inner join that will contain only those members that had a purchase record. The `sqldf()` function will match all the observations by member:

```
join2 <- sqldf("select * from 'member' inner join 'purchases_filtered' on member.memberid=purchases_filtered.memberid2")
```

Immediately after the join, perform a `str()` function on the `join2` dataframe:

```
str(join2)
```

The `str()` function will show that there are 489 observations, indicating that not all members had purchases:

```
> str(join2)
'data.frame':	489 obs. of  16 variables:
 $ memberid    : int  192 676 909 971 384 963 541 9 79 272 ...
 $ Age         : int  23 20 31 29 28 20 33 26 26 24 ...
 $ Gender      : Factor w/ 2 levels "M","F": 2 2 2 2 2 1 1 2 1 1 ...
 $ DOB         : Date, format: "2001-12-16" "2002-09-08" "2001-07-24" "2002-03-26" ...
 $ Income      : num  53330 31842 47418 30076 10282 ...
 $ Children    : int  1 1 3 7 0 4 0 4 0 3 ...
 $ Employment  : Factor w/ 5 levels "Full Time","Part Time",..: 5 1 1 1 1 3 1 5 1 1 ...
 $ Level       : int  4 4 2 3 1 4 3 1 3 4 ...
 $ Grade       : num  78.3 82.8 83.2 91.6 84.4 83.9 82.7 86.9 85.9 85.1 ...
 $ Year        : int  1998 2015 2013 1998 2015 1996 2008 1996 1999 1999 ...
 $ State       : Factor w/ 50 levels "Alabama","Alaska",..: 5 38 43 4 35 44 38 5 43 9 ...
 $ Zip         : chr  "37189" "49835" "45727" "68914" ...
 $ memberid2   : int  192 676 909 971 384 963 541 9 79 272 ...
 $ purch       : int  1 1 2 1 1 1 2 4 1 2 ...
 $ TotalAmount : num  21222 20239 20118 20439 20874 ...
 $ Product     : chr  "C" "C" "A" "C" ...
```

In cases where you do not expect to always have matches from two files, an outer join is usually better. The `join3` dataframe will merge members with their purchase records, but will also result in including all members who didn't have any purchase records. This is accomplished by using the outer join clause. After joining the dataframes, issue the str and nrow functions to verify the number of rows. There should be 1,105 rows in the dataframe. This is more than the number of members. This is due to the fact that members had multiple purchases:

```
join3 <- sqldf("select * from member left outer join purchases_filtered on
member.memberid=purchases_filtered.memberid2 order by member.memberid")
str(join3)
nrow(join3)

#View the output from join 3 for columns 1, and 8-16 corresponding # to the
order #given in str()

View(join3[,c(1,8:16)])
```

The `View()` function is a convenient way to peruse parts of your results to try to reconcile any anomalies. After issuing the `View` command for selected columns of the `join3` dataframe, we can see that memberid 4 had multiple purchases. We can also quickly see which members had no purchases (member ids 7 and 8). In the cases where there were no purchases by a member, the purchase information is included as variables, but NAs are filled in for the purchase variable fields:

	memberid	Level	Grade	Year	State	Zip	purch	purch.f	TotalAmount	Product
1	1	4	93.2	2011	Georgia	49835	NA	NA	NA	NA
2	2	4	85.8	1999	Nebraska	91960	3	3	21428.89	C
3	3	2	85.1	1998	Massachusetts	45727	1	1	21493.89	B
4	4	1	90.1	1996	Texas	82942	2	2	20029.25	C
5	4	1	90.1	1996	Texas	82942	2	2	20153.52	B
6	5	1	86.7	2005	Florida	45727	2	2	20166.95	B
7	5	1	86.7	2005	Florida	45727	3	3	21016.57	C
8	6	1	81.8	2007	New York	22801	1	1	20394.55	B
9	7	3	85.1	2006	Alabama	49835	NA	NA	NA	NA
10	8	3	91.4	1997	Utah	49835	NA	NA	NA	NA

This type of join is known as a **one-to-many** join. For this example, there can only be one member record, but there can be many purchase records.

Identifying members with multiple purchases

Try this query on your own in a new script to determine which members had multiple purchases. There should be 89 of them. In SQL query parlance, the multiple purchases clause is indicated in the query by count (*) > 1:

```
dups <- sqldf("select member.memberid,count(*) from
  member left outer join
  purchases_filtered on
  member.memberid=purchases_filtered.memberid2
  group by member.memberid having count(*) > 1")
```

Eliminating duplicate records

In many cases, you will only want to retain one record that results from a join. Let's say we only want to keep one record for each memberid, and we want it to be the highest TotalPurchase for each member. To eliminate duplicates, we can first sort the data frame by memberid and TotalPurchase amount. Then we will use the rev and duplicated functions to keep only the last purchase record for each memberid. This will leave us with one record for each of the original 1,000 members:

```
join3 <- join3[order(join3$memberid, join3$TotalAmount),]
View(join3)
dedup <- join3[!rev(duplicated(rev(join3$memberid))),]
nrow(join3)
nrow(dedup)

> nrow(join3)
[1] 1105
> nrow(dedup)
[1] 1000
```

Exploring the hospital dataset

Exploratory data analysis is a preliminary step prior to data modeling in which you look at all of the characteristics of data in order t0 get a sense of data distribution, correlation, missing values, outliers, and any other factors that might impact future analyses. It is a very important step, and if performed diligently, will save you a lot of time later on.

For the following examples, we will read the NYC hospital discharges dataset (hospital inpatient discharges (SPARCS De-Identified): 2012, n.d.). This example uses the `read.csv` function to input the delimited file, and then uses the `View` function to graphically display the output. Then the str function is used to display the contents of the df dataframe that was just created, and then finally, the `summary()` function displays all of the relevant statistics on all of the variables. These are all typical first steps to perform when looking at data for the first time:

```
df <-read.csv("C:/PracticalPredictiveAnalytics/Data/NYC Hospital Discharged
2012 Medicare Severe.csv",na.strings= c(" ", ""))
str(df)
```

Output from the str(df) function

The `str()` function is an important function to run after you create a new data object. If you examine the output from the `str(df)` function in the log, you will see that the default `read.csv` function you have just run has defined each of the variables in the data as either numeric or factor. While at this point it is okay to leave it as is, we will eventually want to change the data type for these variables since `Length.of.Stay` is not a factor, it is an integer. Alternatively, we can perform another `read.csv` function that specifies the exact data type that we want, specifying the `ColClasses` vector. I usually like to look at a small dataset sample first, then determine what the data type should be, and then input the data again.

Another thing to notice about the `read.csv` statement is that missing values are specified as blank values via the na.strings option.

The `str()` function is also important in terms of clueing you in as to what variables can be excluded from the analysis, even before frequency distributions have been run.

For example, the `APR.Severity.of.Illness. Description,` and `Payment.Typology.1` variables have only one level, so we will exclude that from the analysis, since there will be no variability in the data:

```
'data.frame':  40052 obs. of  24 variables:
 $ Hospital.County                  : Factor w/ 5 levels "Bronx","Kings",..: 1 1 1 1 1 1 1 1 1 1 ...
 $ Facility.Name                    : Factor w/ 54 levels "Bellevue Hospital Center",..: 13 13 13 13 13 13 13 13 13 13 ...
 $ Age.Group                        : Factor w/ 5 levels "0 to 17","18 to 29",..: 4 4 4 3 5 4 5 3 4 4 ...
 $ Zip.Code...3.digits              : Factor w/ 40 levels "100","101","103",..: 4 4 4 1 4 4 13 4 4 4 ...
 $ Gender                           : Factor w/ 2 levels "F","M": 1 2 2 2 2 2 2 2 2 2 ...
 $ Race                             : Factor w/ 4 levels "Black/African American",..: 4 4 2 2 2 1 2 2 2 2 ...
 $ Ethnicity                        : Factor w/ 3 levels "Not Span/Hispanic",..: 1 1 2 2 2 1 2 1 2 1 ...
 $ Length.of.Stay                   : Factor w/ 120 levels "1","10","100",..: 24 55 25 25 50 42 59 51 35 51 ...
 $ Admit.Day.of.Week                : Factor w/ 7 levels "FRI","MON","SAT",..: 2 3 3 1 5 6 4 2 2 5 ...
 $ Patient.Disposition              : Factor w/ 17 levels "Another Type Not Listed",..: 4 16 17 17 17 12 17 8 7 4 ...
 $ Discharge.Day.of.Week            : Factor w/ 7 levels "FRI","MON","SAT",..: 3 7 6 6 5 6 2 6 2 1 ...
 $ CCS.Diagnosis.Description        : Factor w/ 217 levels "ABDOMINAL HERNIA",..: 3 37 30 190 136 190 95 113 21 190 ...
 $ CCS.Procedure.Description        : Factor w/ 192 levels "ABDOMINAL PARACENTESIS",..: 93 93 3 36 66 76 36 39 111 182 ...
 $ APR.DRG.Description              : Factor w/ 260 levels "ABDOMINAL PAIN",..: 49 82 246 230 172 89 246 89 57 247 ...
 $ APR.MDC.Description              : Factor w/ 24 levels "Alcohol/Drug Use and Alcohol/Drug Induced Organic Mental Disorders",..: 12 4 2 18 5 17 22 17 8 18 ...
 $ APR.Severity.of.Illness.Description: Factor w/ 1 level "Extreme": 1 1 1 1 1 1 1 1 1 1 ...
 $ APR.Risk.of.Mortality            : Factor w/ 4 levels "Extreme","Major",..: 1 1 1 1 1 2 1 1 1 ...
 $ APR.Medical.Surgical.Description : Factor w/ 2 levels "Medical","Surgical": 1 1 2 1 1 1 2 1 1 2 ...
 $ Payment.Typology.1               : Factor w/ 1 level "Medicare": 1 1 1 1 1 1 1 1 1 1 ...
 $ Payment.Typology.2               : Factor w/ 9 levels "Blue Cross/Blue Shield",..: 5 NA 5 5 5 5 5 4 4 ...
 $ Payment.Typology.3               : Factor w/ 9 levels "Blue Cross/Blue Shield",..: NA 4 4 4 4 4 4 NA NA ...
 $ Emergency.Department.Indicator   : Factor w/ 2 levels "N","Y": 2 2 2 2 2 2 2 2 2 2 ...
```

Output from the View function

Aside from using the head and tail commands, a quick view of the data using the `View` command can be helpful. Scroll up and down, and to the left and right, and examine the type of values that are representative, and whether or not they are populated. Viewing the data can also give you some idea on how the data may be sorted or grouped:

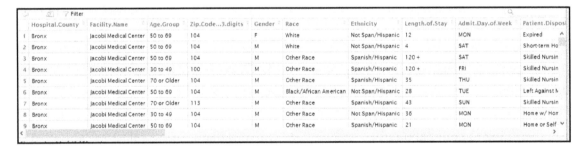

The colnames function

Running the `colnames()` function is a convenient way of obtaining the index numbers for each of the variables. Using index numbers in R functions is a convenient and fast way of referencing variables.

However, changes in file format can change the order, so using this method is only recommended for interactive use:

```
> colnames(df)
 [1] "Hospital.County"                "Facility.Name"                  "Age.Group"                      "Zip.Code...3.digits"
 [5] "Gender"                         "Race"                           "Ethnicity"                      "Length.of.Stay"
 [9] "Admit.Day.of.week"              "Patient.Disposition"            "Discharge.Day.of.week"          "CCS.Diagnosis.Description"
[13] "CCS.Procedure.Description"      "APR.DRG.Description"             "APR.MDC.Description"            "APR.Severity.of.Illness.Description"
[17] "APR.Risk.of.Mortality"          "APR.Medical.Surgical.Description" "Payment.Typology.1"           "Payment.Typology.2"
[21] "Payment.Typology.3"             "Emergency.Department.Indicator"  "Total.charges"                 "Total.Costs"
```

To simplify the example, we will eliminate variables 12, 13, 16, 19, 20, and 21 from the analysis

The summary function

The `summary()` function is a convenient way to get a snapshot of the distribution of the variables. For numeric variables, it will give you the six important distribution statistics (mean, min, max, first, fifth, and third quartiles). The function will return a lot of information quickly. For a large number of variables, the output of the `summary()` function can be overwhelming (and not pretty!).

To limit the output, we will use the column numbers obtained previously and run a `summary()` function that exclude columns 12, 13, 16, 19, 20, and 21:

```
summary(df[,-c(12,13,16,19,20,21)],maxsum=7)
```

Or, if you would rather not use the index numbers and prefer using variable names, you can get the same results with the following code, which uses the NOT sign (!) to exclude the variables specified in the vector: :

```
exclude_vars <- names(df) %in%
c('CCS.Diagnosis.Description','CCS.Procedure.Description','APR.Severity.of.
Illness.Description','Payment.Typology.1','Payment.Typology.2','Payment.Typ
ology.3')

summary(df[!exclude_vars],maxsum=7)
```

Look at the output from the `summary()` function, and observe the distribution of the variables. Look for variables that seem to be under or over represented. Does the distribution for Hospital Country reflect the population of the five NYC boroughs? The age group is skewed toward the older population, but what are the causes of the five cases in the 0-17 age group?

A lot of information can be gained from just looking at summary statistics, and these are the types of questions that should be posed at this point:

```
> summary(df[,-c(12,13,16,19,20,21)],maxsum=7)
  Hospital.County                                           Facility.Name           Age.Group         Zip.Code...3.digits Gender
 Bronx      : 6667   Maimonides Medical Center                       : 2513   0 to 17    :    5   112      :12839          F:20865
 Kings      :11952   Montefiore Medical Center - Henry & Lucy Moses Div : 2002   18 to 29   :  176   104      : 7343          M:19187
 Manhattan:11457     New York Presbyterian Hospital - New York Weill Cornell Center: 1899   30 to 49   : 1251   100      : 7043
 Queens     : 7258   Staten Island University Hosp-North             : 1770   50 to 69   : 9071   113      : 4049
 Richmond : 2718     New York Presbyterian Hospital - Columbia Presbyterian Center : 1689   70 or Older:29549   103      : 2819
                     New York Hospital Medical Center of Queens      : 1633                        (Other): 5942
  (Other)                                                            :28546                        NA's   :    17
          Race              Ethnicity          Length.of.Stay  Admit.Day.of.week                       Patient.Disposition Discharge.Day.of.week
 Black/African American:11256  Not Span/Hispanic:32763  7     : 2399   FRI:5805   Skilled Nursing Home             :13991   FRI:8050
 Other Race       :11311   Spanish/Hispanic : 6193   8     : 2255   MON:6440   Expired                          : 9556   MON:6196
 Unknown          :   65   Unknown          : 1096   6     : 2206   SAT:4856   Home w/ Home Health Services     : 6789   SAT:2733
 white            :17420                             5     : 2118   SUN:4668   Home or Self Care                : 4735   SUN:2050
                                                     9     : 2085   THU:5987   Hospice - Medical Facility       : 1262   THU:6901
                                                     10    : 2027   TUE:6215   Inpatient Rehabilitation Facility: 1192   TUE:7198
                                                     (Other):26962  WED:6081   (Other)                          : 2527   WED:6924
                                    APR.DRG.Description                                                                    APR.MDC.Description
 SEPTICEMIA & DISSEMINATED INFECTIONS              :10256   Infectious and Parasitic Diseases, Systemic or Unspecified Sites:12585
 HEART FAILURE                                     : 1450   Diseases and Disorders of the Respiratory System              : 6356
 PULMONARY EDEMA & RESPIRATORY FAILURE             : 1365   Diseases and Disorders of the Circulatory System              : 5702
 TRACHEOSTOMY W MV 96+ HOURS W/O EXTENSIVE PROCEDURE : 1274   Diseases and Disorders of the Digestive System              : 3411
 OTHER PNEUMONIA                                   : 1131   Diseases and Disorders of the Nervous System                  : 2504
 INFECTIOUS & PARASITIC DISEASES INCLUDING HIV W O.R. PROCEDURE: 1066   Diseases and Disorders of the Kidney and Urinary Tract : 2394
 (Other)                                           :23510   (Other)                                                       : 7100
 APR.Risk.of.Mortality APR.Medical.Surgical.Description Emergency.Department.Indicator Total.Charges       Total.Costs
 Extreme :29274        Medical :32205                  N: 4414                        Min.   :    999   Min.   :    947
 Major   :10060        Surgical: 7847                  Y:35638                        1st Qu.:  36927   1st Qu.:  14183
 Minor   :  108                                                                       Median :  69117   Median :  26725
 Moderate:  610                                                                       Mean   : 109712   Mean   :  43188
                                                                                      3rd Qu.: 130770   3rd Qu.:  50827
                                                                                      Max.   :5166411   Max.   :3719936
```

Sending the output to an HTML file

Since the output from summary is not pretty for a large number of variables, you can also format the output as HTML and send it to a file where you can view the results in a browser. We will illustrate one way to do it via the R2HTML package.

In the following code, all output from HTMLStart to HTMLStop is sent to the file and directory specified:

```
Install.packages("R2HTML")
library(R2HTML)
HTMLStart(outdir="C:/PracticalPredictiveAnalytics/Outputs",file="MedicareNY
CInput",extension="html",HTMLframe=FALSE")
summary(df[,-c(12,13,16,19,20,21)],maxsum=7)
HTMLStop()
```

After the HTMLStop() command is written, the log shows that the output has been written to an HTML file:

```
HTML> HTMLStop()
[1] "C:/PracticalPredictiveAnalytics/Outputs/MedicareNYCInput.html"
>
```

Open the file in the browser

Next, open up the file in the browser of your choice. You will see the summary statistics displayed as one column per variable, which should correspond with output generated from the previous summary. You may need to scroll up/down, or left/right to see all of the variables:

Hospital.County	Facility.Name	Age.Group	Zip.Code...3.digits	Gender	Race	Ethnicity	Length.of.Stay	Admt.Day.of.Week	Patient.Disposition	Discharge.Day.of.Week	APR.DRG.Description	APR.MDC.Description	APR.Risk
Bronx : 6667	Maimonides Medical Center : 2513	0 to 17 : 5	112 :12839	F:20865	Black/African American :11256	Not Span/Hispanic:32763	7 : 2399	FRI:5805	Skilled Nursing Home : 13991	FRI:6050	SEPTICEMIA & DISSEMINATED INFECTIONS :10256	Infectious and Parasitic Diseases, Systemic or Unspecified Sites:12585	Extreme :
Kings :11952	Montefiore Medical Center - Henry & Lucy Moses Div : 2002	18 to 29 : 176	104 : 7343	M:19187	Other Race :11311	Spanish/Hispanic : 6193	8 : 2255	MON:6440	Expired : 9556	MON:6196	HEART FAILURE : 1450	Diseases and Disorders of the Respiratory System : 6356	Major :10
Manhattan:11457	New York Presbyterian Hospital - New York Weill Cornell Center : 1899	30 to 49 : 1251	100 : 7043	NA	Unknown : 65	Unknown : 1096	6 : 2206	SAT:4856	Home w/ Home Health Services : 6789	SAT:2733	PULMONARY EDEMA & RESPIRATORY FAILURE : 1365	Diseases and Disorders of the Circulatory System : 5702	Minor : 10
Queens : 7256	Staten Island University Hosp-North : 1770	50 to 69 : 9071	113 : 4049	NA	White :17420	NA	5 : 2118	SUN:4668	Home or Self Care : 4735	SUN:2050	TRACHEOSTOMY W MV 96+ HOURS W/O EXTENSIVE PROCEDURE : 1274	Diseases and Disorders of the Digestive System : 3411	Moderate :
Richmond : 2718	New York Presbyterian Hospital - Columbia Presbyterian Center : 1689	70 or Older:29549	103 : 2819	NA	NA	NA	9 : 2085	THU:5987	Hospice - Medical Facility : 1262	THU:6901	OTHER PNEUMONIA : 1131	Diseases and Disorders of the Nervous System : 2504	NA
NA	New York Hospital Medical Center of Queens : 1633	NA	(Other): 5942	NA	NA	NA	10 : 2027	TUE:6215	Inpatient Rehabilitation Facility : 1192	TUE:7198	INFECTIOUS & PARASITIC DISEASES INCLUDING HIV W O.R. PROCEDURE: 1066	Diseases and Disorders of the Kidney and Urinary Tract : 2394	NA
NA	(Other) :26549	NA	NA's : 17	NA	NA	NA	(Other):26962	WED:6081	(Other) : 2527	WED:6924	(Other) :23510	(Other) : 7100	NA

Generated on: Wed May 10 09:20:16 2017 - R2HTML

Plotting the distributions

Creating a matrix plot of the variables is also a good preliminary step to perform, since it will immediately let you see the shape and distributions of the variables, and well as point out any gaps in the data. After removing some of the columns from the dataframe that we know we are not going to use, we can see that out dataset is fairly clean, and that the variables line up pretty much as we expect. For example, `Admit.Day.of.Week` is fairly normally distributed, but we can see that there is a null in the number of people discharged at mid-week. Costs are skewed, with very high values (but with low occurrences) at the extremes:

```
df <- df[,-c(12,13,16,19,20,21)]
```

Visual plotting of the variables

Sometimes you may want to generate plots for all of the variables layed out in a matrix. While there are many packages available which will do this automatically, you can also do this yourself in code, as I have shown below. I have also limited to bar plots in which the number of levels are less than or equal to 20. I might want to look at the others later, and possibly condense some of the categories, however this shows me enough variables to get started:

```
colors = c("blue","green3","orange")
numcols <- length(names(df))
par(mfrow=c(3,5))
for(i in 1:numcols){
  if(is.factor(df[,i])){
    if( as.integer(nlevels(df[,i]) <= 20) )
plot(df[,i],main=names(df)[i],col=colors)
  }
else{hist(df[,i],main=names(df)[i],xlim=c(0,300000),breaks=100,xlab=names(df)[i],col=colors)
  }
}
```

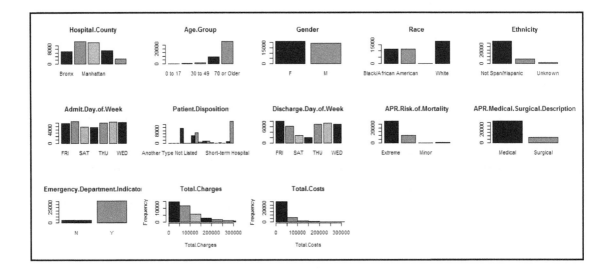

Breaking out summaries by groups

Following an initial inspection of the data, it is a good idea to look at various summary statistics of the target variable broken down by some of the categories (or factors). We could do this using SQL; however, for this example we will use a useful package called dplyr, which has syntax that is SQL-like, and it should be easy for anyone familiar with SQL and/or Linux to pick up.

One of our goals is to break down the Total.Costs by some of the factors to see if we can see any differences in costs among the levels. Let's start with something easy, by breaking out these Total.Costs by the day of the week. We will do this by piping the df dataframe to the dplyr group by command, which will then send it to a summarize() function that will compute the counts, means, and sums of Total.Costs. Finally, the %>% operator will send (or pipe) the output to the View function:

```
library(dplyr)
df %>% group_by(Admit.Day.of.Week) %>%
summarize(total.count=n(),sum(Total.Costs),mean(Total.Costs)) %>% View()
```

	Admit.Day.of.Week	total.count	sum(Total.Costs)	mean(Total.Costs)
1	FRI	5805	258461087	44523.87
2	MON	6440	278940375	43313.72
3	SAT	4856	197503874	40672.13
4	SUN	4668	195987045	41985.23
5	THU	5987	262899265	43911.69
6	TUE	6215	263160240	42342.76
7	WED	6081	272822899	44864.81

The Total.Costs variable seems to be roughly equal for the different days of the week. If you are now running your project with a particular methodology, this might also be a good time to keep track of the results somewhere in one of your results folders, and note that you need to perform a statistical test, such as a t-test or an ANOVA, to test for significant differences among the days of the week.

Standardizing data

There are a couple more transformations that we can perform on our hospital dataset.

We would like to standardize both the `Total.Costs` variable and the `Total.Charges` variable so that we can compare them more easily. Predictive models like to see variables standardized because there is less bias towards any particular variable, since all standardized variables have approximately the same magnitude.

The way we do this is by normalizing the means to 0, with a standard deviation of 1. Computational means that we will take each value, subtract the mean and divide the results by the standard deviation.

In previous examples, we have explicitly referred to variables using their full name (for example, `df$Total.Costs`, which refers to the `Total.Costs` variable within the `df` dataframe). If you will be referring to many variables within a single dataframe, it sometimes makes sense to issue an `attach` statement, which will allow you to use the variable without the dollar sign, if your intent is to always refer to the same dataframe.

Start off by issuing the `attach(df)` command so that we can use these shortcut names to apply to the `df` dataframe:

```
attach(df)
```

Compute a new standardized variable by subtracting the mean of `Total.Costs` variable from each of the `Total.Costs` variable and dividing by the standard deviation of `Total.Costs`:

```
Total.Costs.z <- mean((Total.Costs - mean(Total.Costs)) / sd(Total.Costs))
```

We can also accomplish the same thing by using the `scale()` function, which simplifies the calculation a bit:

```
Total.Costs.z <- scale(df$Total.Costs)
Total.Charges.z <- scale(df$Total.Charges)
```

To prove to yourself that the transformation is accurate, print the `mean` and `sd` of the new variables separately to verify that the mean is 0 and the standard deviation is 1. Note that there will be some minor rounding in the results:

```
mean(Total.Costs.z)
sd(Total.Costs.z)
mean(Total.Charges.z)
sd(Total.Charges.z)
```

Changing a variable to another type

If you examine the preceding `str()` output, you will also see that `Length.of.Stay` is currently defined as a factor. This will need to be transformed to a new variable by using the `as.integer` function. Transform it to an integer, and code a `str()` and `summary()` function to ensure that the transformation is correct:

```
los.int <- as.integer(Length.of.Stay)
head(los.int)
summary(los.int)
```

Appending the variables to the existing dataframe

We will now take the three new variables that we have created, append the new vectors to the existing data frame, and give it a new name:

```
df2 <- cbind(df,Total.Charges.z,Total.Costs.z,los.int)
str(df2)
```

Extracting a subset

Another typical task that you might want to perform is to first extract a particular characteristic of the data (such as patient `"Expired"`), and then perform a similar grouping to try to understand where the differences are. In this next example, we will also use the `dplyr` package to first extract those patients admitted to a hospital who died, and then summarize the `TotalCosts` by each of the major diagnostic classifications. Finally, we will order the costs by the most expensive diagnoses. As you can see from the results, infectious diseases have the highest costs associated with them:

```
df %>% filter(as.character(Patient.Disposition) == "Expired") %>%
group_by(APR.MDC.Description) %>%
summarize(total.count=n(),TotalCosts=sum(Total.Costs)) %>%
arrange(desc(TotalCosts)) %>% head()
```

	APR.MDC.Description	total.count	TotalCosts
	(fctr)	(int)	(dbl)
1	Infectious and Parasitic Diseases, Systemic or Unspecified Sites	4020	163413560
2	Diseases and Disorders of the Respiratory System	1556	59766742
3	Diseases and Disorders of the Circulatory System	1126	56659503
4	Diseases and Disorders of the Digestive System	635	37725309
5	Diseases and Disorders of the Nervous System	723	30941505
6	Diseases and Disorders of the Kidney and Urinary Tract	351	17718863
>			

Transposing a dataframe

You will sometimes be given a format that contains data that is arranged vertically and you want to flip it so that the variables are arranged horizontally. You will also hear this referred to as long format versus wide format. Most predictive analytics packages are set up to use long format, but there are often cases in which you want to switch rows with columns. Perhaps data is being input as a set of key pairs and you want to be able to map them to features for an individual entity. Also, this may be necessary with some time series data in which the data which comes in as long format needs to be reformatted so that the time periods appear horizontally.

Here is a data frame that consists of sales for each member for each month in the first quarter. We will use the `text='` option of the `read.table()` function to read table data that we have pasted directly into the code. For example, this is from data that has been pasted directly from an Excel spreadsheet:

```
sales_vertical <- read.table(header=TRUE, text='
                memberid   Month  sales
       1          1         1       17
       1          2         15
       1          3         11
       2          1          6
       2          2         20
       2          3         11
       3          1          9
       3          2         33
       3          3         43
       4          1         11
       4          3         13
       4          4         12
       ')
```

After running the preceding code, the `sales_vertical` command displays the data in the console similar to how it was coded in the `read.table()` function:

```
>sales_vertical
    memberid Month sales
1          1     1    17
2          1     2    15
3          1     3    11
4          2     1     6
5          2     2    20
6          2     3    11
7          3     1     9
8          3     2    33
9          3     3    43
```

```
10          4       1      11
11          4       3      13
12          4       4      12
```

For switching the rows with the columns, we can use the spread function from the `tidyr` package:

```
install.packages("tidyr")
library(tidyr)
sales_horizontal <- spread(sales_vertical, Month, sales)
sales_horizontal
```

The last line prints the results of the transpose to the console. Take a look at the output of the console to verify that what used to be rows (`memberids`) are now columns. Each of the sales figures also appears as columns, with the column name designating the specific month. Additionally, for each month of data in which a sales figure did not appear for a particular month, NA will appear. For example, in the original data, member 12 was the only member who had sales figures for month 4. That will appear as 12, in the month 4 column, but since the other members had no sales for that month, they will appear as NA:

```
>sales_horizontal <- spread(sales_vertical, Month, sales)
>sales_horizontal
  memberid  1   2   3   4
1         1  17  15  11  NA
2         2   6  20  11  NA
3         3   9  33  43  NA
4         4  11  NA  13  12
```

Dummy variable coding

A dummy variable is a binary flag (0 or 1) that designates the presence or absence of a feature. If you are using dummy variables, you will need to accommodate for as many levels as there are of the dummy variable, minus 1. For example, if you have a category designating humidity with only two levels, such as `High` and `Low`, you only need to create one dummy variable. Let's say it is called `is.humid`. If the value of humidity is `High`, `is.humid=1`. If humidity is `Low`, `is.humid=0`. However, many predictive analytics functions handle the creation of a dummy variable internally, so there is not as much use for coding dummy variables manually as there used to be. But you still may want to create flags that designate the levels of a categorical variable, which can be useful for plotting, creating customized transformations, and for manually creating interactions in a statistical model. There are several ways to do this; you can use Dummies package, which will create dummy variables automatically. But you can also accomplish this via code by using the Model Matrix function.

This takes the Segment categorical variable , which contains five levels (A-E), and expands it into four separate dummy variables:

```
set.seed(10)
model <- data.frame(y=runif(10), x=runif(10),
segment=as.factor(sample(LETTERS[1:5])))
head(model)

A <- model.matrix(y ~ x + segment,model)
head(A)
```

```
> head(model)
           y          x segment
1 0.50747820 0.6516557       E
2 0.30676851 0.5677378       C
3 0.42690767 0.1135090       D
4 0.69310208 0.5959253       A
5 0.08513597 0.3580500       B
6 0.22543662 0.4288094       E

> A <- model.matrix(y ~ x + segment,model)

> head(A)
  (Intercept)         x segmentB segmentC segmentD segmentE
1           1 0.6516557        0        0        0        1
2           1 0.5677378        0        1        0        0
3           1 0.1135090        0        0        1        0
4           1 0.5959253        0        0        0        0
5           1 0.3580500        1        0        0        0
6           1 0.4288094        0        0        0        1
```

Binning – numeric and character

Often numeric variables are binned into categories such as high, low, medium, or high risk and low risk. Even though this results in a loss of information, this can result in being able to use a variable in a logistic regression, or simply using it for the purpose of simplicity. There are different ways to define the cut points that segment a variable, but the simplest way is to divide the variable into equal parts. Taking our `sales_horizontal` data as an example, we can create a new categorical variable that splits the sales data along a high and low category. We will create a new variable called `sales_cat` that segments sales into two parts using the `cut()` function:

```
sales_vertical$sales_cat <- cut(sales_vertical$sales, 2, labels =
c('L','H'))
sales_vertical
```

```
       memberid Month sales sales_cat
1             1     1    17         L
2             1     2    15         L
3             1     3    11         L
4             2     1     6         L
5             2     2    20         L
6             2     3    11         L
7             3     1     9         L
8             3     2    33         H
9             3     3    43         H
10            4     1    11         L
11            4     3    13         L
12            4     4    12         L
```

Binning character data

Character data is usually grouped according to some sort of hierarchy. But occasionally you will want to group it based upon a text pattern contained in the actual string. Here is an example of binning character data based upon the year (the first four characters of `cats`):

```
cats <- as.factor(c('2016-1','2016-2','2016-3'))
sales <- c(10,20,30)
x <- cbind.data.frame(cats,sales)
x
str(x)
binned <- x
binned
levels(binned$cats) <- substring(levels(binned$cats), 1, 4)
binned
> cats <- as.factor(c('2016-1','2016-2','2016-3'))
> sales <- c(10,20,30)
> x <- cbind.data.frame(cats,sales)
> x
    cats sales
1 2016-1    10
2 2016-2    20
3 2016-3    30
> str(x)
'data.frame':   3 obs. of  2 variables:
 $ cats : Factor w/ 3 levels "2016-1","2016-2",..: 1 2 3
 $ sales: num  10 20 30
> binned <- x
> binned
    cats sales
1 2016-1    10
2 2016-2    20
3 2016-3    30
```

```
> levels(binned$cats) <- substring(levels(binned$cats), 1, 4)
> binned
  cats sales
1 2016    10
2 2016    20
3 2016    30
```

Now the all the dates have been binned to the proper year, based upon an embedded text string:

```
aggregate(binned$sales, by=list(binned$cats), sum )
```

The results are written to the console:

```
> aggregate(binned$sales, by=list(binned$cats), sum)
  Group.1  x
1    2016 60
```

Missing values

Missing values denote the absence of a value for a variable. Since data can never be collected in a perfect manner, many missing values can appear due to human oversight, or can be introduced via any systematic process that touches a data element. It can be due to a survey respondent not completing a question, or, as we have seen, it can be created from joining a membership file with a transaction file. In this case, if a member did not have a purchase in a particular year, it might end up as NA or missing.

The first course of action for handling missing values is to understand why they are occurring. In the course of plotting missing values, you not only want to produce counts of missing values, but you want to determine which sub-segments may be responsible for the missing values.

To research this, attempt to break out your initial analysis by time periods and other attributes using some of the bivariate analysis techniques that have been mentioned. This will help you to identify where missing values may be tucked away.

Setting up the missing values test dataset

We will start off by using two groups of generated data. One group is for males, who have a 3% probability of not responding to an age question in a survey, and the other group is for females, who have a 5% probability of not responding to an age question:

```
library(wakefield)
library(dplyr)

#generate some data for Males with a 5% missing value for age

set.seed(10)
f.df <- r_data_frame(
  n = 1000,
  age,
  gender(x = c("M","F"), prob = c(0,1),name="Gender"),
  education
) %>%
  r_na(col=1,prob=.05)

#str(f.df)
summary(f.df)
set.seed(20)
#generate some data for Females with a 3% missing value for age

m.df <- r_data_frame(
  n = 1000,
  age,
  gender(x = c("M","F"), prob = c(1,0),name="Gender"),
  education
) %>%
  r_na(col=1,prob=.03)
summary(m.df)

all.df=rbind.data.frame(m.df,f.df)
```

Note that we have generated missing values by piping the output of the `r_data_frame()` function into the `r_na()` function, which will generate the specified percentage of missing values. After the script completes, switch over to the console to verify that NAs were generated for the age variable. There are 80 of them:

```
summary(all.df)
```

```
> summary(all.df)
      Age         Gender                                              Education
 Min.   :20.00   M:1000   Regular High School Diploma                     :522
 1st Qu.:23.00   F:1000   Bachelor's Degree                               :323
 Median :28.00            Some College, 1 or More Years, No Degree:295
 Mean   :27.54            9th Grade to 12th Grade, No Diploma             :169
 3rd Qu.:32.00            Master's Degree                                 :150
 Max.   :35.00            Associate's Degree                              :140
 NA's   :80               (Other)                                         :401
>
```

The various types of missing data

There are actually three different categories of missing value that you should become familiar with. Understanding the type of missing value will help you determine how to handle them.

Missing Completely at Random (MCAR)

Some percentage of missing values will always occur naturally. When this happens, the missing data is known as Missing Completely at Random (**MCAR**). An example of this is if 2% of a survey was not recorded due to a glitch in a survey response system. If this were the case, one could assume that it was not related to any other variable in the data. MCAR variables are also not correlated with its own data values, that is it would also not be related to any other of the non-missing values that appear in the data.

Testing for MCAR

When you suspect that your data is MCAR, there are various statistical tests can help you determine if MCAR may be occurring. One important test is the Little test, which we will now run on the test missing value dataset.

First, install the `BaylorEdPsych` package, which contains the `LittleMCAR` test:

```
try(require(BaylorEdPsych) ||
install.packages("BaylorEdPsych",dependencies=TRUE))
library(BaylorEdPsych)
```

Now, run the `LittleMCAR` test:

```
test_mcar<-LittleMCAR(all.df)
```

Print the missing values found by the test. 4% of the data was found to be missing. This makes perfect sense, since 5% of the 1,000 males and 3% of the 1,000 females were generated with NAs.

```
print(test_mcar$amount.missing)
print(test_mcar$p.value)
```

```
> print(test_mcar$amount.missing)
                  Age Gender Education
Number Missing  80.00      0         0
Percent Missing  0.04      0         0
```

Print the value of the test statistic. High values of p imply the data is MCAR, while low values imply there is some pattern. At the .05 significance level, it passes the MCAR test (but barely). We also know that we generated our own patterns of NA via the simulation, so that certainly contributed to the p-value of .07:

```
> print(test_mcar$p.value)
[1] 0.06782777
```

Alternatively, you can use Chi-square and regressions tests to determine if the missingness of a variable is related to another variable. If you find that there is no statistical significance between the missing variable and any other variable, you can consider the variable MCAR. These tests can be valuable, although the methods are not fool proof. There are still assumptions that need to be made about the process that generated them. As always, the best course is to investigate the process that generated the values to see how they were generated.

Missing at Random (MAR)

Missing at random (MAR) implies that the missingness of a value is related to another variable in the analysis. It is somewhat of a misnomer, since there is nothing random about it.

So, another question to ask when dealing with missing values is "Is the fact that there are missing values in this variable related to the dynamics of any other variable?" Again, using our survey analogy as an example, missing values for, "What is your Expected Salary?" might occur for certain demographic groups who did not answer the question. If you found a statistically significant number of missing values at one level of a factor, but not as many within another level, that would suggest that the data was missing at random. A variable that is MAR can be found by looking at some of the same techniques used previously, that is, Chi-square, regression, and Little test, and if differences are found you can consider the variable MAR. For our test missing dataset, we might consider this MAR since there is a difference in the number of missing values for males and females.

Not Missing at Random (NMAR)

A variable that is not MCAR and not MAR can be considered **Not Missing at Random** (**NMAR**). That basically means that the missing value is related to the values of the missing value itself, or is related to a variable that's not in the model. NMAR values often show up in survey research and clinical research where subjects are measured over time. For example, a survey respondent who reported severe depression at the beginning of a study may drop out at the end of the study, so if they scored high on a depression scale, that would be related to the fact they have missing scores at a later date, since they might be more inclined to drop out.

NMAR is the most difficult situation to detect, since a variable may seem to be MAR or MCAR and really be NMAR. Missing value analysis is not an exact method, and again, that is where understanding the domain, and the underlying methods of generating data, is so important.

Correcting for missing values

Although it is always important to understand the source of your missing values, how you ultimately handle them depends upon the technique that you use to analyse your data sets. For example, classification methods such as decision trees and random forests know how to deal with missing values, since they can treat them as a separate class, and you can safely leave them in the model. However, if a variable has a large amount of missing values, say > 20%, you might want to look at imputation techniques, or try to find a better variable that measures the same thing.

Listwise deletion

For MCAR, eliminating rows that have missing values is acceptable. In this example (from h
`ttps://en.wikipedia.org/wiki/Listwise_deletion`), observations 3, 4, and 8 will be
removed from the data prior to analysis:

Subject	Age	Gender	Income
1	29	M	$40,000
2	45	M	$36,000
3	81	M	--missing--
4	22	--missing--	$16,000
5	41	M	$98,000
6	33	F	$60,000
7	22	F	$24,000
8	--missing--	F	$81,000
9	33	F	$55,000
10	45	F	$80,000

However, the downside effect of listwise deletion is that you may end up deleting some
non-missing variables that could have an important effect on the model. However, since the
missing data is presumed random, removing some rows would not have a major effect,
assuming your assumptions are correct.

Another consideration is the amount of data you have to work with. You do not want to
end up deleting most of your data if there is one missing value that would cause you to
throw out all of your data! If you will be going down this route, see if you can eliminate this
variable from consideration and start with a list of variables that are reasonably complete.

For example, if you had zip code information on most of the records, but the state variable
was only 50% populated, you wouldn't want to include both zipcode and state together in
an algorithm that performed listwise deletion (such as regression) since that would
eliminate 50% at least of your data. So, the first line of attack would be to see if the variables
were even needed in the first place (possible through a variable importance measure), or if
there was an alternative variable that could serve as a substitute that was better populated.
Principal component analysis or basic pairwise correlation can help you identify this
situation.

Imputation methods

Imputating a missing value means substituting the missing value for another value that is reasonable. What is reasonable can range from substituting the missing value for the mean, median, or mode of a variable to regression techniques, to more advanced techniques involving Monte Carlo simulation.

Imputing missing values using the 'mice' package

In this example we will use the `mice` package to impute some missing values for the `age` variable in the `all.df` dataframe. The value of the `age` variable will be imputed by two other existing variables: `gender` and `education`.

To begin, install and load the `mice` package:

```
install.packages("mice")
library(mice)
```

We will now run the `md.pattern()` function, which will show you the distribution of the missing values over the other columns in the dataframe. The `md.pattern()` function output is useful for suggesting which variables might be good candidates to use for imputing the missing values:

```
md.pattern(all.df)
```

The output from `md.pattern()` function is shown later. Each row shows a count of observation along with a **1** or **0** flag, which indicates if the count contains completely populated values or not:

- The first row indicates that there are 1,920 observations where **Gender, Education,** and **Age** are not missing
- The second row shows the remaining **80** observations also have populated values for **Gender,** and **Education,** but not for **Age**

It is important to examine the `md.pattern()` function to see if there are enough non-missing values in other variables to be able to impute missing values:

```
> md.pattern(all.df)
     Gender Education Age
1920      1         1   1  0
  80      1         1   0  1
          0         0  80 80
>
```

To begin the imputation process, call the `mice()` function and assign it to a new R object:

```
imp <- mice(all.df,m=5,maxit=50, seed=1010,printFlag = TRUE)
```

- In the function call, make sure you supply a random seed value so you can replicate the same results if you run it again
- The `m=5` parameter specifies that you end up with five plausible imputations for the variable
- The `maxit=50` parameter specifies that there will be up to 50 iterations of the algorithm before it converges to a solution and this can be adjusted upward or downward to the desired precision

After you run the `mice()` function you will see the imputation run in real time, so it may take a while depending upon the number of iterations you specified.

When it is done, you can see some of the imputed value for `Age` (or other values) using `head()` function:

```
head(imp$imp$Age)
```

```
> head(imp$imp$Age)
      1    2  3  4  5
38   29   35 20 33 27
49   25   23 30 32 21
79   25   23 25 25 25
99   31   30 22 26 24
157  24   30 24 23 22
180  29   22 26 28 29
```

To actually complete the imputation, you will have to run the `complete()` function and assign the results to a new dataframe. This version of `complete()` function will collect all imputations in the assigned dataframe via the `"long"` parameter:

```
all_imputed_df <- complete(imp, "long", include=TRUE)
```

Run the `table()` function on the new dataframe to calculate a count of the missing values for all of the imputations, plus the original values. The original dataframe containing NAs is designated by `imp=0`.

There are five other imputations of age designated as imp 1-6:

```
table(all_imputed_df$.imp,is.na(all_imputed_df$Age))
```

```
> table(all_imputed_df$.imp,is.na(all_imputed_df$Age))

    FALSE TRUE
0   1920   80
1   2000    0
2   2000    0
3   2000    0
4   2000    0
5   2000    0
```

To see the imputation in action, we will filter the new dataframe for one of the original IDs that contained missing values (#216).

Then we can look to see how the age value changes for each imputation of age. There can be some variation for the imputed values. For this example, it can range from a starting value of 25 up until 34:

```
all_imputed_df %>% filter(.id == 216)
>all_imputed_df %>% filter(.id == 216)
   .imp .id Age Gender                                       Education
1    0 216  NA      M Some College, 1 or More Years, No Degree
2    1 216  25      M Some College, 1 or More Years, No Degree
3    2 216  29      M Some College, 1 or More Years, No Degree
4    3 216  22      M Some College, 1 or More Years, No Degree
5    4 216  34      M Some College, 1 or More Years, No Degree
6    5 216  34      M Some College, 1 or More Years, No Degree
```

Of course, that is for a single observation, if you look at the mean values for imp=1-6 that are all similar:

```
all_imputed_df %>% group_by(.imp) %>% summarize(MeanAge=mean(Age))
> all_imputed_df %>% group_by(.imp) %>% summarize(MeanAge=mean(Age))
# A tibble: 6 × 2
.imp MeanAge
<fctr> <dbl>
1   0   NA
2   1 27.5300
3   2 27.5780
4   3 27.5230
5   4 27.5855
6   5 27.5325
```

Running a regression with imputed values

Now that you have imputed a value for age, you will be able to run models such as linear regression without having to discard missing values.

Let's try a regression with imputation #2.

First, extract impute #2:

```
impute.2 <- subset(all_imputed_df,.imp=='2')
```

Next, run the `summary()` function at the console to insure there are no more NAs:

```
> summary(impute.2)
 .imp    .id    Age    Gender
0: 0 1   : 1 Min.  :20.00 M:1000
1: 0 10  : 1 1st Qu.:23.00 F:1000
2:2000 100 : 1 Median :28.00
3: 0 1000 : 1 Mean  :27.58
4: 0 1001 : 1 3rd Qu.:32.00
5: 0 1002 : 1 Max.  :35.00
   (Other):1994
        Education
Regular High School Diploma    :522
Bachelor's Degree        :323
Some College, 1 or More Years, No Degree:295
9th Grade to 12th Grade, No Diploma  :169
Master's Degree        :150
Associate's Degree      :140
(Other)        :401
```

Finally, run the regression:

```
lm(Age ~ Education + Gender,data=impute.2)

> lm(Age ~ Education + Gender,data=impute.2)

Call:
lm(formula = Age ~ Education + Gender, data = impute.2)

Coefficients:
        (Intercept)
        26.85358
 EducationNursery School to 8th Grade
        0.86901
 Education9th Grade to 12th Grade, No Diploma
        1.02452
 EducationRegular High School Diploma
```

```
              0.33593
EducationGED or Alternative Credential
              1.26967
EducationSome College, Less than 1 Year
              1.53750
EducationSome College, 1 or More Years, No Degree
              0.69232
EducationAssociate's Degree
              0.95965
EducationBachelor's Degree
              0.82072
EducationMaster's Degree
              0.84928
EducationProfessional School Degree
              0.11744
EducationDoctorate Degree
              0.87017
              GenderF
             -0.03037
```

Imputing categorical variables

Imputing categorical variables can be trickier than imputation of numeric variables. Numeric imputation is based upon random variates, but imputation of categorical variables is based upon statistical tests with less power, such as Chi-square, and they can be rule-based, so if you end up imputing categorical variables, use with caution and run the results past some domain experts to see if it makes sense. You can use decision trees or random forests to come up with a prediction path for your missing values, and map them to a reasonable prediction value using the actual decision rules generated by the tree.

Outliers

Outliers are values in the data that are outside the range of what is to be expected. "What is to be expected?" is of course subjective. Some people will define an outlier as anything beyond three standard deviations of a normal distribution, or anything beyond 1.5 times the interquartile ranges. This, of course, may be good starting points, but there are many examples of real data that defies any statistical explanation. These rules of thumb are also highly dependent upon the form of the data. What might be considered an outlier for a normal distribution would not hold for a lognormal or Poisson distribution.

In addition to potential single variable outliers, outliers can also exist in multivariate form, and are more prevalent as data is examined more closely in a high-dimensional space.

Whenever they appear, outliers should be examined closely since they may be simple errors or provide valuable insight. Again, it is best to consult with other collaborators when you suspect deviation from the norm.

Why outliers are important

Outlier detection is important for a couple of reasons. First, it allows you to learn a lot about the extremes in your data. Typical data is usually easy to explain. If you have many values of a certain category, it is usually easy to track down an explanation. It is the extreme values that can add additional insight beyond the typical, or identify faulty processes which can be fixed.

Additionally, outliers have a profound effect upon some algorithms. In particular, regression methods can be biased by the presence of outliers and lose power because of them.

Detecting outliers

Graphical methods are best for initially scanning for outliers. Boxplots, histograms, and normal probability plots are very useful tools.

In this code example, sales data is generated with an average sale of $10,000 and a standard deviation of $3,000. The boxplot shows some data above and below the whiskers of the diagram. Additionally, the histogram shows a gap between the highest bar and the one just below that. These are clues that potential outliers need to be looked at more closely:

```
set.seed(4070)
#generate sales data
outlier.df <-data.frame(sales=rnorm(100,mean=10000,sd=3000))
#plot the data, to possible outliers
par(mfrow=c(1,2))
boxplot(outlier.df$sales, ylab="sales")
hist(outlier.df$sales)
```

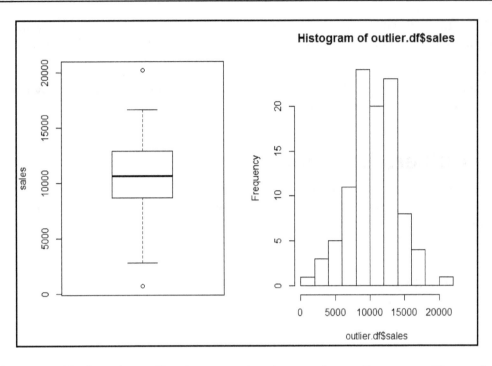

Another way of looking for outliers is to examine the actual quartiles, percentiles, or deciles. These measures are useful for breaking the data into equal buckets, and then observing the difference among the groupings.

Here we can look at all of the deciles of the data using the quantile() function and specifying that we want each breakpoint at each 10% of the data:

```
deciles <- data.frame(quantile(outlier.df$sales,
    prob=c(0.1,0.2,0.3,0.4,0.5,0.6,0.7,0.8,.9,1)))
deciles
>deciles
    quantile.outlier.df.sales..prob...c.0.1..0.2..0.3..0.4..0.5..
10%                                                     5548.897
20%                                                     7409.263
30%                                                     8621.341
40%                                                     9090.793
50%                                                     9741.979
60%                                                    10364.654
70%                                                    11019.190
80%                                                    12175.635
90%                                                    13164.274
100%                                                   15363.606
```

Transforming the data

Another way to look at outliers is by first standardizing them to a normal distribution with a mean of 0 and standard deviation of 1. Using standard normal form is convenient, since the properties of the distribution never change, and some critical cut-off points can be committed to memory. For example, for a standard normal distribution, quartile 1 is always at -.67 and quartile 3 is always at +.67, so it is easy to compute the interquartile range to memory, which is 1.34. Using the interquartile range rule to identify outliers means that we will take 1.5 times this amount to derive the value of 2.01, so we will be considering any data point above .67+2.01=2.68, or -.67-2.01=-2.68, to be a possible outlier. This is an example of how we can use a statistical property of a distribution to identify an outlier. You could also use a rule such as identifying any data point more than three standard deviations from the mean, or by using a Chi-square test to determine if your grouped data differs significantly from the theoretical distribution. The outliers package also contains several other methods and statistical tests for detecting outliers, including the Grubbs test.

Here we will first normalize the data, and then look for data falling above or below plus or minus 2.68:

1. First, use the `scale()` function to standardize the sales vector, and create a new vector, `v1`, that contains the standardized values (or z-scores):

   ```
   outlier.df$v1 <- scale(outlier.df$sales)
   ```

2. Next, we will use the `order()` function to sort the z-scores from lowest to highest. This will make it easy to look at the extremes using the `head()` and `tail()` functions. We can see immediately that there are two values that fall out with the range -2.68 to +2.68:

   ```
   #sort from lowest to highest
   outlier.df <- outlier.df[order(outlier.df$v1),]
   head(outlier.df)

   >head(outlier.df)
         sales         v1
   59   672.6731  -2.917263
   88  2776.8597  -2.295223
   39  3034.5596  -2.219042
   69  3041.7867  -2.216905
   63  4363.3742  -1.826217
   75  4894.2080  -1.669292

   tail(outlier.df)
   >tail(outlier.df)
         sales         v1
   ```

```
77  15434.46  1.446619
22  16286.14  1.698392
71  16319.01  1.708109
26  16455.81  1.748549
66  16624.87  1.798528
35  20176.17  2.848362
```

3. Finally, we will examine the `boxplot()` function for the transformed data. Note the shape of the distribution is exactly the same as the original data. The only difference is that the scale of the data has changed along the *y*-axis:

```
boxplot(outlier.df$v1, ylab="v1")
```

We can still see the potential outliers at the top of the `boxplot` (small circle):

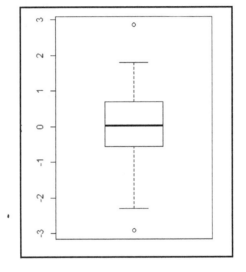

Tracking down the cause of the outliers

Once you have identified a possible outlier, it is always the best course of action to determine why they occurred. We have illustrated an outlier that appears in one set of data; however, more often than not you will be splitting your data into various subsets to try to track down the cause of the outlier. This is assuming that you have enough data to work with. Outlier detection for small samples is a lot tougher.

Ways to deal with outliers

Here are a few ways to deal with the outliers:

- Remove them, or set them to NA. This can make sense if you do not have too many of them, and it will make your model easier to explain. The trade-off is that you may be removing important data, so use with caution.
- Use a transformation to reduce the variability. Choose the appropriate transformation based upon the skewness of the data, or try a **Box-Cox Power Transformation**. One advantage to this is that the correct transformation can reduce the influence of the extreme observations.
- Bring them down to a pre-controlled level. This can be accomplished by using a trimmed or Windsorized mean. This is done in the actuarial profession, since some risk can be capped if the variable exceeds a certain level.
- Choose a classification rather than a regression type algorithm, which will not be as sensitive to outliers. For decision trees, outliers will tend to show up in their own leaves with small counts. At that point, you can choose to ignore the outlier by pruning the tree and collapsing it into a different category.
- For regression type algorithms, you can choose an algorithm that penalizes large coefficients, such as ridge or lasso regression, which are more robust against outliers.

Example – setting the outliers to NA

The next step is of course to start examining these outliers. For our example, the extremes are part of the random number generation process, therefore they are not really outliers. However, if you encountered this situation in your own data, you would begin to track down the reasons these extremes occur. Start by trying to associate these extremes with other data elements. Perhaps these outliers are appearing in certain age groups and not in others.

For our example, we will simply be setting the value to NA for these extreme values. We will also be creating a new variable, v1x, to house the new variable, and will not overwrite the value of the original variable. As you investigate new ways of detecting outliers, you can store the new values in additional variables, with the assurance that you can always refer back to the original variable:

```
outlier.df$v1x<-ifelse( (outlier.df$v1 >= 2.68 | outlier.df$v1 <=
-2.68),NA,outlier.df$v1)
tail(outlier.df)
head(outlier.df)
```

Refer to the console with output of the `head()` and `tail()` command and notice the changes in the data. What was previously considered an outlier (-2.917263) has now been mapped to NA:

```
>tail(outlier.df)
      sales       v1        v1x
77 15434.46 1.446619  1.446619
22 16286.14 1.698392  1.698392
71 16319.01 1.708109  1.708109
26 16455.81 1.748549  1.748549
66 16624.87 1.798528  1.798528
35 20176.17 2.848362        NA
>head(outlier.df)
       sales        v1        v1x
59   672.6731 -2.917263        NA
88  2776.8597 -2.295223 -2.295223
39  3034.5596 -2.219042 -2.219042
69  3041.7867 -2.216905 -2.216905
63  4363.3742 -1.826217 -1.826217
75  4894.2080 -1.669292 -1.669292
```

Also run a boxplot() function and observe that the original upper outlier has been removed:

```
boxplot(outlier.df$v1x, ylab="v1 new")
```

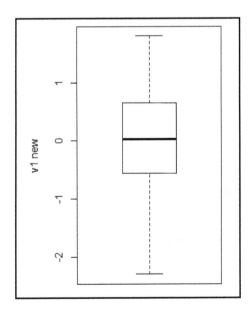

Multivariate outliers

The preceding example has just given an example of looking at outliers from a univariate, or single variable, perspective. However, outliers can also occur in a multivariate or combination form. In these cases, visualizing outliers in two dimensions can be a start, but as the dimensionality increases they can be more difficult to isolate. For multivariate outliers you can use distance and influence measures such as Cook's D or Mahalanobis distances to measure how far they are from a regression line. Principal component analysis can also help by reducing the dimensionality first, and then examining the higher order principal components that could include the outliers.

Data transformations

When you are dealing with continuous skewed data, consider applying a data transformation, which can conform the data to a specific statistical distribution with certain properties. Once you have forced the data to a certain shape, you will find it easier to work with certain models. A simple transformation usually involves applying a mathematical function to the data.

Some of the typical data transformations used are `log`, `exp`, and `sqrt`. Some work better for different kinds of skewed data, but they are not always guaranteed to work, so it is always best practice to try out several basic ones and determine if the transformation becomes workable within the modeling context. As always, the simplest transformation is the best transformation, and do some research on how transformations work, and which ones are best for certain kinds of data.

To illustrate the concept of a transformation, we will start by first generating an exponential distribution, which is an example of a non-linear distribution. Refer to the histogram of X and the normal Q-Q plot in the first row of the following plot quadrant. Both of these plots show the data to be highly skewed. You can see the histogram is heavily weighted toward the lower range of x, and the Q-Q plot is not displaying as a straight line. So, we will need to find a transformation that smooths out the skewness. We will apply the Box Cox algorithm, which will determine an optimal transformation to use.

Generating the test data

Install the packages if needed:

```
install.packages("car")
install.packages("MASS")
```

Assign the libraries:

```
library(car)
library(MASS)
```

Generate the skewed data:

```
set.seed(1010)
x<-rexp(1000)        # exponential sample with parameter 1
par(mfrow=c(2,3)).
```

Plot the histogram and normal probability plots. The `par()` function specified that they will be part of the first row of plots shown in the next section:

```
hist(x)
qqnorm(x)
# Normal probability plot for original variable
```

The Box-Cox Transform

We will now illustrate the Box-Cox Power Transformation (also known as Power Transformation). This is a generic transform that will search for optimal transformations to use on your data. This transformation optimizes an exponent called lambda, which is then applied to your data. It does this by iterating over all exponents between -5 and +5 until it has found the best one to transform your data to a normal distribution:

```
boxcox(x~1)
```

As you can see from the plot produced from the `boxcox()` function (the third plot), the optimal exponent to apply the data will be somewhere between 0 and 1.

Next, we will apply the power function. The `powerTransform()` function will apply the optimal lambda just calculated to the original data:

```
p<-powerTransform(x)
```

You can see what the value is by switching over to the console and looking for the value of `p$lamda`. The console will show that the value is 0.2873638:

```
p$lamda
```

The next step is to apply the power transformation to your existing data and assign the results to a new vector, `y`:

```
y<-bcPower(x,p$lambda) # Box-Cox transformation
```

The histogram of the new data (histogram of y in the following image) shows that the data has been transformed to a normal distribution, and the QQ plot, which measures normality, shows a nice straight line:

```
qqnorm(y)
# Normal probability plot for transformed variable
hist(y)
```

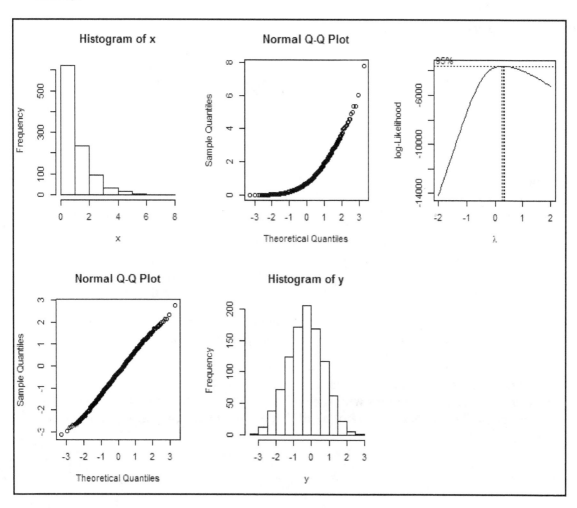

Variable reduction/variable importance

Variable reduction techniques allow you to reduce the number of variables that you need to specify to a model. We will discuss three different methods to accomplish this.

1. Principal Components Analysis (PCA).
2. All subsets Regression.
3. Variable Importance.

Principal Components Analysis (PCA)

Principle Components Analysis (**PCA**) is a variable reduction technique, and can also be used to identify variable importance. An interesting benefit of PCA is that all of the resulting new component variables will all be uncorrelated with each other. Uncorrelated variables are desirable in a predictive model since too many correlated variables confound predictions and make it difficult to tell which of the independent variables have the most influence. So, if you first perform an exploratory analysis of your data and you find that a high number of correlations exist, this would be a good opportunity to apply PCA.

 Models can tolerate some degree of correlated variables. The situations I am speaking of are cases in which you have a large number of variables to consider, and just end up throwing them into a model, hoping the algorithm will determine the model by itself. Most of the time it won't.

In many models where you start with a large number of variables, you will find that many of them are similar to each other and have the same predictive abilities.

A classic example of this is predictors for standardized test scores. While some of them are tailored to measure specific things, such as reading or math aptitude, many of the predictors have high correlations with each other. The bottom line is that using one or two of them in a prediction model may not be all that different that using all eight or nine of them.

PCA has the ability to identify redundancy in the data and can be thought of as a way to determine the minimum number of variables that contribute the most to the model's variation. If you can reduce the explained variability of the data to just two or three components, that will help you reduce the dimensionality of the data. Once you determine the components, you can use them in the following ways:

- Replace the original variables with the principal components.
- Use the principal component analysis to simply identify and keep only the most useful original variables. In this case, useful can mean variables with the highest variance, variables with the highest correlation with the target variable, variables that have the most meaning, and so on.

Therefore, one goal of principal component analysis is to identify a small subset of new variables that explain a very large part of the variance of the original data.

Where is PCA used?

Principal components are used heavily in the social sciences, marketing, and advertising industries. Related to PCA is factor analysis, in which rotating principal components results in creating latent variables. Latent variables attempt to describe the behavior of the data subjectively, as opposed to principal components, which are simply a linear combination of the original variables, and are more or less synthetic linear equations.

A PCA example – US Arrests

As an example, here is the correlation matrix plot for US Arrests, corresponding to the number of arrests per 100,000 residents for assault, murder, and rape in each of the 50 US states in 1973. Also given is the percent of the population living in urban areas. The USArrests dataset should be loaded automatically as part of the datasets package.

You can get description of the USArrests dataset by entering the help command? USArrests dataset at the console.

To see the correlation between all of the variables, enter the following on the console line:

```
library(datasets)
pairs(USArrests)
```

The output is shown here:

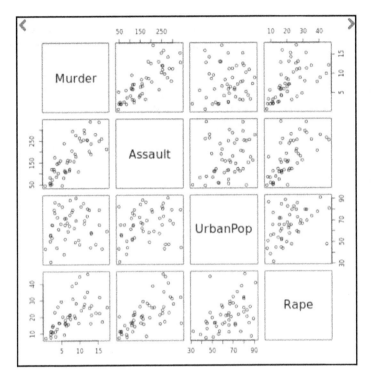

The `pairs()` function creates mini scatterplots for all of the different combinations of continuous variables in the dataframe. To examine a particular pair, look at the cell that intersects the appropriate row and column labels for the variables, which are shown in the diagonal row of the matrix. For example, the scatterplots for **Murder** with **Assault** are shown by locating the cells that these labels intersect. That would be in two places: row 1, column 2 of the matrix, and row 2 and column 1. Note that most of the variables seem strongly correlated with each other. The urban population variable (UrbanPop) seems to be the least correlated variable, at least based upon the scatter that is represented visually. Murder and assault seems to have a stronger correlation. That makes me wonder if we would need to include all of the variables in a prediction model.

To run principal components on this data we will use the `prcomp()` function. Note the comments in the code that scaling (normalization) is appropriate, since the variables have different scales:

```
require(graphics)

## the variances of the variables in the
## USArrests data vary by orders of magnitude, so scaling is appropriate

prcomp(USArrests, scale = TRUE)
```

The output of the `prcomp()` function is shown here. This output describes the loadings of each of the variables on each of the principal components. The original variables are shown as rows, and the new variables, the principal components, are shown as columns. By default, they are named PC1, PC2, PC3, and PC4:

```
Standard deviations: (1, .., p=4):
[1] 1.5748783 0.9948694 0.5971291 0.4164494

Rotation (n x k) = (4 x 4):
                PC1         PC2         PC3         PC4
Murder    -0.5358995  0.4181809  -0.3412327  0.64922780
Assault   -0.5831836  0.1879856  -0.2681484  -0.74340748
UrbanPop  -0.2781909  -0.8728062  -0.3780158  0.13387773
Rape      -0.5434321  -0.1673186  0.8177779  0.08902432
```

The numbers given under each column are the actual coefficients used, which are used to determine the linear combination. So, we can calculate the first, and most important principal component as follows:

```
PC1=Murder * 0.5358995 + Assault*-0.5831836 + UrbanPop*-0.2781909 +
Rape*-0.5434321.
```

Since the variables have been scaled (or standardized) to begin with, the magnitude of the coefficients can give a rough estimate of how much a variable contributes to each of the components. For example, PC1 could be described as the variation due to murder, rape, and assault, while PC2 is more about the variations in urban population. PC3 might be about the effect of rape within urban populations, and PC4 could be about murder when assault is not involved.

The overwhelming power of PC1 can be shown in the following plot. Each succeeding principal component measures the leftover variation unexplained by the previous components:

```
plot(prcomp(USArrests))
```

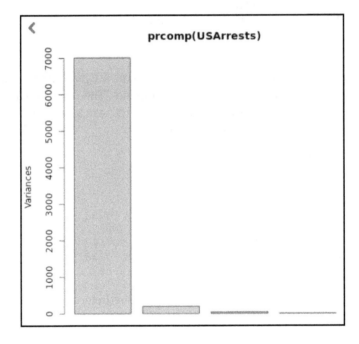

The `prcomp summary` function shows the cumulative percentage of explained variation:

```
summary(prcomp(USArrests, scale = TRUE))
```

This is the following output:

```
Importance of components%s:
                          PC1    PC2     PC3     PC4
Standard deviation     1.5749 0.9949 0.59713 0.41645
Proportion of Variance 0.6201 0.2474 0.08914 0.04336
Cumulative Proportion  0.6201 0.8675 0.95664 1.00000
```

In the last line of the output, `Cumulative Proportion`, you can see that the first component explains 62% of the variation, and the first two principal components explain a total of 87% of the variation in the data.

This was based on four original variables. Principal Components have reduced the number of variables by 50%. Think how many variables could be reduced if you started with a feature set of over 100 variables!

All subsets regression

All subsets regression is another method you can use for variable selection. It works by running separate regressions for different combinations of one variable, two variables, three variables at a time, until it has used all of the variables or until a specified stopping point. As part of the output, the best model for each of the combination of variables is then calculated. That will then give you an idea of which is the best single one variable model, two variable model, and so on, so that you can pare down a large list of variables into a smaller number of important ones using some plots and output statistics.

An example – airquality

In this example, we will use the regsubsets() function contained within the leaps package to determine which variables are important for predicting temperature:

```
install.packages("leaps")
library(leaps)
data(airquality)
str(airquality)
```

In the following regsubsets() function call, we specify that we want the best model for each combination of one, two, and three variables. By default, the function will compute the best model for all variables in the model. In the function call, I illustrate specifying a max value, since I want to be able to stop the algorithm after a certain number of variables has been reached. This becomes important when you use data that has a large number of variables, and you do not want to tie up precious memory:

```
out <-regsubsets(Temp ~ .,data=airquality,nbest=1,nvmax = 99)
```

Run a summary() on the output:

```
summary(out)
```

The following output shows the variables contained in the best 1-5 variable model. Note that there are only five variables, so you cannot have more than a five-variable model:

```
Subset selection object
Call: regsubsets.formula(Temp ~ ., data = airquality, nbest = 1, nvmax =
99)
5 Variables (and intercept)
         Forced in Forced out
Ozone         FALSE      FALSE
Solar.R       FALSE      FALSE
Wind          FALSE      FALSE
Month         FALSE      FALSE
Day           FALSE      FALSE
1 subsets of each size up to 5
Selection Algorithm: exhaustive
         Ozone Solar.R Wind Month Day
1 ( 1 )  "*"    " "    " "   " "   " "
2 ( 1 )  "*"    " "    " "   "*"   " "
3 ( 1 )  "*"    "*"    " "   "*"   " "
4 ( 1 )  "*"    "*"    " "   "*"   "*"
5 ( 1 )  "*"    "*"    "*"   "*"   "*"
```

It is useful to be able to interpret the stars in the output table. The row indicates the number of variables in the model, and the * in the column shows that the variable is part of that combination. So we can see that Ozone is the best single variable predictor, and Ozone, with Month is the best two-variable predictor:

Variables in Model	Ozone	Solar.R	Wind	Month	Day
1	Ozone	"*"	" "	" "	" "	" "
2	Ozone, Month	"*"	" "	" "	"*"	" "
3	Ozone, Month,Solar.R	"*"	"*"	" "	"*"	" "
4	Ozone,Month,Solar.R, Day	"*"	"*"	" "	"*"	"*"
5	Ozone,Month,Solar.R, Day,Wind	"*"	"*"	"*"	"*"	"*"

To see the adjusted R-squares for each of the combinations of variables, run the following at the command line:

```
summary(out)$adjr2
```

This is the following output:

```
[1] 0.4832625 0.5746686 0.5801736 0.5836452 0.5823619
```

You can see that the one-variable model has an adjusted R-Square of .48, while the two-variable model adjusted R-Square is .57. For three variables and beyond it seems as though the increase in R-Square is incremental. So, it would seem that a two-variable model of ozone and month would be adequate for predicting air quality.

Adjusted R-square plot

The adjusted R-square plot is also helpful in selecting a model. Each row of the following plot represents a separate model, with the intercept and all of the variables as columns. The `plot` function shows how adjusted R-square (y-axis) changes for each of the variables in the model:

```
plot(out, scale = "adjr2")
```

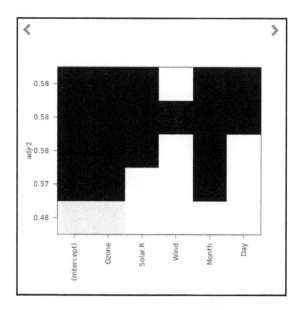

To select an optimal model, look to the point at which variables have black boxes near the top of the y-axis range.

For our example, that would mean using the four-variable model **Ozone, Month, Solar.R,** and **Day**. However, as noted previously, the difference between the two and four variable model seems minimal. However, you can see how you could use this method to reduce your variables from five to two with minimal degradation to a regression model.

Variable importance

For classification targets you can use the random forest algorithm to determine variable importance.

For this example, a simulated sample was generated, with smoking and family history being key factors in determining heart disease among males:

```
set.seed(1020)
#construct a 50/50 sample of Males, and Females
gender <- sample(c("M","F"), 100, replace=T,prob=c(0.50,0.50))

#assign a higher probability of smoking to the Males (95%, WAY to high!)
smokes <- ifelse(gender=="M",
                sample(c("N","Y"), 100, replace=T,prob=c(0.05,0.95)),
                sample(c("N","Y"), 100, replace=T,prob=c(0.45,0.55))
)

#assume they also have a 60% chance of family history of heart disease

familyhistory <- ifelse(gender=="M",
                sample(c("N","Y"), 100, replace=T,prob=c(0.40,0.60)),
                sample(c("N","Y"), 100, replace=T,prob=c(0.50,0.50))
)


HighChol <- sample(c("Y","N"), 100, replace=T,prob=c(0.50,0.50))
heartdisease <- sample(c("Y","N"), 100, replace=T,prob=c(0.05,0.95))

#bind all of the variables together

heart<-
as.data.frame(cbind(smokes,HighChol,familyhistory,gender,heartdisease))
```

Verify some of the generated table with some crosstabs:

```
#row percentages for smoking by gender. Males who smoke came out little bit
higher than the 95%
prop.table(table(heart$gender,heart$smokes),1)
```

This is the following output:

```
> prop.table(table(heart$gender,heart$smokes),1)

           N          Y
  F 0.42592593 0.57407407
  M 0.04347826 0.95652174
```

See the following code:

```
#row percentage for family history by gender. Males with family history of
heart disease came out also a bit higher than 60%
prop.table(table(heart$gender,heart$familyhistory),1)
```

This is the following output:

```
> prop.table(table(heart$gender,heart$familyhistory),1)
             N          Y
  F 0.5370370 0.4629630
  M 0.3913043 0.6086957
```

Finally, check out the occurrence of heart disease by gender as well:

```
> prop.table(table(heart$gender,heart$heartdisease),1)
             N          Y
  F 0.96296296 0.03703704
  M 0.93478261 0.06521739
```

Variable influence plot

Now we can run our variable influence plot. The following plot indicates high cholesterol and family history as the most important variables:

```
require(randomForest)
fit <- randomForest(factor(heartdisease)~., data=heart,ntree=1000)
(VI_F <- importance(fit))
varImpPlot(fit,type=2,main="Random Forest Variable Importance Plot - Heart
Disease Simulation")
```

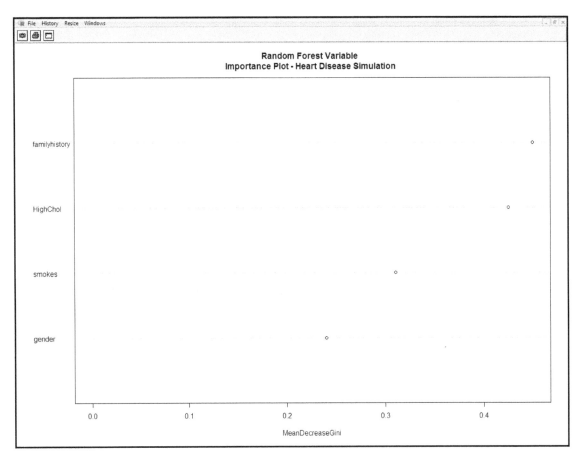

A downside to this method is that it is treating each variable individually, and not considering any correlation between two variables.

References

Hospital Inpatient Discharges (SPARCS De-Identified): 2012. (n.d.). Retrieved from `https://he alth.data.ny.gov/Health/Hospital-Inpatient-Discharges-SPARCS-De-Identified/u 4ud-w55t`.

Summary

In this chapter, we learned all about getting data prepared for analysis so that you can start to run models. It starts with inputting external data in raw form, and we saw that there are several ways you can accomplish these available methods. You also learned how to generate your own data and two different ways you can use to join, or munge data together, one using SQL and the other using `dplyr` function.

We later proceeded to cover some basic data cleaning and data exploration techniques that are sometimes needed after your data is input, such as standardizing and transposing the data, changing the variables type, creating dummy variables, binning, and eliminating redundant data. You now know about the key R functions that are used to take a first glance at the contents of the data, as well as its structure.

We then covered the important concepts of analyzing missing values and outliers, and how to handle them.

We saw a few ways to decrease the number of variables to a manageable level, using techniques such as Principal Component Analysis and all subsets regression.

Finally, we learned to use Random Forest algorithms to identify the most important variables for modeling.

This concludes the data preparation section, and we have just scratched the surface in terms of the ways you can prepare your data for modeling.

In the next chapter, we will cover more detail about Random Forests, as well as regression, decision trees, SVM, and some other things that will allow us to build a solid foundation of basic algorithms that you can use for your own core models.

4

Introduction to Regression Algorithms

"It ain't ignorance causes so much trouble; it's folks knowing so much that ain't so."
- Billings

Every day, the number of predictive analytics techniques seems to be increasing. There is a constant debate about whether we need better algorithms, or whether more or better data is needed in order to attack a predictive analytics problem.

Whatever the case, it is always good to keep abreast of all of the available algorithms at your disposal. It is equally important to hone your skills on the top three or four algorithms that can tackle 90% of the problems that you will face, and be able to understand the situations in which it makes sense to use them.

This chapter is the first of two chapters which will present four basic algorithms which cover a lot of typical business situations that you will encounter. In fact, many of the data science surveys which poll analytics practitioners will often include these techniques in the top techniques that all data scientists should know. Among these techniques, we will discuss regression in detail for this chapter and the three remaining core algorithms in the following chapters. But let's start by introducing all four:

- Regression techniques represent a standard parametric approach to problem solving which assigns a coefficient or weight to each of the independent variables. Variables are related to the outcome variable via a `linear` function.
- Decision trees are an important algorithm class which can be used as an alternative to regression when the relationships of the variables may not necessarily be linear.

- Cluster analysis is also discussed as a form of unsupervised learning, which is more exploratory in nature, but not necessarily predictive.
- Support vector machines are useful in situations in which you have high dimensional data. High dimensional data comes into play when you have a large number of variables appearing in the data, and you have chosen to use all or most of them in the model, without first applying some sort of data reduction technique. This can often occur as you apply analysis to some real-time data in raw form, in which case models need to be applied in split-second time.

Supervised versus unsupervised learning models

We have already discussed the concept of target (dependent) variables and independent variables, or features. Features (or independent variables) are used to describe the relationship with, or to predict values of, a target variable. After defining your independent and depending variables, you will formulate your model. One way to characterize the way in which a model learns from the data, is by classifying it into either a supervised or unsupervised learning model.

Supervised learning models

When the possible values of a target variable are specified and labeled, a model is considered supervised, that is, we know what we want to predict, and the goal is to find the most appropriate predictive model which will predict the outcome.

As an example, if we are predicting the approval rating for a product, we know what we are predicting (approval rating of a product), and we also usually know the range of possible outcomes. It could be a percentage from 0-100, or it could be some category such as high approval or low approval.

When the problem is supervised, the choice of which models to use are usually dependent upon the type of the target variable, that is, whether it is continuous or categorical. It can also be dependent upon factors such as bias/variance (discussed in Chapter 2, *The Modeling Process*), and the various assumptions we are willing to make concerning the model. Regression and decision tree algorithms are considered supervised algorithms since the target variables or target classes (in the case of decision trees) are specified even before the predictive modelling begins.

Unsupervised learning models

Unsupervised problems are more exploratory in nature. In an unsupervised learning context, one doesn't specify a target variable, or even have any idea what something should be. A data scientist is usually given a set of attributes, and then asked to derive some relationships, or discover some new attributes which are not obvious from looking at the data.

As an example, during an exploratory customer analysis, you could look at different attributes of customers, such as age, gender, and sales history, which could then lead you to create new variables (which hadn't existed before), which would describe each customer as best, good, or average. You could then choose an appropriate algorithm to suit this problem which might be a clustering algorithm, a decision tree, or a support vector machine.

Another example would be to use a neural network algorithm with some financial trading data in order to uncover some potential fraud or anomaly findings.

Usually, you will match up an unsupervised algorithm (such as neural networks) cast to an unsupervised setting (find fraud), but that is not always the case. You may find that you are able to incorporate traditional supervised techniques such as regression to find results which are totally unexpected using post-diagnostic tools which would examine such thing as residuals and outliers. That might lead you to other explorations which could cause you to reformulate your problem.

Finally, supervised learning and unsupervised learning often work hand in hand. It is possible to find yourself creating a new variable, discovered through an unsupervised process, which in turn would lead to incorporating this as a latent variable into a traditional supervised algorithm, such as a decision tree.

Regression techniques

Regression analysis (which is considered a supervised learning algorithm) dates back to the early 1800s when Gauss and Legendre utilized these techniques to measure the trajectories of the planets around the sun (`https://en.wikipedia.org/wiki/Regression_analysis`). The regression algorithm's usage is still going strong within the predictive analytics community due to its large base of literature and its ability to adapt to a wide range of problems.

Linear regression is the basic regression technique to use when your target variable is continuous. Linear regression is built upon the concept of ordinary least squares, and the functional form of the model is:

$$y_i = \beta_0 + \beta_{1xi1} + \beta_{2xi2} + \ldots \beta_{pxip} + \varepsilon_i$$

The preceding formula illustrates that linear regression models are additive, that is, the results of the prediction are calculated by summing the cross-product values of all of the independent variables, and then adding an intercept (first term of the formula), and error term (last term of the formula). That calculation yields the *prediction* for the dependent or target variable (y). The linear regression line is fitted via the method of **ordinary least squares (OLS)**, in which the squared (residual) differences between the observed value and the predicted distances on the regression line are minimized. Squared differences are used, rather than the actual differences, since we are really interested in the magnitude, not the direction of the differences. Squaring the results eliminates the negative or positive sign. The residuals are often used to test the errors resulting from the predictive model.

Advantages of regression

One advantage to using linear regression is that it facilitates easy interpretation of the linear coefficients which are attributed to each variable. Specifically, the slope of each variable in a regression model (the β in front of each of the regression terms), will indicate the change in the prediction for each 1-unit change in the corresponding independent variable, with all other variables in the model held constant. There is a fair amount of flexibility in using linear models in that you can also model nominal (categorical) independent variables as well as continuous ones, and incorporate a fair degree of non-linear relationships by using variable transformations and interactions. The body of knowledge for linear regression is vast, and based heavily on probability theory.

While linear regression can be very powerful when used correctly, here are some of the major assumptions of linear regression which you should pay attention to:

- **Independence**: the observations have no relationship with each other. This assumption will often be violated when you are dealing with time-series data. Knowing how the data was sampled will help with understanding whether or not the data is independent and randomly sampled.

- **Linearity**: there is a linear relationship between the independent and dependent variables. Other kinds of relationships can exist; for example there can be a curvilinear relationship between the variables. The second plot of the first row in the Wikipedia reference for *Anscombe's quartet* shows how this can occur.
- **Normality**: the errors term in the regression model is normally distributed. Intuitively, normally distributed residuals are good to have since they imply that the correct variables are all accounted for in your model, and there is nothing left to explain. You are just left with random error.
- **Equal variances of errors**: the error terms also have constant variance. For example, non equality of variances can mean that the errors in prediction are increasing or decreasing as values of the independent variables grow larger or smaller.

If any of the assumptions are grossly violated, you probably should not be using linear regression. I say grossly since there is a certain degree of tolerance that any model has for assumptions, and there are statistical tests that can be used to measure that degree for some of the assumptions. However, if your data meets the assumptions of linear regression, the predictions can be quite powerful.

Generalized linear models

Generalized linear models (**GLMs**) refer to a larger framework of prediction techniques which can include linear regression, logistic regression (used to predict binary outcomes), and poisson regression (used to predict counts). They are a generalization of linear regression techniques which allow you to work with other distributions which have non-normal error terms. GLMs can be implemented in R by using the `glm` package, in which you supply a link function to specify which distribution you are modeling. That makes it easier to work with different types of models within a single package, using standard syntax.

Linear regression using GLM

In Chapter 1, *Getting Started with Predictive Analytics*, our original example that we used to predict womens' heights based upon womens' weights used the lm package. We could also have used the glm package, specifying family=Gaussian as the link function:

```
lm_output <-  lm(women$height ~ women$weight)
```

or:

```
glm_output <-  glm(women$height ~ women$weight,family=gaussian)
```

Logistic regression

A very popular use of GLM is via logistic regression. This is the type of regression to use when your target variable is a binary value, that is, it can only take on two values. These two binary values usually take the form:

- Something occurred (binary value = 1)
- Something did not occur (binary value = 0)

These two values typically vary according to the type of industry. Here are some examples of binary responses in different industries:

- **Marketing**: Did the customer respond to a specific offer or not?
- **Health care**: Was a specific drug effective in treating a condition or was it not?
- **Financial**: Did a specific trading strategy lead to a profit or not?
- **Web tracking**: Did a customer abandon a shopping cart at the checkout or not?

Virtually every industry will have problems which can be formulated in terms of binary outcomes. In fact, sometimes standard linear regression problems are often recast, so instead of predicting the specific values for the target value, the problem will be reformulated into a binary problem. Often this is done to take advantage of some of the relaxed assumptions of logistic regression.

You may ask, "Why not use regular linear regression for these kinds of problems?" Unfortunately, linear regression itself will not work when you have a binary outcome variable for a variety of reasons. Here are two important ones:

- First of all, if regular regression is used, the results will extend way beyond the bounded ranges of 0 and 1, since a line is infinite in both directions.
- Second, one of the requirements of regular regression is that the residual errors are normally distributed, and this is not true in the case of logistic regression. The error term is related to a conditional Bernoulli distribution.

However, logistic regression does share many of the features of regression models:

- It is a low variance algorithm, and as a result it is fairly simple to implement and explain, and does not have as many problems with overfitting as some of the other algorithms.
- It also has good capabilities for feature selection, and the addition of transformed variables and interactions which it shares with linear regression. However, what it *does* predicts (the likelihood of an event), sets it apart from standard regression techniques.

The odds ratio

While linear regression will predict an actual outcome for the dependent variable, logistic regression does not predict actual outcomes or events. What it will predict is the likelihood, (or odds ratio) of one of the events occurring. This is slightly different since it is related to the probability of an event occurrence (rather than the prediction of the event itself).

The odds ratio is defined as the ratio of the probability of an event A occurring divided by the probability of an event not occurring. In functional form, this ratio is expressed as a natural logarithm:

$$\ln\left(\frac{P}{1-P}\right) = a + \beta_1 X_1 + \beta_2 X_2 + \dots \beta_1 X_1$$

The logistic regression coefficients

The coefficients returned from the logistic regression are standardized, in that they measure the effect of a 1-unit change in the independent variable on the log of the odds ratio, and not on the change of the variable itself.

The algorithm determines these coefficients not by using the OLS method used in linear regression, but it determines the coefficients by using a method called **maximum likelihood estimation**. Simply put, this means that the algorithm starts with arbitrary values of the coefficients and then puts forth an initial model. Then the algorithm measures the errors in the model and adjusts the coefficients to new values so that the results of the next model conform better to the values contained in your data. This is performed iteratively until the errors converge to an optimal solution.

Since the predictions from a linear model are determined by summing up the cross products and intercepts from the model, this result can be compared to a 0.5 percent cut-off value, which is used as a decision rule to classify an occurrence into one of the two values of the target variables. So while the output of a logistic regression is really a function of an odds ratio, logistic regression can essentially be used as a classification algorithm.

Example - using logistic regression in health care to predict pain thresholds

This example takes data from a research study which predicts whether or not a subject reported experiencing a reduction of pain for a condition, after being administered various treatments. The Gender, Age, and the Duration columns of any pre-existing pain were also used as independent variables in the model. The outcome variable, Pain, is coded as 1 (reported pain), or 0 (reported no pain). The Treatment column refers to 1 of 2 treatments (A or B), as well as a control group (P).

Reading the data

We will use the read.table with the text= option to read the raw data inline, that is, without the need to first create an external file. This method is useful for analysis in which you are copying and pasting data from another source, for example, a spreadsheet:

```
df <- read.table(text = 'Treatment  Gender  Age  Duration  Pain
                    P         F      68      1       0
                    P         M      66      26      1
                    A         F      71      12      0
```

A	M	71	17	1
B	F	66	12	0
A	F	64	17	0
P	M	70	1	1
A	F	64	30	0
B	F	78	1	0
B	M	75	30	1
A	M	70	12	0
B	M	70	1	0
P	M	78	12	1
P	M	66	4	1
A	M	78	15	1
P	F	72	27	0
B	F	65	7	0
P	M	67	17	1
P	F	67	1	1
A	F	74	1	0
B	M	74	16	0
B	F	67	28	0
B	F	72	50	0
A	F	63	27	0
A	M	62	42	0
P	M	74	4	0
B	M	66	19	0
A	M	70	28	0
P	M	83	1	1
P	M	77	29	1
A	F	69	12	0
B	M	67	23	0
B	M	77	1	1
P	F	65	29	0
B	M	75	21	1
P	F	70	13	1
P	F	68	27	1
B	M	70	22	0
A	M	67	10	0
B	M	80	21	1
P	F	67	30	0
B	F	77	16	0
B	F	76	9	1
A	F	69	18	1
P	F	64	1	1
A	F	72	25	0
B	M	59	29	0
A	M	69	1	0
B	F	69	42	0
P	F	79	20	1
B	F	65	14	0

A	M	76	25	1
B	F	69	24	0
P	M	60	26	1
A	F	67	11	0
A	M	75	6	1
P	M	68	11	1
A	M	65	15	0
P	F	72	11	1
A	F	69	3	0',header =

```
    TRUE)
```

Obtaining some basic counts

Now that the data has been read, switch over to the console window. At the console prompt, enter the command `table(df$Pain)`. This function will give you the raw counts of the number of patients who did or did not experience pain:

```
> table(df$Pain)
```

This is the output that will appear in the console window:

```
 0  1
35 25
```

The `prop.table` function will supply you with the percentages of reported pain:

```
> prop.table(table(df$Pain))
```

This is the following output:

```
        0         1
0.5833333 0.4166667
```

Saving your data

Before we do anything else, let's save this dataframe to disk, since we will be using it again in this chapter. Before saving the file, make sure you set your working directory to the data directory:

```
setwd("C:/PracticalPredictiveAnalytics/Data")
save(df,file="pain_raw.Rda")
```

Fitting a GLM model

Now we will fit a logistic model using the `glm` package. Logistic regression typically predicts the probability of the 1 event, so make sure that the 1 events corresponds to what you want to predict. Often there is some confusion when variables are coded 1 for negative conditions such as not present, or does not exist. For our model, `Pain=1` represents reduction of pain. Be sure to specify `family="binomial"` as an option, since that tells GLM that you will be running a logistic model:

```
PainGLM <- glm(Pain ~ Treatment + Gender + Age + Duration, data=df,
family="binomial")
```

The `summary` function will list the coefficients (`Estimate`), along with the standard error, standardized `z value`, and the p-values. The p-values (last column) which contain an asterisk (`*` or `**`) usually specify the significant variables, and are usually the ones you should look at first. However, please try not to automatically look at just the variables with asterisks. You should look at the coefficients and statistics for all of the variables, since p-values should not be treated as absolute numbers, especially when dealing with people's health:

```
summary(PainGLM)
```

This is the output that is produced:

```
Call:
glm(formula = Pain ~ Treatment + Gender + Age + Duration, family =
"binomial",
    data = df)

Deviance Residuals:
    Min       1Q     Median       3Q       Max
 -2.7638   0.5904    0.1952    0.6151    2.3153

Coefficients:
              Estimate Std. Error z value Pr(>|z|)
(Intercept) -20.588282   7.102883  -2.899  0.00375 **
TreatmentB   -0.526853   0.937025  -0.562  0.57394
TreatmentP    3.181690   1.016021   3.132  0.00174 **
GenderM       1.832202   0.796206   2.301  0.02138 *
Age           0.262093   0.097012   2.702  0.00690 **
Duration     -0.005859   0.032992  -0.178  0.85905
---
Signif. codes:  0 '***' 0.001 '**' 0.01 '*' 0.05 '.' 0.1 ' ' 1

(Dispersion parameter for binomial family taken to be 1)
```

```
    Null deviance: 81.503  on 59  degrees of freedom
Residual deviance: 48.736  on 54  degrees of freedom
AIC: 60.736

Number of Fisher Scoring iterations: 5
```

As mentioned earlier, the output coefficients are expressed as the log of the odd-ratio. To express the coefficients in the original scale, you will need to apply the `exp()` function. Also, in the following code, we will include confidence intervals along with the exponentiated coefficients to get an idea of the ranges. Look for any confidence interval in which 0 is contained within the range, since that implies that the effect may be non-existent or slight.

In the following example, `TreatmentB` and `Duration` all contain 0 within their respective confidence intervals:

```
cbind(exp(coef(PainGLM)),confint(PainGLM))
```

This is the output which results:

```
                                        2.5 %        97.5 %
(Intercept)   0.000000001144518  -36.68451736   -8.30307052
TreatmentB    0.590460426864162   -2.47589653    1.28411227
TreatmentP   24.087421759279735    1.38534008    5.45845778
GenderM       6.247629578965714    0.38227954    3.58627713
Age           1.299647808771851    0.09349231    0.48146218
Duration      0.994158449470197   -0.07338820    0.05768555
```

The `exp()` function will give you the actual likelihood ratios for each of the variables. This allows you to observe the effect of each variable on the likelihood of the predictor occurring. In our previous example, increasing the `Age` by 1 year increases the likelihood of `Pain` by a factor of 1.3. Is that a lot? Start thinking beyond the numbers and consider how you might perceive that result if you happened to be suffering a chronic condition.

Examining the residuals

One of the first things I do after looking at the coefficients is to look at the residuals.

You can see all of the residuals by using the `residuals()` function:

```
residuals(PainGLM, type="deviance") # residuals
```

For many good models, the residuals will be scattered around zero, and will have roughly the same variance at all levels. The deviance of the residuals for this model are listed within the summary section shown previously. We can see that the distribution is balanced since the absolute values of the min and max are approximately equal, as well as 1Q (25th percentile) with 3Q (75th percentile):

```
Deviance Residuals:
    Min       1Q    Median       3Q       Max
 -2.7638  -0.5904  -0.1952   0.6151    2.3153
```

If we want to look at the mean, we can wrap the `mean()` function around the `residuals()` function. Note that the mean value of -0.04 is greater than the median value of -0.195. This means that the residuals have a slightly positive skew:

```
mean(residuals(PainGLM, type="deviance"))
```

Here is the output which will appear in the console:

```
[1] -0.04269042
```

Residual plots

Plots are extremely helpful at showing the residuals, and often are critical at diagnosing problems with a model:

```
plot(residuals(PainGLM, type="deviance"))
```

The plot which is output indicates a good example of neatly distributed residuals. Along the range of index, the residuals look like they are scattered around 0, and there seems to be no major trending upwards or downwards along the range, other than the slight skew noted previously:

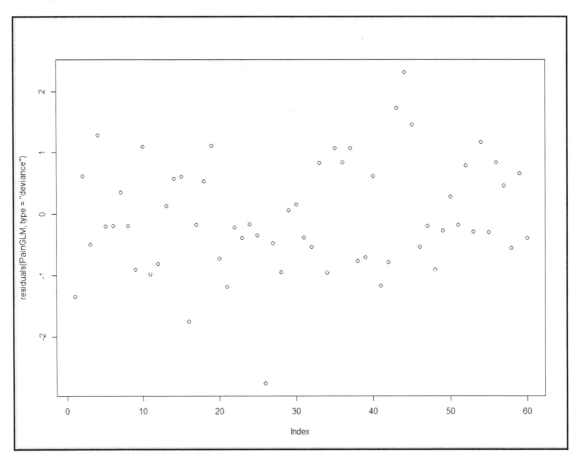

Added variable plots

Added variable plots allow you to examine the effect of a specific variable, while holding the coefficients of the other variables constant. In other words, it visually describes what happens when you add *one more variable* to the model. It can also be seen as one way to examine a specific variable's effect, by projecting a multiple regression line onto a 2-dimensional space. In this way, you can examine which variables have more influence compared to the others.

In the following plots, we will use the `avPlots()` function from the `car` package. You can see the strong linear effect of `Age`, while there is a negligible effect for `Duration`. This is also reflected in the coefficients and significance of the logistic regression model shown previously:

```
library(car)
library(car)
avPlots(PainGLM, id.method="mahal", id.n=2)
```

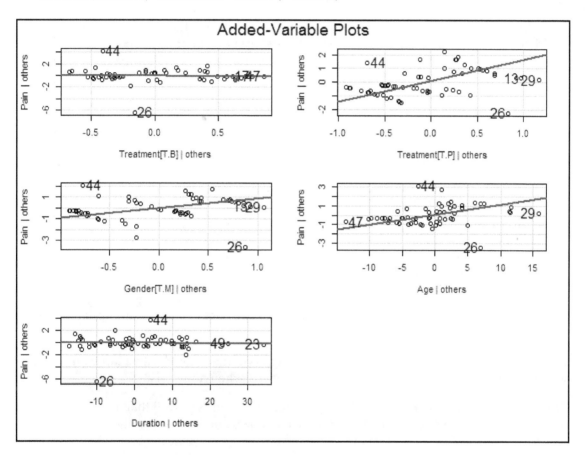

Outliers in the regression

Note that preceding each plot also identifies extreme data points in the dataset which may have an influence upon the regression line (line drawn through the data). The extreme values are represented in bold within the plot itself.

For example, in all of the preceding plots, you can see that observation 26 is considered an outlier with respect to the other covariates.

Print this observation to the console along with some of its neighbors. You can see how this could be considered an outlier just by inspection, since two variables (Duration and Treatment) immediately pop out as being different from the surrounding observations:

```
df[c(26,27,28,25),]
```

This is the output which is sent to the console:

```
   Treatment Gender Age Duration Pain
26         P      M  74        4    0
27         B      M  66       19    0
28         A      M  70       28    0
25         A      M  62       42    0
```

P-values and effect size

P-values have been the traditional way of performing hypothesis testing on output statistics, but have come under criticism in recent year as not being the appropriate measure to use, in many cases.

Datasets are much larger than they used to be. A very large dataset with a large number of variables can always show a significant p-value, even when none exist.

There are also a large number of different kinds of algorithms as well than can produce p-values, and there is a good chance you can pick one which will give you the p-value you want.

There are different p-value cut-off levels that an analyst can use to force significance.

The more dangerous situation is when you can select or alter the data to affect the p-value. This can be often very subtle, and can manifest itself through non-random sampling, data transformations from one level to another, keeping missing values, or deleting or imputing them. All of the decisions made by the modeler prior to applying the statistical test will affect the p-value.

Having said that, p-values are still useful for identifying possible significant predictors, and for understanding if the data fits the model. But it should be treated as only one tool, just as each algorithm you use is only one tool of many which you will use to help reveal the truth. Other tools we have demonstrated (such as confidence intervals, random sampling, and variable influence plots) should be used along with the calculation of p-values to present a complete picture of the data.

Here is an important statement from the **American Statistical Association** on the usage of p-values (*AMERICAN STATISTICAL ASSOCIATION RELEASES STATEMENT ON, 2016*):

- P-values can indicate how incompatible the data is with a specified statistical model
- P-values do not measure the probability that the studied hypothesis is true, or the probability that the data was produced by random chance alone
- Scientific conclusions and business or policy decisions should not be based only on whether a p-value passes a specific threshold
- Proper inference requires full reporting and transparency
- A p-value, or statistical significance, does not measure the size of an effect or the importance of a result
- By itself, a p-value does not provide a good measure of evidence regarding a model or hypothesis

P-values and effect sizes

There has always been this concern regarding p-values with small samples, however using data with large samples can also yield bad results, in that the p-value may be correct, but the magnitude of the change (the effect) is very small.

Take this example in which you are measuring the effect of winning between an average of $1,000,000 or $1,000,001 in a lottery.

We will generate two probability samples:

- X contains 1 million observations with a mean value of 1,000,000
- Y also contains 1 million observations but with a mean value of 1,000,001 and it is only a 1-unit difference

Generate a dataframe with X and Y and print some summary statistics:

```
set.seed(1020)
lottery <- data.frame(
  cbind(x=rnorm(n=1000000,1000000,100),y=rnorm(1000000,1000001,100)   )
)
  summary(lottery)
```

The output shows the simulated X and Y exactly as we expect. Both with the same number of observations, but with only a 1-unit difference in the mean values:

```
         x                    y
 Min.    : 999503    Min.    : 999513
 1st Qu.: 999933    1st Qu.: 999934
 Median :1000000    Median :1000001
 Mean    :1000000    Mean    :1000001
 3rd Qu.:1000067    3rd Qu.:1000068
 Max.    :1000526    Max.    :1000489
```

If we run a statistical t-test on the difference between the means, the p-value shows a very significant difference based upon the p-value. But, for only a $1 difference:

```
t.test(lottery$x,lottery$y)
```

This is the output which is written to the console:

```
    Welch Two Sample t-test

data:  lottery$x and lottery$y
t = -7.4518, df = 2000000, p-value = 9.209e-14
alternative hypothesis: true difference in means is not equal to 0
95 percent confidence interval:
 -1.3303374 -0.7762632
sample estimates:
mean of x mean of y
 999999.9 1000001.0
```

Now let's repeat this simulation, but this time run this same code using a much smaller value of *n*, say n=100000:

```
set.seed(1020)
lottery <- data.frame(
  cbind(x=rnorm(n=100000,1000000,100),y=rnorm(n=100000,1000001,100)   )
)
summary(lottery)
```

This is the output which is written to the console:

```
        x                    y
 Min.   : 999545    Min.    : 999590
 1st Qu.: 999933    1st Qu.: 999934
 Median :1000000    Median :1000000
 Mean   :1000000    Mean    :1000001
 3rd Qu.:1000068    3rd Qu.:1000068
 Max.   :1000446    Max.    :1000450
```

Now re-run the t-test again, and notice we are obtaining a much larger p-value of 0.2492 :

```
t.test(lottery$x,lottery$y)
```

This is the output which is written to the console:

```
    Welch Two Sample t-test

data:  lottery$x and lottery$y
t = -1.1522, df = 200000, p-value = 0.2492
alternative hypothesis: true difference in means is not equal to 0
95 percent confidence interval:
 -1.3899758  0.3607735
sample estimates:
mean of x mean of y
  1000000   1000001
```

Here is the point of this exercise.

If these were amounts won in a lottery, most people would not care whether or not they won $1,000,000 or $1,000,001 (regardless of the sample size), so what comes into play is the effect size, which in this case is simply the difference between the two means ($1). Obviously, for large amounts of money, $1 does not make a difference, but what is important about this is that you need to know approximately how much of a change is meaningful to you in your analytics work.

Variable selection

Stepwise regression can be used as a variable selection method in cases in which you have a large number of variables, and you need to define a starting point in which you can start looking at a limited set of variables. However, all of the caveats regarding p-values come into play here as well. Use this method only to look at a candidate list of variables for model testing. It is not a good idea to use stepwise regression to determine a final model, since there are several methods use to determine the best variables, the final model can yield artificially high and biased results.

However, let's just start with identifying a list of potential variables for our `PainGLM` model, which is small, but will be good to illustrate the process. In the following example, the `stepwise()` function is used to determine a maximum `AIC` using the stepwise regression `forward/backward` options.

The variable selection process starts by adding variables one at a time, and then implementing a form of variable swapping, that is, taking into account whether or not `AIC` would be improved by removing any variable which was already in the model. Once `AIC` cannot be improved, the selection process stops.

- In the `PainGLM` example, the algorithm is illustrated, listing all the steps it goes through to determine the final variables selected. It begins with an initial `AIC` statistic of 83.5 (intercept-only model). Adding all of the variables into the model produces an `AIC` of 73.48. However, the `AIC` can then be improved by removing Duration. Therefore, it ends with a `Treatment`, `Age`, and `Gender` model with an `AIC` of 58.77, since it can no longer improve the AIC:

```
install.packages("RcmdrMisc")
library(RcmdrMisc)
stepwise(PainGLM, direction='forward/backward',
criterion='AIC')
```

The output of the stepwise function is written to the console:

```
Direction:  forward/backward-
Criterion:  AIC
Start:  AIC=83.5
Pain ~ 1
            Df Deviance     AIC
+ Treatment  2   67.480  73.480
+ Age        1   73.056  77.056
+ Gender     1   75.849  79.849
<none>           81.503  83.503
+ Duration   1   79.886  83.886

Step:  AIC=73.48
Pain ~ Treatment
            Df Deviance     AIC
+ Age        1   55.044  63.044
+ Gender     1   59.886  67.886
<none>           67.480  73.480
+ Duration   1   66.688  74.688
- Treatment  2   81.503  83.503

Step:  AIC=63.04
Pain ~ Treatment + Age
```

```
          Df Deviance    AIC
+ Gender   1   48.767 58.767
<none>         55.044 63.044
+ Duration 1   55.036 65.036
- Age      1   67.480 73.480
- Treatment 2  73.056 77.056
Step:  AIC=58.77
Pain ~ Treatment + Age + Gender
          Df Deviance    AIC
<none>         48.767 58.767
+ Duration 1   48.736 60.736
- Gender   1   55.044 63.044
- Age      1   59.886 67.886
- Treatment 2  68.900 74.900
Call:  glm(formula = Pain ~ Treatment + Age + Gender,    family =
"binomial",
    data = df)
Coefficients:
   (Intercept)  Treatment[T.B]   Treatment[T.P]              Age
Gender[T.M]
      -20.8694         -0.5474           3.1790           0.2650
1.8235
Degrees of Freedom: 59 Total (i.e. Null);   55 Residual
Null Deviance:       81.5
Residual Deviance: 48.77   AIC: 58.77
```

Interactions

We have seen that regression is additive, that is, the prediction is mostly calculated via adding crossproducts of the coefficients and independent single variables together. However, often single variables by themselves are not enough to adequately predict an outcome in a simple regression model. Often considering how say, predictor variable A affects predictor variable B can improve the outcome. This also goes a long way in terms of explaining the rationale behind using certain variables. The way two or more variables influence each other is referred to as *interaction*, and using an interaction in a model can produce an effect which is greater than the sum of their individual effects. Usually, two or more interaction variables are involved, and the way that one variable effects the dependent variable is conditional upon the different levels or ranges of the other variables.

In this example, we will take our original `Pain` model and determine if there is a separate effect for the different treatments by age. Interaction effects can be specified in the model by using the `:` separator (the colon). If we also want to include the individual variable effects as well as the interaction we would use the `*` separator.

First we will set up the model as we did before, but specify an `Age:Treatment` effect in the model. We will do this because we already know that Age and the Type of treatment independently can predict the Pain outcome to some degree, but we are interested to see if knowing the Age of the participant together with the type of treatment they received will improve the model. If so, we could research administrating different treatments to the various age groups, and as a result, affect the output variable (`Pain`):

```
install.packages("effects")
library(effects)
output <- glm(Pain ~ Treatment + Gender + Age + Duration + Age:Treatment
             ,data=df, family="binomial")
summary(output)
```

The output of the summary function is written to the console:

```
glm(formula = Pain ~ Treatment + Gender + Age + Duration + Age:Treatment,
    family = "binomial", data = df)

Deviance Residuals:
     Min        1Q    Median        3Q       Max
-2.21745  -0.38598  -0.05829   0.44605   2.53761

Coefficients:
                  Estimate Std. Error z value Pr(>|z|)
(Intercept)     -39.420723  20.276062  -1.944   0.0519 .
TreatmentB       -9.012876  31.965793  -0.282   0.7780
TreatmentP       38.338070  21.827078   1.756   0.0790 .
GenderM           1.957605   0.872107   2.245   0.0248 *
Age               0.524314   0.283665   1.848   0.0646 .
Duration          0.003562   0.036643   0.097   0.9226
TreatmentB:Age    0.100597   0.433846   0.232   0.8166
TreatmentP:Age   -0.504315   0.307248  -1.641   0.1007
---
Signif. codes:  0 '***' 0.001 '**' 0.01 '*' 0.05 '.' 0.1 ' ' 1

(Dispersion parameter for binomial family taken to be 1)

    Null deviance: 81.503  on 59  degrees of freedom
Residual deviance: 41.928  on 52  degrees of freedom
AIC: 57.928

Number of Fisher Scoring iterations: 7
```

In the output that appears preceding, note that instead of having one coefficient for `Treatment`, we have two separate coefficients for `TreatmentB` and `TreatmentP`, as well as the interaction of these levels versus `Age`. Note that none of the new interaction terms have significance codes in the last column.

Interaction effects plot:

The interaction effects can be shown using plot with the `effects()` function:

```
plot(effect("Treatment*Age", output, xlevels=list(age=0:99)),
ticks=list(at=c(.001, .005, .01, .05, seq(.1,.9,by=.2), .95, .99, .995)))
```

As the plots indicate, there is no interaction between `TreatmentP` (Placebo) and `Age`, which is what you would expect in a controlled study. The plots also indicate the relationship between `Age` and `Pain` for the other two treatments, but there is not enough of a significant difference (at the 0.05 level) to justify including this as an individualized coefficient:

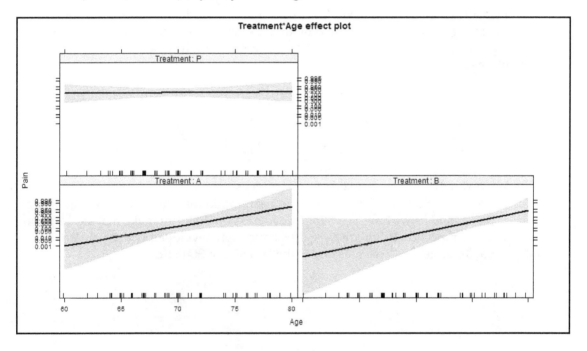

Goodness of fit statistics

Goodness of fit tests determine how well a model fits the data. There are several methods of judging how well the data fits the logistic regression model:

- **Data partitioning**: One way we learned how to do this was by dividing the data into training and testing datasets and measuring the degree to which they produce similar results. That method was demonstrated in `Chapter 2`, *The Modeling Process*.
- **Single metrics**: Another way to do this is to come up with a quantitative measure of how well your independent variable predicts your dependent variables on a scale from 0 to 1, with 0 meaning no predictive power, and 1 meaning the best possible predictive power. **Area Under the Curve (AUC)**, and R-square are examples of these kind of **Goodness of Fit (GOF)** tests.
- R-Square is a popular method of assessing goodness of fit, and it roughly measures the amount of explained variation in a model to the total variation. In linear regression, it is calculated by first taking the ratio of the residual Sum of Squares to the total Sum of Squares and subtracting the result from 1. (*Coefficient of Determination*)

$$R^2 \equiv 1 - \frac{SS_{res}}{SS_{tot}}.$$

- Interestingly enough, logistic regression does not have an R-square statistic. That is because R-Square is based upon the assumption that the model you are fitting is linear, and as we have seen, logistic regression does not make that assumption. However, pseudo R-Square measures have been developed which contain the same 0-1 scale. Of these measure is the McFadden Statistic.

McFadden statistic

The McFadden statistic approximates an R-Square type measure by looking at the ratio of the log-likelihood of the full model (analogous to the sum of squared errors in the OLS R-square model formula previously defined), divided by the log-likelihood of an intercept-only model (similar to the R-square total sum of squares denominator). This approximates the improvement of a logistical model over the intercept-only null model. The McFadden statistic can be considered a *pseudo* R-square since it will try to measure the same thing, and produce similar R-square results within the same 0-1 scale.

Here is the McFadden formula from the UCLA Institute for Digital Research and Education. (*FAQ: WHAT ARE PSEUDO R-SQUAREDS?*):

$$R^2 \equiv 1 - \frac{In\,\hat{L}\left(M_{Full}\right)}{In\,\hat{L}\left(M_{Intercept}\right)}$$

In the following code, the McFadden statistic of 0.40 shows that the model has a reasonably good fit:

```
install.packages("pscl")
library(pscl)
pR2(PainGLM)
```

The output of the pR2() function is written to the console:

```
          llh       llhNull           G2     McFadden          r2ML
  -24.3678589  -40.7515960   32.7674742    0.4020392     0.4208099
         r2CU
    0.5664233
```

Confidence intervals and Wald statistics

A Wald test is used to evaluate the statistical significance of each coefficient in the model and is calculated by taking the ratio of the square of the regression coefficient to the square of the standard error of the coefficient. The idea is to test the hypothesis that the coefficient of an independent variable in the model is not significantly different from zero.

The output shows the 95% confidence interval (with the lower 2.5% limit, and the upper 97.5% limit). Two intervals are given, one for the actual model coefficient, and the other for the exponentiated coefficient. We can again see that 0 is contained within the range for Duration, so we can consider removing the variable from the model:

```
confint(output, level=0.95, type="Wald")
```

The output of the confint() function is written to the console:

```
                      Estimate           2.5 %        97.5 %   exp(Estimate)
(Intercept)      -20.588282035   -34.50967776   -6.66688631    1.144518e-09
Treatment[T.B]    -0.526852662    -2.36338765    1.30968232    5.904604e-01
Treatment[T.P]     3.181689786     1.19032495    5.17305463    2.408742e+01
Gender[T.M]        1.832202124     0.27166722    3.39273703    6.247630e+00
Age                0.262093311     0.07195380    0.45223282    1.299648e+00
Duration          -0.005858679    -0.07052171    0.05880435    9.941584e-01
                         2.5 %          97.5 %
(Intercept)      1.029526e-15    1.272354e-03
Treatment[T.B]   9.410090e-02    3.704997e+00
Treatment[T.P]   3.288150e+00    1.764530e+02
Gender[T.M]      1.312150e+00    2.974726e+01
Age              1.074606e+00    1.571818e+00
Duration         9.319075e-01    1.060568e+00
```

Basic regression diagnostic plots

Plots are very critical for diagnosing fit and any potential problems associated with a regression model. These four plots can help you identify observations which do not fit in neatly with the regression, and should be looked at individually to see if there is anything special about them. It is just a part of the iterative process which is a part of developing your model, and does not by itself indicate a bad model.

Run the basic plot for `PainGLM`. Note that we will plot the four plots in a 2x2 quadrant:

```
oldpar <- par(oma=c(0,0,3,0), mfrow=c(2,2))
plot(PainGLM)
par(oldpar)
```

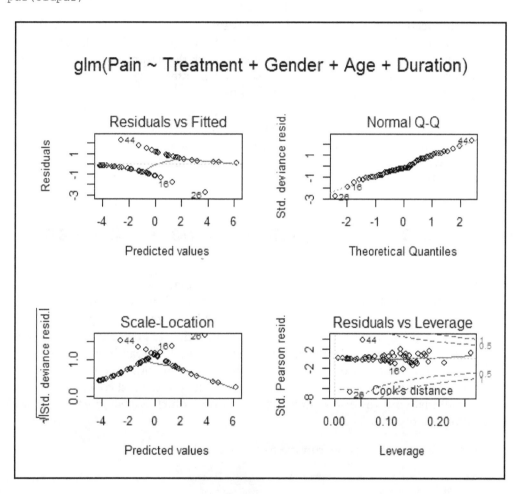

Description of the plots

Residual versus fitted: The residual versus fitted plot helps with determining if there are any patterns in the residuals. Ideally, the pattern (or ideally, no pattern) will be random scatter of the residual around a horizontal line.

If there is any obvious pattern, it is a good idea to revisit some of the bivariate correlations, or partial regression plot to try to tie the area back to some of the original scatterplots:

- **Normal Q-Q**: This plot will indicate if the residuals are normally distributed. It is a good sign if the residuals track the straight line.
- **Scale location**: This plot is used to check for the assumption of equal variances. It is also a good sign if this plot shows if residuals are spread equally along the ranges of predictors. This is how you can check the assumption of equal variance (homoscedasticity). It's good if you see a horizontal (red) reference line with points randomly equidistant from the line.
- **Residuals versus leverage**: This plot will help identify which outliers influence the regression estimates. Not all outliers will influence the regression, even if they are far from the regression line. The outliers outside of the dashed lines are the ones which can affect the regression coefficients, and if they are removed from the analysis, your results can change.

An interactive game – guessing if the residuals are random

When looking at the diagnostic plots, you are only looking at one possible distribution of the residuals. The library `TeachingDemos` has an interesting interactive function named `vis.test` which will challenge you to pick out the residuals which were generated from the regression which was run, with an alternate set of randomly generated residuals from the same regression. Remember, the residuals are supposed to be random, so the test essentially randomizes the residuals. If you are able to discern your own residuals from the other residuals that it generates, the residuals fail the test, and the test concludes (with a p-value of course) that your residuals really aren't random, which will send you back to the modelling drawing board.

To run the test, and play the game, run the following code:

```
install.packages("TeachingDemos")
library(TeachingDemos)
set.seed(1)
if(interactive()) {vis.test(residuals(PainGLM, type="response"), vt.qqnorm,
nrow=4, ncol=4, npage=1)}
```

After the following pattern appears, click on the pattern that you believe matches the normal Q-Q plot in row 1, column 2 previously:

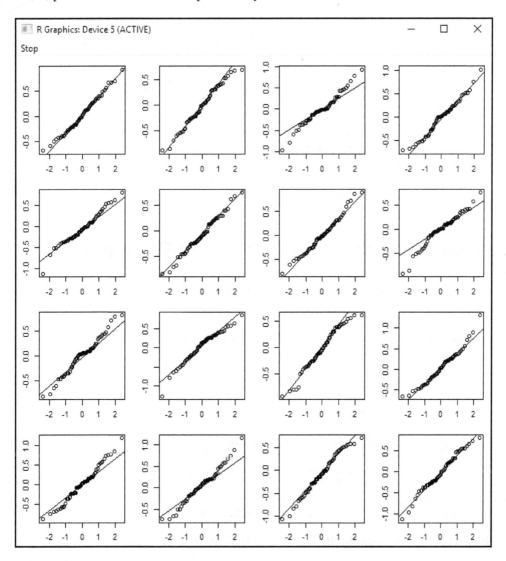

After clicking your answer, the function will test if you matched correctly, and what the probability was. If you keep on getting it wrong, reduce the number of rows and columns until you are able to match the Q-Q plot.

Goodness of fit – Hosmer-Lemeshow test

This goodness of fit test will look at subgroups of the predicted probabilities, for example, the probability ranges grouped into 10 (deciles), and measuring whether or not the prediction of the response variable is significantly different from what would be expected by chance.

First the data is group by their predicted probabilities from lowest to highest, and then binned into equally-sized groups.

Then a chi-square test is used to compare the predicted probability of each binned group to their expected probabilities. In a good model, predictions should do better than what is expected for most of the binned groups. If it does not, the groups which are problematic will be indicated in the predicted vs. expected plot, and you will be able to go back and attempt to identify any potential model problems.

Goodness of fit example on the PainGLM data

In the following example, we will apply the Hosmer-Lemeshow test to the `PainGLM` dataset. We will implement the Hosmer-Lemeshow test via the `hoslem.test()` function contained within the `ResourceSelection` package.

To set up the test, supply the observed values, with the fitted (predicted) values as part of the `hoslem.test()` function:

```
install.packages("ResourceSelection")
library(ResourceSelection)
hoslem.test(PainGLM$y,fitted(PainGLM))
```

The `hoslem.test` output is written to the console:

```
   Hosmer and Lemeshow goodness of fit (GOF) test

data:  PainGLM$y, fitted(PainGLM)
X-squared = 8.4981, df = 8, p-value = 0.3864
```

From the p-value statistic (0.38) the test shows that there is no problem with the fit.

The following plot shows that some of the predicted probabilities are better than expected (above the outperforms some of the bins do better than expected, and others do worse, relative to the ideal straight line).

We can see the bins, predicted, and observed values using a `cbind()` function:

```
cbind(hoslem$observed,hoslem$expected)
```

The first column shows the defined bins for each of the probability ranges.

Columns 2 and 3 give the observed and expected frequencies for each bin:

```
> cbind(hoslem$observed,hoslem$expected)
               y0 y1    yhat0        yhat1
[0.0143,0.02]   6  0 5.8984765 0.1015235
(0.02,0.0668]   6  0 5.7762161 0.2237839
(0.0668,0.128]  5  1 5.4894519 0.5105481
(0.128,0.246]   5  1 4.9134095 1.0865905
(0.246,0.353]   5  1 4.1805425 1.8194575
(0.353,0.502]   4  2 3.4564716 2.5435284
(0.502,0.632]   2  4 2.6816122 3.3183878
(0.632,0.807]   1  5 1.5600375 4.4399625
(0.807,0.903]   0  6 0.9008531 5.0991469
(0.903,0.998]   1  5 0.1429292 5.8570708
```

Regularization

In certain cases in which you have a large number of variables, you can end up overfitting the model. This will result in a biased model with some variables having more of an influence on the prediction than is reasonable to expect.

One way to deal with this is to select a subset of the original variables. We demonstrated all subsets regression which only considers a reduced number of variables for a final model. However, in some cases you may want to keep all or most of the variables in your model. For example, if you know via past studies that particular variables should always be included, you would want to keep that in the model, even though it might drop out of contention after a variable selection procedure has been run.

Regularization in regression is a method by which certain coefficients are reduced or even set to 0 in an effort to reduce their influence. While I believe it is always the better course to simplify the model by reducing the model to the most important variables, regularization can also help to reduce multicollinearity, or correlation between the independent variables, along with some other techniques that we have discussed such as principal components.

If you do choose the regularization path, there are many regularization options. Some of the regularization methods are ridge regression, LASSO, or LARS.

An example – ElasticNet

To illustrate regularization for our `PainGLM` data, we will use the ElasticNet regularization algorithm (contained within the `glmnet` package), which combines several different methods of regularization.

Start by creating some dummy variables using the `model.matrix()` function which we have used previously. Then, merge in the `Duration` variable to form a new matrix:

```
dummy.vars <- model.matrix(df$Pain ~ df$Treatment + df$Gender + df$Age +
df$Duration)[,-1]
x <- as.matrix(data.frame(df$Duration,dummy.vars))
head(x)
```

This is the following output:

	df.Treatment.T.B.	df.Treatment.T.P.	df.Gender.T.M.	df.Age	df.Duration
1	0	1	0	68	1
2	0	1	1	66	26
3	0	0	0	71	12
4	0	0	1	71	17
5	1	0	0	66	12
6	0	0	0	64	17

Next, run Lasso regularization (`alpha=1`) on the model, using matrix x as input, and setting.

The `Pain` as the target variable. Note that the syntax for `glmnet` is similar to that of the `glm` function which we used earlier:

```
install.packages("glmnet")
library(glmnet)
options(scipen = 999)
mod.result<-glmnet(x,y=as.factor(df$Pain),alpha=1,family='binomial')
```

Choosing a correct lamda

The model output will show the ranges of lambda (the regularization parameter), which will smooth out the effects of the various coefficients to different degrees.

A plot of `mod.results` will display the size of the coefficients as lambda changes:

```
plot(mod.result,xvar="lambda")
```

The parameter lambda controls the amount of shrinkage for the coefficients.

Notice that as lambda gets larger, more coefficients will be shrinking towards 0:

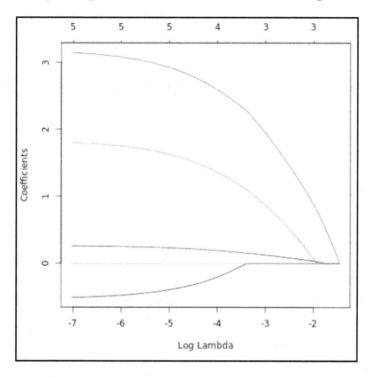

If you print some of the results you will see how many non-zero coefficients are included in the model for each lambda, as well as the percent deviation for each model. This will help you select an appropriate lambda for your model:

```
head(print(mod.result))
```

The table of Lambda's are written to the console:

```
        Df                       %Dev Lambda
[1,]    0  -0.0000000000000004904 0.2357
[2,]    1   0.0284499999999999996 0.2148
[3,]    1   0.0519700000000000023 0.1957
[4,]    2   0.0739900000000000002 0.1783
[5,]    2   0.1071000000000000008 0.1625
[6,]    2   0.1351999999999999869 0.1480

tail(print(mod.result))
        Df    %Dev      Lambda
```

```
[56,]   5 0.4019 0.0014130
[57,]   5 0.4019 0.0012870
[58,]   5 0.4020 0.0011730
[59,]   5 0.4020 0.0010690
[60,]   5 0.4020 0.0009739
[61,]   5 0.4020 0.0008874
```

Printing out the possible coefficients based on Lambda

Using some of the lambda values, you can print out the different coefficients for each model.

This will also help you choose a lambda value that is good for your model:

```
coef(mod.result,s=0.1957000)    #  4 of 5 coefficient are at 0, too much
shrinkage
coef(mod.result,s=0.0131800)    #  only 1 coefficient is set to 0
coef(mod.result,s=0.0120100)    #   All coefficients are included
coef(mod.result,s=0.01)
```

Using a lambda of .01 will use all of the variables, so let's print out the coefficients using that value:

```
> coef(mod.result,s=0.01)
7 x 1 sparse Matrix of class "dgCMatrix"
                                          1
(Intercept)       -17.57297008856023268208
df.Duration        -0.000962546
df.TreatmentB      -0.33638216397784859168
df.TreatmentP       2.82134076268210698402
df.GenderM          1.54779351031200929079
df.Age              0.22139548722788335300
df.Duration.1           .
```

Comparing the regularized coefficients with the original `glm` coefficients, you can observe that the magnitude of the coefficients has been reduced. As an exercise, try experimenting with different lambda values and observe how the coefficients change:

```
Coefficients:
             Estimate Std. Error z value Pr(>|z|)
(Intercept) -20.588282   7.102883  -2.899  0.00375 **
TreatmentB   -0.526853   0.937025  -0.562  0.57394
TreatmentP    3.181690   1.016021   3.132  0.00174 **
GenderM       1.832202   0.796206   2.301  0.02138 *
Age           0.262093   0.097012   2.702  0.00690 **
Duration     -0.005859   0.032992  -0.178  0.85905
```

Summary

In this chapter, we started with a discussion of supervised and unsupervised learning and emphasized the difference between pure predictive and exploratory analytics. We were then introduced to the first of the core algorithms (general linear models) which are important in the predictive analytics world. We then discussed various regression methods, along with its pros and cons, and noted that regression can be an extremely flexible and well researched statistical based modeling tool. We then used a pain threshold study to show examples of logistic regression and regularized regression, along with discussing important regressions concepts such as interaction, p-values and effect sizes.

In the next chapter, we will resume our discussion of the core predictive analytics algorithms by discussing three additional algorithms, that is, decision trees, clustering, and support vector machines.

5
Introduction to Decision Trees, Clustering, and SVM

"My interest is in the future because I am going to spend the rest of my life there"

– Charles F. Kettering.

Decision tree algorithms

Decision trees are considered a good predictive model to start with, and have many advantages. Interpretability, variable selection, variable interaction, and the flexibility to choose the level of complexity for a decision tree all come into play.

Decision trees methods are considered classification methods, so the typical use case for a decision tree is predicting a class or category. However, there are also certain types of decision trees, which are known as regression trees, where the output is a continuous variable. In this way, we can begin development models that are a mix of numeric and categorical variables.

Decision trees are heavily used in marketing and advertising, and in any industry where there is a need to segment customers into different groups. They are also used in healthcare for disease and risk classification.

Advantages of decision trees

Decision trees have many advantages. They can be easily understood by both technical and business people and can be presented in an extremely simplified or detailed way.

They can be specifically tailored to the type of audience, depending upon the inclusion/exclusion of domain-specific variables and the level of complexity. They are most useful when there are a small to medium number of variables that are generally understood, and the goal is to learn about the interactions between them. Decision trees are also good vehicles for storytelling since the natural presentation of a tree, and its splitting mechanism, corresponds well with business rule decision making and each specific node can be examined and questioned if need be.

Decision trees can handle both categorical and number variables, and deal with missing values. There is no need to discard or impute them.

Disadvantages of decision trees

Most decision trees utilize what are known as **greedy** algorithms. There are many definitions of what *greedy* means, but I like the one that suggests that it always makes the optimal choice based upon whatever information happens to be available at that moment. There is no hindsight that is used when building trees. Slight changes in data can alter results, and if you run the algorithm on a subsequent sample, the results may not replicate in exactly the same way. It is also difficult to force the tree to split the way you want it to when running in an automated fashion. If you want to control splits exactly, you may be better off using *interactive decision trees* in which you are able to split a node by pointing and clicking. Unfortunately there are not a lot of open source options for this.

Additionally, there is a built-in bias in decision tree algorithms in that they favor variables with a large number of categories. This enables the algorithm to be able to split over a large category, even when the result would not make any sense (we will see this in an example). Large trees can produce invalid or silly results, especially when the size of the tree is very large. Over-fitting is common, but there is a technique known as **pruning** which can be used to reduce this. Random forest trees can help with these disadvantages somewhat, since not all variables are included in every tree, and it uses consensus building to generate a result.

Despite these disadvantages of decision trees, I advocate their use as more of an exploratory tool (unsupervised learning), and you will find that they are very good at uncovering many important relationships that exist in your data when the analysis is performed in an organized and methodical method. It is also a good way to validate results obtained from other types of models. If you find that other models obtain much better results that you cannot replicate visually in a decision tree model, chances are good that the results from the more complex model will not replicate in the future.

Basic decision tree concepts

Decision trees algorithm are analogous to the game of 20 questions, or animal, vegetable, mineral. A basic decision tree algorithm will start at the root of the tree, representing all of the data, and continue to break each category into two separate categories that are based upon optimal methods, to be able to guess the best characteristics to identify each of the two categories. This is known as **splitting a node**. Then the algorithm will continue to split the data until it either cannot split any more, or stops in other ways based upon the control parameters.

For example, if we want to classify gender based upon the presence of osteoporosis, ischemic heart disease, and the average number of prescriptions, we could develop a tree that looked something like this:

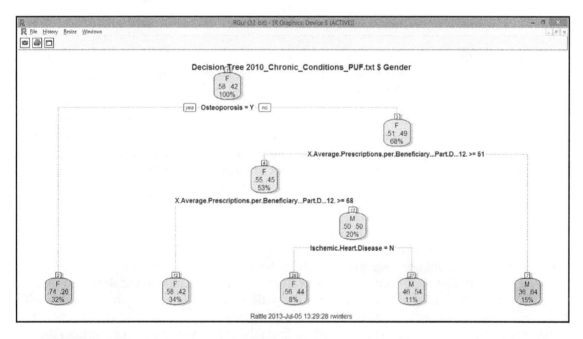

Notice that the first question is "Does the patient have Osteopororis?". Then based upon the answer, another series of question are asked which will ultimately place a patient into a final node of the tree, in which no more questions can be asked which will improve the results.

Growing the tree

Our original node always starts at the root of the tree. In the preceding diagram, the first node merely starts with a description of how the population breaks down by gender. In this case, females make up the majority class at 58% of the population. The goal in decision of tree algorithms is to always grow a tree and improve predictions. So, at this point, we want to do better than 58% prediction for gender.

As we grow the tree, two questions will always need to be taken into consideration:

- Which variable will best improve the prediction for each of the classes of the target variable at that point?
- For that variable, what is the best split point that will segment a categorical variable into two parts, or divide a continuous variable into two parts, and will improve the prediction for that class?

The outcome of this decision will be a new tree node, or leaf. In a classical decision tree, there are typically two paths (yes or no, high or low) that are followed, but there can be more than two paths depending upon the algorithm.

In our preceding example, the algorithm will first run through all of the variables and determine which one will improve the prediction. That variable happens to be the presence of osteoporosis. If osteoporosis is present, one could predict that the patient is female with 74% accuracy. However, when osteoporosis is not present, the probability of being female actually decreases to 51%, which is slightly worse than the original 58% representation of females in the study.

But wait. The partitioning algorithm will continue to try to split the data again. This time it looks at the average prescriptions variable as a way to improve the prediction. The average number of prescriptions per year per beneficiary for this analysis runs from about 15 per year to about 200. The algorithm will try all values in this range to split the data into two parts. For example, it might try to first compare patients with 10 or more prescriptions, with those with 9 or less prescriptions. It will then look at the prediction for that cutoff. Then it will continue to change to cutoff value until it finds the cutoff value which optimizes the separation between the two classes.

In this instance, it has found that 51 prescriptions is the cutoff that optimizes the split for those patients without osteoporosis. When the number of prescriptions is greater than 50, there is a 64% probabiltity that the patient is male.

Impurity

One a node is split according to the best criteria, the resulting nodes are examined for impurity. Impurity measures the separation of the classes, based upon what the expected frequencies should be at that point. The most impure case is when a node is split 50/50 for a binary class. This essentially designates a random class assignment. The least impure case is when a decision rule places all the observations completely in one class, and 0 observations are placed in the other class. This is the more desirable case, since it allows us to make a *perfect* prediction for that node.

Once an impurity measure is calculated, the algorithm will compute an information gain measure, which calculates how much the impurity decreases by splitting each of the variables, and proceeds to calculate all possible split points for a continuous variable.

Controlling the growth of the tree

One characteristic of the cart (implemented as rpart in R) is that it will try all possible variables and split points until it finds the best one to use. Depending upon how the algorithm is configured, it can be, the one that achieves the highest information gain. However, in a real-world setting, very few trees are grown with unlimited boundaries. Trees are grown with constraints. Examples of constraints would be specifying the maximum number of branches that can be grown, or the minimum number of observations contained within a leaf. As a result, the predictive modeler can construct a tree to be as simple or as complex as needed.

Types of decision tree algorithms

In R, two types of decision tree algorithms are illustrated. We will first look at the traditional algorithm, known as rpart and we will analyze the `state.x77` data to determine life expectancy, based upon a number of attributes.

Here is a description of the metadata for the `state.x77` data. You can also get more information able this table by entering `?x77.data` at the R console.

Population	Population estimate as of July 1, 1975
Income	Per capita income (1974)
Illiteracy	Illiteracy (1970, percent of population)
Life experience	Life expectancy in years (1969-71)

Murder	Murder and non-negligent manslaughter rate per 100,000 population (1976)
HS graduate	Percentage high-school graduates (1970)
Frost	Mean number of days with minimum temperature below freezing (1931-1960) in capital or large city
Area	Land area in square miles

First, we will concatenate this data with two other reference datasets. Use the R help system to obtain more information about the adjunct tables as well:

- `state.abb`: To obtain the state abbreviation
- `state.region`: To obtain the state"s geographical region

```
statedf <- as.data.frame(state.x77)
x <- data.frame(statedf, state.abb, state.region)
summary(x)
```

The output from the `summary()` function appears in the console:

```
> summary(x)
   Population         Income        Illiteracy        Life.Exp         Murder          HS.Grad          Frost
 Min.   :  365   Min.   :3098   Min.   :0.500   Min.   :67.96   Min.   : 1.400   Min.   :37.80   Min.   :  0.00
 1st Qu.: 1080   1st Qu.:3993   1st Qu.:0.625   1st Qu.:70.12   1st Qu.: 4.350   1st Qu.:48.05   1st Qu.: 66.25
 Median : 2838   Median :4519   Median :0.950   Median :70.67   Median : 6.850   Median :53.25   Median :114.50
 Mean   : 4246   Mean   :4436   Mean   :1.170   Mean   :70.88   Mean   : 7.378   Mean   :53.11   Mean   :104.46
 3rd Qu.: 4968   3rd Qu.:4814   3rd Qu.:1.575   3rd Qu.:71.89   3rd Qu.:10.675   3rd Qu.:59.15   3rd Qu.:139.75
 Max.   :21198   Max.   :6315   Max.   :2.800   Max.   :73.60   Max.   :15.100   Max.   :67.30   Max.   :188.00

      Area          state.abb          state.region
 Min.   :  1049   AK     : 1   Northeast    : 9
 1st Qu.: 36985   AL     : 1   South        :16
 Median : 54277   AR     : 1   North Central:12
 Mean   : 70736   AZ     : 1   West         :13
 3rd Qu.: 81163   CA     : 1
 Max.   :566432   CO     : 1
                  (Other):44
```

Examining the target variable

A quick histogram of the target variable, `Life.Exp`, shows a considerable amount of variation. Therefore, it can be considered a good potential target variable.

```
hist(x$Life.Exp)
```

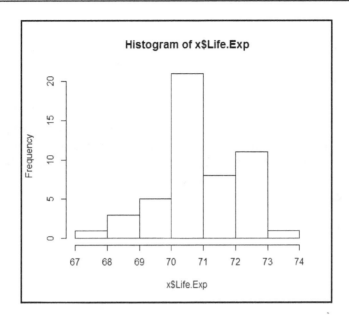

Using formula notation in an rpart model

We have already seen how to specify regression models in R using formula notation. For example, we use `lm(women$height ~ women$weight))` to predict height based upon weight.

The general form of formula notation in regression models is:

Dependent variable ~ Independent variables

Where the dependent variable is on the left side of the tilde (~), and the independent variables are on the right side of the tilde.

An rpart model can be set up using formula notation as well, with a slight change in terminology. In an rpart model, we can specify the target variable (`Life.Exp`) on the left side of the tilde (~), and the predictor variables on the right side of the tilde. We will use dot notation (`.`) to designate that we will be considering *all* variables.

TIP

Dot notation is a convenient way to specify all your variables; however, as you build out your model, you may want to avoid using this, and instead specify the specific list of the variables that you are interested in. This will speed up processing, and will avoid unnecessary splits.

In the following example, you can see that rpart will select `state` as the best initial split variable. While this may ultimately grow a very accurate tree, in terms of prediction ability, splitting initially on a high dimensional variable such as state does not offer great insight into what causes variation in life expectancy. There is always the possibility that the states will be broken out into geographic areas. But often you will obtain a split of states that do not make any sense.

In the following example we will use the `rpart()` function to generate a simple decision tree. We will also use the `prp()` function from the package `rpart.plot` to visualize the tree:

```
install.packages("rpart")
install.packages("rattle")
install.packages("rpart.plot")
install.packages("RColorBrewer")

library(rpart)
library(rattle)
library(rpart.plot)
library(RColorBrewer)
set.seed(1020)
y1 <- rpart(Life.Exp ~ .,data=x,cp=.01)
prp(y1, type=4, extra=1)
```

Interpretation of the plot

In the following plot, the splitting of the nodes is purely based upon state, with no insights on how the states were grouped. Notice that `state.region` does not factor at all in the splitting algorithm, so it would be a good guess that much of the splitting is purely mechanical and visually, no obvious grouping is reflected in many of the splits:

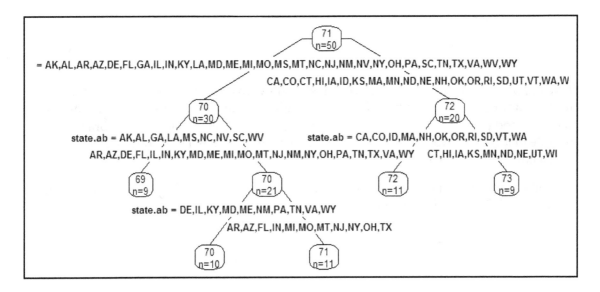

Printing a text version of the decision tree

Printing the rpart object will also give you the text output, which will show you the members of each class after each split point. Entries with an asterisk (*) are terminal nodes. Terminal nodes cannot be split any further. Often, segmentation can be performed based on terminal nodes only, assuming the sizes are large enough to make decisions made upon them actionable:

```
> print(y1)
```

This `print()` function sends this output to the console:

```
n= 50

node), split, n, deviance, yval
      * denotes terminal node

1) root 50 88.2990000 70.87860
2)
state.abb=AK,AL,AR,AZ,DE,FL,GA,IL,IN,KY,LA,MD,ME,MI,MO,MS,MT,NC,NJ,NM,NV,NY
,OH,PA,SC,TN,TX,VA,WV,WY 30 21.0890000 69.98000
4)  state.abb=AK,AL,GA,LA,MS,NC,NV,SC,WV 9  2.2790220 68.82556 *
5)  state.abb=AR,AZ,DE,FL,IL,IN,KY,MD,ME,MI,MO,MT,NJ,NM,NY,OH,PA,TN,TX,VA,WY
21  1.6747240 70.47476
10) state.abb=DE,IL,KY,MD,ME,NM,PA,TN,VA,WY 10  0.1656400 70.21400 *
11) state.abb=AR,AZ,FL,IN,MI,MO,MT,NJ,NY,OH,TX 11  0.2109636 70.71182 *
```

```
3) state.abb=CA,CO,CT,HI,IA,ID,KS,MA,MN,ND,NE,NH,OK,OR,RI,SD,UT,VT,WA,WI 20
6.6488550 72.22650
6) state.abb=CA,CO,ID,MA,NH,OK,OR,RI,SD,VT,WA 11  0.7760909 71.78091 *
7) state.abb=CT,HI,IA,KS,MN,ND,NE,UT,WI 9  1.0192890 72.77111 *
```

If we remove state from the model, we will start off with a much more understandable model. After `prp()` function has plotted the result, you can see that the left branches of the tree are based purely on the high murder rate. The two terminal loads for this branch indicate that the life expectance for an area with murder rate >= 11% is one year less than with a murder rate < 11%.

The right branches of the tree concentrate on lower murder rates. For these branches, region is considered. The North and Southern regions have a 1 year. lower life expectancy than the West or North Central regions:

```
y2 <- rpart(Life.Exp ~ Population + Income + Illiteracy +
            Murder +
            HS.Grad +
            Frost +
            Area +
            state.region,method='anova',
data=x
)

prp(y2, type=4, extra=1)
```

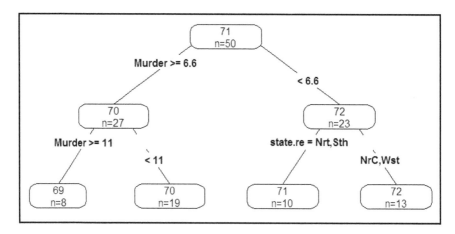

The ctree algorithm

The ctree function gives some advantages over rpart in that the results produced can be a bit more intuitive. Rather than optimizing a result node based purely upon the purity of the resultant node, ctree uses statistical hypothesis testing to determine if the results of the split are statistically significant. It uses chi-square test statistics to test the association, only keeping the associations that are significant, and thus removing bias due to a large number of categories. So, while accuracy may suffer in some cases, benefit is gained by having the results be more explanatory:

```
install.packages("partykit")
library(partykit)
y2 <- ctree(Life.Exp ~ .,data=x)
y2
plot(y2)
```

As you can see from the following plot, **ctree** and **rpart** both agree on the first split (murder), and the cutoff points are very similar. This can add additional credence to the first split since the split is corroborated by two different algorithms:

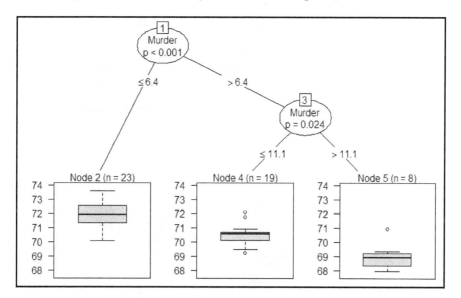

Pruning

Pruning is another way to defend against overfitting. If you visually examine a tree and find that you want to stop the growth of branches at a particular point, you can prune all branches below that node, so that all of the results under that node are collapsed into a single node. That may give you more interpretable results for the decision rules displayed at that point.

The rpart has a unique interactive pruning feature using the prp() function which can help you do this.

In the previous states example, you might want to rid yourself of all of the nodes below node 70 in order to balance the tree and keep it at two levels deep. Balanced trees can also be considered a desirable feature:

```
PrunedTree <- prp(y1,type=4, extra=1,snip=TRUE)$obj
```

Click on node 70 and observe the delete node 5 message in the console. After you see that message, click **Quit** in the plot:

```
> PrunedTree <- prp(y1,type=4, extra=1,snip=TRUE)$obj
Click to snip ...
Delete node 5        state.ab = DE,IL,KY,MD,ME,NM,PA,TN,VA,WY
        var   n wt dev yval complexity ncompete nsurrogate
5 state.abb 21 21 1.7   70      0.015        4          5
```

Display the results of the tree and note the nodes have been eliminated:

```
prp(PrunedTree, type=4, extra=1)
```

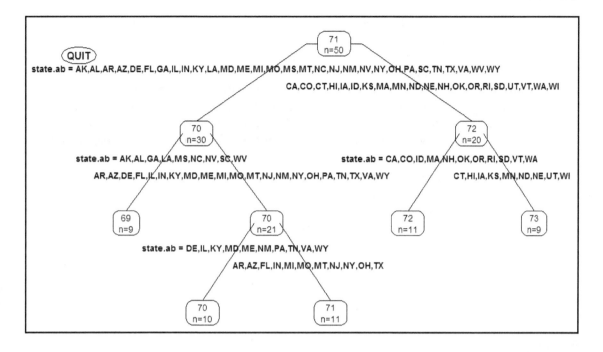

Other options to render decision trees

These are the important control parameters that are used by rpart to grow a tree. You can often play with these values to get a tree to render in a reasonable form, and to control its complexity:

- cp parameters: The cp (complexity parameter) is an option used in rpart that controls how liberal you want the splitting algorithm to be when it decides whether or not to split a node. Utilizing a small cp value (< 0.01) can generate an enormous tree that can contain unexplainable splits, while a tree with a high cp value (> 0.05) can produce a tree containing only obvious information. Therefore, it is important to set the cp level at a number that generates a fair amount of nodes, yet remains explainable.

- Maximum depth: If you want the number of levels of the tree to stop at a certain level, specify this number as an option within the function call. Some people will stop a decision tree after 10 levels or so, assuming that there will be no interpretable information beyond that point. However, if you suspect that there may be single nodes that pop up that could contain the information you are looking for, by all means continue to grow the tree. However, remember as you extend the number of levels, that will increase the computation time and memory needed. It is always a good idea to see limits on the growth of the tree, even if it is a high number.

- `Minbucket`: Many analysts like to concentrate on terminal nodes. However, a terminal node needs to be a minimum size for it to have statistical meaning. The only exception would be if you were looking for true outliers or anomalies. But generally, for segmentation, we want groups that are large enough to have meaning.

- `Minsplit`: This option controls how many observations a node has to have in order to even be considered for a split.

Cluster analysis

Cluster analysis has many uses. At its very basic level, a cluster is a group of people or objects that share similar characteristics. In the marketing and sales industries, clustering is important, since customers (or potential customers) can be grouped by characteristics such as average spending, frequency of purchase, and recency of purchases, and assigned a cluster that represents one single measure of the different levels contained in all of the attributes that make up that cluster. So, for our RFM example, cluster A might represent frequent purchasers who spend a lot of money, and spend often (every marketers dream). Cluster B could represent people who are just average consumers across all three of those RFM metrics, and there might even be a cluster Z which represents things that seem to be impossible, such as customers who buy Halloween costumes only on Tuesdays.

Data analysts can often get good results by using tools such as SQL, or by having great insights in customers behavior. So, while cluster analysis is not necessarily an end in itself, clustering algorithms allow you to cut to the chase rather quickly and enable you to begin to look at groupings in different ways.

Clustering is used in diverse industries

Clustering is often related to other terms that you may hear in different industries:

- In marketing and sales, you will hear the term product segmentation, which refers to how we cluster people according to their product preferences along various dimensions. It can also refer to a customer's willingness to buy a product with the ultimate goal of being able to cluster customers into those two groups (willing and not willing) and only marketing to those customers who we predict are willing to buy.
- An insurance company might cluster customers according to how often they file a claim, or cluster customers according to a certain risk profile.

What is a cluster?

A cluster can be defined as a group of objects with similar characteristics. Clusters can vary in size. There is no requirement that a cluster must have a certain number of members. It can even have a single member. This might be useful in fraud applications, in which you want to identify anomalies in the data. In this case, very small clusters can act as outliers.

Clusters are often constructed to have an equal number of members in each group, as in partitioning clustering. In this case, all of the members in each cluster are homogeneous within each cluster group.

Furthermore, clusters are constructed so they have distinct differences from the remaining clusters. Differences are usually calculated based upon measurements between each of the clusters centroids, which is the middle of each cluster, and the centroid of each cluster can be thought of as the average representative values of the attributes for the cluster that it represents.

Clustering is usually done on numeric variables only. That is because clustering utilizes distance measures, and as we have seen, categorical variables have no measure between them. However, there are ways to incorporate similarity using categorical variables, which we will see later on.

Types of clustering

There are two types of clustering that are often utilized, partional clustering and hierarchical clustering:

Partitional clustering

This is also known as non-hierarchical clustering. In partitional clustering, each object is divided into smaller non-overlapping subsets (partition) that have similar characteristics. An observation can belong to one, and only one, cluster.

Here is a classic example of a three-cluster partitioned model. However, you may wonder why some of the yellow observations end up in the yellow group cluster, rather than the red group. That is because k-means has determined what the linear boundaries are for each of the clusters (right diagram), and any point that falls within any particular decision boundary is defined by the boundaries of that cluster:

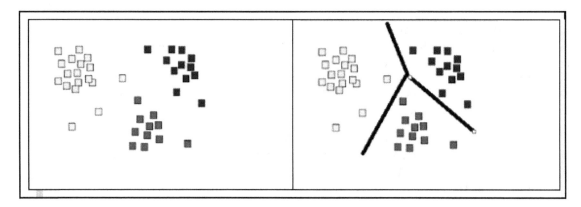

K-means clustering

K-means clustering is the most popular algorithm used for partition clustering. In k-means clustering, similarity between clusters is based, in part, upon distance measures. Generally, the goal is to group similar clusters together with each observation having a relatively small distance from other observations in the same clusters. On the other hand, another goal is to have the maximum distance from one cluster to the next, so that the distances can be discerned. It is essentially a balancing act in which there is a tradeoff between defining similarities within groups, and defining opposing dissimilarities between groups.

The k-means algorithm

The k-means algorithm is based upon an iterative process.

First, we decide how many clusters we desire. The number of clusters can be determined by a number of methods, but bear in mind that there is really no correct number of clusters. Typically, between 3 and 20 clusters can be used as a range.

As an initial step, cluster members are randomly assigned to one of the three clusters that have been specified. In the following example, we have 12 observations (in gray), and three centroids (solid colors) which have been randomly generated. For this example let's make believe we have only two variables, let's say there were `age`, and `height`. We will represent them on an x and y axis but we won't label them:

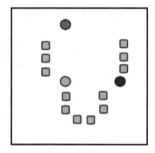

The next step is to assign each observation to the nearest cluster. The nearness of each cluster will be discussed in the next section, but for now let's say that each of the observations have been assigned to each of the three clusters randomly as shown below. The solid lines define the boundaries of the cluster. Visually you can see that that some adjustment could help the random assignment. For example, would the green observation at the border between the red and green cluster border could be a better fit if it was assigned to the red (top) cluster? That could be true since it looks like it could be closer to the cluster at the top than the one it was randomly assigned to:

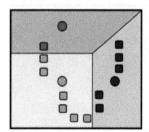

After the random assignment, the cluster assignment are recalibrated. What that means is that the centroids of each cluster are recomputed (we will see how that is done later), and then each data point is then moved to the new closest centroid. This movement is demonstrated in the following figure showing the centroids being shifted:

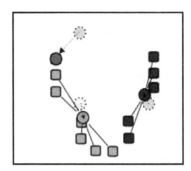

This process is repeated. Centroids are recalculated, and the data points move again to their nearest centroid until there can be no additional improvement. When done the final centroids are computed, the clusters are finalized as in the diagram below. You can see that the observations are clustered slightly better than the original random assignment. Note that the data point in each cluster tend to be closer together than the original random assignment, and that there is more separation between at least two of the clusters (the one on the left, and the other in the middle):

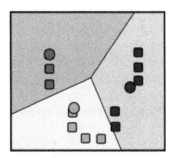

Measuring distance between clusters

K-means clustering uses Euclidian distances to determine how far apart each of the clusters are from each other. For clusters of just one variable, the computation is trivial. You just take the centroids from any two clusters and subtract them from one another. As you add more variables, the computation becomes slightly more involved since you will be summing the squared difference between all of the variables that comprise each of the clusters, and summing them all together to determine the total distance.

Here is an example of how the centroid is determined for three cluster members that have been assigned to cluster 1. Centroid 1 has been calculated, the vector [186,45] where 186 is the average of the weight of the three members, 1, 2, and 3, and 45 is the average age of members 1, 2, and 3. These will not be the final cluster assignments, but merely a best guess at this point:

Member	Weight	Age
1	146	25
2	175	43
3	236	68
Centroid 1	186	45

The next step is to get a better estimate for each cluster assignment. Each member's dimensions are then compared to the centroids of all of the clusters, and then reassigned to the cluster to which it is the closest. This is done using the concept of Euclidean distances.

The formula for Euclidean distance is as follows:

$$\sqrt{\sum_{i=1}^{n} (q_i - p_i)^2}$$

For a cluster that contains only two variables, this is equivalent to:

$$\sqrt{(q_1 - p_1)^2 + (q_2 - p_2)^2}$$

In our age and weight example previously defined, the Euclidean distances have been computed for member 1 between cluster 1 (the first cluster assignment that it is currently a member of), and an alternative cluster 2. The distance is calculated using the preceding formula, and the results of the final sum of squares is listed in the final column. As you can see, cluster 2 is computed as being closer to member 1, since the distance is smaller, and as a result, member 1 is moved into cluster 2:

	Weight	Age		Weight Squared	Age Squared	square root of sums
Member 1	146	25	Distance to Cluster 1	1600	400	45
	146	25	Distance to Cluster 2	16	1225	35
Cluster 1	186	45				
Cluster 2	150	60				

After the distances have been computed for all members, and each member has been moved into its closest cluster, the centroids for each cluster will change, since members will have been added or removed. So, the process is repeated until no more members can be moved into more suitable clusters.

Clustering example using k-means

This example will illustrate a simple RFM clustering example. RFM analysis is simple database marketing that can be used to segment out your best (and worst) customers. It is a good example to use for demonstrating cluster analysis since there are only three variables, and can be segmented, theoretically, into a much larger number of marketing segments.

The data comes from the CDNOW database, which contains the entire purchase history up to the end of June 1998 of the cohort of 23,570 individuals who made their first-ever purchase at CDNOW in the first quarter of 1997 (Fader, 2001).

Here are three variables that we will be using:

- **Date of purchase**: This is the date that the item was purchased and will be used to determine the recency part of the RFM analysis.
- **Units bought**: This corresponds to the number of items purchased in the cart, and roughly corresponds to the frequency of the customer.
- **Total paid**: This is the total amount of the purchase. This reflects the monetary portion of the RFM.

As a first step, we will read on the data, transform the dates to date values, and then compute the number of days since purchase.

Then we will assign column names to the variables:

```
library(graphics)
library(dplyr)
x <- read.table("C:/PracticalPredictiveAnalytics/Data/CDNOW_master.txt",
quote="\", stringsAsFactors=FALSE)
```

Next we will transform the purchase date to date format, and calculate how long it has been since that purchase. Use July 1, 1998 as the reference date:

```
x$xd <- as.Date(as.character(x$V2), "%Y%m%d")
x$diffdate <- as.integer(as.Date("1998-07-01")  - x$xd)
#rename the columns

colnames(x) <-
c("id","orig.date","units.bought","TotalPaid","purch.date","Days.since")
str(x)
summary(x)
```

We will illustrate the k-means function to perform k-means clustering on the variables units.bought, TotalPaid, and Days.since. One characteristic of k-means clustering is that each observation can be categorized into one and only one cluster. K-means requires all variables to be numeric, you cannot use categorical variables in the kmeans function.

One decision you will need to make is how many clusters you would like kmeans to produce. I usually like to aim for between 5 and 15 clusters. Anything more than that will make it difficult to explain the meaning behind each individual cluster, but you can certainly do that. One problem with increasing the number of clusters is that the k-means algorithm specifies approximately equal size clusters, so as you increase the number of clusters, some of the outlier clusters will have a smaller number of members.

The output from k-means will give you a general idea of the goodness of fit of your clusters. The within cluster sum of squares indicates the separation of the individual data points within each cluster. Smaller numbers show the cluster is more homogeneous. The ratio betweenss/totss is a single metric that you can use as a measure of how all of the clusters are separated as a group. A higher number indicates a better separation of clusters.

For this example, we will generate clusters of size 3, 5, and 7:

```
attach(x)
#cluster on the RFM variables
y <- subset(x, select = c(units.bought,TotalPaid,Days.since))

#perform kmeans producing 3 and 5 clusters
```

K-means relies on a random seed in order to initially populate a pseudo-random cluster assignment. Changing the seed may change your results. Since clustering involves some degree of human interpretation, it is common to run the algorithm several times using different seeds, and observe how well they conform (or not) with each other.

```
#always set seed before clustering

set.seed(1020)
clust3 <- kmeans( y,3)
clust3$betweenss/clust3$totss
clust5 <- kmeans( y,5)
clust5$betweenss/clust5$totss
clust7 <- kmeans( y,7)
clust7$betweenss/clust7$totss
```

After creating the three clusters, print the ratio of the cluster between sum of squares to the cluster total sum of squares. That will give you a starting metric to begin comparing clusters. A higher number implies better separation between the clusters:

```
> set.seed(1020)
> clust3 <- kmeans( y,3)
> clust3$betweenss/clust3$totss
[1] 0.8706681
> clust5 <- kmeans( y,5)
> clust5$betweenss/clust5$totss
[1] 0.9178001
> clust7 <- kmeans( y,7)
> clust7$betweenss/clust7$totss
[1] 0.9381889
```

So, based on the output above, cluster 7 has the highest `betweenss/totss` ratio, and having seven clusters would be considered the optimal number of clusters. But, if you run the analysis, increasing the number of clusters each time, you will always see an increase in the ratio. So, we need to determine where the law of diminishing returns kicks in.

Cluster elbow plot

One way to determine this is by using an automated method known as the `elbow` method in which you plot the total within clusters sum of squares for all values within a range, and look at where an `elbow` method develops in the plot:

```
#elbow method
set.seed(1020)
# Compute and plot wss for k = 3 to k = 15
df <- sapply(3:15,function(k){kmeans(y,k)$tot.withinss})
```

```
plot(3:15, df,type='b',xlab="# of clusters",ylab="Total Within Clusters
SS")
```

In the following plot, you might see two elbows, one at 5-6 cluster, and one at 8-9. We will assume for now that five is the optimal number, only because there is an elbow in that area, and the names given to the clusters will be easier to explain:

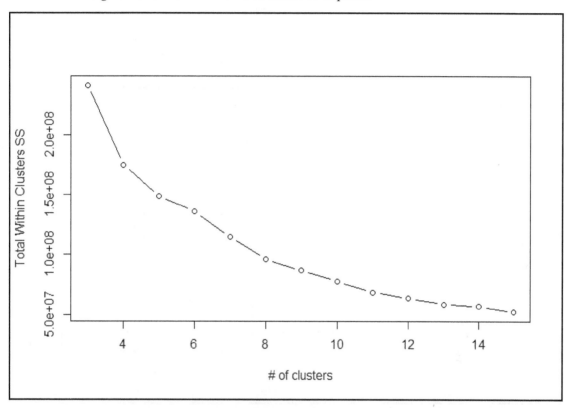

Extracting the cluster assignments

Let's extract the cluster assignments from the `clust` objects, and then compare the counts for each cluster with clusters of size 3, 4, and 7:

```
#cluster assignments
clusters3 <- clust3$cluster
clusters5 <- clust5$cluster
clusters7 <- clust7$cluster
```

Graphically displaying the clusters

We can plot the clusters in many different ways. The first thing you would want to look at would be histograms of the cluster segments. Remember, k-means likes to see approximately equal clusters:

```
#usually but now always the middle cluster is the average cluster
par(mfrow=c(1,3))
hist(clusters3)
hist(clusters5)
hist(clusters7)
```

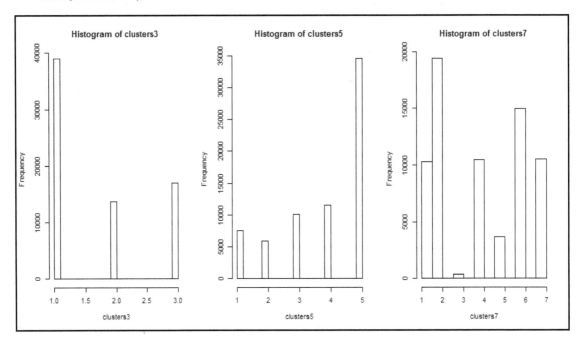

Cluster plots

We can also plot the assigned clusters with the original data, to see if there are any problems with cluster assignment.

First, we need to append the cluster assignment to the original dataset:

```
#append the clusters the original data
append.clust <- data.frame(x, clusters3,clusters5,clusters7)
```

For illustration purposes, let's sample from the `append.clust` dataset. We will set the sample size to 100, but you can set it to any number that makes the diagram readable:

```
library(cluster)
set.seed(1020)
sampleit <- append.clust[sample(nrow(append.clust), 100), ]
```

Generating the cluster plot

We will use the `clusplot` package from the `cluster` library to plot the cluster assignments based upon the first two principal components. If you recall, principal components are a way to reduce the number of variables in this exercise to two, mainly so that we can graph it on a two-dimensional x and y axis.

If you run the following command, you will see that the first component is a measure of the price and number of units bought, and the second component is a measure of time since the last purchase. That is what is represented on the x and y axis. This is trivial for this case since the cluster model only has three variables as input, but becomes more important as the number of variables you use increases:

```
prcomp(append.clust[,c(3,4,6)], scale = TRUE)
```

```
par(mfrow=c(1,3))
clusplot(sampleit[,c(3,4,6)], sampleit$clusters3, color=TRUE,
shade=TRUE,labels=2, lines=0)
clusplot(sampleit[,c(3,4,6)], sampleit$clusters5, color=TRUE,
shade=TRUE,labels=2, lines=0)
clusplot(sampleit[,c(3,4,6)], sampleit$clusters7, color=TRUE,
shade=TRUE,labels=2, lines=0)
```

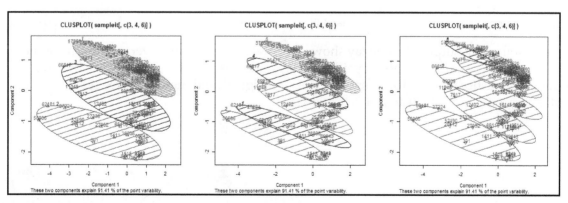

Based on the preceding plots, I would eliminate `clusters7`, since the third centroid seems to have a small `count.p`.

Let's look at the makeup of each of the clusters and see how they relate to the original variables.

Look at the output from the `head()` function. Notice that each row contains three different cluster assignments. Let's look at the means and counts of the original variables grouped by each of the cluster assignments:

```
head(append.clust)
```

```
> head(append.clust)
  id orig.date units.bought TotalPaid purch.date Days.since clusters3 clusters5 clusters7
1  1  19970101            1     11.77 1997-01-01        546         1         5         2
2  2  19970112            1     12.00 1997-01-12        535         1         5         2
3  2  19970112            5     77.00 1997-01-12        535         1         5         5
4  3  19970102            2     20.76 1997-01-02        545         1         5         2
5  3  19970330            2     20.76 1997-03-30        458         1         5         6
6  3  19970402            2     19.54 1997-04-02        455         1         5         6
```

We will use `dplyr` to get the average values and counts for each cluster:

```
library(dplyr)
attach(append.clust)
append.clust %>% select(units.bought,TotalPaid,Days.since,clusters3) %>%
  group_by(clusters3) %>%
    summarise_each(funs(n(),mean))
append.clust %>% select(units.bought,TotalPaid,Days.since,clusters5) %>%
  group_by(clusters5) %>%
    summarise_each(funs(n(),mean))
append.clust %>% select(units.bought,TotalPaid,Days.since,clusters7) %>%
  group_by(clusters7) %>%
    summarise_each(funs(n(),mean))
```

In the following output, the display shows the total counts and the averages for the number of units purchased, total amount paid, and days since last purchased. Each line lists the specific statistics relevant to the specific cluster assigned, and there are three sets of statistics, one each for clusters of 3, 5, and 7:

```
>
> append.clust %>% select(units.bought,TotalPaid,Days.since,clusters3) %>%
+    group_by(clusters3) %>%
+      summarise_each(funs(n(),mean))
Source: local data frame [3 x 7]

  clusters3 units.bought_n TotalPaid_n Days.since_n units.bought_mean TotalPaid_mean Days.since_mean
      (int)          (int)       (int)        (int)             (dbl)          (dbl)           (dbl)
1         1          39001       39001        39001          2.273942       34.36202       485.85334
2         2          13657       13657        13657          2.558102       37.02813        98.91748
3         3          17001       17001        17001          2.603317       38.49593       293.54491
> append.clust %>% select(units.bought,TotalPaid,Days.since,clusters5) %>%
+    group_by(clusters5) %>%
+      summarise_each(funs(n(),mean))
Source: local data frame [5 x 7]

  clusters5 units.bought_n TotalPaid_n Days.since_n units.bought_mean TotalPaid_mean Days.since_mean
      (int)          (int)       (int)        (int)             (dbl)          (dbl)           (dbl)
1         1           7561        7561         7561          2.608121       38.06974       138.7954
2         2           5948        5948         5948          2.505884       35.89042        45.8228
3         3          10089       10089        10089          2.587075       37.91040       250.6387
4         4          11521       11521        11521          2.619651       39.12428       376.5500
5         5          34540       34540        34540          2.228547       33.75117       495.1166
> append.clust %>% select(units.bought,TotalPaid,Days.since,clusters7) %>%
+    group_by(clusters7) %>%
+      summarise_each(funs(n(),mean))
Source: local data frame [7 x 7]

  clusters7 units.bought_n TotalPaid_n Days.since_n units.bought_mean TotalPaid_mean Days.since_mean
      (int)          (int)       (int)        (int)             (dbl)          (dbl)           (dbl)
1         1          10298       10298        10298          2.391532       35.17277       342.13138
2         2          19416       19416        19416          1.748146       25.58429       512.46127
3         3            330         330          330         18.075758      305.69979       371.37273
4         4          10461       10461        10461          2.522417       36.73229       216.94523
5         5           3668        3668         3668          6.151854      101.58269       485.78190
6         6          14969       14969        14969          1.843142       26.49776       456.32394
7         7          10517       10517        10517          2.548636       36.79511        77.25055
```

We can explain the clusters in terms of the original variables:

For the three-cluster assignment:

- Cluster 1 has the lowest average number of units bought, as well as the lowest `TotalPaid` amount of all of the three clusters. It also has customers who purchased items a long time ago, relative to the other customers.
- Cluster 2 is categorized by customers who have purchased recently, since they have the lowest Day.since mean statistic.
- Cluster 3 is categorized by those customers who purchase a relatively high number of units, and have a higher total invoice, but are not necessarily recent buyers.

Based upon these cluster definitions, a marketing department can customize different offerings for each customer group.

Hierarchical clustering

As an alternative to k-means, you can perform hierarchical clustering, which does not require you to specify the number of clusters beforehand. In hierarchical clustering, you can either start with one cluster and then continue to subdivide two clusters at a time, or start with every record being in its own cluster, and then merge them together to become a larger cluster. In any case, it is easy to scan up and down the tree, known as a dendrogram, and identify the grouping of clusters that suit your needs, rather than having to run the clustering one at a time. However, for large computational processing, partitioning clustering (k-means) definitely has a performance edge, which is why it is favored in industry.

We will use the `hclust` R function with the `Pain` dataframe to demonstrate hierarchical clustering. After reading in the data, we will scale or normalize the data by centering the mean to 0. The reason we do this is that we do not want the clustering procedure to favor any variable over another, by nature of its size or variance, so we try to equalize the magnitude as best we can.

First, we will load the `pain_raw` data we saved earlier into a dataframe object:

```
require(graphics)
setwd("C:/PracticalPredictiveAnalytics/Data")
load("pain_raw.Rda")

df2 <- subset(df, select=c(Age,Duration,Pain))
df2 <- scale(df2)
head(df2)
```

Next, we will compute a distance matrix, and run the hierarchical clustering algorithm using the average linkage method:

```
fit <- hclust(dist(df2), "average")
```

Before plotting the dendrogram, we will specify that we want to show a red border around the three groups of clusters that are the most similar:

```
groups <- cutree(fit, k=3)
rect.hclust(fit, k=3, border=""red"")
```

The dendrogram is plotted and it should look similar to the following plot. Observation numbers are shown at the ends of the vertical lines, so it will be easy to subset the original dataframe and inspect the data:

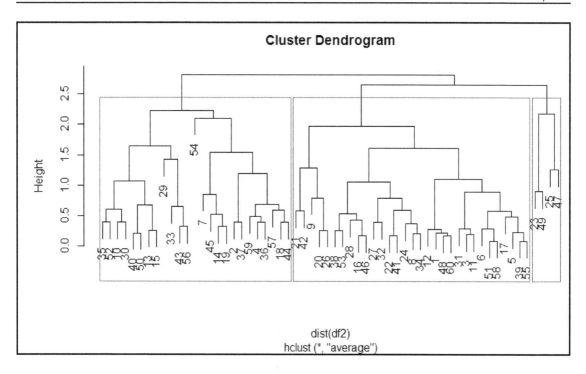

Examining some examples from cluster 1

From the bottom of the dendrogram, we can see some of the observations associated with cluster1. Extract them from the original dataframe (df):

```
cluster1 <- df[c(35,52,10,30),]
```

Examine the output using the View command. The output shows that cluster1 may be associated with males in their 70s, who are reporting pain with a duration between 21 and 29 days:

```
View(cluster1)
```

	Treatment	Gender	Age	Duration	Pain
35	B	M	75	21	1
52	A	M	76	25	1
10	B	M	75	30	1
30	P	M	77	29	1

Examining some examples from cluster 2

Similarly, pull some observations from cluster 2, and view them:

```
cluster2 <- df[c(23,49,25,47),]
View(cluster2)
```

This cluster looks like it could be related to those who were administered treatments **A** and **B**, who reported no pain, within the age range of 59-72:

	Treatment	Gender	Age	Duration	Pain
23	B	F	72	50	0
49	B	F	69	42	0
25	A	M	62	42	0
47	B	M	59	29	0

Examining some examples from cluster 3

Extract and view some examples from `cluster3`:

```
cluster3 <- df[c(20,26,38,53),]
View(cluster3)
```

Cluster 3 could be patients who reported no pain. However, they are characterized by a much shorter duration than `cluster2`:

	Treatment	Gender	Age	Duration	Pain
20	A	F	74	1	0
26	P	M	74	4	0
38	B	M	70	22	0
53	B	F	69	24	0

Note that in the preceding examples we only pulled four observations from each cluster. However, you need not pull only four of them. Pull as many as necessary, and try to give it a name that categorizes the clusters characteristics.

Support vector machines

We have already seen some examples in which we use a straight line to separate classes.

As the dimensionality, or feature space, of a model increases, there may be many different ways to separate classes, in both linear and non-linear ways.

In the cases of support vector machines, data is first transformed into a higher dimensional space using a mapping function known as a kernel, and an optimal hyperplane is used to segment the higher dimensional space. A hyperplane uses one dimension less than the space it is trying to measure, so a straight line is used to segment a two-dimensional space, and a 2-dimensional sheet of paper is used to segment a three-dimensional space. The hyperplane can be either linear or non-linear.

Hyperplanes use support vectors which are important training tuples and are used to define the boundaries of each class. They are the most critical points in the data, and they are the most important points used which support the definition of the hyperplane. The hyperplane is used do define the boundaries beween the different classes. A class is often a binary class, such as 0 or 1. The boundaries between the classes can also be wide or thin. That characteristic is measured by the margins which define a maximum separation that can be optimized between the classes.

Here is an example of a dataset with two features, **x** and **y**. The lines **A** and **B** could be considered as two separate linear classifiers for a decision rule that separates the red observations from the blue observations. The **A** line is preferable, since it contains a *larger margin, separation value* between the decision line and the nearest observation. The observations that are close to the line are known as the support vectors:

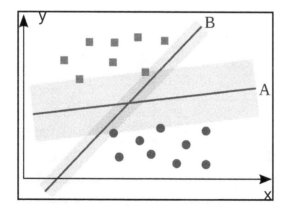

Simple illustration of a mapping function

To illustrate how a kernel mapping function can help in defining a linear boundary, look at the following plots and see how creating a new variable z will help differentiate among the new transformed points that are mapped by the polynomial function t2$Latitude^2*t2$High.Low.Temp^2 in two-dimensional space. However, a kernel mapping will take place in a higher dimension, and the results of the mapping reverse mapped back into the original space:

```
#generate a non-linear circle of point

radius <- 2
t2 <- data.frame(x=radius * cos(seq(0,6,length = 20)),y = radius *
sin(seq(0, 6, length = 20)))
names(t2) <- c("Latitude","High.Low.Temp")
plot(t2$Latitude,t2$High.Low.Temp)

# create a new variable and plot it against on the original points
t2$z = (t2$Latitude^2*t2$High.Low.Temp^2)

plot(t2$High.Low.Temp,t2$z)
```

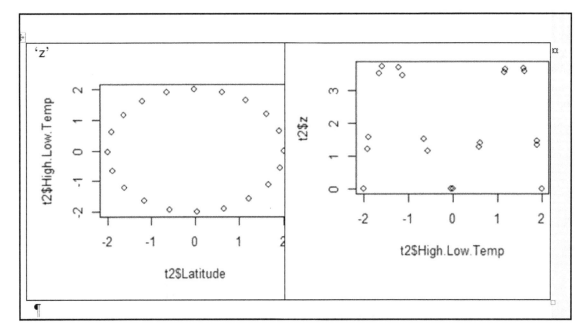

Typically, SVMs are used with data that is very high dimensional. That could include applications involving object and facial recognition. SVM can be very accurate, but its disadvantage includes interpretability and performance. SVMs can also overfit the data, since the decision boundaries are highly dependent upon the choice of the kernel that is used to perform the mapping. There are a large number of kernel choices available and the choice of a kernel should not be made based upon the best model fit. This would not be unlike using higher order polynomial functions to overfit a regression model.

Analyzing consumer complains data using SVM

In this example, we will use a text classification model to define a linear SVM model. Unstructured text data is a perfect way to illustrate SVM since the data is very high dimensional.

To illustrate SVM classifiers, we will begin by reading in some consumer complaint data regarding student loans. We will be using two packages, e1071 and RTextTools:

```
install.packages("e1071")
install.packages("RTextTools")
library(e1071)
library(RTextTools)
```

Begin by loading the data from the CSV file. The data frame simply consists of some consumer narrative regarding student loans, along with how the complaint was classified. The goal is to develop a SVM model which will classify future customer complaints into the various issue categories:

```
data <-
read.csv("C:\\PracticalPredictiveAnalytics\\Data\\Consumer_Complaints.csv",
sep=",")
str(data)
```

Subset the data and keep only the columns we will need:

```
data <- subset(data,1 select=c(Issue,Consumer.complaint.narrative))
```

Take a sample of the first 50 records and view:

```
data.samp <- subset(data[1:50,],
select=c(Issue,Consumer.complaint.narrative))
View(data.samp)
```

	Issue	Consumer.complaint.narrative
1	Dealing with my lender or servicer	Was not contacted 4 years later about some private l...
2	Can't repay my loan	This is a continuation of a previous issue with Citiba...
3	Can't repay my loan	Navient informed me that I can afford nearly {$150.0...
8	Dealing with my lender or servicer	My husband lost his job in XX/XX/XXXX and was une...
9	Dealing with my lender or servicer	Mohela called me on XXXX/XXXX/15, I told the rep I ...
4	Dealing with my lender or servicer	In 2008 I attended XXXX University in XXXX off XXXX ...
7	Dealing with my lender or servicer	I was behind on my loans, and I called about two mon...
5	Dealing with my lender or servicer	I received a private student loan from XXXX XXXX (n...
6	Can't repay my loan	I have a private loan with Sallie Mae. I called them to ...
10	Can't repay my loan	I ca n't pay for my private student loans. They have b...

Converting unstructured to structured data

Notice that complaint data is in unstructured format. Certain text mining algorithms treat unstructured text as a *bag of words*, which means that in analyzing documents, one disregards semantics and grammar, and ends up treating each word as its own feature or variable.

An important data structure in text mining is a **term document matrix** (**TDM**), which simply indicates which words appear in each document.

The `create_matrix()` function will do this for us. However, before we do this, we will want to clean the data and impose some restrictions on the creation of the term document matrix.

First, we do not want to include any words, such as *the*, *an*, or *it*, that would not add any value to the TDM and would force it to be quite large. These are known as **stopwords**. So, we will filter these words using the option `removeStopwords=TRUE`. Similarly, we will also eliminate any numbers and punctuation, and only consider words that have a minimum length of four. These options are not arbitrary. It is up to the text miner to set these options at the optimal value, tempering the need to capture the most value from the data, while keeping the size of the data at a minimum. Knowledge of the domain is extremely helpful when setting these options. For example, had I set `minwordLength=5`, I would have not included words such as `Paid`:

```
# Create the document term matrix
dtMatrix <-
create_matrix(data.samp[""Consumer.complaint.narrative""],minDocFreq = 1,
removeNumbers=TRUE,
minWordLength=4,removeStopwords=TRUE,removePunctuation=TRUE,stemWords =
FALSE)
```

The TDM is a data structure that is optimized for text mining. It can be difficult to view as the number of documents and words increase. However, in our example, we only have 50 documents, and since we have started by taking a sample of the data, only have a limited number of words, so we can view a small TDM using the `transpose()` function:

```
xx = as.data.frame( t(as.matrix(  dtMatrix )) )
head(xx)
```

Notice that even in this small sample, we can see the document contains several references to `access`, `able`, and `ability`. The column indicates the documents that the word occurs in, along with the number of references. There is a column for every document, even though any particular word (listed as rows) do not appear in the document:

```
> head(xx)
               1 2 3 4 5 6 7 8 9 10 11 12 13 14 15 16 17 18 19 20 21 22 23 24 25 26 27 28 29 30 31 32 33 34 35 36 37 38 39 40 41 42 43 44 45 46 47 48 49 50
ability        0 0 0 0 0 0 0 0 0 0  0  0  0  0  0  0  0  0  0  0  0  0  0  0  1  0  0  0  0  0  0  0  0  0  0  0  0  0  2  0  0  0  0  0  0  0  0  0  0  0
able           0 0 0 0 0 0 0 0 0 0  0  0  0  0  0  0  0  0  0  0  0  0  0  0  0  0  0  0  3  0  0  0  3  0  0  0  0  1  1  0  0  1  0  0  0  0  0  1  0  0
abovementioned 0 0 0 0 0 0 0 0 0 0  0  0  0  0  0  0  0  0  0  0  0  0  0  0  0  0  0  0  0  0  0  0  0  0  0  0  0  0  0  0  0  0  0  1  0  0  0  0  0  0
accept         0 0 0 0 0 0 0 0 0 0  0  0  0  0  0  0  0  0  0  0  0  0  0  0  0  0  0  0  0  0  0  0  0  0  0  0  0  0  0  0  0  0  0  1  0  0  0  0  0  0
access         0 0 0 0 0 0 0 0 0 0  0  0  0  0  0  0  0  0  0  0  0  0  0  0  0  0  0  0  0  0  0  0  0  0  0  0  1  0  0  5  0  0  0  0  0  0  0  0  0  0
accomplish     0 0 0 0 0 0 0 0 0 0  0  0  0  0  0  0  0  0  0  0  0  0  0  0  0  0  0  0  0  0  0  0  0  0  0  0  0  0  0  0  0  0  0  0  0  0  0  1  0  0
```

Now that we have viewed a TDM for a sample, let"s run it for the entire dataframe.

```
dtMatrix <- create_matrix(data[""Consumer.complaint.narrative""],minDocFreq
= 1, removeNumbers=TRUE,
minWordLength=4,removeStopwords=TRUE,removePunctuation=TRUE,stemWords =
FALSE)
```

Instead of viewing the TDM (which in this case would be quite large), let's perform a frequency on the terms, by adding up the number of times that they occurred. By scrolling through the dataframe, you will get a very good idea of the single terms that are popping up. You would also want to compute these terms in combination (bi-grams, and N-grams), which would give you insight into the kinds of things that the customers are complaining about:

```
freq <- colSums(as.matrix(dtMatrix))
length(freq)
head(freq)
freq.df <- as.data.frame(freq)
View(freq.df)
```

The output of the `View` command will display the following terms in the TDM, in alphabetical order. Use the elevator bars to scroll through the list:

	freq
aaron	1
abhorrent	1
abide	2
abided	2
abiding	2
abilities	1
ability	82
able	771
ablethe	1
ableye	1

The `RTextTools` package uses containers to hold different kinds of R objects. We will create a container that will be used as a holding object to train the first 500 customer comments:

```
container <- create_container(dtMatrix, data$Issue,
trainSize=1:500,virgin=FALSE)
str(container)
```

Once the container is created, we can use it to train many different kinds of models. We will be using an SVM with a linear kernel.

That means that we will be using linear hyperplanes to separate the data into segments within the high dimensional text space:

```
# train a SVM Model
model <- train_model(container, ""SVM"", kernel=""linear"", cost=1)
str(model)
head(model)
summary(model)
```

The output from the summary model appears as follows; 349 support vectors where created, which were used to separate the data into three classes:

```
Call:
svm.default(x = container@training_matrix, y = container@training_codes,
kernel = kernel, cost = cost, cross = cross, probability = TRUE,
    method = method)


Parameters:
   SVM-Type:  C-classification
 SVM-Kernel:  linear
       cost:  1
      gamma:  9.832842e-05

Number of Support Vectors:  349

 ( 189 143 17 )


Number of Classes:  3

Levels:
 Can''t repay my loan Dealing with my lender or servicer Getting a loan
```

Now that the data has been trained, we will take the next 500 observations to do the testing, and see how the model performs. Similar to what we did for training, we will create a TDM for the test data, but use the same labels, or terms that we created for the training data:

```
predictionData <- data$Consumer.complaint.narrative[501:1000]

# create a prediction document term matrix
predMatrix <- create_matrix(predictionData, originalMatrix=dtMatrix)

# create the corresponding container

plength = length(predictionData);
predictionContainer <- create_container(predMatrix, labels=rep(0,plength),
testSize=1:plength, virgin=FALSE)
```

To see how the model performs, we will use the classify model function to score the test dataset based on the model. Then we will aggregate the data based upon the issue type, and the average SVM probability. As the output shows, the model does best in classifying `Dealing with my lender or servicer`, and is not able to discern `Getting a loan` as well. This all provides valuable information for a loan lender, since we now can see what types of topics a caller is discussing:

```
# predict
results <- classify_model(predictionContainer, model)
head(results)
aggregate(results$SVM_PROB, by=list(results$SVM_LABEL), FUN=mean,
na.rm=TRUE)

> head(results)
```

The output appears in the console as shown as follows:

```
                          SVM_LABEL   SVM_PROB
1 Dealing with my lender or servicer 0.5436438
2 Dealing with my lender or servicer 0.7521835
3 Dealing with my lender or servicer 0.5153998
4 Dealing with my lender or servicer 0.7611152
5 Dealing with my lender or servicer 0.7225702
6 Dealing with my lender or servicer 0.7590674
> aggregate(results$SVM_PROB, by=list(results$SVM_LABEL), FUN=mean,
na.rm=TRUE)
                             Group.1         x
1              Can''t repay my loan 0.6211851
2 Dealing with my lender or servicer 0.6967735
3                   Getting a loan 0.4779246
```

References

- *AMERICAN STATISTICAL ASSOCIATION RELEASES STATEMENT ON STATISTICAL SIGNIFICANCE AND P-VALUES. (2016, March 7).* Retrieved from ASA news: `http://www.amstat.org/asa/files/pdfs/P-ValueStatement.pdf`
- *Anscombe's quartet.* Retrieved from Wikipedia: `https://en.wikipedia.org/wiki/Anscombe%27s_quartet`

- *Coefficient of determination*. Retrieved from Wikipedia:https://en.wik ipedia.org/wiki/Coefficient_of_determination
- *Fader, P. S. (2001, May-June). Forecasting Repeat Sales at CDNOW. Interfaces, 31 (May-June), Part 2 of 2, S94-S107.*
- *FAQ: WHAT ARE PSEUDO R-SQUAREDS?* Retrieved from UCLA Institute for Digital Research and Education: http://stats.idre.ucla.edu/other/mult-pkg /faq/general/faq-what-are-pseudo-r-squareds/

Summary

In this chapter, we added three more algorithms to our arsenal, and these 3, along with regression form the core basic algorithms that can cover a lot of ground in terms of the typical problems a predictive analyst will face. We saw that a good knowledge of decision tree methodologies allows you to start developing models quickly, they are easily interpretable, and are the basis for more advanced techniques such as random forests. We then went on to clustering. Clustering allows you to begin to grasp the concepts of similarity and dissimilarity, and we introduced distance measures. We then ended with a basic introduction to support vector machines, which were demonstrated in the context of text mining.

In the next chapter, we will begin to look at some examples of creating models that predict how long a customer will stay with a company, or for predicting how long it will be until a patient develops a certain medical condition.

6
Using Survival Analysis to Predict and Analyze Customer Churn

What is survival analysis?

Survival analysis covers a broad range of topics. Here is the list of topics that we will cover in this chapter:

- Survival analysis
- Time-based variables and regression
- R survival objects
- Customer attrition or churn
- Survival curves
- Cox regression
- Plotting methods
- Variable selection
- Model concordance

Often, predictive analytic problems deal with various situations concerning the tracking of important events along a customer's journey, and predicting when these events will occur. Survival analysis is a form of analysis that is based upon the concept of time to event. The time to event is simply the number of units of time that have elapsed until something happens. The event can be just about anything; a car crash, a stock market crash, or a devastating phenomenon.

Survival analysis originated in the studying of patients who developed terminal diseases, such as cancer, hence the term survival. However, conceptually, it can even be applied to marketing applications in which you are following the occurrence of an event over a customer's lifetime. In this case, the time to event can mean a customer response or purchase.

In our example, we will use a customer churn example. Customer churn is a term that you will hear often in the context of how a company retains its customers. Churn is very important, since it often costs more to acquire new customers than it would to offer some discounts or promotions to existing customers, in order to keep them happy so they don't leave.

There are many different statistical modeling techniques you can choose for churn analysis, including regression, decision trees, random forests, naive bayes, and neural networks.

Survival analysis is a good technique to use with customer churn problems since it is able to deal specifically with two aspects of marketing data, which other techniques have problems with. These involve the concepts of time-dependent data and censoring.

Time-dependent data

In many analytic techniques, all data is treated as static at the time of analysis, and these techniques are not well equipped to deal with data that changes over time. Any event that measures a change in a variable over time, such as age, or changes in attitudes via surveys can be treated as time-dependent variables, and are handled well by survival techniques. This works well within a marketing concept since the treatment of different customer segments can change, and we need a mechanism to measure the effect of interventions such as promotions and advertising that can change customer behavior over time.

Censoring

In general, censoring is a term that is used to describe data that is only partially known. The reason it is considered partially known is that all data is constrained between the starting and ending periods of an observational study. This can be information that occurs before a study has begun or after a study has ended. If all the information is contained within the study period itself, the data is not censored. However, this rarely happens.

Censored data can be left or right censored.

Left censoring

In a marketing context, studies usually begin with customers already in place, and without any knowledge of how they were acquired.

Additionally, not all customers start at the same time. When a customer has started prior to the beginning of a study or analysis, some customer attributes can be referred to as left censored. If you start an analysis that includes all of your customers, you will not have knowledge of some of the events that preceded the start of the study. This knowledge may include very important information, such as customer dissatisfaction with a prior customer policy that was implemented way before the start of the study, but there is not much we can do about it if we don't have the information. In a survival analysis, everyone starts off on an even footing.

Right censoring

Studies also have an ending period, and customers who may leave a day after the study ends would still be considered active. This is another example of data that wouldn't be recorded. Therefore, a customer is considered right censored if a study ends before the customer terminates. However, it also includes some other special situations, such as when a customer is still active at the end of the study, or is lost due to events not related to the study's variables.

For example, a customer who has been active only for 10 days would still be expected to be active if the study happens to be ending a short time after that; or if a customer did not respond to follow-up questionnaires due to a change of address, they could be thrown out of the study. These are all naturally occurring events.

In the following diagram, the black vertical lines indicate the beginning and end dates of a hypothetical churn study. The first dot in each row indicates the point at which the customer was acquired, and the last dot indicates the point in time that the customer left. Only the data available within the begin and end date period is available for analysis. The diagram shows vertical lines in places where a customer could be considered as left or right censored:

- As indicated in the top bar, we see that a customer was acquired after the study began and left before the study ended. Therefore, we have complete information about the customer with regard to tenure, and the customer is considered not censored.
- The middle bar shows a customer that was acquired after the study began; however, the customer is still active at the end of the study, and the dot slightly past the right vertical line shows that the customer left shortly after the end of the study. However, this churn activity will not be reflected in the data, so this is an example of right censored data.
- The bottom bar shows a customer who was acquired prior to the start of the study, with an unknown start date. This is an example of a left censored observation:

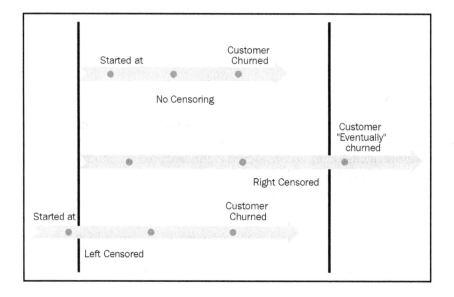

Our customer satisfaction dataset

In this chapter, we will be looking at a dataset of hypothetical customers who are subscribed to an online service, and who have responded to a customer satisfaction survey prior to the beginning of the study. This survey was then matched to transactional as well as demographic data to produce this simple analysis dataset, consisting of an event variable (churn), which will represent whether or not a customer unsubscribed from the service. We will also include some transaction data (number of purchases last month), as well as some demographic data (gender, educational level), as well as an overall satisfaction survey administered prior to the start of the study:

Variable	Description
Monthly.Charges	Average dollar amount of previous purchases
Purch.last.Month	Number of purchases in the month before the study begins
Satisfaction	Overall satisfaction with the service supplied on a Likert scale
Satisfaction2	Follow-up satisfaction score
Gender	Male or female
Education Level	Bachelors/masters/doctorate
Churn	1 if customer left before the study ended; 0 if customer was still active at the end of the study

Generating the data using probability functions

Rather than use a pre-existing dataset, we will generate our own data by using some built-in sampling and probability functions. This will be a valuable way to learn how to perform analysis, since it will enable you to alter the makeup of your own data and observe how it changes the models produced. Some of the code that you will see also incorporate some of the concepts of reproducible research that we discussed in Chapter 1, *Getting Started with Predictive Analytics*.

To ensure that these examples run correctly, make sure that `setwd()` is set to the correct folder on your computer. This function is illustrated in the first few lines of the following code. In addition to `setwd()`, you will also see a few other functions within the code examples given that will help promote reproducibility:

- `Set.seed()`: this is always supplied with a constant. This guarantees that any sampled data can be reproduced exactly on different computers that use the same seed. In this example I will use the number 1 as a seed.

- `Dev.copy()`: This copies the plot that is displayed on the screen to the filename specified within the directory set by `setwd()`. That way, you can keep all of your images in the appropriate directory applicable to the project or sub-project you are working on. When you are done with your `dev.copy()`, use `dev.off()` to reset the plots. Note: you may need to specify `dev.off()` twice for it to complete.

- `Clearhistory()`, `Savehistory()`: All code contained between these two functions are copied to the filename specified in `Savehistory()`. This will allow you to keep a permanent record of the code, separate from the code editor. This is important if you are manually keeping track of versions, or are using it to include in other word processing programs.

- Code labels: You will see some code labels that start with # and end with ==== (four equals signs). While they are technically comments, they also serve as labels or bookmarks that identify specific sections of the code. For example, our first section of code will begin using the `#simulate churn====` label, as shown in the following figure:

> In Rstudio, use the up/down arrows at the bottom of the source pane to jump to an area in the code that has a defined label.

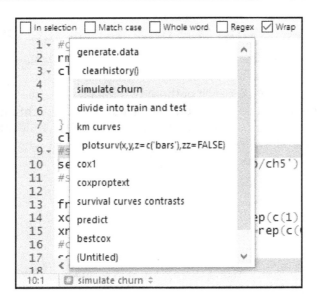

After locating the code in the next section, select and run it. Here is a brief outline of what the code does by the labeled sections. For each item, jump to the code label indicated.

Creating the churn and no churn dataframes

The code begins by simulating data for the response variable (xchurn). Remember, this variable can take on only two values, 0 and 1. Since we want these groups to behave differently, we will simulate separate data separately for each of the two groups, the churners (xchurn) and those that remained active at the end of the 12 month period (xnochurn):

```
#simulate churn data====
setwd('C:/PracticalPredictiveAnalytics/Outputs')
frame.size <- 1000
xchurn <- data.frame(Churn=rep(c(1),frame.size))
xnochurn <- data.frame(Churn=rep(c(0),frame.size))
```

Creating and verifying the new simulated variables

This section simulates the independent variables Xeducation, Xgender, Xsatisfaction, Xpurch.last.month, and Xmonthly.charges. The code uses the sample() function to generate slightly different data for each of those two data frames based upon a probability vector. Some of the generated data distributions will have only slight differences between the churners and non-churners (for example, education levels), while other variables will be generated specifically to show the differences between members who stayed and who left (tenure2, and purchases last month):

```
#create new vars====
# set the seed for reproduceability

set.seed(1)

#set the gender and Education Vectors.
ed.vector <- c("Bachelor's Degree", "Master's Degree", "Doctorate Degree")
gen.vector <- c("M", "F")
#sample from each of the vector elements with the associated probabilities
given in the probability vector.

xchurn$Xeducation <- sample(ed.vector, nrow(xchurn),replace = TRUE, prob =
c(.8,.15,.05))
xnochurn$Xeducation <- sample(ed.vector, nrow(xnochurn),replace = TRUE,
prob = c(.7, .10, .05))
xchurn$Xgender <- sample(gen.vector, nrow(xchurn),replace = TRUE, prob =
c(.8,.2))
xnochurn$Xgender <- sample(gen.vector, nrow(xnochurn),replace = TRUE, prob
= c(.75,.25))

#do the same for the service vector. 1=not at all satisfied, 5=very
satisfied.

serv.vector <- c("1","2","3","4","5",NA)
#make the churners not very satisfied. Note that the probability is higher
for the lower service categories than for the higher satisfaction scores.
(e.g .35 vs. .01)

xchurn$Xsatisfaction <- sample(serv.vector, nrow(xchurn),replace = TRUE,
prob = c(.35,.35,.2,.2,.2,.01))
#non churners get an increased probability of a higher satisfaction score

xnochurn$Xsatisfaction <- sample(serv.vector, nrow(xnochurn),replace =
TRUE, prob = c(.2,.2,.2,.35,.35,.01))

# simulate incremental increase in satisfaction after the 2nd survey for
the churners category (by adding 1 across the board).  This is to simulate
```

something the company did to get them to stay.

```
xchurn$Xsatisfaction2 <- as.integer(xchurn$Xsatisfaction) + 1
```

#For the 2nd survey. keep the satisfaction level the same for the others

```
xnochurn$Xsatisfaction2 <- sample(serv.vector, nrow(xnochurn),replace =
TRUE, prob = c(.2,.2,.2,.35,.35,.01))
```

#simulate a higher increase in calls to customer service for the churners.

```
xchurn$Xservice.calls <- sample(c(0,1,2,3,4,5), nrow(xchurn),replace =
TRUE, prob = c(.80, .20, .05, .03, .05, .01))
xnochurn$Xservice.calls <- sample(c(0,1,2,3,4,5), nrow(xnochurn),replace =
TRUE, prob = c(.80, .10, .05, .03, .02, .01))
```

#Simulate tenure of 12 months to 1 month. Notice, for example, that
churners have a lower probability of being assigned a tenure of 12 months
(.8) than the nonchurners do. (.9)

```
xchurn$Xtenure2 <- sample(c(12:1), nrow(xchurn),replace = TRUE, prob =
c(.8,.7,.7,.6,.5,.4,.3,.2,.1,.3,.3,.1))
xnochurn$Xtenure2 <- sample(c(12:1), nrow(xnochurn),replace = TRUE, prob =
c(.9,.8,.7,.6,.5,.4,.3,.2,.1,.1,.1,.1))
```

#simulate the number of purchases last month. We do the simulation a bit
differently this time, since there is no predefined vector to sample from.
The rep() function is used to repeat a value a specified number of time.
For churners, 1 purchase last month has the highest probability of being
selected since it is repeated 150 times.

```
xchurn$Xpurch.last.month <-
sample(c(rep(10,5),rep(1,150),rep(3,10)),nrow(xchurn),replace = TRUE)
xnochurn$Xpurch.last.month <-
sample(c(rep(0,5),rep(1,20),rep(3,10)),nrow(xnochurn),replace = TRUE)
```

#monthly charges are selected via a normal distribution. Churners will end
up having average monthly charges of $215. This is used to simulate "High
Charges" as a reason for leaving

```
xchurn$Xmonthly.charges <- rnorm( nrow(xchurn), mean=215,sd=70)
xnochurn$Xmonthly.charges <- rnorm( nrow(xnochurn), mean=75,sd=50)
#also convert to a list
xchurn.list <-lapply(xchurn, function(x) sample(x,replace=TRUE))
xnochurn.list <-lapply(xnochurn, function(x) sample(x,replace=TRUE ))
```

After the data has been generated, you can use some additional R functions to verify that
the data has been generated as intended. For example, in the command line, you can use the
prop.table() function to verify that the percentages were generated correctly:

```
> prop.table(table(xchurn$Xeducation))
```

This is the following output:

```
Bachelor's Degree  Doctorate Degree   Master's Degree
          0.802             0.053             0.145
```

Check the following code:

```
> prop.table(table(xnochurn$Xeducation))
```

This is the following output:

```
Bachelor's Degree  Doctorate Degree   Master's Degree
          0.819             0.060             0.121
```

This shows the data for the churners was generated correctly from the original parameters specified in the `sample(ed.vector)` code line. There are only minor differences between the two churn/nochurn groups.

However, note that since this is simulated data, you could alter the `prob=` option in the `sample()` function to correspond to whatever scenario is applicable to your industry. This is desirable since it will ultimately suggest to you how robust your model is when the assumptions change. If you wish, you can experiment with some different scenarios by changing the probability vector.

For example, if we wanted to drastically alter the makeup of the education levels by increasing the occurrence of doctorate degrees, we would increase the probability of the third slot of the probability vector again:

```
Xeducation_PHD <- sample(ed.vector, 1000,replace = TRUE, prob = c(.7, .10,
.95))
```

We can then see the differences by plotting the percentages:

```
par(mfrow=c(1,3))
barplot(table(xchurn$Xeducation),names.arg=c('B.A','Ph.D','Masters'),cex.na
mes=.75,ylim=c(0,800),main='Slightly higher proportion of Bachelors and
Masters Degree',cex.main=1)
barplot(table(xnochurn$Xeducation),names.arg=c('B.A','Ph.D','Masters'),cex.
names=.75,ylim=c(0,800),main='Slightly lower  proportion of Bachelors and
Masters Degree',cex.main=1)
barplot(table(Xeducation_PHD),names.arg=c('B.A','Ph.D','Masters'),cex.names
=.75,ylim=c(0,800),main='Exaggered number of Doctorate Degrees',cex.main=1)
```

This is the following output:

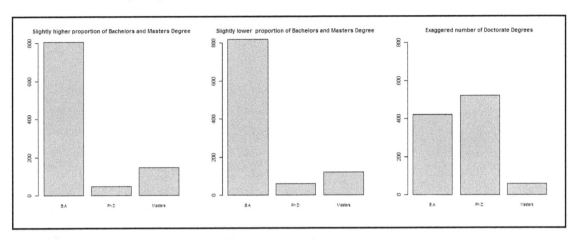

Recombining the churner and non-churners

Now that we have simulated the variables separately for the two groups, we will recombine them and then remove some of the NAs:

```
#bind them back together====

d1 <- data.frame(xchurn.list)
d2 <- data.frame(xnochurn.list)
ChurnStudy <- rbind(d1,d2)
ChurnStudy <- na.omit(ChurnStudy)
summary(ChurnStudy)
nrow(ChurnStudy)
savehistory (file="ch5 generate churn data")
```

The `str`, `summary`, and `nrow` functions will output to the console, and the `savehistory()` function will save all of the commands that were run to an external file:

```
'data.frame': 1984 obs. of  9 variables:
 $ churn           : num  1 1 1 1 1 1 1 1 1 ...
 $ xeducation      : Factor w/ 3 levels "Bachelor's Degree",..: 1 3 3 1 1 3 2 1 1 3 ...
 $ xgender         : Factor w/ 2 levels "F","M": 2 2 1 1 2 2 2 2 2 ...
 $ xsatisfaction   : Factor w/ 5 levels "1","2","3","4",..: 1 1 4 1 4 5 1 1 5 3 ...
 $ xsatisfaction2  : chr  "3" "6" "2" "2" ...
 $ xservice.calls  : num  0 0 0 1 0 1 0 0 0 0 ...
 $ xtenure2        : int  12 5 11 12 6 7 6 11 6 10 ...
 $ xpurch.last.month: num  1 1 1 1 3 1 1 1 1 ...
 $ xmonthly.charges : num  233 217 269 168 299 ...
 - attr(*, "na.action")=Class 'omit'  Named int [1:16] 19 86 398 554 676 743 993 996 1207 1297 ...
  .. ..- attr(*, "names")= chr [1:16] "19" "86" "398" "554" ...
> summary(x3)
      churn                  xeducation      xgender   xsatisfaction  xsatisfaction2        xservice.calls         xtenure2      xpurch.last.month  xmonthly.charges
 Min.   :0.0   Bachelor's Degree:1593   F: 452   1:419         Length:1984        Min.   :0.0000   Min.   : 1.000   Min.   : 0.000   Min.   :-97.53
 1st Qu.:0.0   Doctorate Degree : 122   M:1532   2:448         Class :character   1st Qu.:0.0000   1st Qu.: 7.000   1st Qu.: 1.000   1st Qu.: 67.80
 Median :0.5   Master's Degree  : 269            3:304         Mode  :character   Median :0.0000   Median : 9.000   Median : 1.000   Median :131.48
 Mean   :0.5                                     4:456                            Mean   :0.4718   Mean   : 8.449   Mean   : 1.479   Mean   :143.74
 3rd Qu.:1.0                                     5:357                            3rd Qu.:1.0000   3rd Qu.:11.000   3rd Qu.: 1.000   3rd Qu.:221.42
 Max.   :1.0                                                                      Max.   :5.0000   Max.   :12.000   Max.   :10.000   Max.   :381.82
> nrow(x3)
[1] 1984
> savehistory (file="ch5 generate churn data")
>
```

Notice that the summary output shows satisfaction as a factor and `satisfaction2` as a character variable. We will alter the format and the values of `satisfaction2` later in the chapter when we discuss the follow-up survey.

Try plotting some of the histograms which show the difference in tenure and the number of purchases last month for the two groups, the churners and those who remained active:

```
par(mfrow=c(2,2))
hist(xchurn$Xtenure2,main="Churners Tenure")
hist(xnochurn$Xtenure2,main="Non-Churners Tenure")
hist(xchurn$Xpurch.last.month, col = "grey", labels = FALSE,main="Churners
Purch last Month")
hist(xnochurn$Xpurch.last.month, col = "black", labels = FALSE,main="Non-
Churners Purch last Month")
dev.copy(jpeg,'Ch5 - Plots after dataset creation.jpg'); dev.off()
```

Compare the churners to the non-churners with respect to tenure and number of purchases in the last month:

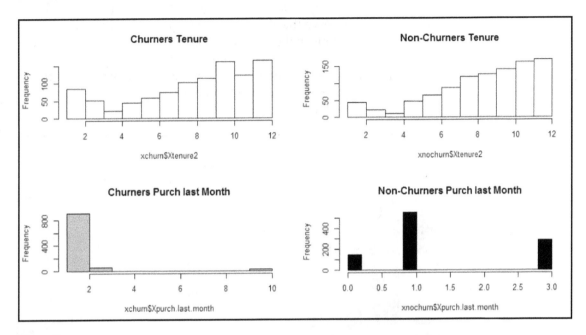

We can see from the preceding plots that the churners generally have a lower number of purchases last month than those who remained active. For the churners, there seems to be some churn activity after 1 or 2 months, but this is a premature assessment, since we do not know at what point in time the customer came aboard.

Creating matrix plots

If we want to explore tenure a bit further for the churners, we could also produce a matrix plot showing the association between tenure and any other variables we choose. In this example we will use the ggpairs() function to plot the matrix plots for tenure, gender, satisfaction, and monthly charges:

```
str(xchurn)
install.packages("GGally")
library(GGally)
library(ggplot2)
ggpairs(xchurn,c(3,4,7,8),lower=list(combo=wrap("facethist",binwidth=30)))
```

We can see from the plot that males churn quicker than females. This is indicated by the matrix plot in the first row and third column. Note that a boxplot is produced since a continuous variable (tenure) is being compared with a categorical variable (gender). The matrix plot is a great way to quickly observe the single variable distribution as well as the pairwise plots. Single variable intersections that are continuous typically show density plots for that variable. For example, monthly charges (row 4, column 4) is clearly normally distributed with an average monthly charge of about $240. For count variables, barcharts are typically shown. However, you can override the default presentation, so check the documentation for the ggpairs() function:

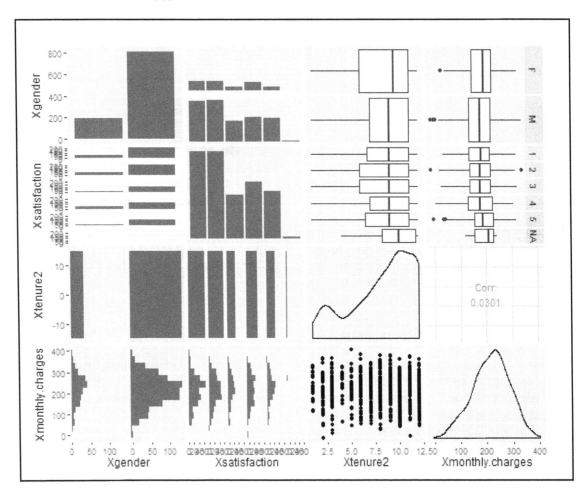

Partitioning into training and test data

Next, we will generate test and training datasets so that we can validate any models produced. There are many ways of generating test and training sets.

In earlier chapters, we used the `createDataPartition` function. For this example, we will generate the test and training data using native R functions. Please refer to the outline of the code here, and then run the code that follows:

- Set a variable corresponding to the percentage of the data to designate as training data (`TrainingRows`). In this example, we will use 75%.
- Use the `sample()` function to randomize the rows and assign to a new dataframe named `ChurnStudy`.
- Then select the first `TrainingRows` rows. Since the `df` dataframe has already been sampled, selecting a percentage of rows sequentially from a random sample is a convenient and valid way to select a training sample.
- The remaining rows (`TrainingRows+1` to the end) will be the testing dataset. Assign it to ChurnStudy.test.

Once we have generated the test and training validation dataset, we will use the `stargazer` package (which we used in `Chapter 1`, *Getting Started with Predictive Analytics*) to generate HTML output for the original `ChurnStudy` dataset, as follows:

```
#divide into train and test====
TrainingRows <- round(.75 * nrow(ChurnStudy))
TrainingRows
set.seed(1020)
#randomize rows
df <- ChurnStudy[sample(nrow(ChurnStudy)), ]
rows <- nrow(df)
ChurnStudy <- df[1:TrainingRows, ]   #training set
ChurnStudy.test <- df[(TrainingRows+1):rows, ]      #test set
nrow(ChurnStudy)
nrow(ChurnStudy.test)
str(ChurnStudy)
str(ChurnStudy.test)
library(stargazer)
stargazer(ChurnStudy[1:10,1:9],out=c("ch 5
AnalysisDataFrame.html"),summary=FALSE,type='html')
browseURL("ch 5 AnalysisDataFrame.html")
savehistory (file="ch5 generate test and train")
```

Towards the end of the code shown, the `browseURL()` function will open up your browser and view the HTML file that has been generated:

	Churn	Xeducation	Xgender	Xsatisfaction	Xsatisfaction2	Xservice.calls	Xtenure2	Xpurch.last.month	Xmonthly.charges	SurvObj
43	1	Bachelor's Degree	F	1	5	0	7	1	295.502908	7
219	1	Bachelor's Degree	F	3	5	0	9	1	215.769268	9
44	1	Bachelor's Degree	M	4	5	0	6	1	230.142292	6
1412	0	Bachelor's Degree	M	3	2	4	11	1	84.775160	11+
12	1	Bachelor's Degree	F	4	3	1	11	1	167.735122	11
1458	0	Bachelor's Degree	M	3	1	0	1	0	174.883747	1+
519	1	Bachelor's Degree	M	1	5	0	4	1	154.264568	4
562	1	Doctorate Degree	M	4	3	0	12	1	212.801643	12
668	1	Bachelor's Degree	M	4	2	0	12	1	291.822605	12
135	1	Bachelor's Degree	M	4	2	1	3	10	318.343811	3
1979	0	Bachelor's Degree	M	2	4	0	12	3	71.934505	12+

Setting the stage by creating survival objects

Coding survival analysis in R usually starts with creating what is known as a survival object using the `Surv()` function. A `survival` object contains more information than a regular dataframe. The purpose of the `survival` object is to keep track of the time and the event status (0 or 1) for each observation. It is also to designate what the response (dependent) variable is.

At a minimum, you need to supply a single time variable and an event when defining a `survival` object. In our case, we will use the tenure time (`Xtenure2`) as the time variable, and a formula that designates the defining event. In our case, this will be `Churn == 1`, since that means that the customer churned in that month:

```
install.packages("survival")
library(survival)
ChurnStudy$SurvObj <- with(ChurnStudy, Surv(Xtenure2, Churn == 1))
```

As I mentioned in earlier chapters, I always like to issue a `str()` command after I create a new dataframe, just to make sure the results are as expected:

```
> str(ChurnStudy$SurvObj)
 Surv [1:1488, 1:2]  7   9   6  11+ 11    1+  4  12  12   3 ...
 - attr(*, "dimnames")=List of 2
  ..$ : NULL
  ..$ : chr [1:2] "time" "status"
 - attr(*, "type")= chr "right"
```

From the preceding output we can see that the survival object created contains 1488 rows, with columns named time and status. Note that the + sign after the number of months means that the member was censored at the end of the study period, that is, the subscriber remained active and did not churn. The attr(*, "type") line shows the model is incorporating right censoring.

Once the survival object is created, we can perform some rudimentary operations on it. Type the following command at the console to see the first few elements:

```
> head(ChurnStudy$SurvObj)
[1]  7   9   6  11+ 11    1+
```

You can also treat the survival object as a matrix and display a subset of the data. Here we will display the first 10 observations:

```
> ChurnStudy$SurvObj[1:10,1:2]
        time status
 [1,]     7      1
 [2,]     9      1
 [3,]     6      1
 [4,]    11      0
 [5,]    11      1
 [6,]     1      0
 [7,]     4      1
 [8,]    12      1
 [9,]    12      1
[10,]     3      1
```

You can also tabulate the data by time and event. We can see that at the end of the study period, approximately 50% of the members have churned:

```
> table(ChurnStudy$SurvObj[,1],ChurnStudy$SurvObj[,2])

        0    1
 1     18   15
 2     10   52
 3     17   34
 4      7   20
 5     31   39
 6     47   42
 7     76   60
 8    102   68
 9     96   89
10    115  115
11    105  105
12    113  112
```

If you prefer to work using column names rather than column numbers, try converting the `survival` object to a dataframe first. This will produce the same results as here, but will allow you to use column names instead of indices. This is a handier way of referencing a large number of columns:

```
Surv.df <- data.frame(ChurnStudy$SurvObj[,1:2])
table(Surv.df$time,Surv.df$status)
```

Let's try a summary. The summary function shows an average tenure of ~8.5 months:

```
> summary(ChurnStudy$SurvObj)
      time                status
 Min.    : 1.000    Min.    :0.000
 1st Qu.: 7.000    1st Qu.:0.000
 Median : 9.000    Median :0.000
 Mean    : 8.474    Mean    :0.495
 3rd Qu.:11.000    3rd Qu.:1.000
 Max.    :12.000    Max.    :1.000
```

When we created the `survival` object, we created it as part of the original `ChurnStudy` dataframe. To view the full data frame with the `survival` data appended, use the `View(ChurnStudy)` command.

Note that the `SurvObj` time corresponds to the `Xtenur2` time. However, the + designation after the number indicates that the customer was still active at the end of the study period.

Examining survival curves

Kaplan Meir survival curves are usually a good place to start when examining the effect of different single factors upon the survival rate, since they are easy to construct and visualize. Later on, we will example cox regression, which can examine multiple factors.

Kaplan Meir (KM) curves are actually step functions in which the `survival` object, or hazard rate, is estimated at each discrete time point. This survival rate is computed by calculating the number of customers who have survived (are still active), divided by the number of customers at risk. The number of customers at risk (which is the denominator) excludes all customers who have already churned, or haven't achieved the tenure specified at any particular time point.

To illustrate, if we table `ChurnStudy` by the number of months active (`Xtenure2`), we can see that for month 1, there were 44 members whose survival rate is calculated as (1984 -19) (Number left after end of month 1 / 1984):

```
table(ChurnStudy$Xtenure2,ChurnStudy$Churn)
         0    1
 1     25   19
 2     12   69
 3     24   45
 4      9   29
 5     50   50
 6     63   61
 7    100   73
 8    124   98
 9    132  114
10    150  159
11    144  129
12    159  146
```

Three elements are needed to construct a KM curve:

- A serial time, which is simply the time interval (months, day, years) from the start of the study. What that means for customer retention is that a subscriber who has been with a company for five years is treated the same as someone who joined one month ago, if the start period for the study begin an a month ago. The five years prior are considered censored information.
- An event flag, usually 0 or 1, which designates whether or not the event has occurred during that time period. A customer will have multiple event flags corresponding to each month in the study.
- A classification or grouping variable. This is usually a single variable.

KM survival curves are then generated by using the `Survfit()` function, which is contained within the `survival` package.

We can begin by examining the survival curve for the entire dataset, without grouping. In this case we use a unity operator, or 1 using formula notation, to designate the entire dataset as a single group:

```
km <- survfit(SurvObj ~ 1, data = ChurnStudy, conf.type = "log-log")
plot(km,col='red')
title(main = "Survival Curve Baseline")
dev.copy(jpeg,'Ch5 - Survival Plot Baseline.jpg'); dev.off()
```

The curve shows all members as being active at the beginning of the study. As members leave, the plot monotonically decreases in value. You can see that the variance of each estimate (the dashed lines that appear above and below the estimate) is much larger as the time period extends in duration. That is because the sample size becomes smaller as the number of customers shrink, and the estimates become less accurate. For the baseline estimate, we can see that at 6 months, the (theoretical) estimate shows that about 86% customers have remained:

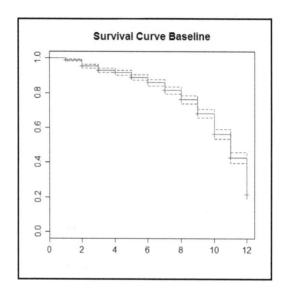

Plots are great for visually observing where the major churn occurs, but you will also want to look at the underlying data.

First, look at how `summary(km)` describes the `survival` object. The output is a bit different from how the `summary` object typically describes a normal R dataframe:

- The output will first list the function call that was used to produce the `km` survival object:

  ```
  > summary(km)
  Call: survfit(formula = SurvObj ~ 1, data = ChurnStudy, conf.type =
  "log-log")
  ```

- Next, the output lists the data points that were plotted, along with the probability of survival for that point and the 95% confidence intervals:

time	n.risk	n.event	survival	std.err	lower 95% CI	upper 95% CI
1	1488	15	0.990	0.00259	0.983	0.994
2	1455	52	0.955	0.00543	0.943	0.964
3	1393	34	0.931	0.00660	0.917	0.943
4	1342	20	0.917	0.00720	0.902	0.930
5	1315	39	0.890	0.00820	0.873	0.905
6	1245	42	0.860	0.00914	0.841	0.877
7	1156	60	0.815	0.01032	0.794	0.835
8	1020	68	0.761	0.01155	0.738	0.783
9	850	89	0.681	0.01307	0.655	0.706
10	665	115	0.564	0.01472	0.534	0.592
11	435	105	0.428	0.01608	0.396	0.459
12	225	112	0.215	0.01638	0.184	0.248

You can see by looking at the survival percentages that the survival rate is cumulative and monotonically descending. What that means is that every subsequent time interval has a decreasing survival probability from the last period.

You can also calculate the survival rate for a given month, given that the customer has remained. For example, in month 12 it will be 48% (146 customers churned/305 customers who were at risk for churning)

Better plots

There is another function that you could use that gives you better graphics and is a bit more customizable than the generic plot function. It is the survplot() function, which is contained in the rms library. Since we will want to demonstrate this function in a few different ways with varying parameters, we will wrap a few of the native functions into a new function called Plotsurv(), which will allow us to customize some of the plots.

First, define the function:

```
library(rms)
plotsurv <- function(x,y,z=c('bars'),zz=FALSE){
   objNpsurv <- npsurv(formula = Surv(Xtenure2,Churn ==1) ~ x, data =
ChurnStudy)
   class(objNpsurv)
survplot(objNpsurv,col=c('green','red','blue','yellow','orange','purple'),
label.curves=list(keys=y),xlab='Months',conf=z,conf.int=.95,n.risk=zz)
   mtext(date(),side=3,line=0,adj=1,cex=.5)

}
```

We will call the baseline plot again, but this time we will include the number of members at risk, which can be found at the top of the horizontal time access. You can verify that these numbers conform to the `summary(km)` function that was run earlier. These numbers correspond to the number of subscribers that were still active at the end of the time period specified. The confidence intervals have also been replaced by short error bars at each marking point:

```
#baseline plot again
par(mfrow=c(1,1))
ChurnStudy$unity <- 1
plotsurv(ChurnStudy$unity,c(1),c('bars'),TRUE)
title(main = "1 KM Curve with Bands and number at risk")
dev.copy(jpeg,'Ch5 - baseline again.jpg');
dev.off()
```

A simpler plot is now produced that contains additional data and is easier on the eyes:

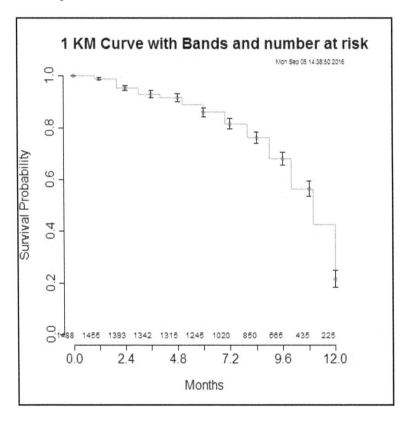

Contrasting survival curves

A baseline survival curve by itself is useful, but the most meaningful analysis comes from looking at the different curves that are generated by different segments of groups. That way, you can see where any intervention might be required. To generate this curve for gender, we will again use the `survfit()` function and specify `XGender` on the right side of the ~ operator. This code will give us separate survival curves for male and female:

```
km.gender <- survfit(SurvObj ~ Xgender, data = ChurnStudy, conf.type =
"log-log")
km.gender
plot(km.gender,col=c('red','blue') ,lty=1:2)
legend('left', col=c('red','blue') ,c('F', 'M'), lty=1:2)
title(main = "Survival Curves by Gender")
dev.copy(jpeg,'Ch5 - Survival Plot by Gender.jpg'); dev.off()
```

The two curves plotted here indicate that females are more likely to be retained over all time periods, and suggests that useful marketing incentives could target males early on:

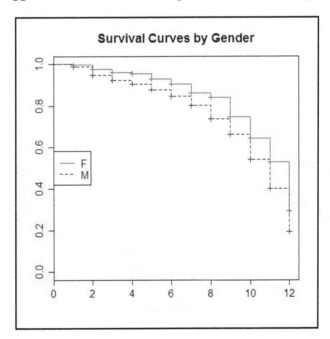

Testing for the gender difference between survival curves

On examination of the survival curve, it is apparent that females are surviving longer than males at every time period. However, we are judging this purely based upon visual inspection. Often, the results are not as obvious. Even if they were obvious, it is good statistical practice to construct a statistical hypothesis test for this. We will use the log-rank test, which is implemented in R using the `survdiff()` function.

The output from the function prints the chi-square statistics associated with the test, which will demonstrate any significant difference between the two curves, along with the associated p-value.

For gender, there is a significant difference at the .01 level, as shown by the low p-value, which is much less than this cutoff:

```
> survdiff(SurvObj ~ Xgender, data = ChurnStudy)
Call:
survdiff(formula = SurvObj ~ Xgender, data = ChurnStudy)

              N Observed Expected (O-E)^2/E (O-E)^2/V
Xgender=F   341      137      177      9.24      14.5
Xgender=M  1147      614      574      2.86      14.5

 Chisq= 14.5  on 1 degrees of freedom, p= 0.000143
```

Testing for the educational differences between survival curves

Now run the `survdiff` function for any differences in education:

```
> survdiff(SurvObj ~ Xeducation, data = ChurnStudy)
Call:
survdiff(formula = SurvObj ~ Xeducation, data = ChurnStudy)

                                   N Observed Expected (O-E)^2/E (O-E)^2/V
Xeducation=Bachelor's Degree 1186      592    594.8   0.01291   0.07392
Xeducation=Doctorate Degree    88       45     45.4   0.00301   0.00382
Xeducation=Master's Degree    214      114    110.9   0.08896   0.12417

 Chisq= 0.1  on 2 degrees of freedom, p= 0.94
```

Now look at the p value. The p value for the chi-square test is 0.94. That means that we cannot conclude that a significant difference exists for the education survival curves.

This also suggests having a closer look at the following plot. We can see that, often, the three levels of education cluster within one standard deviation of the point estimate. Overlapping data points within confidence intervals suggest that there is not enough separation between the means to attain significance:

```
#
plotsurv(ChurnStudy$Xeducation,c(1:3),c('bars'))
title(main = "3 KM Curve Education")
dev.copy(jpeg,'Ch5 - 3 KM Curve Education.jpg'); dev.off()
```

Time 12 (the end of the study) is a perfect example of illustrating this. The three confidence intervals encompass a large swatch of survival probability for the three education levels, so it is difficult to discern any difference. As a follow up, it would make sense to combine master's and doctorate degrees into an advanced degree category and then measure the difference between two categories instead of three:

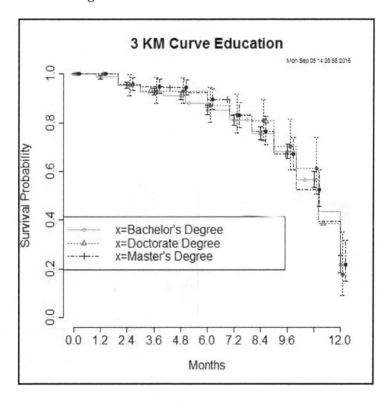

Plotting the customer satisfaction and number of service call curves

We will also generate two more curves, corresponding to the satisfaction and number of service calls variables:

```
par(mfrow=c(1,1))
plotsurv(ChurnStudy$Xsatisfaction,c(1:5),c('bars'))
title(main = "2 KM Curve Satisfaction")/
dev.copy(jpeg,'Ch5 - 2 KM Curve Satisfaction.jpg'); dev.off()
plotsurv(as.factor(ChurnStudy$Xservice.calls),c(1:6),c('none'))
dev.copy(jpeg,'Ch5 - 4 KM Curve Service Calls.jpg');
title(main = "4 KM Curve Service Calls")

dev.off()
```

The plots for the curves are sent to the output window, and are copied to the file specified in the preceding code:

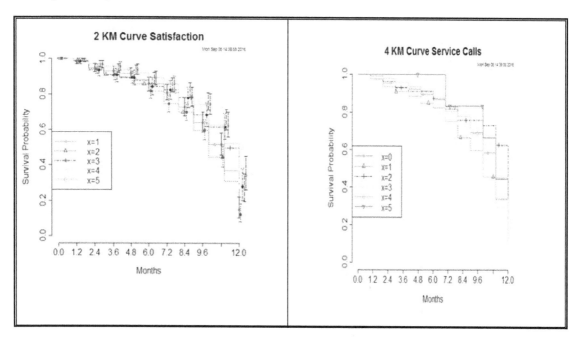

User exercise:

Plot the preceding survival curves and run the log-rank test using `survdiff()` to see if there is a significant difference.

```
survdiff(SurvObj ~ Xsatisfaction, data = ChurnStudy)
survdiff(SurvObj ~ Xpurch.last.month, data = ChurnStudy)
survdiff(SurvObj ~ Xservice.calls, data = ChurnStudy)
```

Improving the education survival curve by adding gender

As we have seen, we cannot conclude that a significant difference exists among the education levels. Often analyzing interaction effects can uncover significance when other covariates are added. If we are interested in seeing if there is a difference in education levels that depends on gender, we can create a new variable that contains dummy variables for each combination of education and gender:

- We will first create this new variable (`factorC`) by using the `interaction()` function. Then we will use our new `plotsurv()` function, to plot the curve based upon all interactions of education and gender.
- Next, we will use the `survdiff()` function to test for the significance of these effects:

```
#create a new factor with interaction between education and gender
#first check the number of satisfaction levels
#
levels(ChurnStudy$Xsatisfaction)
#
#create and store it in the data frame
#
ChurnStudy$factorC <- with(ChurnStudy,    interaction(Xeducation,
Xgender))
#
```

Now plot the survival curves for each level of education (three levels) and gender (two levels). That will be a total of six plots. However, not all combinations survive to month 12, since there are only five levels at the end:

```
plotsurv(ChurnStudy$factorC,c(1:6),c('none'))
title(main = "4 KM Curve Gender*Education")
#
dev.copy(jpeg,'Ch5 - 4 KM Curve Gender Education.jpg');
dev.off()
```

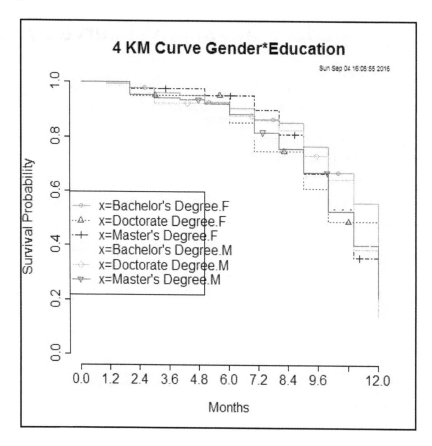

Call the `survdiff()` function to see if there is a significant difference between the curves. The output from the `survdiff()` function is shown here:

```
options(scipen=3)
survdiff(SurvObj ~ ChurnStudy$factorC, data = ChurnStudy)
#
#
> survdiff(SurvObj ~ ChurnStudy$factorC, data = ChurnStudy)
Call:
survdiff(formula = SurvObj ~ ChurnStudy$factorC, data = ChurnStudy)


                                      N Observed Expected (O-E)^2/E (O-E)^2/V
ChurnStudy$factorC=Bachelor's Degree.F 279      111   150.49 10.361225
15.550628
ChurnStudy$factorC=Doctorate Degree.F    22        8     8.21  0.005201
0.006050
ChurnStudy$factorC=Master's Degree.F     40       18    18.81  0.034461
0.041049
ChurnStudy$factorC=Bachelor's Degree.M  907      481   444.28  3.034267
8.884136
ChurnStudy$factorC=Doctorate Degree.M    66       37    37.16  0.000714
0.000903
ChurnStudy$factorC=Master's Degree.M    174       96    92.05  0.169101
0.230200

 Chisq= 16.3  on 5 degrees of freedom, p= 0.00597
```

The chi-square test looks at all of the groups together, and will indicate significance if any one of the groups is significantly different from the others. To see which particular group behaves differently, you need to examine the observed and expected column, as well as the squared error terms in the last two columns. Higher values indicate deviation from the expected. On examination of the output, we see that there are two effects that seem to be the significant groups:

- Females with bachelor's degrees. We expected 150 churners and we observed 111. This is a group that has relatively lower churn than the others.
- Males with doctorate degrees. The observed survival rate is higher than what would be expected.

Earlier, we saw that a college degree by itself didn't make much of difference. But adding gender to the mix can identify specific cohorts that can be targeted.

Save the history:

```
savehistory (file="ch5 interaction plot km curves.log")
```

Transforming service calls to a binary variable

Variables with a higher number of levels will often be difficult to manage even though there may be statistically significant differences shown in the curves. This can be due to the smaller sizes of the groups. Rather than try to analyse all the groups at once, it often makes more sense to first find a cutoff point that collapses the variable into a binary outcome.

For example, running the `survdiff()` function on the number of service calls (ranging from 0 to 5) shows a significant difference between the individual survival curves:

```
> survdiff(SurvObj ~ Xservice.calls, data = ChurnStudy)
Call:
survdiff(formula = SurvObj ~ Xservice.calls, data = ChurnStudy)

                      N Observed Expected (O-E)^2/E (O
E)^2/V
Xservice.calls=0 1103      507   542.87     2.371    10.322
Xservice.calls=1  222      154   116.77    11.873    16.992
Xservice.calls=2   58       23    32.72     2.888     3.711
Xservice.calls=3   51       33    28.43     0.734     0.923
Xservice.calls=4   47       31    25.95     0.985     1.215
Xservice.calls=5    7        3     4.26     0.373     0.448

 Chisq= 23.3  on 5 degrees of freedom, p= 0.000301
```

The last two columns give the chi-square values, and you can see that most of the higher values are for the lower number of service calls. There seems to be a break between `Xservice.calls` 1 and 2. So, we can treat that as a natural breakpoint.

Alternatively, we can formulate a hypothesis that there is difference between low and high service calls; we can create a new binary variable that simply designates whether there were any service calls or not.

We can then plot the results and use the log-rank test again to test for the difference:

```
ChurnStudy$called.binary <- as.factor(ifelse(ChurnStudy$Xservice.calls
==0,'NONE','CALLED'))
survdiff(SurvObj ~ ChurnStudy$called.binary, data = ChurnStudy)
plotsurv(ChurnStudy$called.binary,c(1:2),c('none'))
title(main = "5 KM Curve Called")
dev.copy(jpeg,'Ch5 - 5 KM Curve Called.jpg'); dev.off()

survdiff(SurvObj ~ ChurnStudy$called.binary, data = ChurnStudy)
```

The `plotsurv` call specified here produces the following plot:

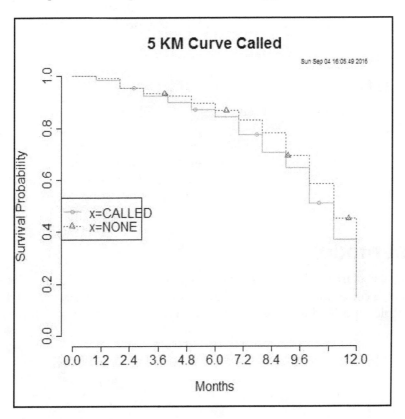

Testing the difference between customers who called and those who did not

Calling the `survdiff()` function produces the chi-square test:

```
> survdiff(SurvObj ~ ChurnStudy$called.binary, data = ChurnStudy)
Call:
survdiff(formula = SurvObj ~ ChurnStudy$called.binary, data = ChurnStudy)

                                    N Observed Expected (O-E)^2/E (O-E)^2/V
ChurnStudy$called.binary=CALLED   385      244      208      6.18      10.3
ChurnStudy$called.binary=NONE    1103      507      543      2.37      10.3

 Chisq= 10.3  on 1 degrees of freedom,  p= 0.00131
```

This shows a clear break between a customer calling or not, and indicates that customer calls might require an intervention plan so that any potential churn can be addressed.

Cox regression modeling

KM tests can be satisfactory in many situations, especially during preliminary analysis; however, KM tests are non-parametric, and typically are less powerful than parametric equivalents. Cox regression extends survival analysis to a parametric regression type framework under which it assumes more power. If there are several independent variables that need to be incorporated into a model, and some of them are continuous, it is advantageous to perform cox proportional hazard modeling rather than KM.

Our first model

Cox modeling also starts with creating a `survival` object, as we did in previous examples. Other than that, a cox model looks very similar to a standard regression model with the response variables specified to the left of the ~ and the independent variables specified to the right.

In cox regression modeling, we use the `coxph()` function over the `surv()` function to specify the dependent variable. This can be done directly in the formula, or by assigning it to a new variable and specifying the new variable to the left of the ~.

Recall that in defining our original survival object we defined `Xtenure2` as the time variable and `Churn` as the outcome of interest. In our example, we will specify `coxph(Surv(Xtenure2, Churn)` as the left side of the predictive model.

Proceed with this next part of the exercise by running the following code, which will run a cox regression model that predicts churn using education, gender, customer satisfaction, number of service calls, monthly charge, and number of purchases last month as independent variables:

```
clearhistory()
#start CoxModel.1====
rm(CoxModel.1)
ChurnStudy$SurvObj <- with(ChurnStudy, Surv(Xtenure2, Churn == 1))
CoxModel.1 <- coxph(Surv(Xtenure2, Churn) ~
                    Xeducation + Xgender + Xsatisfaction + Xservice.calls
+
                    Xpurch.last.month + Xmonthly.charges,
                data=ChurnStudy)
```

To view the results, we will use the `stargazer` library:

```
library(stargazer)
stargazer(CoxModel.1,single.row=TRUE,multicolumn=TRUE,font.size='large',
no.space = TRUE,column.separate = c(1,2,3),
out=c("CoxModel1.html"),type='html')
browseURL("CoxModel1.html")
```

The `browseURL` command will display the output written from stargazer to your browser:

	Dependent variable:
	Xtenure2
XeducationDoctorate Degree	-0.007 (0.157)
XeducationMaster's Degree	-0.041 (0.103)
XgenderM	0.281*** (0.095)
Xsatisfaction2	-0.003 (0.101)
Xsatisfaction3	-0.231* (0.124)
Xsatisfaction4	-0.250** (0.111)
Xsatisfaction5	-0.188 (0.125)
Xservice.calls	0.030 (0.034)
Xpurch.last.month	-0.016 (0.024)
Xmonthly.charges	0.008*** (0.0004)
Observations	1.488
R^2	0.298
Max. Possible R^2	0.999
Log Likelihood	-4.611.885
Wald Test	494.750*** (df = 10)
LR Test	526.196*** (df = 10)
Score (Logrank) Test	551.558*** (df = 10)
Note:	*p<0.1; **p<0.05; ***p<0.01

	Dependent variable:
	Xtenure2
XeducationDoctorate Degree	-0.007 (0.157)
XeducationMaster's Degree	-0.041 (0.103)
XgenderM	0.281*** (0.095)
Xsatisfaction2	-0.003 (0.101)
Xsatisfaction3	-0.231* (0.124)
Xsatisfaction4	-0.250** (0.111)
Xsatisfaction5	-0.188 (0.125)
Xservice.calls	0.030 (0.034)
Xpurch.last.month	-0.016 (0.024)
Xmonthly.charges	0.008*** (0.0004)
Observations	1.488
R^2	0.298
Max. Possible R^2	0.999
Log Likelihood	-4.611.885
Wald Test	494.750*** (df = 10)
LR Test	526.196*** (df = 10)
Score (Logrank) Test	551.558*** (df = 10)
Note:	*p<0.1; **p<0.05; ***p<0.01

Alternatively, you could run a `summary(CoxModel.1)` command to print a more detailed version in the console:

```
> summary(CoxModel.1)
Call:
coxph(formula = Surv(Xtenure2, Churn) ~ Xeducation + Xgender +
    Xsatisfaction + Xservice.calls + Xpurch.last.month + Xmonthly.charges,
    data = ChurnStudy)

  n= 1488, number of events= 751

                                coef  exp(coef)   se(coef)        z Pr(>|z|)
XeducationDoctorate Degree -0.0067422  0.9932804  0.1568365  -0.043  0.96571
XeducationMaster's Degree  -0.0411774  0.9596589  0.1031115  -0.399  0.68964
XgenderM                    0.2809885  1.3244384  0.0954112   2.945  0.00323
**
Xsatisfaction2             -0.0031029  0.9969019  0.1010203  -0.031  0.97550
Xsatisfaction3             -0.2305492  0.7940974  0.1240880  -1.858  0.06318
.
Xsatisfaction4             -0.2503191  0.7785523  0.1105464  -2.264  0.02355
*
Xsatisfaction5             -0.1879801  0.8286312  0.1247098  -1.507  0.13172
Xservice.calls              0.0303329  1.0307976  0.0336934   0.900  0.36798
Xpurch.last.month          -0.0160869  0.9840418  0.0243041  -0.662  0.50803
Xmonthly.charges            0.0082750  1.0083093  0.0003928  21.064  < 2e-16
***
---
Signif. codes:  0 '***' 0.001 '**' 0.01 '*' 0.05 '.' 0.1 ' ' 1
```

Examining the cox regression output

Since we are essentially running an adapted logistic regression, the coefficients in a cox model are always in log form. To transform them to a likelihood ratio you need to take the exponent. This is also part of the summary output.

First, take a look at the value of the exponentiated coefficient, listed under the `exp(coef)` column. Any coefficients significantly greater than 1 indicate that the customer is more likely to churn than not. On the other hand, `exp(coef)` < 1 indicates that the variable is less likely to churn. The magnitude of the difference from 1 will indicate higher probabilities in one direction.

The model results indicate that `gender (males)`, `satisfaction`, and `monthly charges` are the significant variables.

Males and those customers with higher monthly charges have a higher propensity to churn, as indicated by their likelihood score that's above 1 with low p-values

Customers with satisfaction scores of 4 have a lower propensity to churn, as indicated by the likelihood score below 1 with a low p-value. Even though customers with a satisfaction score of 5 were not found significant, it would make sense to include them as well, since their coefficients indicate that they are likely to stay, and their p-value is somewhat low (but not significant at the .05 level). It would also be interesting to pull these customers out separately and see if there are any other factors that lead to some of them churning. We indicate that an interation factor might be needed in the model.

Proportional hazards test

Some follow up tests are needed after a cox regression is run. One assumption of cox regression that needs to be tested is that the hazard for an event is purely dependent upon the variables, and not dependent upon time. If it was, time could not be treated as an independent variable. So, we need to test for what is known as proportional hazards. This can be done using the `cox.zph` function.

Run the following portion of the code, which is listed under the label `#coxproptext====`

It will do the following:

- Assign the output of the proportional hazard test to the `temp` object
- Print the results of the test to the console

- Loop through all of the model variables contained in the `temp` object and plot the proportional hazards:

```
#coxproptext====
#test for proportional hazards
temp <- cox.zph(CoxModel.1, transform = 'log')
print(temp)
par(mfrow=c(2,5))
for (i in 1:10){
plot(temp[i])
}
dev.copy(jpeg,'Ch5 - Coxmodel1 zph.jpg');
dev.off()
savehistory (file="Ch5 CoxModel zph.txt")
```

First, look at the output of the `print(temp)` command:

```
> print(temp)
                               rho     chisq        p
XeducationDoctorate Degree  0.02283  0.40067 0.5267
XeducationMaster's Degree   0.06161  2.88733 0.0893
XgenderM                   -0.05593  2.36508 0.1241
Xsatisfaction2             -0.01517  0.17429 0.6763
Xsatisfaction3             -0.06778  3.47926 0.0621
Xsatisfaction4              0.01274  0.12252 0.7263
Xsatisfaction5             -0.00120  0.00111 0.9735
Xservice.calls              0.02364  0.41897 0.5175
Xpurch.last.month           0.00987  0.10354 0.7476
Xmonthly.charges            0.01265  0.07633 0.7823
GLOBAL                           NA 11.43649 0.3245
```

For the printed output, you will notice the chi-square (column 4) and associated p-value (column 5), which test the assumption that each regression covariate is dependent on time. For the model to pass the assumption, you want to see higher p-values, all of which are above a critical significance level. In this case, they are all above p=.05, so all of the variables pass the assumptions of proportional hazards.

Proportional hazard plots

The plots produced also show that all of the variables are dispersed in a uniform fashion as time increases. Any change due to time would be indicated by a pronounced line that slopes upward or downward:

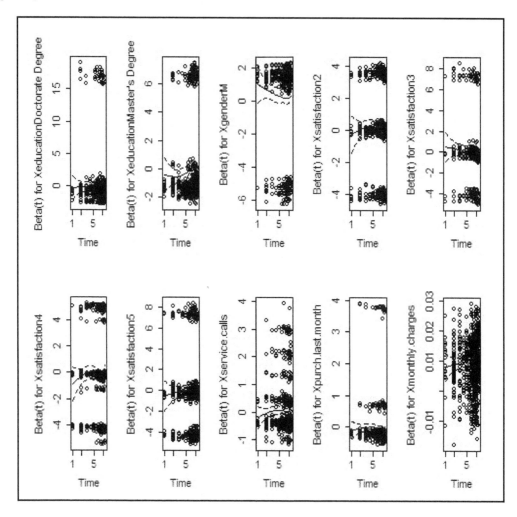

Obtaining the cox survival curves

We can obtain survival curves for the Cox model in a similar fashion as we did for the KM models. To obtain the data points for the curve, use `summary(survfit(CoxModel.1))`, which will also display the confidence intervals, count of the number of members who churned (`n.event`), and the number of members at risk (`n.risk`):

```
> summary(survfit(CoxModel.1))
Call: survfit(formula = CoxModel.1)
```

time	n.risk	n.event	survival	std.err	lower 95% CI	upper 95% CI
1	1488	15	0.993	0.00185	0.989	0.996
2	1455	52	0.967	0.00404	0.960	0.975
3	1393	34	0.950	0.00505	0.940	0.960
4	1342	20	0.940	0.00559	0.929	0.951
5	1315	39	0.919	0.00655	0.906	0.932
6	1245	42	0.896	0.00752	0.881	0.911
7	1156	60	0.861	0.00884	0.844	0.879
8	1020	68	0.818	0.01033	0.798	0.838
9	850	89	0.754	0.01233	0.731	0.779
10	665	115	0.657	0.01500	0.628	0.687
11	435	105	0.536	0.01789	0.502	0.572
12	225	112	0.278	0.02226	0.237	0.325

Plotting the curve

The curve can be plotted using the generic plot function:

```
plot(survfit(CoxModel.1),col=c('red','blue') ,lty=1,xlab="Months",
ylab="Hazard")
title(main = "Model Survival Curve")
dev.copy(jpeg,'Ch5 - Coxmodel1 plot.jpg'); dev.off()
```

You can also plot a prettier version of the curve using `ggplot` and `ggfortify`:

```
library(ggplot2)
library(ggfortify)

autoplot(survfit(CoxModel.1), surv.linetype = 'dashed', surv.colour =
'blue',
        conf.int.fill = 'dodgerblue3', conf.int.alpha = 0.5, censor =
FALSE)
```

Here is a side by side comparison of the curves produced by the native plot function (left plot) and `autoplot` functions (right plot). The major difference is that the shaded bands replace the confidence interval dotted lines:

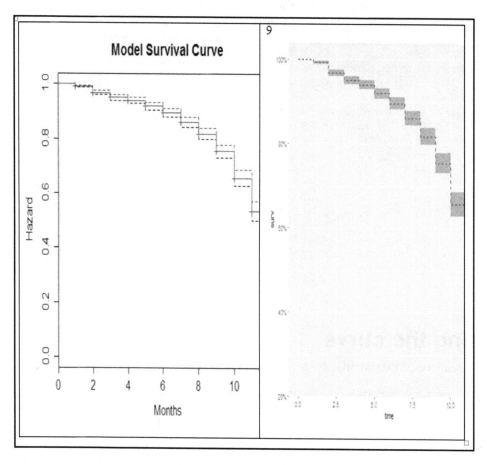

Partial regression plots

Partial regression plots are useful in regression to observe the effect of the individual variables independently of the other variables. Use the `termplot()` function to view the variables in the model separately. The termplot curves roughly correspond to the slopes of the regression line, so you can visually observe the effect of each variable as the levels or continuous values change.

For the regression that we just ran, males, satisfaction levels 3 and 4, and monthly charges are all marked as significant in the regression output, so we can observe their individual slopes by looking at the plots.

The following code will loop through all the variables in the model and produce the following plots. The sixth term (monthly charges), which is a continuous variable, is produced with standard error bars. Notice the increasing variance as the monthly charges increase:

```
par(mfrow=c(3,3))
for(i in 1:5)
termplot(CoxModel.1,term=i,col.se='grey',se=TRUE,partial.resid
=FALSE,smooth=panel.smooth)
termplot(CoxModel.1,term=6,col.se='grey',se=TRUE,partial.resid
=TRUE,smooth=panel.smooth)
dev.copy(jpeg,'Ch5 - Coxmodel1 termplot.jpg');
dev.off()
```

Each `termplot()` call produces the following three plots in a 3*3 matrix format, as defined by the supplied `mfrow` specification:

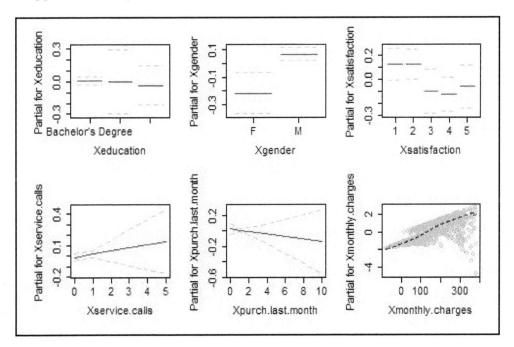

Examining subset survival curves

As we did with the KM curves, we can also produce separate plots for subsets of the data. We will do this by applying the regression coefficients we obtained previously to subsets of the data, with each subset containing an approximately equal number of rows. That way, we will be able to compare the density across groups:

- In the following code, we will first subset our original dataset (ChurnStudy) by gender
- Then we will score the new subsets by applying the coefficients of CoxModel.1
- We will then reduce the density of the plots by sampling 300 observations each from the males and females subsets
- Finally, we will plot the results

Run the following code to produce some interesting subsets of the survival curves:

```
par(mfrow=c(1,2))
#
males <-subset(ChurnStudy,Xgender=='M')
males.nrow <- nrow(males)
females <-subset(ChurnStudy,Xgender=='F')
nrow(females)
females.fit <- survfit(CoxModel.1, newdata=females)
plot(females.fit,col=c('blue') ,lty=1,xlab="Months", ylab="Hazard")
title(main = "Females Survival Curve")
mtext(paste("Observations=",nrow(females)),side=3,line=0,adj=1,cex=1)
#
males.fit <- survfit(CoxModel.1, newdata=males)
plot(males.fit,col=c('red') ,lty=1,xlab="Months", ylab="Hazard")
title(main = "Males Survival Curve")
mtext(paste("Observations=",nrow(males)),side=3,line=0,adj=1,cex=1)
#
par(mfrow=c(1,2))
#
#sample the males population
#
males.sample <- sample(males)[1:300,]
males.sample.fit <- survfit(CoxModel.1, newdata=males.sample)
plot(males.sample.fit,col=c('orange') ,lty=1,xlab="Months", ylab="Hazard")
title(main = "Males (Sample) Survival Curve")
mtext(paste("Observations=",nrow(males.sample.fit)),side=3,line=0,adj=1,cex
=1)
#
#sample the females population
#
females.sample <- sample(females)[1:300,]
```

```
females.sample.fit <- survfit(CoxModel.1, newdata=females.sample)
plot(females.sample.fit,col=c('red') ,lty=1,xlab="Months", ylab="Hazard")
title(main = "FeMales (Sample) Survival Curve")
mtext(paste("Observations=",nrow(females.sample.fit)),side=3,line=0,adj=1,c
ex=1)
#
dev.copy(jpeg,'Ch5 - CoxModel1 Gender.jpg'); dev.off()
sat.fit.low <- survfit(CoxModel.1,
newdata=subset(ChurnStudy[1:300,],as.integer(Xsatisfaction) == 1))
plot(sat.fit.low,col=c('red') ,lty=1,xlab="Months", ylab="Hazard")
title(main = "Sat (Lowest) Survival")
#
sat.fit.high <- survfit(CoxModel.1,
newdata=subset(ChurnStudy[1:300,],as.integer(Xsatisfaction) == 5))
plot(sat.fit.high,col=c('blue') ,lty=1,xlab="Months", ylab="Hazard")
title(main = "sat (Highest) Survival")
dev.copy(jpeg,'Ch5 - CoxModel1 sat.jpg'); dev.off()
savehistory (file="Ch5 CoxModel Contrast Curves.txt")
```

Comparing gender differences

In the comparison of males (left plot) with females (right plot), we can see that there is slightly more density in the upper left quadrant for males than there is for females. This supports the hypothesis that the males will churn earlier:

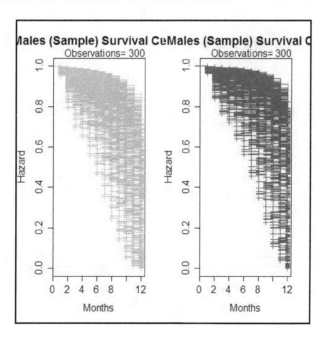

Comparing customer satisfaction differences

First, extract a sample for the highest and lowest satisfaction scores satisfaction=1 indicates more early churners than satisfaction=5, due to the density of the points:

```
sat.fit.low <- survfit(CoxModel.1,
newdata=subset(ChurnStudy[1:300,],as.integer(Xsatisfaction) == 1))
plot(sat.fit.low,col=c('red') ,lty=1,xlab="Months", ylab="Hazard")

title(main = "Sat (Lowest) Survival")
#
sat.fit.high <- survfit(CoxModel.1,
newdata=subset(ChurnStudy[1:300,],as.integer(Xsatisfaction) == 5))
plot(sat.fit.high,col=c('blue') ,lty=1,xlab="Months", ylab="Hazard")
title(main = "sat (Highest) Survival")
dev.copy(jpeg,'Ch5 - CoxModel1 sat.jpg'); dev.off()
```

Here is the side-by-side comparison of the highest and lowest satisfaction scores:

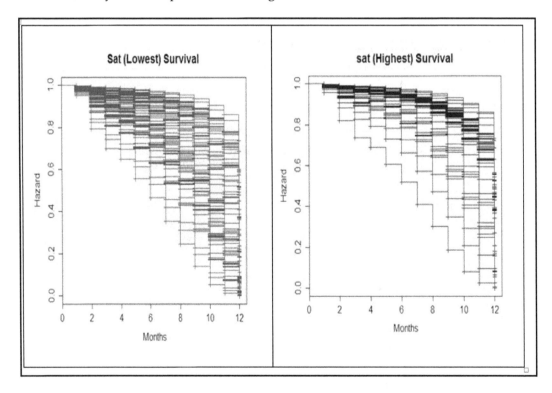

Validating the model

Earlier, we created the `ChurnStudy.test` testing dataset and did not use it to train our cox regression model. After we created it, we just put it off to the side. We will demonstrate one way to use this hold out dataset to validate the training results obtained from `CoxModel1`.

Locate the `#predict===` label and run the following code:

```
#predict====
par(mfrow=c(1,1))
#
```

Computing baseline estimates

We will first determine the baseline (or average) estimates for the regression model we have just run, using the `basehaz()` function. We will assign it to an object named base, and then we will print and plot it.

```
#Let's start by looking at the baseline estimates for each time period.
#
base <- basehaz(CoxModel.1)
print(base)
> print(base)
        hazard time
1   0.007174321    1
2   0.033151848    2
3   0.051088747    3
4   0.062057960    4
5   0.084305023    5
6   0.109773610    6
7   0.149493300    7
8   0.200891166    8
9   0.281904190    9
10  0.420681696   10
11  0.623702585   11
12  1.281690658   12
```

Recall that the hazard is the likelihood that an event (churn) will happen, given that it hasn't already happened. This terminology is slightly different from the term survival rate, which we originally discussed, which is the percentage of the population in which the event did not happen.

We can see that the likelihood of churn always increases as time progress.

Churn seems to increase linearly until month 7 or 8, and then begins to increase exponentially with the greatest churn at the end of 12 months. This could occur as customers begin to approach the end of any contract that is in place.

Plot the baseline `hazard` for each time period:

```
ggplot(base, aes(base$time, base$hazard)) + geom_bar(stat =
"identity",fill='blue') +
  ggtitle("Churn Baseline Hazard by Time") +
  labs(x="Month",y="Hazard")
dev.copy(jpeg,'Ch5 - baseline hazard.jpg');
dev.off()
```

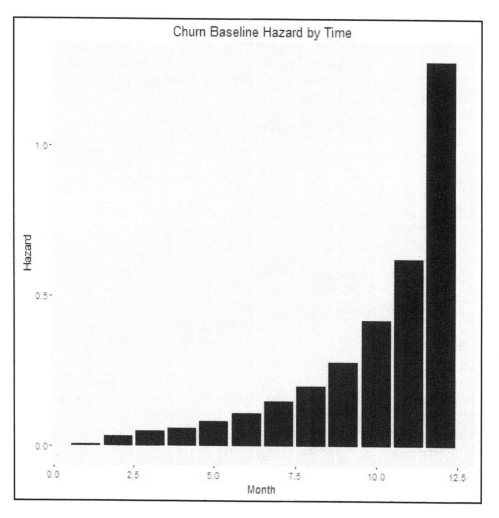

Running the predict() function

Next, we will use the `predict()` function to score the test data in `ChurnStudy.test`, based upon the prediction model trained on `ChurnStudy`. The `newdata=` label designates the new dataset to be stored. The `lp` type is one of several types used for prediction, and this method uses the linear predictor:

```
pred_validation <- predict(CoxModel.1, newdata=ChurnStudy.test, type='lp')
```

The resulting predictions will be in log form.

Predicting the outcome at time 6

The predictions are in log form. Take the exponent and multiply by the base hazard estimate to obtain the predicted value at 6 months:

```
#
head(pred_validation)
#
pred.val <- base[6,1]*exp(pred_validation)
```

Let's assume we want to predict the risk of churn that occurs halfway through the analysis period (time=6):

First, we will first take the exponents of the prediction and multiply them by the base hazard estimate that was shown in the hazard column at time=6. This method, in effect, adds the predictive power of the coefficients to the base hazard rate:

```
pred.val <- base[6,1]*exp(pred_validation)
```

We will now merge the predicted values in with the raw values from the test dataset and view the results after verifying that the number of rows is what we expect:

```
combine <- cbind(ChurnStudy.test,pred_validation,pred.val)
> nrow(combine)
[1] 496
View(combine)
```

The `View` function opens up the dataframe so that it can be examined:

	Churn	Xeducation	Xgender	Xsatisfaction	Xsatisfaction2	Xservice.calls	Xtenure2	Xpurch.last.month	Xmonthly.charges	pred_validation	pred.val
1081	0	Master's Degree	M	3	3	0	9	1	115.098475	-0.326359648	0.07920667
691	1	Master's Degree	M	4	2	0	9	1	372.688733	1.785420280	0.65447961
1413	0	Bachelor's Degree	F	3	5	0	10	0	120.539268	-0.505061482	0.06624491
1699	0	Bachelor's Degree	M	3	1	1	7	1	-2.017806	-1.223982249	0.03227968
1111	0	Bachelor's Degree	M	5	3	3	7	1	67.455601	-0.545857524	0.06359677
1962	0	Bachelor's Degree	M	1	5	0	9	1	31.944160	-0.742731950	0.05223163

Look at the last column, which contains the prediction. The prediction is essentially a risk score that ranges from 0 to 1.

Examine the predicted value (`pred_val`) with the actual churn output (`Churn`) to get an idea of how the predicted values vary with the outcomes. Also examine the relationship between the independent variables and the predicted values. For example, you can see within the first few rows that the churn=1 event contains a much higher monthly charge than the other surrounding rows.

To see the difference in the average scores between the churners and non-churners, we can take some mean aggregate functions and print the results. After running the following code, we can see difference between the churners (who have higher risk scores) and the non-churners:

```
y <- aggregate(combine$pred.val, by=list(combine$Churn),FUN=mean,
na.rm=TRUE)
print(y)
> print(y)
  Group.1          x
1       0 0.0646759
2       1 0.2326843
```

Determining concordance

A concordance index is another measure that is used in survival analysis to determine how well the model is able to discern between the observed and predicted responses. For our churn example, we would expect the churners to have higher hazard rates than those customers who remain active. If the concordance index is more than .5, that indicates that there is some predictive ability built into the model.

To compute the index we will use the `concordance.index()` function from the `survcomp` package to measure the agreement of the `pred_validation` statistic, with the actual churn outcome.

As in previous examples, one needs to supply the predictions, time variable, and event variable as arguments to the function. We will also print the associated confidence intervals:

```
library(survcomp)
cindex_validation = concordance.index (pred_validation, surv.time =
ChurnStudy.test$XTenure2,
                              surv.event=ChurnStudy.test$Churn)
#
print(cindex_validation$c.index)
print(cindex_validation$upper)
```

```
print(cindex_validation$lower)
```

For our example, the computed index is 70%, with confidence intervals showing that it can range between 60 and 77%:

```
> print(cindex_validation$c.index)
[1] 0.6973212
> print(cindex_validation$upper)
[1] 0.7736508
> print(cindex_validation$lower)
[1] 0.6082843
```

Time-based variables

Up until now, we have treated all of our variables as static, that is, they maintained their original values measured from the beginning of the measurement period.

In reality, values such as age and marital status change over time, and these changes can be accounted for by the model. In the marketing context, surveys might be administered after the study has begun. Based upon changes in some of these variables, coupons and other incentives might be offered (interventions) with the purpose of changing customer behavior. In the model, these interventions can also be accounted for.

In our example, we will introduce a hypothetical second survey, which was introduced 6 months into the measurement period and measured the effect of treating some of the unsatisfied customers.

Changing the data to reflect the second survey

The following code uses the survSplit function to create a new record a time period 6 that will reflect the response to a second hypothetical customer survey administered at that time.

Copy the following code and run it in a new script window:

```
library(survival)
SURV2 <- survSplit(data = ChurnStudy, id="ID.char", cut = 6, end =
"Xtenure2",  start = "time0", event = "Churn", episode="period")
SURV2$CustomerID <- as.integer(SURV2$ID.char)
SURV2 <- SURV2[order(SURV2$CustomerID),]
```

In the R console, execute the following commands to see how the dataframe has grown larger. Because we are splitting records at the mid-point (6 months), we have almost doubled the original records:

```
> nrow(ChurnStudy)
[1] 1984
> nrow(SURV2)
[1] 3512
```

How survSplit works

We will look a bit closer at the `survSplit` function and how it affects the satisfaction variable. Since we need to keep track of how customer satisfaction changed at time period 6, `survSplit` function will alter the dataframe by creating new rows and adjusting the time periods to reflect the change in customer satisfaction. In our example, that means that the function would create additional rows after the 6 months cutoff (cut=6) based upon the values of `Xtenure2`.

As an example of how this would work, first look at the original `ChurnStudy` dataframe and observe that the very first record has a tenure of 7 months. This customer would have been around long enough for a second survey:

```
ChurnStudy$seqid <- seq(1:nrow(ChurnStudy))
View(subset(ChurnStudy, select = c(seqid,Xtenure2,Xsatisfaction,
Xsatisfaction2, Churn)))
```

	seqid	Xtenure2	Xsatisfaction	Xsatisfaction2	Churn
43	1	7	1	5	1
219	2	9	3	6	1
44	3	6	4	6	1
1412	4	11	3	2	0
12	5	11	4	3	1
1458	6	1	3	1	0
519	7	4	1	5	1
562	8	12	4	3	1
668	9	12	4	2	1
135	10	3	4	2	1

Now look at the output produced by `survSplit()` function. You can see that the first record (`CustomerID=1`) has been split into two records, one record starting from the first month that the member was active (`time0=0`) and the other record from the sixth month onward (`time 0=6`).

On the other hand, `CustomerID=2` only has one record, since the member was only around for 5 months, which is less than the `cut=6` cutoff:

```
View(subset(SURV2, select = c(CustomerID,time0,period, Xsatisfaction,
Xsatisfaction2, Xtenure2, Xmonthly.charges, Churn)))
```

	CustomerID	time0	period	Xsatisfaction	Xsatisfaction2	Xtenure2	Xmonthly.charges	Churn
1174	1	0	0	1	3	6	233	0
2662	1	6	1	1	3	12	233	1
213	2	0	0	1	6	5	217	1
1307	3	0	0	4	2	6	269	0
2795	3	6	1	4	2	11	269	1
1266	4	0	0	1	2	6	168	0
2754	4	6	1	1	2	12	168	1
1268	6	0	0	5	3	6	164	0
2756	6	6	1	5	3	7	164	1
1372	7	0	0	1	2	6	89	1
681	8	0	0	1	5	6	175	0
2169	8	6	1	1	5	11	175	1
45	9	0	0	5	3	6	106	1

At this point, nothing has really changed analytically. There have been two records created with the exact same information, except that one record shows the information as it exists at the end of period 6, and the other the information at the end of period 12.

We can see how months 1-12 align with the periods by running a simple crosstab:

```
> table(SURV2$period, SURV2$Xtenure2)

     1    2    3    4    5    6    7    8    9   10   11   12
0   33   62   51   27   70 1245    0    0    0    0    0    0
1    0    0    0    0    0    0  136  170  185  230  210  225
```

Adjusting records to simulate an intervention

Now that we have multiple records, we will be able to adjust for the new survey information which changed after month 6 and include that as a time dependent variable.

Recall that we initially simulated the second survey data for the churners by increasing the satisfaction rating by 1 (Xsatisfaction2). This resulted in some satisfaction scores of 6 for some members, which would be impossible. So we will first clean those by setting the 6 ratings to 5:

```
#fix up some "6" satisfaction scores, that are not possible, and make them
"5"
SURV2$Xsatisfaction2 <-
as.factor(ifelse(SURV2$Xsatisfaction2=="6","5",SURV2$Xsatisfaction2))
```

Assume that at month 5 there was a promotion targeted to those members who gave low satisfaction ratings (1 or 2) in the initial survey. This result in an increased satisfaction score for some members who would have churned.

We will simulate a positive response to the survey by upgrading their satisfaction score (Xsatisfaction2) for those that churned from 1 or 2 to 3. This is to simulate a slight increase in satisfactions. This is only performed for period=1, which is the period following the survey. Technically, this is the period assigned by survSplit() function after the cut (Period 1). Period 0 is the period before the cut:

```
#an intervention increased low satisfaction scores to "Average".
SURV2$Xsatisfaction2 <- ifelse(SURV2$period==1 & SURV2$Churn==1 &
SURV2$Xsatisfaction %in% c("1","2"),"3",SURV2$Xsatisfaction)
```

We will also simulate the change in retention status for these survey2 customers by changing the Churn status from 1 (left) to 0 (retained), indicating that the promotion had enough of an effect to keep them from leaving:

```
#Simulate retaining these customers by changing their status to active
#change is detected when the new score is higher than the old score
SURV2$Churn2 <-ifelse(SURV2$period==1 & SURV2$Churn==1 &
                      (as.integer(SURV2$Xsatisfaction2) >
as.integer(SURV2$Xsatisfaction)),
                      0, SURV2$Churn)fe
SURV2$ChurnChanged <- ifelse(SURV2$Churn==SURV2$Churn2,'N','Y')
```

Now, sort the dataframe by ID and view the results. Records that have multiple IDs have been split by the algorithm:

```
attach(SURV2)
tmp <- SURV2[order(CustomerID),]
str(tmp)


tmp2 <- subset(tmp, select = c(CustomerID,ChurnChanged,time0,period,
Xsatisfaction, Xsatisfaction2, Churn,Churn2))


View(tmp2)
```

	CustomerID	ChurnChanged	time0	period	Xsatisfaction	Xsatisfaction2	Churn	Churn2
1174	1	N	0	0	1	1	0	0
2662	1	Y	6	1	1	3	1	0
213	2	N	0	0	1	1	1	1
1307	3	N	0	0	4	4	0	0
2795	3	N	6	1	4	4	1	1
1266	4	N	0	0	1	1	0	0
2754	4	Y	6	1	1	3	1	0
1268	6	N	0	0	5	5	0	0
2756	6	N	6	1	5	5	1	1
1372	7	N	0	0	1	1	1	1
681	8	N	0	0	1	1	0	0
2169	8	Y	6	1	1	3	1	0
45	9	N	0	0	5	5	1	1

Observe that any customer who has had a tenure of more than 6 months has also had an additional record added. This additional record reflects the customer's updated status and updates the value of variables that have changed.

In this case, we have performed one cut at 6 months. The data also includes two new variables: time0, which designates the starting period; and an episode variable, which we named period, and is incremented sequentially for every time-based change in a variable. We only showed an example with one change in a time-based variable. For longer observation periods you can have many more changes.

Running the time-based model

Now that we have reformatted the data, we are already ready to run the second time-based model.

The `CoxModel.2` variable is created in a similar fashion as `CoxModel.1`, however `Xsatisfaction2` is substituted for `Xsatisfaction` to account for the change in satisfaction due to the follow-up study. The new `time0` variable is also substituted for the original tenure variable, and `Churn2` is substituted for the original churn response variable:

```
CoxModel.2 <- coxph(Surv(time0,Xtenure2, Churn2) ~
                    Xeducation + Xgender + Xsatisfaction2 +
Xservice.calls +
                    Xpurch.last.month + Xmonthly.charges,
                data=SURV2)
```

Avoid overwriting existing variable names. Either create new variables within an existing dataframe or preserve the old one and create a new frame.

After the model is run, we can use the `stargazer` command (or `summary(CoxModel.2)`) to view the model output.

The asterisks after gender, satisfaction, and monthly charges indicate that they are the most significant variables in the model.

The R-square of .13 is not a standard linear regression type measure, but is a pseudo-R square measure that we discussed earlier, which is a number between 0 and 1 that measures the difference between the fitted model and a null model. If you are curious to see how this particular pseudo R-square is calculated for a cox regression, you can issue the following command:

```
getS3method("summary","coxph")
```

However, it is not as high as the original `CoxModel.1`. This is possibly due to the artificial changing of the data. In any case, it is not a good idea to rely on a single measure, and we will see shortly how the model does improve the retention.

```
library(stargazer)
stargazer(CoxModel.2,single.row=TRUE,type='text')


> stargazer(CoxModel.2,single.row=TRUE,type='text')


===========================================================
                        Dependent variable:
```

	time0
XeducationDoctorate Degree	−0.160 (0.210)
XeducationMaster's Degree	−0.200 (0.140)
XgenderM	0.091 (0.120)
Xsatisfaction22	0.160 (0.200)
Xsatisfaction23	−0.600*** (0.200)
Xsatisfaction24	0.520*** (0.180)
Xsatisfaction25	0.580*** (0.180)
Xservice.calls	0.013 (0.044)
Xpurch.last.month	−0.007 (0.029)
Xmonthly.charges	0.009*** (0.001)
Observations	2,644
R2	0.130
Max. Possible R2	0.900
Log Likelihood	−2,869.000
Wald Test	370.000*** (df = 10)
LR Test	380.000*** (df = 10)
Score (Logrank) Test	399.000*** (df = 10)
Note:	*p<0.1; **p<0.05; ***p<0.01

Let's start by generating another survival curve:

```
par(mfrow=c(1,1))
autoplot(survfit(CoxModel.1), surv.linetype = 'dashed', surv.colour =
'blue',
        conf.int.fill = 'dodgerblue3', conf.int.alpha = 0.5, censor =
FALSE)
dev.copy(jpeg,'Ch5 - time based variable 1.jpg');
dev.off()

autoplot(survfit(CoxModel.2), surv.linetype = 'dashed', surv.colour =
'red',
        conf.int.fill = 'orange', conf.int.alpha = 0.5, censor = FALSE)
dev.copy(jpeg,'Ch5 - time based variable 2.jpg');
dev.off()
savehistory (file="Ch5 time based variable.txt")
```

Here are the original (left plot) and time-based survival plots side by side:

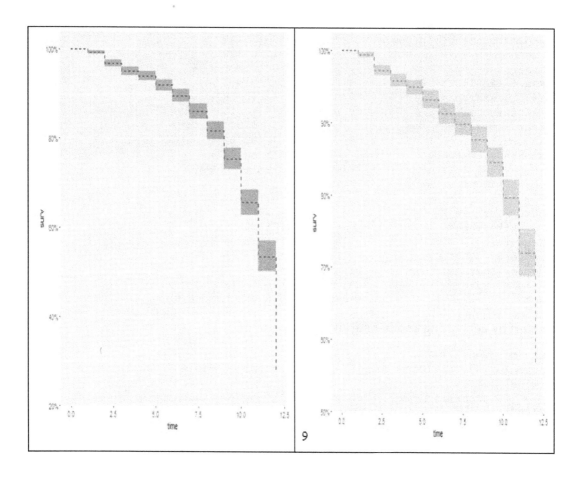

Comparing the models

Even though the survival curves are similar, we can see that at the end of 12 months, 56% of the customers were retained, as opposed to the original 27%. We could attribute that to the intervention that took place at month 6.

Use the `summary(survfit)` function to compare the modes:

> summary(survfit(CoxModel.2)) Call: survfit(formula = CoxModel.2) v time n.risk n.event survival std.err lower 95% CI upper 95% CI 1 1488 15 0.994 0.00157 0.991 0.997 2 1455 52 0.973 0.00359 0.966 0.980 3 1393 34 0.958 0.00461 0.949 0.967 4 1342 20 0.950 0.00518 0.940 0.960 5 1315 39 0.932 0.00624 0.920 0.945 6 1245 42 0.913 0.00736 0.898 0.927 7 1156 24 0.898 0.00801 0.883 0.914 8 1020 32 0.877 0.00902 0.859 0.895 9 850 40 0.846 0.01052 0.825 0.866 10 665 51 0.797 0.01293 0.772 0.822 11 435 54 0.721 0.01688 0.688 0.755 12 225 55 0.569 0.02518 0.522 0.621	> summary(survfit(CoxModel.1)) Call: survfit(formula = CoxModel.1) time n.risk n.event survival std.err lower 95% CI upper 95% CI 1 1488 15 0.993 0.00185 0.989 s0.996 2 1455 52 0.967 0.00404 0.960 0.975 3 1393 34 0.950 0.00505 0.940 0.960 4 1342 20 0.940 0.00559 0.929 0.951 5 1315 39 0.919 0.00655 0.906 0.932 6 1245 42 0.896 0.00752 0.881 0.911 7 1156 60 0.861 0.00884 0.844 0.879 8 1020 68 0.818 0.01033 0.798 0.838 9 850 89 0.754 0.01233 0.731 0.779 10 665 115 0.657 0.01500 0.628 0.687 11 435 105 0.536 0.01789 0.502 0.572 12 225 112 0.278 0.02226 0.237 0.325

Variable selection

The model we just worked with had a limited number of variables, so mechanical variable selection methods when dealing with a large number of variables were not really that pertinent. We were able to pinpoint the important ones via the regression model. However, for a model with a large number of variables we could use the `glmulti` package for the purpose of performing variable selection.

For the churn example that was generated, we have a small number of variables, so it is easy to demonstrate a variable selection and not so time consuming.

In the following code, we will set the maximum number of terms to include in the best regression to 10 in order to limit the computational time needed to perform an exhaustive search. We will also use the genetic algorithm option (`method = "g"`) which can be much faster with larger datasets, since it only considers the best subsets of all of the combinations.

If you wish to perform an exhaustive search, use `method = "h"`. However, be forewarned, this may tie up your machine for a very long time:

- Run the following code to begin the variable selection process:

```
library(glmulti)
glmulti.coxph.out <-
   glmulti(Surv(Xtenure2, Churn) ~ Xeducation + Xgender +
   Xsatisfaction + Xservice.calls +
         Xpurch.last.month + Xmonthly.charges, data =
   ChurnStudy,
         maxsize=10,

         level = 2,              # interaction considered
         method = "g",           # Genetic Algorithm
         crit = "aic",           # AIC as criteria
         confsetsize = 5,        # Keep 5 best models
         plotty = T, report = F, # produce AIC plot
         fitfunction = "coxph")  # coxph function
```

- You will receive the following message in the console when the algorithm has completed. It should complete in 5 minutes or less:

```
TASK: Genetic algorithm in the candidate set.
Initialization...
Algorithm started...
Improvements in best and average IC have bebingo en below the
specified goals.
Algorithm is declared to have converged.
Completed.
```

- Print a summary of the output object. The summary includes the best model found from the candidate set. Notice that the best model does not include the education variable:

```
> print(glmulti.coxph.out)
glmulti.analysis
Method: g / Fitting: coxph / IC used: aic
Level: 2 / Marginality: FALSE
From 5 models:
Best IC: 9214.89853563887
Best model:
[1] "Surv(Xtenure2, Churn) ~ 1 + Xgender + Xsatisfaction +
Xservice.calls + "
[2] " Xmonthly.charges + Xpurch.last.month:Xservice.calls +
Xmonthly.charges:Xservice.calls + "
[3] " Xgender:Xmonthly.charges +
```

```
Xsatisfaction:Xmonthly.charges"
Evidence weight: 0.257101917192717
Worst IC: 9216.1617086134
5 models within 2 IC units.
4 models to reach 95% of evidence weight.
Convergence after 120 generations.
Time elapsed: 55.2994699478149 minutes.
```

- Since we specified that interactions should be considered in the model, the algorithm has found several interactions that should be looked at for further model improvement:

```
Xpurch.last.month:Xservice.calls
Xmonthly.charges:Xservice.calls
Xmonthly.charges:Xpurch.last.month
Xgender:Xpurch.last.month
Xsatisfaction:Xpurch.last.month
Xsatisfaction:Xmonthly.charges
```

- Two important ones are those that relates gender to the number of purchases last month, and the interaction that relates satisfaction and monthly charges. Both of these interactions are specified in the best model.

Incorporating interaction terms

To incorporate these interactions in a future model we specify them directly in the right side of the model formula. For example, this specification includes service calls, as well as the interaction between service calls and the number of purchases last month, as model terms:

```
CoxModel.2 <- coxph(Surv(time0,Xtenure2, Churn2) ~
                    Xeducation + Xgender + Xsatisfaction2 +
Xservice.calls + Xpurch.last.month:Xservice.calls +
                    Xpurch.last.month + Xmonthly.charges,
                data=SURV2)
```

Displaying the formulas sublist

If you don't like typing out all of the terms, you can display a formulas sub list, which will list all of the formulas for the top 5 models. That will help in cutting and pasting:

```
> glmulti.coxph.out@formulas
[[1]]
Surv(Xtenure2, Churn) ~ 1 + Xgender + Xsatisfaction + Xservice.calls +
  Xmonthly.charges + Xpurch.last.month:Xservice.calls +
```

```
  Xmonthly.charges:Xservice.calls +
    Xgender:Xmonthly.charges + Xsatisfaction:Xmonthly.charges
  <environment: 0x0000000034599328>

[[2]]
Surv(Xtenure2, Churn) ~ 1 + Xgender + Xsatisfaction + Xservice.calls +
    Xmonthly.charges + Xpurch.last.month:Xservice.calls +
  Xmonthly.charges:Xservice.calls +
    Xmonthly.charges:Xpurch.last.month + Xgender:Xmonthly.charges +
    Xsatisfaction:Xmonthly.charges
  <environment: 0x0000000034599328>

[[3]]
Surv(Xtenure2, Churn) ~ 1 + Xgender + Xsatisfaction + Xservice.calls +
    Xmonthly.charges + Xpurch.last.month:Xservice.calls +
  Xmonthly.charges:Xservice.calls +
    Xsatisfaction:Xmonthly.charges
  <environment: 0x0000000034599328>

[[4]]
Surv(Xtenure2, Churn) ~ 1 + Xgender + Xsatisfaction + Xservice.calls +
    Xpurch.last.month + Xmonthly.charges + Xpurch.last.month:Xservice.calls +
    Xmonthly.charges:Xservice.calls + Xgender:Xmonthly.charges +
    Xsatisfaction:Xmonthly.charges
  <environment: 0x0000000034599328>

[[5]]
Surv(Xtenure2, Churn) ~ 1 + Xgender + Xsatisfaction + Xservice.calls +
    Xpurch.last.month + Xmonthly.charges + Xpurch.last.month:Xservice.calls +
    Xmonthly.charges:Xservice.calls + Xmonthly.charges:Xpurch.last.month +
    Xgender:Xmonthly.charges + Xsatisfaction:Xmonthly.charges
  <environment: 0x0000000034599328>
```

Comparing AIC among the candidate models

As mentioned in earlier chapters, AIC is a metric that you can use to help you select a model. The `plotty='T'` option also produced a plot of the AICs for the top models found. In the function call, we indicate that we wanted to see up to five.

According to the author of the package, a reasonable rule of thumb is to consider models that fall below the horizontal red line.

According to that definition, that would eliminate models 4 and 5, and leave models 1, 2, and 3 to consider.

Here is the plot of the AICs for the top five models:

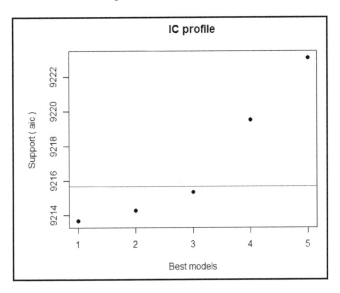

We can also specify a variable importance plot by using the plot statement with `type='s'`:

```
plot(glmulti.coxph.out,type = "s")
```

This plot gives a nice simple horizontal barchart ordered by the most important features:

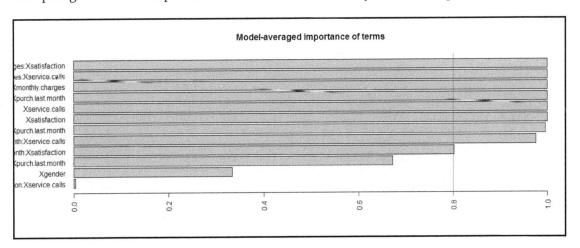

Summary

In this chapter, we learned about what survival analysis is, and how two main techniques, Kaplan-Meir and Cox Regression, can be used to explain and predict customer churn.

We also learned how we can generate our own data to test assumptions and test the robustness of the models.

Finally, we included some coding techniques to help us reproduce and save our generated code and images.

In the next chapter, we will not be concerned with a customer leaving, but will cover how to keep customers happy by predicting what they will purchase next using a technique known as **Market Basket Analysis**.

7
Using Market Basket Analysis as a Recommender Engine

"It's not wise to violate the rules until you know how to observe them."

- T.S. Eliot

In this chapter, we will cover the following topics:

- Market basket analysis using the arules package
- Data transformation and cleaning techniques using semi-structured market basket transaction data
- Learn how to transform transaction objects into dataframes
- Use cluster analysis for prediction using the flexclus package
- Utilize some text mining using RTextTools and tm packages

What is market basket analysis?

If you have survived the last chapter, you will now be introduced to the world of **market basket analysis** (**MBA**). Market basket analysis (also sometimes called **affinity analysis**), is a predictive analytics technique that is used heavily in the retail industry in order to identify baskets of items that are purchased together. The typical use case for this is the supermarket shopping cart in which a shopper would typically purchase an assortment of items such as milk, bread, cheese, and so on, and the algorithm will predict how purchasing certain items together will affect the purchase of other items. It is one of those methods that retailers use to know to start sending you coupons and emails for things that you didn't know you needed!

One often quoted example of MBA is the relationship between diapers and beer:

> *"One super market chain discovered in its analysis that customers that bought diapers often bought beer as well, have put the diapers close to beer coolers, and their sales increased dramatically"*
> - http://en.wikipedia.org/wiki/Market_basket

However, it is not only restricted to the retail industry. MBA can be used in the insurance industry to look at the various products that an insured person currently has, such as a car, home, and so on, and suggest other possible products such as life, disability, or investment products.

MBA is generally considered an unsupervised learning algorithm, in that target variables are usually not specified. However, as you will see later it is possible to refine the association rules, so that specific items can be specified as target variables.

MBA is also considered a type of recommender engine in which purchases of a set of items imply the purchase of others. Certainly, MBA and other recommender engines can share the same types of input data. However, MBA was developed before the advent of collaborative filtering techniques, as pioneered by Amazon, and is more suggestive of the integration of collected web data, while MBA is more associated with the RFID bar coding technologies found in scanners. However, in both cases suggestions of future purchases based on past purchases is the goal.

Examining the groceries transaction file

Critical to the understanding of MBA are the concepts of support, confidence, and lift. These are the measures that evaluated the *goodness of fit* for a set of association rules. You will also learn some specific definitions that are used in MBA, such as consequence, antecedent, and itemsets.

To introduce these concepts, we will first illustrate these terms through a very simplistic example. We will use only the first 10 transactions contained in the Groceries transaction file, which is contained in the `arules` package:

```
library(arules)
```

After the `arules` library is loaded, you can see a short description of the Groceries dataset by entering `?Groceries` at the command line. The following description appears in the **help** window:

"The `Groceries` data set contains 1 month (30 days) of real-world point-of-sale transaction data from a typical local grocery outlet. The data set contains 9835 transactions and the items are aggregated to 169 categories".

For more information about how this dataset was collected, refer to the original publication (*Michael Hahsler, 2006*).

Once the `arules` package is loaded, load the `Groceries` dataset into memory:

```
data(Groceries)
```

Format of the groceries transaction Files

The `Groceries` is a transaction class object, not a dataframe. This R object represents transaction data used for mining item sets or rules. Logically, it is organized as a list of grocery receipts along with the items that were purchased together. Every individual line is referred to as a transaction and every column of the transaction represents a specific item purchased.

For example, here are three transactions consisting of a varying number of purchases:

Transaction 1	Milk	Cereal	
Transaction 2	Beef		
Transaction 3	Butter	Sugar	Cream

However, a transaction object is not physically organized in strict database table format. It is in a special R object format known as transactions.

You can also run a `summary(Groceries)`, which will give you some high level information about the structure of the transactions file, as well as the most frequent individual items found in the market basket:

```
> summary(Groceries)
transactions as itemMatrix in sparse format with
 9835 rows (elements/itemsets/transactions) and
 169 columns (items) and a density of 0.026

most frequent items:
      whole milk other vegetables      rolls/buns          soda          yogurt        (Other)
            2513           1903            1809          1715 |          1372          34055
```

You will see later on how we can convert dataframes to transaction objects, and vice versa. For more information about this object, you can enter `?transactionInfo` at the console line.

To see an example of a simple market basket for the `Groceries` file, run the following code:

Examine the output produced from the `inspect()` function, which prints transactions 10-19 from the market basket. Note that each transaction can consist of a single transaction ID, along with a list of purchased items. It can be a single purchased item (Transaction #4, Beef purchased by itself), or consist of multiple purchases (Transaction #1, Milk and Cereal):

```
inspect(Groceries[10:19])
```

This is the following output:

```
         items
[1]  {whole milk,cereals}
[2]  {tropical fruit,other vegetables,white bread,bottled water,chocolate}
[3]  {citrus fruit,tropical fruit,whole
      milk,butter,curd,yogurt,flour,bottled water,dishes}
[4]  {beef}
[5]  {frankfurter,rolls/buns,soda}
[6]  {chicken,tropical fruit}
[7]  {butter,sugar,fruit/vegetable juice,newspapers}
[8]  {fruit/vegetable juice}
[9]  {packaged fruit/vegetables}
[10]{chocolate}
```

The sample market basket

Each transaction numbered 1-10 listed previously represents a basket of items purchased by a shopper. These are typically all items that are associated with a particular transaction or invoice. Each basket is enclosed within braces {}, and is referred to as an itemset. An itemset is a group of items that occur together.

Market basket algorithms construct rules in the form of:

```
Itemset{x1,x2,x3 ...} --> Itemset{y1,y2,y3...}.
```

This notation states that buyers who have purchased items on the left-hand side of the formula (lhs) have a propensity to purchase items on the right-hand side (rhs). The association is stated using the à symbol, which can be interpreted as implies.

 The lhs of the notation is also known as the antecedent, and the rhs is known as the consequence. If nothing appears on either the left-hand side or right-hand side there is no specific association rule for those items; however, it also means that those items have appeared in the basket.

Association rule algorithms

Without an association rule algorithm, you are left with the computationally very expensive task of generating all possible pairs of itemsets, and then trying to mine the data in order to identify the best ones yourself. Associate rule algorithms help with filtering this.

The most popular algorithm for MBA is the apriori algorithm, which is contained within the `arules` package (the other popular algorithm is the eclat algorithm).

Running apriori is fairly simple. We will demonstrate this using our demo 10 transaction itemset that we just printed.

The apriori algorithm is based upon the principle that if a particular itemset is frequent, then all of its subsets must also be frequent. That principle itself is helpful for reducing the number of itemsets that need to be evaluated, since it only needs to look at the largest items sets first, and then be able to filter down:

- First, some housekeeping. Fix the number of printable digits to 2:

  ```
  options(digits = 2)
  ```

- Next, run the apriori algorithm. However, only run it on rows 10 through 19 of the `Groceries` dataset since we will want to keep the output small for now. We will also adjust the `supp` =, and `conf` = parameters to produce enough output so that we can illustrate some points in the next sections:

```
rules <- apriori(Groceries[10:19], parameter = list(supp = 0.1,
conf = 0.6))
```

- The output shows that 2351 rules were created. This is a large number of rules relative to the 10 transactions we are inspecting. The large number of rules is due to the low support level that we specified (0.10). That yields transactions that only contain a single combination. This is also indicated by the warning message produced by the log:

```
> Apriori
>
> Parameter specification:
> confidence minval smax arem aval originalSupport support minlen
maxlen
>          0.6    0.1     1 none FALSE TRUE      0.1 1 10
> target ext
> rules FALSE
>
> Algorithmic control:
> filter tree heap memopt load sort verbose
>    0.1 TRUE TRUE   FALSE TRUE    2    TRUE
>
> Absolute minimum support count: 1
> Warning in apriori(Groceries[10:19], parameter =  list(supp = 0.1,
conf =
    0.6)): You chose a very low absolute support count of    1. You might
run out
    of memory! Increase minimum support.
> set item appearances ...[0 item(s)] done [0.00s].
> set transactions ...[22 item(s), 10 transaction(s)] done [0.00s].
> sorting and recoding items ... [22 item(s)] done [0.00s].
> creating transaction tree ... done [0.00s].
> checking subsets of size 1 2 3 4 5 6 7 8 9 done [0.00s].
> writing ... [2351 rule(s)] done [0.00s].
> creating S4 object ... done [0.00s].
```

- Sort the rules by support, which is one of the important evaluation metrics that measures how frequently different items occur together. This will be discussed further in the next section:

```
rules <- sort(rules, by = "support", decreasing = TRUE)  # 'high-
confidence' rules.
```

- Look at the first five rules using the `arules inspect` function. The output columns are designated: index number (blank header), lhs (left-hand side), rhs (right-hand side), support, confidence, and lift. Note that each support and confidence measure is at least equal to the parameter specified in the call to the `apriori` function specified previously:

```
inspect(head(rules, 5))
```

This is the following output:

```
      lhs                   rhs              support confidence lift
[1] {bottled water}   => {tropical fruit} 0.2       1.00      3.3
[2] {tropical fruit}  => {bottled water}  0.2       0.67      3.3
[3] {cereals}         => {whole milk}     0.1       1.00      5.0
[4] {chicken}         => {tropical fruit} 0.1       1.00      3.3
[5] {soda}            => {rolls/buns}     0.1       1.00      10.0
```

Antecedents and descendants

The rules shown previously are expressed as an implication between the antecedent (left-hand side) and the consequence (right-hand side).

The first rule, describes customers who buy a bottle of water also buying tropical fruit. The third rule states that customers who buy cereals have a tendency to buy whole milk.

Evaluating the accuracy of a rule

Three main metrics have been developed that measure the importance, or accuracy of an association rule: support, confidence, and lift.

Support

Support measures how frequently the items occur together. Imagine having a shopping cart in which there can be a very large number of combinations of items. Some items that occur rarely could be excluded from the analysis. When an item occurs frequently you will have more confidence in the association among the items, since it will be a more popular item. Often your analysis will be centered around items with high support.

Calculating support

Calculating support is simple. You first calculate a proportion by counting the number of times that the items in the rule appear in the basket divided by the total number of occurences in the itemsets:

Examples

- We can see that for the first rule (index #63), {bottled water} and {tropical fruit} appear together in the same transaction in two different transactions (2 and 3), therefore the support for that rule is 2/10 or 20%
- The last rule shown, rule (index #3) has a support of 0.10, since soda with rolls/buns only appears once in the 10 transactions (1/10)

Confidence

Confidence is the conditional probability that the event on the right-hand side (rhs or consequence) will occur, given the items on the left-hand has occurred (lhs or antecedent). This can be computed manually by counting the number of occurrences in the transactions.

For example, let's take a closer look at the following rule:

- {tropical fruit} => {bottled water}
- We can see that tropical fruit occurs in three separate transaction itemsets, itemset 2, 3, and 6 and therefore the denominator of the formula is 3
- Of those three itemsets, bottled water occurs in two of them (itemsets 2 and 3 only, but not 6), so the confidence is 2/3 or 67% and also note that the confidence for the reverse itemset {bottled water} => {tropical fruit} is higher, since every time bottled water is purchased, tropical fruit is purchased as well and you can easily verify that by inspecting and counting the elements by hand

Lift

Lift is determined by dividing the confidence just calculated by the independent probability of the consequent. Lift can be a better measure than either support or confidence, since it incorporates features of both.

To calculate the lift for the second rule (index #64), we only need to determine the unconditional probability of the consequence we just calculated. Since `{bottled water}` appears two out of 10 times (20%) as the consequence, we divide .67 by .20 to yield 3.4, which is the lift for rule 64.

Evaluating lift

The factors when dealing with the evaluation are as follows:

- When evaluating the lift metric, use 1 as a baseline lift measure, since a lift of 1 implies no relationship between the antecedent and the consequence.

- As the value of lift increases, it will help you target more interesting rules. If you are able to identify rules with a high confidence level that occur more than you expect, that could lead to enhanced revenue from developing customer incentives to purchase the same or similar products again.

Preparing the raw data file for analysis

Now that we have had a short introduction to the association rules algorithm, we will illustrate applying association rules to a more meaningful example.

We will be using the online retail dataset, which can be obtained from the UCI machine learning repository at:

`https://archive.ics.uci.edu/ml/datasets/Online+Retail.`

As described by the source, the data is:

"A transnational data set which contains all the transactions occurring between 01/12/2010 and 09/12/2011 for a UK-based and registered non-store online retail. The company mainly sells unique all-occasion gifts. Many customers of the company are wholesalers".

For more information about how the dataset was created, please refer to the original journal article (*Daqing Chen, 2012*).

Reading the transaction file

We will input the Groceries data using the read.csv() function.

We can use the file.show() function to directly examine the input file if needed. This is sometimes needed if you find that there are errors in the input. It has been commented out in the code, but you are encouraged to try it out yourself.

The knitr library will be used mostly for the purposes of display formatted text output via the kable function. If you wish, you can replace kable function calls with head or print functions:

```
rm(list = ls())
library(sqldf)
library(knitr)

setwd("C:/PracticalPredictiveAnalytics/Data")
```

Set stringsAsFactors to FALSE since we will be manipulating the variables as character strings later:

```
options(stringsAsFactors = F)
OnlineRetail <- read.csv("Online Retail.csv", strip.white = TRUE)
 #we are done reading, so set the output directory
setwd("C:/PracticalPredictiveAnalytics/Outputs")
```

capture.output function

This code also illustrates the capture.output() function. The capture.output function will save the metadata for the raw input file. This is done because we want to track changes done to the input, and we want to capture the contents of the same dataframe at different points in time. That will enable us to save the values of metadata and compare them at different points:

```
# Save it in case we need to look at the metadata later on.
OnlineRetail.Metadata <- capture.output(str(OnlineRetail))

# print it now.  We can see that the capture.output contains the output of
the original str function, and that there are 541,909 observations
```

```
> cat(OnlineRetail.Metadata, sep = "\n")
'data.frame':    541909 obs. of  8 variables:
 $ InvoiceNo  : chr  "536365" "536365" "536365" "536365" ...
 $ StockCode  : chr  "85123A" "71053" "84406B" "84029G" ...
 $ Description: chr  "WHITE HANGING HEART T-LIGHT HOLDER" "WHITE METAL LANTERN" "CREAM CUPID HEARTS COAT HANGER" "KNITTE... <truncated>
 $ Quantity   : int  6 6 8 6 6 2 6 6 6 32 ...
 $ InvoiceDate: chr  "12/1/2010 8:26" "12/1/2010 8:26" "12/1/2010 8:26" "12/1/2010 8:26" ...
 $ UnitPrice  : num  2.55 3.39 2.75 3.39 3.39 7.65 4.25 1.85 1.85 1.69 ...
 $ CustomerID : int  17850 17850 17850 17850 17850 17850 17850 17850 17850 13047 ...
 $ Country    : chr  "United Kingdom" "United Kingdom" "United Kingdom" "United Kingdom" ...
```

Set `stringsAsFactors` back to `TRUE`:

```
options(stringsAsFactors = T)
```

Analyzing the input file

After reading in the file, the `nrow()` function shows that the transaction file contains 541909 rows:

```
nrow(OnlineRetail)
```

This is the following output:

```
> [1] 541909
```

We can use our handy `View()` function to peruse the contents. Alternatively, you can use the `kable()` function from the `knitr` library to display a simple tabular display of the dataframe in the console, as indicated later.

Look at the first few records. The `kable()` function will attempt to fit a simple table in the space providing, and will also truncate any long strings:

```
kable(head(OnlineRetail))
```

We can still see the last column is truncated (United Kingdom), but all of the columns fit without wrapping to the next line:

```
|InvoiceNo |StockCode |Description                        | Quantity|InvoiceDate    | UnitPrice| CustomerID|Country       ... <truncated>
|:---------|:---------|:----------------------------------|--------:|:--------------|---------:|----------:|:-----------... <truncated>
|536365    |85123A    |WHITE HANGING HEART T-LIGHT HOLDER |        6|12/1/2010 8:26 |      2.5|      17850|United King... <truncated>
|536365    |71053     |WHITE METAL LANTERN                |        6|12/1/2010 8:26 |      3.4|      17850|United King... <truncated>
|536365    |84406B    |CREAM CUPID HEARTS COAT HANGER     |        8|12/1/2010 8:26 |      2.8|      17850|United King... <truncated>
|536365    |84029G    |KNITTED UNION FLAG HOT WATER BOTTLE|        6|12/1/2010 8:26 |      3.4|      17850|United King... <truncated>
|536365    |84029E    |RED WOOLLY HOTTIE WHITE HEART.     |        6|12/1/2010 8:26 |      3.4|      17850|United King... <truncated>
|536365    |22752     |SET 7 BABUSHKA NESTING BOXES       |        2|12/1/2010 8:26 |      7.6|      17850|United King... <truncated>
```

Using an R Notebook with the `kable()` function.

Note that when using the `Rmarkdown` package, or an R Notebook in RStudio, the output from the `kable()` function can be formatted to appear as an HTML table in the markdown file. Otherwise, it will appear as plain ASCII text.

For example, you may choose to run your code in RStudio using an R Notebook. IF you choose to run code in this manner follow these steps to try out the `kable()` command and see how the results are formatted as HTML.

From the RStudio menu open up a new R notebook, using the menu sequence `File/New File/R Notebook`.

A skeleton R notebook will appear, instead of an R script:

Code is organized in chunks. That means that all R code must appear between ...{r} and ... shaded lines. Inserting the following `kable()` function within this code chunk will output the identical data as before, however, it will be embedded in the R Notebook following the code that you have just written, and formatted as HTML.

Insert the following line into the first code chunk:

```
kable(head(OnlineRetail),format='html')
```

The `kable()` function output appears embedded in the R notebook code, just following the code chunk:

```
1  ---
2  title: "R Notebook"
3  output: html_notebook
4  ---
5
6  ```{r}
7  kable(head(OnlineRetail),format='html')
8  ```
```

	InvoiceNo	StockCode	Description	Quantity	InvoiceDate	UnitPrice	CustomerID	Country	itemcount	Desc2
5	536365	71053	METAL LANTERN	6	12/1/2010 8:26	3.4	17850	United Kingdom	7	MetalLantern
6	536365	21730	GLASS STAR FROSTED T-LIGHT HOLDER	6	12/1/2010 8:26	4.2	17850	United Kingdom	7	GlassStarFrost
2	536365	22752	SET 7 BABUSHKA NESTING BOXES	2	12/1/2010 8:26	7.6	17850	United Kingdom	7	Set7Babushka
4	536365	84029E	WOOLLY HOTTIE HEART.	6	12/1/2010 8:26	3.4	17850	United Kingdom	7	WoollyHottieH
			CREAM CUPID							

Analyzing the invoice dates

We can also look at the distribution plots of `InvoiceDate`. But first, the date will need to be transformed to date format (`Capture.output` shows it as a string) and sorted first:

```
InvoiceDate <- gsub(" .*$", "", OnlineRetail$InvoiceDate)
InvoiceDate <- (as.Date(InvoiceDate, format = "%m/%d/%Y"))
InvoiceDate <- sort(InvoiceDate, decreasing = FALSE)
```

First, observe from the output of the `str()` function that `InvoiceDate` is now truly in date format:

```
> str(InvoiceDate)
```

This is the following output:

```
Date[1:541909], format: "2010-12-01" "2010-12-01" "2010-12-01" "2010-12-01"
"2010-12-01" "2010-12-01" "2010-12-01" "201... <truncated>
```

We can see from the `head` and `tail` commands, as well as the plots, that the invoices encompass the period from 12/1/2011 through 12/9/2011. We can also see several spikes in orders around the December holiday season:

```
> head(as.data.frame(InvoiceDate))
```

This is the following output:

```
  InvoiceDate
1  2010-12-01
2  2010-12-01
3  2010-12-01
4  2010-12-01
5  2010-12-01
6  2010-12-01
```

Similarly, these are the last six records in the file. These records contain the most recent dates:

```
> tail(as.data.frame(InvoiceDate))
```

This is the resulting output:

```
         InvoiceDate
541904   2011-12-09
541905   2011-12-09
541906   2011-12-09
541907   2011-12-09
541908   2011-12-09
541909   2011-12-09
```

Plotting the dates

The individual dates and labels will be too dense to plot, so we will reduce the dates to Month/Year:

First, extract the year and month from the invoice date (first seven characters of YYYY-MM-DD), and then obtain the counts using the `table()` function. Then plot the results. You can see that the last month's transactions are lower than the previous month's since the data only goes through December 9th:

```
par(las = 2)
barplot(table(substr(InvoiceDate,1,7)), cex.lab = 1, cex.main = 1.5,
cex.names = 1,
col = c("blue"),main="Invoices by Year/Month")
```

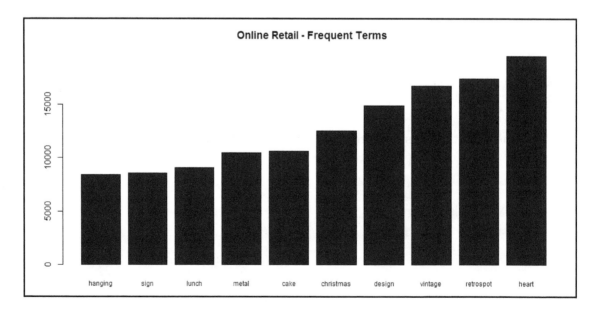

Scrubbing and cleaning the data

Here comes the cleaning part!

Print some of the groceries contained within the description field of `OnlineRetail`:

```
kable(OnlineRetail$Description[1:5],col.names=c("Grocery Item
Descriptions"))
|Grocery Item Descriptions               |
|:---------------------------------------|
|WHITE HANGING HEART T-LIGHT HOLDER      |
|METAL METAL LANTERN                     |
|CREAM CUPID HEARTS COAT HANGER          |
|KNITTED UNION FLAG HOT WATER BOTTLE     |
|RED WOOLLY HOTTIE WHITE HEART.          |
```

Although each line contains a separate grocery item, the items are in a uniform format, that is, the number of words describing each item can vary, and some words are adjectives and some are nouns. Additionally, the retailer may deem certain words to be irrelevant to a particular marketing campaign (such as colors, or sizes, which may be standard across all products). This type of data can be referred to as semi-structured data, since it incorporates certain definitions of structured data (the topic is only groceries, all capitalized, products that are pre-known, and so on), as well as some elements of unstructured data (varying lengths of products, variations in text strings). For optimal results, unstructured data such as text usually needs to be scrubbed and cleaned before it is in a form that is suitable for analysis. Fortunately, there are several R functions available that help you do that.

Removing unneeded character spaces

We can start by removing leading and trailing blanks from each of the product descriptions, since they add no value to the analysis and just take up extra space. trimws is a handy function to accomplish this, since it removes both leading and trailing spaces. The `nchar()` function will count the number of bytes in a character string, so we can run this function on `OnlineRetail$Description` before and after performing the string trim to see how much space we will actually be saving:

```
sum(nchar(OnlineRetail$Description))
```

This is the resulting output:

```
> [1] 14284888
```

Continue the following code:

```
OnlineRetail$Description <- trimws(OnlineRetail$Description)
sum(nchar(OnlineRetail$Description))
```

This is the resulting output:

```
> [1] 14283213
```

We see that `trimws` reduced the size of the Description. Had the number increased after using the function, that would be a clue to check your code!

Simplifying the descriptions

Market basket analysis using color choice analysis is an interesting topic in itself. However, for this analysis, we will remove some of the colors in order to simplify some of the descriptions. We will use the `gsub()` function to remove some of the specific colors that appear as part of the product description. Since the `gsub()` function only works on a single string or pattern at one time, set up a function to pass multiple strings to the `gsub()` function.

This `gsub_multiple` function will take a character vector (x), and change all strings supplied in `from` to their corresponding values in `to`. In our case, we want to eliminate them from the text, so our `to` strings will always be `""`:

```
gsub_multiple <- function(from, to, x) {
  updated <- x
  for (i in 1:length(from)) {
    updated <- gsub(from[i], to[i], updated)
  }
  return(updated)
}


OnlineRetail$Description <-
gsub_multiple(c("RED","PINK","GREEN","SMALL","MEDIUM","LARGE","JUMBO","STRA
WBERRY"), rep("",8), OnlineRetail$Description)
```

Removing colors automatically

If you did not want to bother specifying colors, and you wanted to remove colors automatically, you could accomplish that as well.

The colors() function

The `colors()` function returns a list of colors that are used in the current palette. We can then perform a little code manipulation in conjunction with the `gsub()` function that we just used to replace all of the specified colors from `OnlineRetail$Description` with blanks.

We will also use the `kable()` function, which is contained within the `knitr` package, in order to produce simple HTML tables of the results:

```
# compute the length of the field before changes
 before <- sum(nchar(OnlineRetail$Description))

 # get the unique colors returned from the colors function, and remove any
digits found at the end of the string

 # get the unique colors
 col2 <- unique(gsub("[0-9]+", "", colors(TRUE)))


 #Now we will filter out any colors with a length > 7. This number is
somewhat arbitrary but it is just done for illustration, and to reduce the
number of colors to some of the more 'popular' colors (RED, WHITE, GREEN,
BLACK etc.) We may miss a couple ("STRAWBERRY"), but we can put them back
later.


for (i in 1:length(col2)) {
    col2[i] <- ifelse(nchar(col2[i]) > 7, "", col2[i])
 }

 col2 <- unique(col2)
```

After running the code, double-check the output to ensure that the colors are the ones that you want:

```
cat("Unique Colors\n")
 > Unique Colors
 kable(head(data.frame(col2), 10))
```

This is the resulting output:

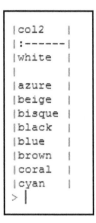

```
|col2    |
|:------|
|white   |
|        |
|azure   |
|beige   |
|bisque  |
|black   |
|blue    |
|brown   |
|coral   |
|cyan    |
> |
```

Cleaning up the colors

Clean up the colors a little more by capitalizing all of the colors and inserting a delimiter:

```
col <- topper(paste0(col2, collapse = "|"))
```

Now pass the results to gsub():

```
cat("Pass to gsub\n", head(col, 9))
> Pass to gsub
 >
WHITE||AZURE|BEIGE|BISQUE|BLACK|BLUE|BROWN|CORAL|CYAN|DARKRED|DIMGRAY|GOLD|
GRAY|GREEN|HOTPINK|IVORY|KHAKI|LINEN|MAGENTA|MAROON|NAVY|OLDLACE|ORANGE|ORC
HID|PERU|PINK|PLUM|PURPLE|RED|SALMON|SIENNA|SKYBLUE|SNOW|TAN|THISTLE|TOMATO
|VIOLET|WHEAT|YELLOW
```

For example, to replace the colors in the dataframe with blanks:

```
OnlineRetail$Description <- gsub(col, "", OnlineRetail$Description)
```

Check the length to see how much was removed. As before, print the character count before and after, to ensure that the Description is reduced in size:

```
after <- sum(nchar(OnlineRetail$Description))
 print(before)
> [1] 13682222
print(after)
> [1] 13341097
```

Verify that there are no more colors by inspection. We will look at the first five, although you will probably want to look at more, all from different parts of the dataset. We will leave "Cream" in for now, but we would remove that as well if we felt it would not help in the analysis:

```
kable(OnlineRetail$Description[1:5],col.names=c("Grocery Item
Description"))
```

The first five rows are shown here:

```
|Grocery Item Description                           |
|:--------------------------------------------------|
|WHITE HANGING HANGING HEART T-LIGHT HOLDER         |
|WHITE METAL LANTERN                                |
|CREAM CUPID HEARTS COAT HANGER                     |
|KNITTED UNION FLAG HOT WATER BOTTLE                |
|WOOLLY HOTTIE WHITE HEART.                         |
```

Filtering out single item transactions

Since we will want to have a basket of items to perform some association rules on, we will want to filter out the transactions that only have one item per invoice. That might be useful for a separate analysis of customers who only purchased one item, but it does not help with finding associations between multiple items, which is the goal of this exercise.

- Let's use `sqldf` to find all of the single item transactions, and then we will create a separate dataframe consisting of the number of items per customer invoice:

  ```
  library(sqldf)
  ```

- First construct a query: How many distinct invoices were there? We see that there were 25900 separate invoices:

  ```
  sqldf("select count(distinct InvoiceNo) from
  OnlineRetail")
  > Loading required package: tcltk
  >    count(distinct InvoiceNo)
  > 1                      25900
  ```

- How many invoices contain only single transactions? First, extract the single item invoices:

```
single.trans <- sqldf("select InvoiceNo, count(*) as itemcount from
OnlineRetail group by InvoiceNo having   count(*)==1")
```

- Next, add them up. This shows us that there are not a lot of single transaction items (5841):

```
sum(single.trans$itemcount)
  > [1]  5841
```

- SQL query: How many have multiple transactions? Instead of using count(*) == 1, use count(*) > 1 to obtain the multiple transactions. There are 536068 of them:

```
 x2 <- sqldf("select InvoiceNo, count(*) as itemcount from
OnlineRetail group by InvoiceNo having count(*) > 1")

sum(x2$itemcount)
  > [1] 536068
```

- Show a tabulation of the number of items per invoice, in x2, to verify that they all have at least two items:

```
kable(head(x2))
```

```
|InvoiceNo | itemcount|
|:---------|---------:|
|536365    |        7|
|536366    |        2|
|536367    |       12|
|536368    |        4|
|536370    |       20|
|536372    |        2|
```

Looking at the distributions

Now we can take a look at the distribution of the number of items. We can see by using the mean() function that there is an average of ~27 items. This will be a large enough assortment of items to do a meaningful analysis:

```
mean(x2$itemcount)
```

This is the following output:

```
> [1] 27
```

We can also plot a histogram:

```
hist(x2$itemcount, breaks = 500, xlim = c(0, 50))
```

The histogram shown next shows a definite spike at the low end. We know that the data cannon contains single invoices (count=1), since we have already filtered them out:

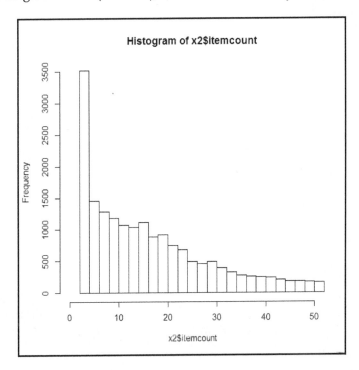

To verify this, we can inspect the itemcount frequencies via a table. Run the following `table()` command at the console:

```
head(table(x2$itemcount) add, 20)
```

We can verify that single item counts no longer appear:

```
> head(table(x2$itemcount),20)

   2    3    4    5    6    7    8    9   10   11   12   13   14   15   16   17   18   19   20   21
1612 1095  815  788  670  652  631  629  553  573  496  519  521  548  569  454  434  481  438  408
```

Merging the results back into the original data

We will want to retain the number of total items for each invoice on the original data frame. That will involve joining the number of items contained in each invoice back to the original transactions, using the `merge()` function, and specifying `Invoicenum` as the key.

If you count the number of distinct invoices before and after the merge, you can see that the invoice count is lower than prior to the merge:

```
#first take a 'before' snapshot

nrow(OnlineRetail)
> [1] 541909

#count the number of distinct invoices

sqldf("select count(distinct InvoiceNo) from OnlineRetail")
```

The output shows a total of 25900 distinct invoices:

```
>    count(distinct InvoiceNo)
> 1                    25900
```

Now merge the counts back with the original data:

```
OnlineRetail <- merge(OnlineRetail, x2, by = "InvoiceNo")
```

Check the new number of rows, and the new count of distinct invoices (20059 versus 25900). Note these counts compared to the original. The reduction is due to eliminating some of the members who only have one invoiced item:

```
> nrow(OnlineRetail)
[1] 536068
> sqldf("select count(distinct InvoiceNo) from OnlineRetail")
  count(distinct InvoiceNo)
1                    20059
```

Print the `OnlineRetail` table along with the merged itemcount:

```
kable(OnlineRetail[1:5,
1:9],col.names=c("Inv#","StockCode","Desc","Quant","InvDate","UnitPrice","C
ustID","Country","ItemCount"), padding = 0)
```

Itemcount appears as the last column in this table:

```
|Inv#   |StockCode|Desc                          |Quant|InvDate
|UnitPrice|CustID|Country        |
|:-----|:--------|:-----------------------------|----:|:-------------|-----
---:|-----:|:-------------|
|536365|84406B   |CREAM CUPID HEARTS COAT HANGER|    8|12/1/2010 8:26|
2.8| 17850|United Kingdom|        7|
|536365|22752    |SET 7 BABUSHKA NESTING BOXES  |    2|12/1/2010 8:26|
7.6| 17850|United Kingdom|        7|
|536365|85123A   |HANGING HEART T-LIGHT HOLDER  |    6|12/1/2010 8:26|
2.5| 17850|United Kingdom|        7|
|536365|84029E   |WOOLLY HOTTIE   HEART.        |    6|12/1/2010 8:26|
3.4| 17850|United Kingdom|        7|
|536365|71053    |METAL LANTERN                 |    6|12/1/2010 8:26|
3.4| 17850|United Kingdom|        7|
```

Compressing descriptions using camelcase

For long descriptions, sometimes it is beneficial to compress them into camelcase to improve readability. This is especially valuable when viewing descriptions that are labels on *x* or *y* axes.

Camelcase is a method that some programmers use for writing compound words, where spaces are first removed, and then each word begins with a capital letter. It is also a way of conserving space.

To accomplish this, we can write a function called .simpleCap, which performs this function. To illustrate how it works, we will pass it a two element character vector c("A certain good book","A very easy book"), and observe the results.

Custom function to map to camelcase

This is a simple example use of this function that maps the two character vector c("A certain good book", "A very easy book") to camelcase. This vector is mapped to two new elements:

```
[1] "ACertainGoodBook", and  [2] "AVeryEasyBook"

# change descriptions to camelcase maybe append to itemnumber for
uniqueness
.simpleCap <- function(x) {
    # s <- strsplit(x, ' ')[[1]]
```

```
    s <- strsplit(tolower(x), " ")[[1]]

    aa <- paste(toupper(substring(s, 1, 1)), substring(s, 2), sep = "",
collapse = " ")
    gsub(" ", "", aa, fixed = TRUE)

}


a  <- c("A certain good book", "A very easy book")
a4 <- gsub(" ", "", .simpleCap(a), fixed = TRUE)
a4
> [1] "ACertainGoodBook"
lapply(a, .simpleCap)
> [[1]]
> [1] "ACertainGoodBook"
>
> [[2]]
> [1] "AVeryEasyBook"
```

Let's use the `.simpleCap` function to create a new version of description from our `OnlineRetail` dataset, and call it `Desc2`, which removes the blanks and capitalizes the first letter of each word:

```
OnlineRetail$Desc2 <- lapply(as.character(OnlineRetail$Description),
.simpleCap)

kable(OnlineRetail[1:5, c(3, 10)], padding = 0)
```

```
|Description                     |Desc2                         |
|:-------------------------------|:-----------------------------|
|CREAM CUPID HEARTS COAT HANGER  |CreamCupidHeartsCoatHanger    |
|SET 7 BABUSHKA NESTING BOXES    |Set7BabushkaNestingBoxes      |
|WHITE HANGING HEART T-LIGHT HOLDER|WhiteHangingHeartT-lightHolder|
|WOOLLY HOTTIE WHITE HEART.      |WoollyHottieWhiteHeart.       |
|WHITE METAL LANTERN             |WhiteMetalLantern             |
> |
```

Extracting the last word

Often the first and last word of product descriptions contain useful information, and sometimes you can use a single word or phrase in place of the original longer description. This may not always be the case, but it is worth trying. In order to extract the last word from the descriptions, we can use the word function from the `stringr` package:

```
library(stringr)
OnlineRetail$lastword <- word(OnlineRetail$Description, -1)    #supply -1 to
extract the last word
OnlineRetail$Description <- trimws(OnlineRetail$Description, "l")
OnlineRetail$firstword <- word(OnlineRetail$Description, 1)
# use head(OnlineRetail) if you are no using Rmarkdown

kable(OnlineRetail[1:5, c(3, 10:12)], padding = 0)
```

Firstword appears as the last column in the following output:

```
|Description                       |Desc2                            |lastword|firstword|
|:---------------------------------|:--------------------------------|:-------|:--------|
|CREAM CUPID HEARTS COAT HANGER    |CreamCupidHeartsCoatHanger       |HANGER  |CREAM    |
|SET 7 BABUSHKA NESTING BOXES      |Set7BabushkaNestingBoxes         |BOXES   |SET      |
|WHITE HANGING HEART T-LIGHT HOLDER|WhiteHangingHeartT-lightHolder   |HOLDER  |WHITE    |
|WOOLLY HOTTIE WHITE HEART.        |WoollyHottieWhiteHeart.          |HEART.  |WOOLLY   |
|WHITE METAL LANTERN               |WhiteMetalLantern                |LANTERN |WHITE    |
> |
```

In order to see if this `lastword` mapping makes any sense, we will sort the results so that we can see the most frequently occurring ending words. We could ultimately use this information to create category subproducts, such as cases, bags, signs, and so on:

```
kable(head(as.data.frame(sort(table(OnlineRetail$lastword[]), decreasing =
TRUE)),
    10))
```

The sorted results appear. Note that this is formatted as a table, although the default output from the `kable()` function will appear as plain text in the console.

The `lastword` description looks useable (other than the large count of NAs), but we will still retain the columns as part of the analytics dataset:

```
|Var1       |   Freq|
|:----------|-----:|
|DESIGN     |  25557|
|           |  24321|
|HOLDER     |  13528|
|RETROSPOT  |  13013|
|BOX        |  12939|
|SIGN       |  12210|
|CASES      |  10888|
|BAG        |   9723|
|SET        |   9056|
|CHRISTMAS  |   7868|
> |
```

Creating the test and training datasets

Now that we are finished with our transformations, we will create the training and test data frames. We will perform a 50/50 split between training and test:

```
# Take a sample of full vector
nrow(OnlineRetail)
> [1] 536068
pctx <- round(0.5 * nrow(OnlineRetail))
set.seed(1)

# randomize rows

df <- OnlineRetail[sample(nrow(OnlineRetail)), ]
rows <- nrow(df)
OnlineRetail <- df[1:pctx, ]   #training set
OnlineRetail.test <- df[(pctx + 1):rows, ]   #test set
rm(df)

# Display the number of rows in the training and test datasets.

nrow(OnlineRetail)
> [1] 268034
nrow(OnlineRetail.test)
> [1] 268034
```

Saving the results

It is a good idea to periodically save your data frames, so that you can pick up your analysis from various checkpoints.

In this example, I will first sort them both by `InvoiceNo`, and then save the test and train data sets to disk, where I can always load them back into memory as needed:

```
setwd("C:/PracticalPredictiveAnalytics/Data")
 OnlineRetail <- OnlineRetail[order(OnlineRetail$InvoiceNo), ]
 OnlineRetail.test <- OnlineRetail.test[order(OnlineRetail.test$InvoiceNo),
]

save(OnlineRetail,file='OnlineRetail.full.Rda')
save(OnlineRetail.test,file='OnlineRetail.test.Rda')

load('OnlineRetail.full.Rda') load('OnlineRetail.test.Rda')

 nrow(OnlineRetail)
> [1] 268034
nrow(OnlineRetail.test)
> [1] 268034
nrow(OnlineRetail)
> [1] 268034
```

At this point, we have prepared our analytics data sets and are ready to move on to the actual analysis.

If you wish, you can save the entire workspace to disk as follows:

```
save.image(file = "ch6 part 1.Rdata")
```

Loading the analytics file

If you are still in a session in which `OnlineRetail` is still in memory, you are OK! However, if you are picking up where we left off, you will need to load the data that we saved in the last session. Start by setting the working directory and then loading the `OnlineRetail` training dataset:

```
rm(list = ls())
setwd("C:/PracticalPredictiveAnalytics/Data")
load("OnlineRetail.full.Rda")
# works for small data
OnlineRetail <- OnlineRetail[1:10000,]
```

```
cat(nrow(OnlineRetail), "rows loaded\n")
> 10000 rows loaded
```

The `cat` function in the previous step should reflect the number of rows in the training data set, which is `268034`.

Determining the consequent rules

We have seen in the data prep stage that there are a large number of itemsets generated for each invoice. To begin to demonstrate the algorithm, we will extract one representative word from each product description, and use that word as the consequent (or rhs) to build some association rules. We have already saved the first and last words from each product description. We would examine those words more closely and see if we can filter them to result in a manageable set of transactions.

Let's first preview the frequency of the first and last word of the descriptions in descending order. That should give us a clue as to what the popular products are:

```
library(arules)
> Loading required package: Matrix
>
> Attaching package: 'arules'
> The following objects are masked from 'package:base':
>
>     abbreviate, write
  library(arulesViz)
> Loading required package: grid
```

Print the popular first words of the description. We will do that by sorting the frequency of first words in descending order:

```
kable(head(as.data.frame(sort(table(OnlineRetail$firstword[]), decreasing =
TRUE)), 10))
```

	sort(table(OnlineRetail$firstword[]), decreasing = TRUE)
SET	17381
BAG	8720
LUNCH	7692
RETROSPOT	7155
PACK	6861

VINTAGE	6204
HEART	4799
HANGING	4457
DOORMAT	4175
REGENCY	3452

Similarly, print the popular last words of the description:

```
kable(head(as.data.frame(sort(table(OnlineRetail$lastword[]), decreasing =
TRUE)),
      10))
```

	sort(table(OnlineRetail$lastword[]), decreasing = TRUE)
	18376
DESIGN	12713
HOLDER	6792
BOX	6528
RETROSPOT	6517
SIGN	6184
CASES	5465
BAG	4826
SET	4418
CHRISTMAS	3963

Looking at the popular terms shows that many transactions concern the purchases of boxes, cases, signs, bags, and so on.

Replacing missing values

We see from the frequencies of `lastword` that there are some blank values. The `lastword` seems to contain mostly nouns, and `firstword` seems to be a mix of adjectives and nouns as well (bag, heart). If we treat the text strings as a *Bag of Words*, we can rationalize combining the two into one token. However, we will give `lastword` priority, and populate it with the value of `firstword` only if it is missing:

```
# replace blank values in lastword, with first word.

OnlineRetail$lastword <- ifelse(OnlineRetail$lastword == "",
OnlineRetail$firstword,
OnlineRetail$lastword)
```

After we are done with this, we will take another look at the frequencies and observe that the blank values have disappeared:

```
head(as.data.frame(sort(table(OnlineRetail$lastword[]), decreasing =
TRUE)),
     10)
>              sort(table(OnlineRetail$lastword[]), decreasing = TRUE)
 > DESIGN                                                        12713
 > HOLDER                                                         6792
 > RETROSPOT                                                      6574
 > BOX                                                            6528
 > SIGN                                                           6184
 > BAG                                                            5761
 > CASES                                                          5465
 > SET                                                            4418
 > HEART                                                          4027
 > CHRISTMAS                                                      4005
```

Making the final subset

Based upon these frequencies, we will filter the data to only include a subset of the top categories. We will exclude some of the terms that do not apply to the physical product, such as design, set, and any associated colors:

```
# Testing OnlineRetail2 <- OnlineRetail
 OnlineRetail2 <- subset(OnlineRetail, lastword %in% c("BAG", "CASES",
"HOLDER",
     "BOX", "SIGN", "CHRISTMAS", "BOTTLE", "BUNTING", "MUG", "BOWL",
"CANDLES",
     "COVER", "HEART", "MUG", "BOWL"))
```

Run the `table()` function again on the results to see the new frequencies:

```
head(as.data.frame(sort(table(OnlineRetail2$lastword[]), decreasing =
TRUE)),
  10)
> sort(table(OnlineRetail2$lastword[]), decreasing = TRUE)
> HOLDER 6792
> BOX 6528
> SIGN 6184
> BAG 5761
> CASES 5465
> HEART 4027
> CHRISTMAS 4005
> BOTTLE 3795
> BUNTING 3066
> MUG 2900
```

Use the `nrow()` function to see how much of the data was filtered from the original:

```
cat(nrow(OnlineRetail), "Original before subsetting\n")
> 268034 Original before subsetting
cat(nrow(OnlineRetail2), "After Subsetting\n")
> 55609 After Subsetting
```

Creating the market basket transaction file

We are almost there! There is an extra step that we need to do in order to prepare our data for market basket analysis.

The association rules package requires that the data be in transaction format. Transactions can either be specified in two different formats:

1. One transaction per itemset with an identifier and this shows the entire basket in one line, just as we saw with the `Groceries` data.
2. One single item per line with an identifier.

Additionally, you can create the actual transaction file in two different ways, by either:

1. Physically writing a transactions file.
2. Coercing a dataframe to transaction format.

For smaller amounts of data, coercing the dataframe to a transaction file is simpler, but for large transaction files, writing the transaction file first is preferable, since append files can be fed from large operational transaction systems. We will illustrate both ways.

Method one – Coercing a dataframe to a transaction file

Now we are ready to coerce the dataframe. We will create a temporary data frame containing just the transaction ID (InvoiceNo), and the descriptor (lastword).

First, we will verify the column names and numbers for these two variables. We can see that they correspond to columns 1 and 12 of the dataframe by first running a colnames function on OnlineRetail2:

```
colnames(OnlineRetail2)
>   [1] "InvoiceNo"   "StockCode"   "Description" "Quantity"
"InvoiceDate"
>   [6] "UnitPrice"   "CustomerID"  "Country"     "itemcount"   "Desc2"
> [11] "lastword"    "firstword"
```

As a double-check, display the first 25 rows, specifying the indices found previously:

```
kable(head(OnlineRetail2[, c(1, 11)], 5))
```

```
|    |InvoiceNo |lastword |
|:--|:---------|:--------|
|6  |536365    |HOLDER   |
|45 |536370    |BOX      |
|39 |536370    |BOX      |
|57 |536373    |HOLDER   |
|59 |536373    |BOTTLE   |
> |
```

First, create the dataframe with only two columns, named TransactionID and Items:

```
tmp <- data.frame(OnlineRetail2[, 1], OnlineRetail2[, 11])
names(tmp)[1] <- "TransactionID"
names(tmp)[2] <- "Items"

tmp <- unique(tmp)
nrow(tmp)
> [1] 33182
```

Verify the results:

```
kable(head(tmp))
```

This is the following output:

```
|    |TransactionID |Items  |
|:--|:-------------|:------|
|1  |536365        |HOLDER |
|2  |536370        |BOX    |
|4  |536373        |HOLDER |
|5  |536373        |BOTTLE |
|7  |536373        |MUG    |
|9  |536375        |HOLDER |
> |
```

We will now use the `split()` function to group the descriptions (`lastword`, which is column 2), by `InvoiceID` (column 1). The `as()` function is the critical keyword, as it converts the results of the split to transaction form:

```
trans4 <- as(split(tmp[, 2], tmp[, 1]), "transactions")
```

Inspecting the transaction file

Once the data has been coerced to transaction form, we can use the inspect function to examine the data.

 When inspecting transaction files, you do not use normal print, or head functions directly, since the objects are in sparse format. You use an `inspect()` function instead.

If you happen to have the `tm` package loaded (which we will use later), you must preface inspect with `arules::inspect`, since there is also an inspect function in the `tm` package that serves a different purpose.

If you run an inspect command on the first five records, you can see that the data is in basket format, that is, each invoice shows the itemsets, delimited by { }, that are associated with each invoice:

```
arules::inspect(trans4[1:5])
>    items                     transactionID
> 1 {HOLDER}                  536365
> 2 {BOX}                     536370
> 3 {BOTTLE,HOLDER,MUG}       536373
> 4 {BOTTLE,HOLDER}           536375
> 5 {HOLDER}                  536376
```

Another way of displaying transactions, other than using inspect, is to first coerce it to a matrix and then display the items as Boolean values. If you have many items, you will need to subset the column vectors so that they fit on the screen:

```
as(trans4, "matrix")[1:5, 1:5]
>             BAG BOTTLE  BOWL    BOX BUNTING
> 536365 FALSE  FALSE FALSE FALSE    FALSE
> 536370 FALSE  FALSE FALSE  TRUE    FALSE
> 536373 FALSE   TRUE FALSE FALSE    FALSE
> 536375 FALSE   TRUE FALSE FALSE    FALSE
> 536376 FALSE  FALSE FALSE FALSE    FALSE
as(trans4, "matrix")[1:5, 6:ncol(trans4)]
>          CANDLES CASES CHRISTMAS COVER HEART HOLDER   MUG  SIGN
> 536365    FALSE FALSE     FALSE FALSE FALSE   TRUE FALSE FALSE
> 536370    FALSE FALSE     FALSE FALSE FALSE  FALSE FALSE FALSE
> 536373    FALSE FALSE     FALSE FALSE FALSE   TRUE  TRUE FALSE
> 536375    FALSE FALSE     FALSE FALSE FALSE   TRUE FALSE FALSE
> 536376    FALSE FALSE     FALSE FALSE FALSE   TRUE FALSE FALSE
```

Obtaining the topN purchased items

Even before we run any association rules we can obtain counts of the topN items, as shown in the first plot.

If we are looking for items with a specified support level, we can include that as a parameter to the function as well.

The second plot is another way of plotting the items, which specifies support as a filter, and it indicates higher support for bags, boxes, cases, and holders:

```
par(mfrow = c(1, 2), bg = "white", col = c("blue"))

 itemFrequencyPlot(trans4, topN = 10, type = "absolute", cex.names = 0.7)
 itemFrequencyPlot(trans4, support = 0.2, cex.names = 0.75)
```

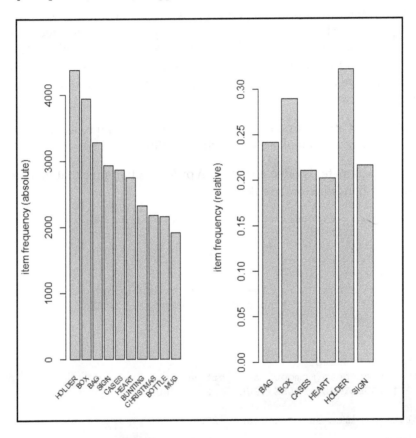

Reset the graphics parameters. The output will show null device, indicating that it has been reset:

```
dev.off()
> null device
>            1
```

Finding the association rules

As shown earlier, the association rules are run using the `apriori()` function. The `apriori()` function has several filtering parameters that are used to control the number of rules that are produced. In our example, we will specify the minimum support and confidence threshold that a rule needs to pass in order to be considered.

The number that you pass to apriori depends upon how you want to look at the rules. It can be an initial screening, or it can be a deeper dive, after you have performed several passes. But generally, if we want many rules we can decrease the `support` and `confidence` parameters. If we want to focus on items that appear frequently, we raise the support threshold. If we want to concentrate on higher quality and more accurate rules, we would raise the confidence level.

These numbers are not absolutes. They are numbers that you can tweak in order to limit the number of rules that you will look at, versus their quality.

The `minlen = 2` parameter is often specified in order to guarantee that there are itemsets included in the left-hand side of the rule:

```
rulesx <- apriori(trans4, parameter = list(minlen = 2, support = 0.02,
confidence = 0.01))
> Apriori
>
> Parameter specification:
>  confidence minval smax arem  aval originalSupport support minlen maxlen
>        0.01    0.1    1 none FALSE           TRUE    0.02      2     10
> target   ext
>  rules FALSE
>
> Algorithmic control:
>  filter tree heap memopt load sort verbose
>     0.1 TRUE TRUE  FALSE TRUE    2    TRUE
>
> Absolute minimum support count: 272
>
> set item appearances ...[0 item(s)] done [0.00s].
> set transactions ...[13 item(s), 13617 transaction(s)] done [0.00s].
> sorting and recoding items ... [13 item(s)] done [0.00s].
> creating transaction tree ... done [0.00s].
> checking subsets of size 1 2 3 4 5 done [0.00s].
> writing ... [829 rule(s)] done [0.00s].
> creating S4 object  ... done [0.00s].
```

The output from the apriori algorithm will tell us how many rules were generated. If you also perform a `str()` function on `rulesx`, that will show you all of the sublists that are contained within the `rulesx` object, which can get complex. Ordinarily the output is sufficient for analyzing the rules, but these sublists can be used programmatically to print the number of rules generated if you vary the paramaters in a loop. For our example, printing the second column of one of the sublists (`rulesx@lhs@data@Dim`[2]) shows that here 829 rules have been generated. This is a manageable number of rules to look at:

```
str(rulesx)
> Formal class 'rules' [package "arules"] with 4 slots
  >   ..@ lhs    :Formal class 'itemMatrix' [package "arules"] with 3 slots
  >   .. .. ..@ data        :Formal class 'ngCMatrix' [package "Matrix"] with
5 slots
  >   .. .. .. .. ..@ i       : int [1:1752] 8 5 8 7 8 11 8 2 8 4 ...
  >   .. .. .. .. ..@ p       : int [1:830] 0 1 2 3 4 5 6 7 8 9 ...
  >   .. .. .. .. ..@ Dim     : int [1:2] 13 829
  >   .. .. .. .. ..@ Dimnames:List of 2
  >   .. .. .. .. .. ..$ : NULL
  >   .. .. .. .. .. ..$ : NULL
  >   .. .. .. .. ..@ factors : list()
  >   .. .. ..@ itemInfo   :'data.frame': 13 obs. of  1 variable:
  >   .. .. .. ..$ labels: chr [1:13] "BAG" "BOTTLE" "BOWL" "BOX" ...
  >   .. .. ..@ itemsetInfo:'data.frame': 0 obs. of  0 variables
  >   ..@ rhs    :Formal class 'itemMatrix' [package "arules"] with 3 slots
  >   .. .. ..@ data        :Formal class 'ngCMatrix' [package "Matrix"] with
5 slots
  >   .. .. .. .. ..@ i       : int [1:829] 5 8 7 8 11 8 2 8 4 8 ...
  >   .. .. .. .. ..@ p       : int [1:830] 0 1 2 3 4 5 6 7 8 9 ...
  >   .. .. .. .. ..@ Dim     : int [1:2] 13 829
  >   .. .. .. .. ..@ Dimnames:List of 2
  >   .. .. .. .. .. ..$ : NULL
  >   .. .. .. .. .. ..$ : NULL
  >   .. .. .. .. ..@ factors : list()
  >   .. .. ..@ itemInfo   :'data.frame': 13 obs. of  1 variable:
  >   .. .. .. ..$ labels: chr [1:13] "BAG" "BOTTLE" "BOWL" "BOX" ...
  >   .. .. ..@ itemsetInfo:'data.frame': 0 obs. of  0 variables
  >   ..@ quality:'data.frame':   829 obs. of  3 variables:
  >   .. ..$ support   : num [1:829] 0.0239 0.0239 0.0206 0.0206 0.0245 ...
  >   .. ..$ confidence: num [1:829] 0.278 0.21 0.24 0.129 0.285 ...
  >   .. ..$ lift      : num [1:829] 2.43 2.43 1.5 1.5 2.03 ...
  >   ..@ info   :List of 4
  >   .. ..$ data          : symbol trans4
  >   .. ..$ ntransactions: int 13617
  >   .. ..$ support      : num 0.02
  >   .. ..$ confidence   : num 0.01
rulesx@lhs@data@Dim[2]
> [1] 829
```

Examining the rules summary

The rule length distribution indicates the number of itemsets that appear in both the left and right side of the association. The most frequent number of item is 3, which either means that the purchase of two items together, implies purchasing a single item, or conversely, purchasing a single item implies purchasing two additional items.

Examining the rules quality and observing the highest support

The quality measures tell you something about the distribution of support, confidence, and lift. The quality function will give the support, lift, and confidence for each of the rules. You can also sort the rules by each of these important measures and observe which rules have the highest measures.

We can see from the low support distribution that there are no particular itemsets that occur more than others. If you inspect the rules sorted by the support level, you will see the highest support level at 0.046. Notice that this agrees with the Max. support level given in the summary. The top three support levels are for those customers who purchase holders, boxes, or signs:

```
summary(rulesx)
> set of 829 rules
>
> rule length distribution (lhs + rhs):sizes
>   2   3   4   5
> 156 438 220  15
>
>    Min. 1st Qu.  Median   Mean 3rd Qu.    Max.
>   2.000   3.000   3.000  3.113   4.000   5.000
>
> summary of quality measures:
>     support             confidence            lift
>  Min.   :0.02005   Min.   :0.1293   Min.   :1.000
>  1st Qu.:0.02210   1st Qu.:0.3672   1st Qu.:1.948
>  Median :0.02512   Median :0.5110   Median :2.393
>  Mean   :0.02987   Mean   :0.5068   Mean   :2.444
>  3rd Qu.:0.03202   3rd Qu.:0.6533   3rd Qu.:2.899
>  Max.   :0.09885   Max.   :0.8571   Max.   :5.419
>
> mining info:
>    data ntransactions support confidence
>  trans4          13617    0.02       0.01
head(quality(rulesx))   #also look at the quality measures for each of the
```

```
rules
>       support confidence      lift
> 1 0.02394066  0.2779199 2.432156
> 2 0.02394066  0.2095116 2.432156
> 3 0.02063597  0.2395567 1.500480
> 4 0.02063597  0.1292548 1.500480
> 5 0.02452816  0.2847400 2.026819
> 6 0.02452816  0.1745949 2.026819

tmp <- as.data.frame(inspect(head(sort(rulesx, by = "support"), 10)))
>       lhs          rhs       support    confidence lift
> 155 {BOX}    => {HOLDER} 0.09884703 0.3417111   1.063075
> 156 {HOLDER} => {BOX}    0.09884703 0.3075166   1.063075
> 135 {HEART}  => {HOLDER} 0.09620328 0.4768839   1.483602
> 136 {HOLDER} => {HEART}  0.09620328 0.2992918   1.483602
> 151 {BAG}    => {BOX}    0.09304546 0.3859275   1.334139
> 152 {BOX}    => {BAG}    0.09304546 0.3216552   1.334139
> 149 {SIGN}   => {HOLDER} 0.09069545 0.4203540   1.307736
> 150 {HOLDER} => {SIGN}   0.09069545 0.2821567   1.307736
> 141 {CASES}  => {BOX}    0.08511420 0.4048201   1.399451
> 142 {BOX}    => {CASES}  0.08511420 0.2942371   1.399451
```

Confidence and lift measures

Similar to previously, sort the rules and examine the highest confidence and lift measures:

```
tmp <- as.data.frame(arules::inspect(head(sort(rulesx, by = "confidence"),
10)))
>       lhs                        rhs       support    confidence lift
> 815 {BAG,BOWL,BOX,SIGN}     => {HOLDER} 0.02070941 0.8571429   2.666601
> 631 {BAG,BOTTLE,BOWL}       => {BOX}    0.02181097 0.8510029   2.941890
> 643 {BOWL,HEART,SIGN}       => {HOLDER} 0.02151722 0.8492754   2.642125
> 820 {BAG,BOX,HEART,SIGN}    => {HOLDER} 0.02137035 0.8434783   2.624090
> 632 {BOTTLE,BOWL,BOX}       => {BAG}    0.02181097 0.8413598   3.489734
> 816 {BAG,BOWL,HOLDER,SIGN}  => {BOX}    0.02070941 0.8392857   2.901385
> 817 {BOWL,BOX,HOLDER,SIGN}  => {BAG}    0.02070941 0.8392857   3.481131
> 707 {BOTTLE,HEART,SIGN}     => {HOLDER} 0.02144378 0.8366762   2.602929
> 651 {BAG,BOWL,HEART}        => {HOLDER} 0.02115003 0.8347826   2.597038
> 719 {BOTTLE,CASES,SIGN}     => {BAG}    0.02063597 0.8289086   3.438089

tmp <- as.data.frame(arules::inspect(head(sort(rulesx, by = "lift"), 10)))
>       lhs                        rhs       support    confidence lift
> 602 {BAG,HOLDER,SIGN}       => {COVER} 0.02012191 0.4667802   5.418710
> 598 {BAG,BOX,SIGN}          => {COVER} 0.02019534 0.4661017   5.410833
> 819 {BAG,BOX,HOLDER,SIGN}   => {BOWL}  0.02070941 0.6698337   5.254105
> 610 {BAG,BOX,HOLDER}        => {COVER} 0.02070941 0.4483307   5.204534
> 606 {BOX,HOLDER,SIGN}       => {COVER} 0.02004847 0.4333333   5.030435
```

```
> 634 {BAG,BOTTLE,BOX}        => {BOWL}  0.02181097 0.6279070  4.925236
> 638 {BAG,HEART,SIGN}        => {BOWL}  0.02034222 0.6141907  4.817647
> 662 {BAG,CASES,SIGN}        => {BOWL}  0.02144378 0.6134454  4.811801
> 159 {BAG,BOWL}              => {COVER} 0.02092972 0.4025424  4.672992
> 670 {CASES,HOLDER,SIGN}     => {BOWL}  0.02078284 0.5811088  4.558156
```

Filtering a large number of rules

Once we have the rules built, we can use special subsetting functions to filter items from itemsets on either the left (lhs) or right (rhs) side of the association rule. This is valuable if you are looking for particular items within the itemsets.

Use the %in% operator to perform an exact match, or %pin% to perform a partial match:

```
# to see what 'Christmas' purchases imply.

lhs.rules <- subset(rulesx, subset = lhs %pin% "CHRISTMAS")
lhs.rules
> set of 44 rules
inspect(lhs.rules)
>      lhs                      rhs        support    confidence lift
> 4    {CHRISTMAS}           => {COVER}    0.02063597 0.1292548  1.500480
> 26   {CHRISTMAS}           => {CANDLES}  0.02702504 0.1692732  1.481358
> 47   {CHRISTMAS}           => {MUG}      0.02379379 0.1490340  1.060845
> 49   {CHRISTMAS}           => {BOWL}     0.02680473 0.1678933  1.316937
> 51   {CHRISTMAS}           => {BUNTING}  0.03018286 0.1890524  1.108191
> 53   {CHRISTMAS}           => {BOTTLE}   0.04553132 0.2851886  1.797876
> 55   {CHRISTMAS}           => {HEART}    0.03708600 0.2322907  1.151475
> 57   {CHRISTMAS}           => {CASES}    0.04751414 0.2976081  1.415484
> 59   {CHRISTMAS}           => {SIGN}     0.03547037 0.2221711  1.029715
> 61   {CHRISTMAS}           => {BAG}      0.04663289 0.2920883  1.211504
> 63   {CHRISTMAS}           => {BOX}      0.05500477 0.3445262  1.191016
> 65   {CHRISTMAS}           => {HOLDER}   0.05133289 0.3215271  1.000282
> 253  {BOTTLE,CHRISTMAS}    => {CASES}    0.02210472 0.4854839  2.309058
> 254  {CASES,CHRISTMAS}     => {BOTTLE}   0.02210472 0.4652241  2.932850
> 256  {BOTTLE,CHRISTMAS}    => {BAG}      0.02283910 0.5016129  2.080555
> 257  {BAG,CHRISTMAS}       => {BOTTLE}   0.02283910 0.4897638  3.087552
> 259  {BOTTLE,CHRISTMAS}    => {BOX}      0.02489535 0.5467742  1.890181
> 260  {BOX,CHRISTMAS}       => {BOTTLE}   0.02489535 0.4526035  2.853288
> 262  {BOTTLE,CHRISTMAS}    => {HOLDER}   0.02504223 0.5500000  1.711069
> 263  {CHRISTMAS,HOLDER}    => {BOTTLE}   0.02504223 0.4878398  3.075423
> 265  {CHRISTMAS,HEART}     => {BAG}      0.02004847 0.5405941  2.242239
> 266  {BAG,CHRISTMAS}       => {HEART}    0.02004847 0.4299213  2.131139
> 268  {CHRISTMAS,HEART}     => {BOX}      0.02203128 0.5940594  2.053645
> 269  {BOX,CHRISTMAS}       => {HEART}    0.02203128 0.4005340  1.985465
> 271  {CHRISTMAS,HEART}     => {HOLDER}   0.02247191 0.6059406  1.885102
> 272  {CHRISTMAS,HOLDER}    => {HEART}    0.02247191 0.4377682  2.170036
```

```
> 274 {CASES,CHRISTMAS}   => {BAG}      0.02291254 0.4822257  2.000142
> 275 {BAG,CHRISTMAS}     => {CASES}    0.02291254 0.4913386  2.336904
> 277 {CASES,CHRISTMAS}   => {BOX}      0.02548285 0.5363215  1.854047
> 278 {BOX,CHRISTMAS}     => {CASES}    0.02548285 0.4632844  2.203473
> 280 {CASES,CHRISTMAS}   => {HOLDER}   0.02283910 0.4806801  1.495412
> 281 {CHRISTMAS,HOLDER}  => {CASES}    0.02283910 0.4449213  2.116135
> 283 {CHRISTMAS,SIGN}    => {BAG}      0.02137035 0.6024845  2.498943
> 284 {BAG,CHRISTMAS}     => {SIGN}     0.02137035 0.4582677  2.123973
> 286 {CHRISTMAS,SIGN}    => {BOX}      0.02342660 0.6604555  2.283174
> 287 {BOX,CHRISTMAS}     => {SIGN}     0.02342660 0.4259012  1.973961
> 289 {CHRISTMAS,SIGN}    => {HOLDER}   0.02276566 0.6418219  1.996731
> 290 {CHRISTMAS,HOLDER}  => {SIGN}     0.02276566 0.4434907  2.055484
> 292 {BAG,CHRISTMAS}     => {BOX}      0.02687817 0.5763780  1.992521
> 293 {BOX,CHRISTMAS}     => {BAG}      0.02687817 0.4886515  2.026795
> 295 {BAG,CHRISTMAS}     => {HOLDER}   0.02460160 0.5275591  1.641255
> 296 {CHRISTMAS,HOLDER}  => {BAG}      0.02460160 0.4792561  1.987825
> 298 {BOX,CHRISTMAS}     => {HOLDER}   0.02812661 0.5113485  1.590823
> 299 {CHRISTMAS,HOLDER}  => {BOX}      0.02812661 0.5479256  1.894162
# what purchases yielded Candles?

 rhs.rules <- subset(rulesx, subset = rhs %pin% c("CANDLES"))
 rhs.rules
> set of 26 rules
tmp <- as.data.frame(arules::inspect(head(sort(rhs.rules, by = "support"),
10)))
>     lhs               rhs       support    confidence lift
 > 46  {HOLDER}      => {CANDLES} 0.04920320 0.1530729  1.339584
 > 44  {BOX}         => {CANDLES} 0.04714695 0.1629855  1.426333
 > 38  {CASES}       => {CANDLES} 0.03958287 0.1882641  1.647552
 > 42  {BAG}         => {CANDLES} 0.03789381 0.1571733  1.375469
 > 36  {HEART}       => {CANDLES} 0.03473599 0.1721878  1.506865
 > 40  {SIGN}        => {CANDLES} 0.03429537 0.1589517  1.391031
 > 34  {BOTTLE}      => {CANDLES} 0.02908130 0.1833333  1.604402
 > 30  {BOWL}        => {CANDLES} 0.02805317 0.2200461  1.925686
 > 252 {BOX,HOLDER}  => {CANDLES} 0.02768598 0.2800892  2.451140
 > 32  {BUNTING}     => {CANDLES} 0.02739223 0.1605682  1.405178

inspect(head(sort(rhs.rules, by = "confidence")))
>     lhs                rhs       support    confidence lift
 > 219 {BAG,HEART}      => {CANDLES} 0.02056253 0.3517588  3.078342
 > 213 {BOWL,BOX}       => {CANDLES} 0.02019534 0.3467844  3.034809
 > 216 {BOTTLE,HOLDER}  => {CANDLES} 0.02026878 0.3183391  2.785876
 > 222 {BOX,HEART}      => {CANDLES} 0.02247191 0.3122449  2.732544
 > 237 {BAG,SIGN}       => {CANDLES} 0.02232503 0.3111566  2.723020
 > 234 {CASES,HOLDER}   => {CANDLES} 0.02232503 0.3095723  2.709156
```

The `plot()` function in the `arules` package is also very flexible. You can look at various scatterplots across the various metrics, or even count and group a small number of rules and show the metrics as bubbles:

```
plot(rhs.rules, method = "scatterplot")
```

Here is the scatter plot for 26 rules, with each individual point color coded according to the lift for that rule:

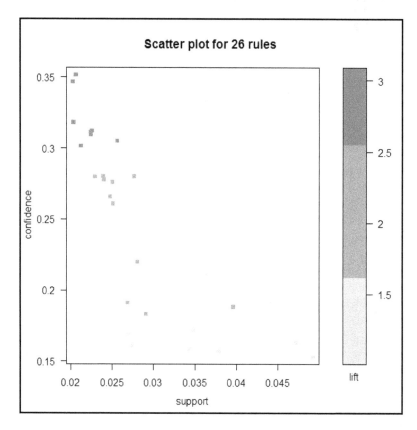

```
set.seed(1)
high_lift <- subset(rules,lift >= 1)
plot(high_lift, method = "grouped",control=list(col=grey.colors(10),
gp_labels=gpar(col='black',cex=1)))
```

Grouped matrix for 2351 rules

Generating many rules

If you wish to generate as many rules as possible, set support and confidence to a very low number:

```
many_rules <- apriori(trans4, parameter = list(minlen = 1, support = 0.01,
confidence = 0.01)) > Apriori
>
> Parameter specification:
> confidence minval smax arem aval originalSupport support minlen maxlen
> 0.01 0.1 1 none FALSE TRUE 0.01 1 10
> target ext
> rules FALSE
>
> Algorithmic control:
> filter tree heap memopt load sort verbose
> 0.1 TRUE TRUE FALSE TRUE 2 TRUE
>
> Absolute minimum support count: 136
>
> set item appearances ...[0 item(s)] done [0.00s].
> set transactions ...[13 item(s), 13617 transaction(s)] done [0.00s].
> sorting and recoding items ... [13 item(s)] done [0.00s].
> creating transaction tree ... done [0.00s].
> checking subsets of size 1 2 3 4 5 6 7 8 done [0.00s].
```

```
> writing ... [8898 rule(s)] done [0.00s].
> creating S4 object ... done [0.00s]. many_rules > set of 8898 rules
```

Plotting many rules

Plots are especially helpful for scenarios in which there are many rules generated, and you need to filter on specific support and confidence ranges.

Here is a plot that shows two of the three metrics, along the *x* and *y* axis, and the third metric (`lift`, `support`, or `confidence`) as shading:

```
sel <- plot(many_rules, measure = c("support", "confidence"), shading =
"lift",
  interactive = FALSE)
```

As the following plot suggests, there is a cluster of rules with high lift (>8), high confidence (> 0.6), but all with low support:

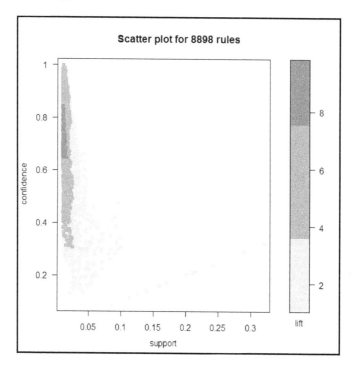

Method two – Creating a physical transactions file

Now that you know how to run association rules using the `coerce to dataframe` method, we will now illustrate the `write to file` method:

- In the `write to file` method, each item is written to a separate line, along with the identifying key, which in our case is the `InvoiceId`

- The advantage to the `write to file` method is that very large data files can be accumulated separately, and then combined together if needed

- You can use the `file.show` function to display the contents of the file that will be input to the association rules algorithm:

```
setwd("C:/PracticalPredictiveAnalytics/Data")
load("OnlineRetail.full.Rda")
OnlineRetail <- OnlineRetail[1:100,]
nrow(OnlineRetail)
> [1] 268034
head(OnlineRetail)
> InvoiceNo StockCode  Description                   Quantity
  > 5   6365      71053  METAL LANTERN                      6
  > 6   536365    21730  GLASS STAR FROSTED T-LIGHT HOLDER 6
  > 2   536365    22752  SET 7 BABUSHKA NESTING BOXES       2
  > 4   536365    84029E WOOLLY HOTTIE HEART.               6
  > 1   536365    84406B CREAM CUPID HEARTS COAT HANGER     8
  > 8   536366    22632  HAND WARMER POLKA DOT              6
  > InvoiceDate UnitPrice CustomerID Country itemcount
  > 5 12/1/2010 8:26 3.39 17850 United Kingdom 7
  > 6 12/1/2010 8:26 4.25 17850 United Kingdom 7
  > 2 12/1/2010 8:26 7.65 17850 United Kingdom 7
  > 4 12/1/2010 8:26 3.39 17850 United Kingdom 7
  > 1 12/1/2010 8:26 2.75 17850 United Kingdom 7
  > 8 12/1/2010 8:28 1.85 17850 United Kingdom 2
  > Desc2 lastword firstword
  > 5 MetalLantern LANTERN METAL
  > 6 GlassStarFrostedT-lightHolder HOLDER GLASS
  > 2 Set7BabushkaNestingBoxes BOXES SET
  > 4 WoollyHottieHeart. HEART. WOOLLY
  > 1 CreamCupidHeartsCoatHanger HANGER CREAM
  > 8 HandWarmerPolkaDot DOT HAND # concatenate the Invoice Number to the
Description separated by a delimiter
  data2 <- paste(OnlineRetail$InvoiceNo, OnlineRetail$Desc2, sep = "!")
```

```
# eliminate duplicates
data2 <- unique(data2)
#

write(data2, file = "demo_single")
file.show('demo_single') #not run
```

Reading the transaction file back in

Use the `read.transaction` file to read the delimited file back into memory formatted as a transaction file. This will have the same results as coercing the dataframe to a transaction file, which we did earlier.

The difference is that the transactions are formatted one transaction per line, as specified by the `format='single'` option. We also specify where the `TransactionID` and item descriptions are via the `cols` option. It is possible to have multiple descriptors and transaction IDs, and identify them with the cols options. The `sep` keyword designates the delimiter, which in this case is the `!` character. There is also a remove duplicate transactions option, which is a logical value that determines whether or not you want to eliminate duplicates.

The returned object, `trans`, is an `itemMatrix`. You can type `trans` to see the dimension, or run the `dim(trans)` to see the dimensions. This will tell you how many transactions the `itemMatrix` is based upon.

As before, to view the items in the `trans` object, use the `inspect()` function:

```
library(arules)
 library(arulesViz)
 setwd("C:/Users/randy/Desktop/ch6")

file.show('demo_single')
 trans <- read.transactions("demo_single", format = "single", sep = "!",
cols = c(1,
 2), rm.duplicates = FALSE, quote = "")
 trans > transactions in sparse format with
 > 19403 transactions (rows) and
 > 3462 items (columns) dim(trans) > [1] 19403 3462 inspect(trans[1:5]) >
items transactionID
 > 1 {CreamCupidHeartsCoatHanger,
 > GlassStarFrostedT-lightHolder,
 > MetalLantern,
 > Set7BabushkaNestingBoxes,
 > WoollyHottieHeart.} 536365
```

```
>  2 {HandWarmerPolkaDot} 536366
>  3 {FeltcraftPrincessCharlotteDoll,
>  KnittedMugCosy,
>  LoveBuildingBlockWord,
>  Poppy'sPlayhouseKitchen} 536367
>  4 {CoatRackParisFashion} 536368
>  5 {CircusParadeLunchBox,
>  LunchBoxILoveLondon,
>  MiniJigsawSpaceboy,
>  PandaAndBunniesStickerSheet,
>  Postage,
>  RoundSnackBoxesSetOf4Woodland,
>  SpaceboyLunchBox,
>  ToadstoolLedNightLight} 536370 dim(trans) > [1] 19403 3462
# look up any item in labels to see if it is there.
```

Take a look at some of the frequently purchased items. Use the `itemFrequencePlot()` function to see a simple bar chart of the top item purchases:

```
itemFrequencyPlot(trans, topN = 10, cex.names = 1)
```

The following chart shows two heart items among the top purchases:

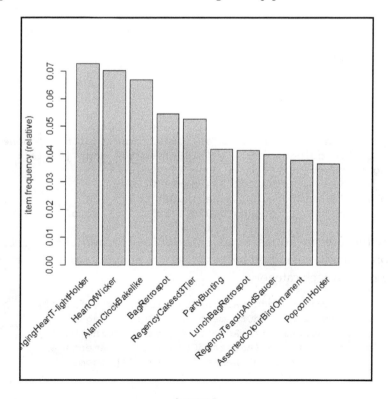

The `itemLabels()` function lists all of the labels associated with the itemset. Since the top ranked item has an unusual abbreviation in it (T-light), you could check to see if there are other items that have that term in it. To accomplish this, use the `grep()` function:

```
result <- grep("T-light", itemLabels(trans), value = TRUE)
str(result)
> chr [1:96] "6ChocolateLoveHeartT-lights" ... head(result)
> [1] "6ChocolateLoveHeartT-lights" "AgedGlassSilverT-lightHolder"
> [3] "AntiqueSilverT-lightGlass" "AssortedColourT-lightHolder"
> [5] "BeadedChandelierT-lightHolder" "BonneJamJarT-lightHolder"
```

Apply the rules engine again. We will use a small `support` and `confidence` level to generate many rules:

```
rules1 <- apriori(trans, parameter = list(minlen = 1, support = 0.001,
confidence = 0.001))
> Apriori
>
> Parameter specification:
> confidence minval smax arem aval originalSupport support minlen maxlen
> 0.001 0.1 1 none FALSE TRUE 0.001 1 10
> target ext
> rules FALSE
>
> Algorithmic control:
> filter tree heap memopt load sort verbose
> 0.1 TRUE TRUE FALSE TRUE 2 TRUE
>
> Absolute minimum support count: 19
>
> set item appearances ...[0 item(s)] done [0.00s].
> set transactions ...[3462 item(s), 19403 transaction(s)] done [0.03s].
> sorting and recoding items ... [2209 item(s)] done [0.01s].
> creating transaction tree ... done [0.01s].
> checking subsets of size 1 2 3 4 done [0.20s].
> writing ... [63121 rule(s)] done [0.02s].
> creating S4 object ... done [0.02s]. rules1 > set of 63121 rules
```

Sort the rules by the three measures: `support`, `confidence`, and `lift` to get an idea of some of the more valuable rules. Sort by `confidence`, `support`, and `lift` to look at the highest scoring rules in each category:

```
tmp <- as.data.frame(inspect(tail(sort(rules1, by = "lift")))) > lhs rhs
> 38860 {AssortedColourBirdOrnament} => {StorageBagSuki}
> 38861 {StorageBagSuki} => {AssortedColourBirdOrnament}
> 38893 {BagRetrospot} => {AssortedColourBirdOrnament}
> 38892 {AssortedColourBirdOrnament} => {BagRetrospot}
```

```
> 11539 {AlarmClockBakelike} => {RexCash+carryShopper}
> 11538 {RexCash+carryShopper} => {AlarmClockBakelike}
> support confidence lift
> 38860 0.001030768 0.02724796 0.8976097
> 38861 0.001030768 0.03395586 0.8976097
> 38893 0.001700768 0.03122044 0.8252999
> 38892 0.001700768 0.04495913 0.8252999
> 11539 0.001082307 0.01621622 0.7183636
> 11538 0.001082307 0.04794521 0.7183636 tmp <-
as.data.frame(inspect(head(sort(rules1, by = "support")))) > lhs rhs
support confidence lift
> 2207 {} => {HangingHeartT-lightHolder} 0.07256610 0.07256610 1
> 2208 {} => {HeartOfWicker} 0.07004072 0.07004072 1
> 2209 {} => {AlarmClockBakelike} 0.06674226 0.06674226 1
> 2205 {} => {BagRetrospot} 0.05447611 0.05447611 1
> 2201 {} => {RegencyCakesd3Tier} 0.05251765 0.05251765 1
> 2190 {} => {PartyBunting} 0.04184920 0.04184920 1 tmp <-
as.data.frame(inspect(head(sort(rules1, by = "confidence")))) > lhs rhs
support confidence lift
> 1 {PolkadotCup,
> RetrospotCharlotteBag,
> SpotCeramicDrawerKnob} => {AlarmClockBakelike} 0.001082307 1.0000000
14.98301
> 2 {AlarmClockBakelike,
> Charlie+lolaHotWaterBottle,
> ChristmasGinghamTree} => {BabushkaNotebook} 0.001185384 0.9200000
48.24530
> 3 {ChristmasHangingStarWithBell,
> RegencyTeacupAndSaucer} => {AlarmClockBakelike} 0.001133845 0.9166667
13.73443
> 4 {PolkadotBowl,
> RetrospotCharlotteBag,
> SpotCeramicDrawerKnob} => {AlarmClockBakelike} 0.001133845 0.9166667
13.73443
> 5 {AlarmClockBakelikeChocolate,
> PolkadotCup} => {AlarmClockBakelike} 0.001030768 0.9090909 13.62092
> 6 {BabushkaNotebook,
> Charlie+lolaHotWaterBottle,
> HeartMeasuringSpoons} => {AlarmClockBakelike} 0.001339999 0.8965517
13.43304
```

You can also coerce the rules to a dataframe and use the `kable()` function to print the first 10 rows, or subset as you choose:

```
rules1 <- sort(rules1, by = "confidence")
rules1.df <- as(rules1, "data.frame")
cat("using kable to print rules")
> using kable to print rules library(knitr)
```

```
kable(rules1.df[1:10,],digits=6,col.names=c("Rules","Supp","Conf","Lift"),a
lign=c("l","l","l","l"))
```

	Rules	Supp	Conf	Lift
62966	{PolkadotCup,RetrospotCharlotteBag,SpotCeramicDrawerKnob} => {AlarmClockBakelike}	0.0011	1.00	15
62971	{AlarmClockBakelike,Charlie+lolaHotWaterBottle,ChristmasGinghamTree} => {BabushkaNotebook}	0.0012	0.92	48
51467	{ChristmasHangingStarwithBell,RegencyTeacupAndSaucer} => {AlarmClockBakelike}	0.0011	0.92	14
62982	{PolkadotBowl,RetrospotCharlotteBag,SpotCeramicDrawerKnob} => {AlarmClockBakelike}	0.0011	0.92	14
51338	{AlarmClockBakelikeChocolate,PolkadotCup} => {AlarmClockBakelike}	0.0010	0.91	14
63058	{BabushkaNotebook,Charlie+lolaHotWaterBottle,HeartMeasuringSpoons} => {AlarmClockBakelike}	0.0013	0.90	13
62970	{BabushkaNotebook,Charlie+lolaHotWaterBottle,ChristmasGinghamTree} => {AlarmClockBakelike}	0.0012	0.88	13
62972	{AlarmClockBakelike,BabushkaNotebook,ChristmasGinghamTree} => {Charlie+lolaHotWaterBottle}	0.0012	0.88	77
51347	{AlarmClockBakelikeChocolate,DinerWallClock} => {AlarmClockBakelike}	0.0011	0.88	13
51356	{AlarmClockBakelikeChocolate,BoxOf24CocktailParasols} => {AlarmClockBakelike}	0.0011	0.88	13

`>`

Plotting the rules

The default plot of the rules will give you a scatterplot of all of the rules showing support
on the *x* axis and confidence on the *y* axis. We can see from the density that confidence can
vary from high to low with most of the density occurring at the 0.5 level. Support tends to
be low, and the highest support level attains ~0.07:

```
plot(rules1)
```

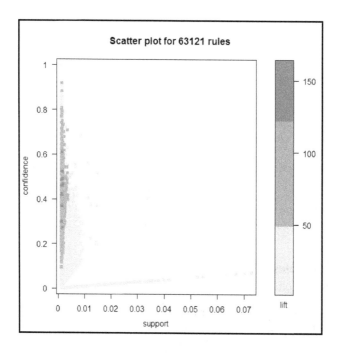

Creating subsets of the rules

As we did before, we can look at some of the subsets by parsing the left or right side.

For example, we might be interested in seeing what items yielded purchasing chocolate things:

- Subset the rules set using the `%pin%` operator (partial match), and look for any transactions where chocolate appears in the right-hand side:

```
purchased.this <- "Chocolate"

lhs.rules <- subset(rules1, subset = rhs %pin%
purchased.this)
```

- Printing `lhs.rules` shows that there are 487 of them:

```
print(lhs.rules) > set of 487 rules
```

- Sort them by lift, inspect them, and plot the first 15 as a graph:

```
lhs.rules <- sort(lhs.rules, by = "lift")

inspect(head(sort(lhs.rules, by = "lift"))) > lhs rhs support confidence
lift
 > 1 {CakeTowelSpots} => {CakeTowelChocolateSpots} 0.001185384 0.2911392
89.66626
 > 2 {BiscuitsBowlLight,
 > DollyMixDesignBowl} => {ChocolatesBowl} 0.001030768 0.4444444 68.98844
 > 3 {BakingMouldHeartChocolate} => {BakingMouldHeartMilkChocolate}
0.001030768 0.2941176 57.64409
 > 4 {BakingMouldHeartMilkChocolate} => {BakingMouldHeartChocolate}
0.001030768 0.2020202 57.64409
 > 5 {BiscuitsBowlLight} => {ChocolatesBowl} 0.001700768 0.3586957 55.67817
 > 6 {MarshmallowsBowl} => {ChocolatesBowl} 0.002422306 0.2397959 37.22208
```

- The directional graph is a good way to illustrate which purchases influence other purchases once you have narrowed down the number of itemset to a small number:

```
plot(lhs.rules[1:15], method = "graph", control = list(type =
"items", cex = 0.5))
```

- The following plot shows that `DollyMixDesignBowl` and `MarshmallowsBowl` appear as larger and darker bubbles, indicating that they are better predictors for chocolate purchase relative to `support`, `confidence`, and `lift`:

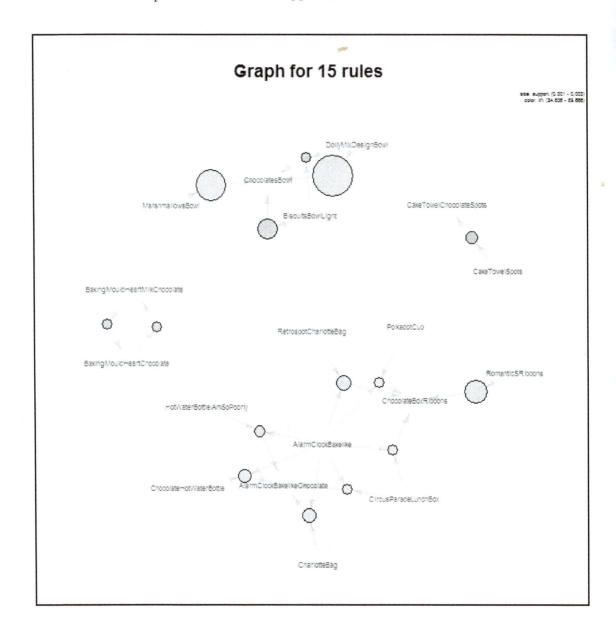

- Finally, if you wish to save your workspace, use the `save.image` command:

```
save.image(file = "ch6 part 2.Rdata")
```

Text clustering

In the previous sections, we used the `lastword` technique for categorizing types of purchases by simple keywords. We could also use more sophisticated techniques such as word clustering to try to identify which types of purchasing clusters occur and then use that to subset the association rules. To illustrate text clustering on our `OnlineRetail` dataset, we will first need to load our training and test dataframes that we previously saved. Also, issue a set.seed command since we will be doing some sampling later on:

```
setwd("C:/Users/randy/Desktop/ch6")
# load the training data
load("OnlineRetail.full.Rda") set.seed(1)
```

We previously demonstrated some text mining examples using a package called `RTextTools`. Another popular text mining package is tm. The tm package has been around for a long time, and it will be useful to know how this package works. Tm requires that all text data be converted to a corpus first. That can be done using the `VCorpus()` function. We can use vector input, since we already have the data available in an existing data frame, and there is no need to read in additional external data:

```
library(tm)
> Loading required package: NLP attach(OnlineRetail)
nrow(OnlineRetail)
> [1] 268034 corp <- VCorpus(VectorSource(OnlineRetail$Description))
```

Displaying the `corp` object shows you some information about the metadata:

```
head(corp) > <<VCorpus>>
> Metadata: corpus specific: 0, document level (indexed): 0
> Content: documents: 6
```

Converting to a document term matrix

Once we have a corpus, we can proceed to convert it to a document term matrix. When building DTM, care must be given to limiting the amount of data and resulting terms that are processed. If not parameterized correctly, it can take a very long time to run. Parameterization is accomplished via the options. We will remove any stopwords, punctuation, and numbers. Additionally, we will only include a minimum word length of four:

```
library(tm)
 dtm <- DocumentTermMatrix(corp, control = list(removePunctuation = TRUE,
wordLengths = c(4,
 999), stopwords = TRUE, removeNumbers = TRUE, stemming = FALSE, bounds =
list(global = c(5,
 Inf))))
```

We can begin to look at the data by using the `inspect()` function.

This is different from the `inspect()` function in an `arules` package, and if you have the `arules` package loaded, you will want to preface this inspect with `tm::inspect`:

```
inspect(dtm[1:10, 1:10]) > <<DocumentTermMatrix (documents: 10, terms:
10)>>
> Non-/sparse entries: 0/100
> Sparsity : 100%
> Maximal term length: 8
> Weighting : term frequency (tf)
>
> Terms
> Docs abstract acapulco account acrylic address adult advent afghan aged
> 1 0 0 0 0 0 0 0 0 0
> 2 0 0 0 0 0 0 0 0 0
> 3 0 0 0 0 0 0 0 0 0
> 4 0 0 0 0 0 0 0 0 0
> 5 0 0 0 0 0 0 0 0 0
> 6 0 0 0 0 0 0 0 0 0
> 7 0 0 0 0 0 0 0 0 0
> 8 0 0 0 0 0 0 0 0 0
> 9 0 0 0 0 0 0 0 0 0
> 10 0 0 0 0 0 0 0 0 0
> Terms
> Docs ahoy
> 1 0
> 2 0
> 3 0
> 4 0
> 5 0
```

```
> 6 0
> 7 0
> 8 0
> 9 0
> 10 0
```

After the DTM has been created, we can look at the metadata that has been produced by issuing a `print(dtm)` command. We can see the number of documents and terms by looking at the first line:

```
print(dtm) > <<DocumentTermMatrix (documents: 268034, terms: 1675)>>
> Non-/sparse entries: 826898/448130052
> Sparsity : 100%
> Maximal term length: 20
> Weighting : term frequency (tf)
```

Removing sparse terms

Most TDMs are initially filled with a lot of empty space. That is because every word in a corpus is indexed, and there are many words that occur so infrequently that they do not matter analytically. Removing sparse terms is a method in which we can reduce the number of terms to a manageable size, and also save space at the same time.

The `removeSparseTerms()` function will reduce the number of terms in the description from 268034 to 62:

```
dtms <- removeSparseTerms(dtm, 0.99)
dim(dtms) > [1] 268034 62
```

As an alternative to inspect, we can also `View()` it in matrix form:

```
View(as.matrix(dtms))
```

Here is the output from the `View` command. A 1 indicates that the term occurs, and 0 indicates it did not occur:

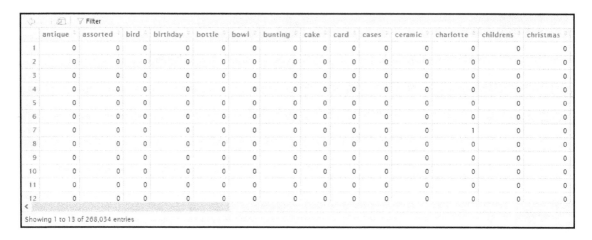

	antique	assorted	bird	birthday	bottle	bowl	bunting	cake	card	cases	ceramic	charlotte	childrens	christmas
1	0	0	0	0	0	0	0	0	0	0	0	0	0	0
2	0	0	0	0	0	0	0	0	0	0	0	0	0	0
3	0	0	0	0	0	0	0	0	0	0	0	0	0	0
4	0	0	0	0	0	0	0	0	0	0	0	0	0	0
5	0	0	0	0	0	0	0	0	0	0	0	0	0	0
6	0	0	0	0	0	0	0	0	0	0	0	0	0	0
7	0	0	0	0	0	0	0	0	0	0	0	1	0	0
8	0	0	0	0	0	0	0	0	0	0	0	0	0	0
9	0	0	0	0	0	0	0	0	0	0	0	0	0	0
10	0	0	0	0	0	0	0	0	0	0	0	0	0	0
11	0	0	0	0	0	0	0	0	0	0	0	0	0	0
12	0	0	0	0	0	0	0	0	0	0	0	0	0	0

Showing 1 to 13 of 268,034 entries

Finding frequent terms

The `tm` package has a useful function called `findFreqTerms`, which is useful to find the frequency of the popular terms used. The second argument to the function restricts the results to terms that have a minimum frequency specified. We can also compute the occurrences by summing up the 1s and 0s for each term in the TDM. Then we can sort the list and display the highest and lowest frequency occurrences:

```
data.frame(findFreqTerms(dtms, 10000, Inf)) >
findFreqTerms.dtms..10000..Inf.
 > 1 cake
 > 2 christmas
 > 3 design
 > 4 heart
 > 5 metal
 > 6 retrospot
 > 7 vintage freq <- colSums(as.matrix(dtms))
 # there are xx terms
 length(freq) > [1] 62 ord <- order(freq)
 # look at the top and bottom number of terms
 freq[head(ord, 12)] > union skull zinc bird wood wall birthday
 > 2752 2770 2837 2974 2993 3042 3069
 > colour charlotte star antique silver
 > 3089 3114 3121 3155 3175 freq[tail(ord, 10)] > hanging sign lunch metal
cake christmas design
 > 8437 8580 9107 10478 10623 12534 14884
```

```
> vintage retrospot heart
> 16755 17445 19520
```

For presentation purposes, a barplot is also useful for displaying the relative frequencies:

```
barplot(freq[tail(ord, 10)], cex.names = 0.75, col = c("blue"))
```

The most popular term is heart:

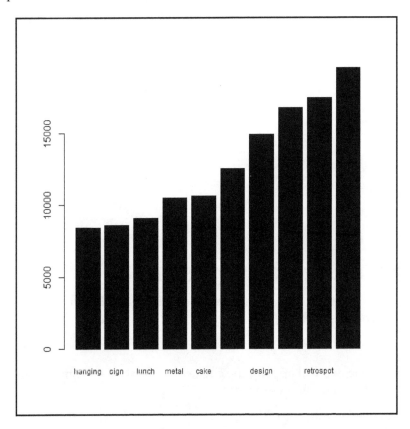

We could also do a little code manipulation to only display the topN most frequent terms:

```
dtmx <- dtms[, names(tail(sort(colSums(as.matrix(dtms))), 12))]
inspect(dtmx[1:10, ]) > <<DocumentTermMatrix (documents: 10, terms: 12)>>
> Non-/sparse entries: 3/117
> Sparsity : 98%
> Maximal term length: 9
> Weighting : term frequency (tf)
>
> Terms
```

```
> Docs pack holder hanging sign lunch metal cake christmas design vintage
> 1 0 0 0 0 0 1 0 0 0 0
> 2 0 1 0 0 0 0 0 0 0 0
> 3 0 0 0 0 0 0 0 0 0 0
> 4 0 0 0 0 0 0 0 0 0 0
> 5 0 0 0 0 0 0 0 0 0 0
> 6 0 0 0 0 0 0 0 0 0 0
> 7 0 0 0 0 0 0 0 0 0 0
> 8 0 0 0 0 0 0 0 0 0 0
> 9 0 0 0 0 0 0 0 0 0 0
> 10 0 0 0 0 0 0 0 0 0 0
> Terms
> Docs retrospot heart
> 1 0 0
> 2 0 0
> 3 0 0
> 4 0 1
> 5 0 0
> 6 0 0
> 7 0 0
> 8 0 0
> 9 0 0
> 10 0 0
```

K-means clustering of terms

Now we can cluster the term document matrix using k-means. For illustration purposes, we will specify that five clusters be generated:

```
kmeans5 <- kmeans(dtms, 5)
```

Once k-means is done, we will append the cluster number to the original data, and then create five subsets based upon the cluster:

```
kw_with_cluster <- as.data.frame(cbind(OnlineRetail, Cluster =
kmeans5$cluster))

# subset the five clusters
cluster1 <- subset(kw_with_cluster, subset = Cluster == 1)
cluster2 <- subset(kw_with_cluster, subset = Cluster == 2)
cluster3 <- subset(kw_with_cluster, subset = Cluster == 3)
cluster4 <- subset(kw_with_cluster, subset = Cluster == 4)
cluster5 <- subset(kw_with_cluster, subset = Cluster == 5)
```

Examining cluster 1

Print out a sample of the data:

```
> head(cluster1[10:13])
 Desc2 lastword firstword Cluster
  50 VintageBillboardLove/hateMug MUG VINTAGE 1
  86 BagVintagePaisley PAISLEY BAG 1
 113 ShopperVintagePaisley PAISLEY SHOPPER 1
 145 ShopperVintagePaisley PAISLEY SHOPPER 1
 200 VintageHeadsAndTailsCardGame GAME VINTAGE 1
 210 PaperChainKitVintageChristmas CHRISTMAS PAPER 1
```

Table the frequencies and print out the most popular terms in the clusters. Observe that many of these items have to do with christmas and paisley items, which seem to occur together:

```
tail(sort(table(cluster1$lastword)), 10) MUG GAME BUNTING CARDS DESIGN LEAF
 427 431 456 482 535 717 911
 DOILY PAISLEY CHRISTMAS
 1073 1699 1844
```

Examining cluster 2

After tabling cluster 2, look at a portion of the file. When looking at both the first and last words together, it seems like this cluster has something to do with hanging holders:

```
> head(cluster2[10:13]) Desc2 lastword firstword Cluster 6
GlassStarFrostedT-lightHolder HOLDER GLASS 2 57 HangingHeartT-lightHolder
HOLDER HANGING 2 62 GlassStarFrostedT-lightHolder HOLDER GLASS 2 70
HangingHeartT-lightHolder HOLDER HANGING 2 81 HangingHeartT-lightHolder
HOLDER HANGING 2 156 ColourGlassT-lightHolderHanging HANGING COLOUR 2
```

Rather than looking just at records, look at the frequencies of the most popular words. Heart, hanging, and folder are the three most frequently occurring words in cluster 2:

```
tail(sort(table(cluster2$lastword)), 10)
```

ANTIQUE	LANTERN	HLDR	DECORATION	GLASS	T-LIGHT	HANGING	HEART	HOLDER	
167	181	226	260	319	361	531	639	668	6792

Examining cluster 3

Cluster 3 may have to do with customers purchasing sets of different signs. Set, sign, box, and design are the four most common words:

```
head(cluster3[10:13]) Desc2 lastword firstword Cluster 5 MetalLantern
LANTERN METAL 3 2 Set7BabushkaNestingBoxes BOXES SET 3 4 WoollyHottieHeart.
HEART. WOOLLY 3 1 CreamCupidHeartsCoatHanger HANGER CREAM 3 8
HandWarmerPolkaDot DOT HAND 3 10 FeltcraftPrincessCharlotteDoll DOLL
FELTCRAFT 3
> tail(sort(table(cluster3$lastword)),10)
CANDLES POLKADOT BUNTING BAG DECORATION SET SIGN BOX DESIGN
2307 2539 2610 3084 3156 3844 6184 6277 10975 16627
```

Examining cluster 4

Cluster 4 could be looked at as customers who purchased retrospot products:

```
> head(cluster4[10:13]) Desc2 lastword firstword Cluster 100
LunchBoxWithCutleryRetrospot RETROSPOT LUNCH 4 102
PackOf72RetrospotCakeCases CASES PACK 4 84 60TeatimeFairyCakeCases CASES 60
4 94 3PieceRetrospotCutlerySet SET 3 4 91 LunchBagRetrospot RETROSPOT LUNCH
4 127 RetrospotMilkJug JUG RETROSPOT 4
tail(sort(table(cluster4$lastword)), 10) APRON NAPKINS BANK PC TINS DESIGN
 486 511 512 514 531 664 1203
 BAG CASES RETROSPOT
 1395 4318 6485
```

Examining cluster 5

Finally, cluster 5 seems to be concerned with the purchases of Bottles, possibly having to do with perfumes, elixirs, and tonics:

```
head(cluster5)

> head(cluster5[10:13])
                              Desc2 lastword firstword Cluster
59   KnittedUnionFlagHotWaterBottle    BOTTLE    KNITTED       5
68   KnittedUnionFlagHotWaterBottle    BOTTLE    KNITTED       5
181          AssortedBottleTopMagnets   MAGNETS   ASSORTED       5
206          EnglishRoseHotWaterBottle   BOTTLE    ENGLISH       5
229    RetrospotHeartHotWaterBottle    BOTTLE   RETROSPOT       5
261    HotWaterBottleTeaAndSympathy  SYMPATHY       HOT       5
tail(sort(table(cluster5$lastword)), 10)
```

BABUSHKA	MAGNETS	TONIC	ELIXIR	PERFUME	OPENER	SYMPATHY	POORLY
CALM	BOTTLE						
87	95	108	112	132	149	318	345
418	3795						

Predicting cluster assignments

The goal in this exercise is to score the test dataset, by assigning clusters based upon the predict method for the training dataset.

Using flexclust to predict cluster assignment

The standard `kmeans` function does not have a prediction method. However, we can use the `flexclust` package which does. Since the prediction method can take a long time to run, we will illustrate it only on a sample number of rows and columns. In order to compare the test and training results, they also need to have the same number of columns. For illustration purposes, we will set the number at 10.

To begin, take a sample from the `OnlineRetail` training data:

```
set.seed(1)
 sample.size <- 10000
 max.cols <- 10

library("flexclust") OnlineRetail <- OnlineRetail[1:sample.size, ]
```

Next, create the document term matrix from the description column in the sampled dataset. We will use the `create_matrix` function from the `RTextTools` package, which can create a TDM first without having a separate step of creating a corpus:

```
require(tm)
 library(RTextTools) #Create the DTM for the training data

 dtMatrix <- create_matrix(OnlineRetail$Description, minDocFreq = 1,
removeNumbers = TRUE,
 minWordLength = 4, removeStopwords = TRUE, removePunctuation = TRUE,
stemWords = FALSE,
 weighting = weightTf)
```

Next, check the dimensions of the data. We can see that there are 1300 terms. Virtually all of them are sparse terms, so we will remove them from the matrix:

```
dim(dtMatrix)
> [1] 10000 1300 dtMatrix <- removeSparseTerms(dtMatrix, 0.99)
```

Removing the sparse terms reduces the number of columns from 1300 to 62!

```
dim(dtMatrix) > [1] 10000 62
```

We will only keep the same number of terms (max.cols) in test and train:

```
dtMatrix <- dtMatrix[, 1:max.cols]
```

In order to view rows of the dtMatrix that have at least two occurrences of the first 10 terms, we can use the rowSums function to add up the 1 and 0 indicators for each term:

```
tmp <- rowSums(as.matrix(dtMatrix)) tmp3 <- data.frame(tmp[tmp>1])
```

Then we will extract the row indices for the >1 condition:

```
selected <- as.numeric(rownames(tmp3)) head(selected) > head(selected) [1]
3 38 68 83 92 111
```

Print out the first 10 rows of the DTM of the first 10 terms that meet this condition:

```
kable(tm::inspect(dtMatrix[selected[1:10],]))
```

	alarm	antique	assorted	babushka	bakelike	bird	bottle	boxes	cake	candle
3	0	0	0	1	0	0	0	1	0	0
38	0	0	0	1	0	0	0	1	0	0
68	1	0	0	0	1	0	0	0	0	0
83	0	0	1	0	0	0	1	0	0	0
92	1	0	0	0	1	0	0	0	0	0
111	1	0	0	0	1	0	0	0	0	0
113	1	0	0	0	1	0	0	0	0	0
115	0	0	1	0	0	1	0	0	0	0
121	0	0	0	1	0	0	0	1	0	0
155	0	0	1	0	0	0	0	0	1	0

Running k-means to generate the clusters

Run `kmeans` function using the `kcca` package to generate five cluster assignments:

```
# repeat kmeans using the kcca function. Clusters=5

clust1 = kcca(dtMatrix, k = 5, kccaFamily("kmeans"))
clust1 > kcca object of family 'kmeans'
>
> call:
> kcca(x = dtMatrix, k = 5, family = kccaFamily("kmeans"))
>
> cluster sizes:
>
> 1 2 3 4 5
> 360 120 152 387 8981
```

Print the number categorized for each cluster:

```
table(clust1@cluster) >
> 1 2 3 4 5
> 360 120 152 387 8981
```

Merge the clusters with the training data, and show some sample records displaying the cluster assigned to each:

```
kw_with_cluster2 <- as.data.frame(cbind(OnlineRetail, Cluster =
clust1@cluster))

head(kw_with_cluster2) > InvoiceNo StockCode Description Quantity
> 5 536365 71053 METAL LANTERN 6
> 6 536365 21730 GLASS STAR FROSTED T-LIGHT HOLDER 6
> 2 536365 22752 SET 7 BABUSHKA NESTING BOXES 2
> 4 536365 84029E WOOLLY HOTTIE HEART. 6
> 1 536365 84406B CREAM CUPID HEARTS COAT HANGER 8
> 8 536366 22632 HAND WARMER POLKA DOT 6
> InvoiceDate UnitPrice CustomerID Country itemcount
> 5 12/1/2010 8:26 3.39 17850 United Kingdom 7
> 6 12/1/2010 8:26 4.25 17850 United Kingdom 7
> 2 12/1/2010 8:26 7.65 17850 United Kingdom 7
> 4 12/1/2010 8:26 3.39 17850 United Kingdom 7
> 1 12/1/2010 8:26 2.75 17850 United Kingdom 7
> 8 12/1/2010 8:28 1.85 17850 United Kingdom 2
> Desc2 lastword firstword Cluster
> 5 MetalLantern LANTERN METAL 5
> 6 GlassStarFrostedT-lightHolder HOLDER GLASS 5
> 2 Set7BabushkaNestingBoxes BOXES SET 5
> 4 WoollyHottieHeart. HEART. WOOLLY 5
```

```
> 1 CreamCupidHeartsCoatHanger HANGER CREAM 5
> 8 HandWarmerPolkaDot DOT HAND 5
```

Run the predict method on the training set. We will eventually apply it to the test data:

```
pred_train <- predict(clust1)
```

Creating the test DTM

Now let's switch over to the test data set. First, take an identical sample size as was taken for the training data, and repeat the procedure starting with creating the term document matrix on the sample:

```
OnlineRetail.test <- OnlineRetail.test[1:sample.size, ]
dtMatrix.test <- create_matrix(OnlineRetail.test$Description, minDocFreq =
1,
 removeNumbers = TRUE, minWordLength = 4, removeStopwords = TRUE,
removePunctuation = TRUE,
 stemWords = FALSE, weighting = weightTf)
```

As we did before, remove sparse terms from the matrix. Then, use the dim() function to see how many non-sparse terms remain:

```
dtMatrix.test <- removeSparseTerms(dtMatrix.test, 0.99)

dim(dtMatrix.test) # reduced to 61 terms

> [1] 10000 61
```

Take the first max.col (10) terms:

```
dtMatrix.test <- dtMatrix.test[, 1:max.cols]

dtMatrix.test > <<DocumentTermMatrix (documents: 10000, terms: 10)>>
> Non-/sparse entries: 2072/97928
> Sparsity : 98%
> Maximal term length: 8
> Weighting : term frequency (tf)
```

Display a portion of files where terms appear at least twice. Note that the first 10 terms of the test DTM is different from the DTM of the training set, although some of the terms occur in both. Since we are taking the first 10 terms just to illustrate the technique, this is normal and expected:

```
tmp <- rowSums(as.matrix(dtMatrix.test))
tmp3 <- data.frame(tmp[tmp>1])
selected <- as.numeric(rownames(tmp3))
head(selected)
#library(knitr)
kable(tm::inspect(dtMatrix.test[selected[1:10],]))
```

	antique	assorted	babushka	bird	bottle	cake	candle	card	cases	ceramic
9	0	1	0	1	0	0	0	0	0	0
44	0	0	0	0	0	1	0	0	1	0
45	0	0	0	0	0	1	0	0	1	0
136	0	1	0	1	0	0	0	0	0	0
144	0	0	0	0	0	1	0	0	1	0
177	0	0	0	1	1	0	0	0	0	0
202	0	0	1	0	1	0	0	0	0	0
209	0	0	0	0	0	1	0	0	1	0
210	0	0	0	0	0	1	0	0	1	0
219	0	0	0	0	0	1	0	0	1	0

Verify that the test and training data have the same number of dimensions. This is important since the predict method will fail if the number of columns are different:

```
dim(dtMatrix)
> [1] 10000 10
dim(dtMatrix.test)
> [1] 10000 10
```

Run the prediction function on the training data, and apply it to the test data:

```
pred_test <- predict(clust1, newdata = dtMatrix.test)
```

First, look at the table the cluster assignments for the test data:

```
table(pred_test)
> pred_test
> 1  2  3  4  5
> 171 113 201 146 9369
```

Finally, merge the clusters with the test data, and show the cluster categories assigned to each. For this demonstration, display two transactions for each cluster:

```
kw_with_cluster2_score <- as.data.frame(cbind(OnlineRetail.test,
Cluster=pred_test))
head(kw_with_cluster2_score)
clust1.score=head(subset(kw_with_cluster2_score,Cluster==1),2)
clust2.score=head(subset(kw_with_cluster2_score,Cluster==2),2)
clust3.score=head(subset(kw_with_cluster2_score,Cluster==3),2)
clust4.score=head(subset(kw_with_cluster2_score,Cluster==4),2)
clust5.score=head(subset(kw_with_cluster2_score,Cluster==5),2)
head(clust1.score[,10:13])
head(clust2.score[,10:13])
head(clust3.score[,10:13])
head(clust4.score[,10:13])
head(clust5.score[,10:13])
```

```
> head(clust1.score[,10:13])
                    Desc2 lastword firstword Cluster
89  PackOf60PaisleyCakeCases    CASES     PACK       1
96 PackOf60DinosaurCakeCases    CASES     PACK       1

> head(clust2.score[,10:13])
                         Desc2 lastword firstword Cluster
61             WoodenFrameAntique            WOODEN       2
140 AntiqueGlassDressingTablePot      POT   ANTIQUE       2

> head(clust3.score[,10:13])
                   Desc2 lastword firstword Cluster
148 3TierCakeTinAndCream    CREAM        3       3
143 3TierCakeTinAndCream    CREAM        3       3

> head(clust4.score[,10:13])
                       Desc2 lastword firstword Cluster
126 ZincWillieWinkieCandleStick    STICK      ZINC       4
488             LoveBirdCandle   CANDLE      LOVE       4

> head(clust5.score[,10:13])
                          Desc2 lastword firstword Cluster
3         HangingHeartT-lightHolder   HOLDER   HANGING       5
7 KnittedUnionFlagHotWaterBottle   BOTTLE   KNITTED       5
```

Running the apriori algorithm on the clusters

Circling back to the apriori algorithm, we can use the predicted clusters that were generated instead of lastword, in order to develop some rules:

- We will use the coerce to dataframe method to generate the transaction file as previously generated

- Create a `rules_clust` object, which builds association rules based upon the itemset of clusters {1,2,3,4,5}

- Inspect some of the generated rules by lift:

```
library(arules)
colnames(kw_with_cluster2_score)
kable(head(kw_with_cluster2_score[,c(1,13)],5))
tmp <-
data.frame(kw_with_cluster2_score[,1],
kw_with_cluster2_score[,13])
names(tmp) [1] <- "TransactionID"
names(tmp) [2] <- "Items"
tmp <- unique(tmp)
trans4 <- as(split(tmp[,2], tmp[,1]), "transactions")    rules_clust
<- apriori(trans4,parameter =    list(minlen=2,support =
0.02,confidence = 0.01))    summary(rules_clust)
tmp <- as.data.frame(inspect( head(sort(rules_clust, by="lift"),10)

> tmp <- as.data.frame(inspect( head(sort(rules_clust,
by="lift"),10) ) )
      lhs    rhs support    confidence lift
22 {2,5} => {4} 0.03065693 0.3088235  3.022059
1  {2}   => {4} 0.03065693 0.3043478  2.978261
2  {4}   => {2} 0.03065693 0.3000000  2.978261
23 {4,5} => {2} 0.03065693 0.3000000  2.978261
32 {1,5} => {4} 0.02773723 0.2087912  2.043171
9  {4}   => {1} 0.02773723 0.2714286  2.020963
10 {1}   => {4} 0.02773723 0.2065217  2.020963
31 {4,5} => {1} 0.02773723 0.2714286  2.020963
35 {3,5} => {4} 0.03357664 0.1965812  1.923687
11 {4}   => {3} 0.03357664 0.3285714  1.891357
```

Summarizing the metrics

Running a summary on the `rules_clust` object indicates an average support of 0.05, and average confidence of 0.43.

This demonstrates that using clustering can be a viable way to develop association rules, and reduce resources and the number of dimensions at the same time:

```
    support            confidence           lift
Min.    :0.02044   Min.    :0.09985   Min.    :0.989
1st Qu.:0.02664    1st Qu.:0.19816    1st Qu.:1.006
Median :0.03066    Median :0.27143    Median :1.526
Mean    :0.05040   Mean    :0.43040   Mean    :1.608
3rd Qu.:0.04234    3rd Qu.:0.81954    3rd Qu.:1.891
Max.    :0.17080   Max.    :1.00000   Max.    :3.022
```

References

- Daqing Chen, S. L. (2012). Data mining for the online retail industry: A case study of RFM model-based customer segmentation using data mining. Journal of Database Marketing and Customer Strategy Management, Vol. 19, No. 3.
- Michael Hahsler, K. H. (2006). Implications of probabilistic data modeling for mining association rules. In R. K. M. Spiliopoulou, Data and Information Analysis to Knowledge.
- Engineering, Studies in Classification, Data Analysis, and Knowledge Organization (pp. 598-605). Springer-Verlag.

Summary

In this chapter, we learned about a specific type of recommender engine, under the umbrella term market basket analysis.

We saw that market basket analysis enabled you to mine large quantities of transactions containing semi-structured data to derive association rules among the itemsets contained in each basket.

Some additional data cleaning techniques were used on the market basket data, in order to standardize and consolidate some of the descriptions of the purchased items. We also learned how to isolate the most powerful rules, using plotting techniques, along with metrics such as lift, support, and confidence.

Finally, we showed you how to generate clusters from your market basket data training data, and to predict cluster assignments based upon a test data set.

8
Exploring Health Care Enrollment Data as a Time Series

Time series data

Time series data is usually a set of ordered data collected over equally spaced intervals. Time series data occurs in most business and scientific disciplines, and the data is closely tied to the concept of forecasting, which uses previously measured data points to predict future data points based upon a specific statistical model.

Time series data differs from the kind of data that we have been looking at previously; because it is a set of ordered data points, it can contain components such as trend, seasonality, and autocorrelation, which have little meaning in other types of analysis, such as "Cross-sectional" analysis, which looks at data collected at a static point in time.

Usually, time series data is collected in equally spaced intervals, such as days, weeks, quarters, or years, but that is not always the case. Measurement of events such as natural disasters is a prime example. In some cases, you can transform uneven data into equally spaced data. In other cases, you can use specialized techniques such as Croston's method for forecasting intermittent or unexpected demand for goods and services in certain cases.

Exploring time series data

Many time series studies start out by exploring one data metric which has been measured across equally spaced time intervals. From a data science perspective, we could be interested in identifying various segments of a time series which could be exhibiting interesting trends, or cyclical or seasonal patterns. So, we always begin time series by looking at the data graphically, and producing aggregate measures before proceeding with the modeling.

Health insurance coverage dataset

We will start by reading in a dataset which contains health care enrollment data over a period for several categories. This data has been sourced from *Table HIB-2*, health insurance coverage status and type of coverage all persons by age and sex: 1999 to 2012, and it is available from the CMS website at
`http://www.census.gov/data/tables/time-series/demo/health-insurance/historical-series/hib.html`.

This table shows the number of people covered by government and private insurance, as well as the number of people not covered.

This table has several embedded time series across all the 14 years represented. 14 data points would not be considered an extremely long time series; however, we will use this data to demonstrate how we can comb through many time series at once. Since it is small, it will be easy enough to verify the results via visual inspection and printing subsets of the data. As you become familiar with the methodology, it will enable you to expand to larger complex datasets with more data points, in order to isolate the most significant trends.

Housekeeping

As we have done in other chapters, we will first clear the workspace, and set our working directory. Obviously, change the `setwd()` function to the path that you are using to store your files:

```
rm(list = ls())
setwd("C:/PracticalPredictiveAnalytics/Data")
```

Chapter 8

Read the data in

Next, we will read in a few rows of the file (using the nrow parameters), and then run a str() function on the input to see which variables are contained within the file. There are several metrics in the file related to medicare enrollment. We will just concentrate on the total enrollment metrics, and not utilize some of the other sub-segments (such as military and private insurance) for this chapter:

```
x <- read.csv("x <- read.csv("hihist2bedit.csv", nrow = 10)"
str(x)
> 'data.frame': 10 obs. of  13 variables:
> $ Year        : Factor w/ 10 levels "2003","2004 (4)",..: 10 9 8 7 6 5
4 3 2 1
> $ Year.1       : int   2012 2011 2010 2009 2008 2007 2006 2005 2004 2003
> $ Total.People: num   311116 308827 306553 304280 301483 ...
> $ Total        : num   263165 260214 256603 255295 256702 ...
> $ pritotal      : num   198812 197323 196147 196245 202626 ...
> $ priemp       : num   170877 170102 169372 170762 177543 ...
> $ pridirect     : num   30622 30244 30347 29098 28513 ...
> $ govtotal      : num   101493 99497 95525 93245 87586 ...
> $ govmedicaid   : num   50903 50835 48533 47847 42831 ...
> $ govmedicare   : num   48884 46922 44906 43434 43031 ...
> $ govmilitary   : num   13702 13712 12927 12414 11562 ...
> $ Not.Covered   : num   47951 48613 49951 48985 44780 ...
> $ cat           : Factor w/ 1 level "ALL AGES": 1 1 1 1 1 1 1 1 1 1
```

Subsetting the columns

For this exercise, we will be using a restricted set of columns from the CSV file. We can either select the specific columns from the dataframe just read in (if we just read in the whole file), or reread the csv file using the colClasses parameter to only read the columns that are required. Often, this method is preferable when you are reading a large file, and will instruct read.csv to only retain the first three and the last two columns, and ignore the columns priemp through govmilitary.

After rereading in the file, with a subset of the columns, we print a few records from the beginning and end of the file. We can do this using a combination of the rbind(), head(), and tail() functions. This will give us all of the columns we will be using for this chapter, except for some columns, which we will derive in the next section:

```
x <- read.csv("hihist2bedit.csv", colClasses = c(NA,NA, NA, NA, rep("NULL",
7)))
```

```
rbind(head(x), tail(x))
>           Year Year.1 Total.People      Total Not.Covered
> 1         2012   2012     311116.15 263165.47  47950.6840
> 2         2011   2011     308827.25 260213.79  48613.4625
> 3    2010 (10)   2010     306553.20 256602.70  49950.5004
> 4         2009   2009     304279.92 255295.10  48984.8204
> 5         2008   2008     301482.82 256702.42  44780.4031
> 6         2007   2007     299105.71 255017.52  44088.1840
> 331  2004 (4)    2004       20062.67  19804.54    258.1313
> 332       2003   2003       19862.49  19615.92    246.5703
> 333       2002   2002       19705.99  19484.01    221.9879
> 334       2001   2001       19533.99  19354.19    179.8033
> 335  2000 (3)    2000       19450.52  19250.63    199.8871
> 336  1999 (2)    1999       19378.56  19189.17    189.3922
>                                           cat
> 1                               ALL AGES
> 2                               ALL AGES
> 3                               ALL AGES
> 4                               ALL AGES
> 5                               ALL AGES
> 6                               ALL AGES
> 331 FEMALE 65 YEARS AND OVER
> 332 FEMALE 65 YEARS AND OVER
> 333 FEMALE 65 YEARS AND OVER
> 334 FEMALE 65 YEARS AND OVER
> 335 FEMALE 65 YEARS AND OVER
> 336 FEMALE 65 YEARS AND OVER
```

Description of the data

Year and Year.1 (columns 1 and 2): Year is the year for which the annual enrollment figures are taken. You will notice that year appears twice, in column 1 (as a factor) and then again in column 2 (integer). This is because the data has been previously preprocessed, and appears twice merely for convenience, since there are certain instances in which we will prefer to use a factor, and other instances in which we prefer to use an integer. The numbers in parentheses in Year refer to footnotes in the original data sources. Please refer the the reference notes at the CMS website for a full explanation of how the data was collected. While you could always create integers from factors and vice versa in the code, this saves valuable processing time if certain transformations can be made available beforehand.

Total people (column 3): Total people is the population size of the category. They may either enrolled for health coverage (total) or not (Not.Covered).

Total (column 4): Total is the number of people who were enrolled for health coverage for that year and in the cat category.

Not.Covered (Column 5): The `Not.Covered` column is the number of people not enrolled in the specified year and category.

Cat (Column 6): Cat is the time series subset. This column, along with `Year`, defines the particular row. It defines the specific demographic data for enrollment for that year.

The `ALL AGES` category represents the entire population for the specified year. All of the other subsets in the file should roll up to this category when totaled together.

For example, the last category (printed as part of `tail ()`) represents females over 65, which is a subset of the `ALL AGES` category.

Target time series variable

The variable that we will begin to look at initially will be the variable `Not.Covered`. We will be interested in examining any possible enrollment trends using this variable. Since the population size will differ depending upon the category, we will calculate the percentage of people not covered in a given year by dividing the raw number corresponding to this variable by the total in the population for that category. This will give us a new variable named `Not.Covered.Pct`. This will also standardize the metric across the different-sized categories, large and small, and enable us to compare.

After calculating the variable, we can print the first few records, and also print some summary statistics for this one variable:

 Note that the average non covered percentage was 14.5% of all of the years, but you can see that there is a considerable able of variation by just looking at the difference between the 1st and 3rd quartile (.15 - .11) = .04. That can translate to a lot of people.

```
x$Not.Covered.Pct <- x$Not.Covered/x$Total.People
  head(x)
>           Year  Year.1  Total.People    Total  Not.Covered      cat
> 1         2012    2012    311116.2   263165.5     47950.68  ALL AGES
> 2         2011    2011    308827.2   260213.8     48613.46  ALL AGES
> 3 2010   (10)    2010    306553.2   256602.7     49950.50  ALL AGES
> 4         2009    2009    304279.9   255295.1     48984.82  ALL AGES
> 5         2008    2008    301482.8   256702.4     44780.40  ALL AGES
> 6         2007    2007    299105.7   255017.5     44088.18  ALL AGES
>    Not.Covered.Pct
```

```
> 1          0.1541247
> 2          0.1574131
> 3          0.1629424
> 4          0.1609860
> 5          0.1485338
> 6          0.1474000
summary(x$Not.Covered.Pct)
Min. 1st Qu. Median  Mean 3rd Qu.  Max.
0.009205 0.109400 0.145300 0.154200 0.210400 0.325200
```

As typical with a target variable, we also like to see basic plots showing the distribution of the variable:

```
hist(x$Not.Covered.Pct)
```

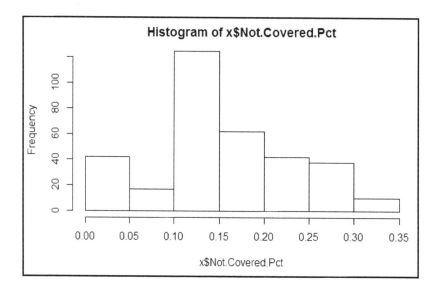

Saving the data

This may be a good time to save the current data to a file, since we may want to read it back later, starting from the analysis stage. This will avoid having to reread the same file again unless, of course, the source data changes:

```
save(x, file = "x.RData")
```

Determining all of the subset groups

Since we have only looked at parts of the file (via `head()` or `tail()` functions), we do not know how many categories there are and how they differ in terms of health care coverage. So we will start off by looking at some of the groupings.

In previous chapters, we have used `sql()` and the `aggregate()` function to group data. For this example, we will use the `dplyr` package. One advange of the `dplyr()` package is that it can also be used with pipe syntax, which allows the result of one function to be passed to the next function without intermediate assignments:

```
library(dplyr)
>
> Attaching package: 'dplyr'
> The following objects are masked from 'package:stats':
>
>       filter, lag
> The following objects are masked from 'package:base':
>
>       intersect, setdiff, setequal, union
# str(x)
```

The `by.cat` object will show the average number insured, and the average total population for each category. Remember, this data is also grouped by year; however, we just want to get a sense of what the averages are across all of the years for now. Since the arrange function will end up sorting the data by the total population sizes, from largest to smallest, we can see that the numbers line up as expected:

- `ALL AGES` is the largest category
- This is followed by `FEMALE ALL AGES`
- Then `MALE ALL AGES`

```
by.cat <- x %>% select(cat, Total, Total.People) %>%
group_by(cat) %>%
summarise(Avg.Total.Insured = mean(Total),Avg.People
= mean(Total.People)) %>%
arrange(desc(Avg.People))
by.cat
```

As a sanity check, if you add the totals for the latter two categories, you can see that they sum to the `ALL AGES` category.

From the console, we can see from the `str(by.cat)` function that there are 24 categories:

```
str(by.cat)
> Classes 'tbl_df', 'tbl' and 'data.frame': 24 obs. of  3 variables:
>  $ cat             : Factor w/ 24 levels "18 to 24 YEARS",..: 7 14 22 24
3 4 2 23  6 15 ...
>  $ Avg.Total.Insured: num  251243 130201 121042 66200 34762 ...
>  $ Avg.People       : num  294700 150330 144371 73752 42433 ...
by.cat
> Source: local data frame [24 x 3]
>
>
>                       cat Avg.Total.Insured Avg.People
>                     (fctr)             (dbl)      (dbl)
> 1               ALL AGES          251242.96  294700.47
> 2        FEMALE ALL AGES          130200.90  150329.73
> 3          MALE ALL AGES          121042.06  144370.74
> 4        UNDER 18 YEARS           66200.46   73752.50
> 5         35 to 44 YEARS           34761.74   42433.12
> 6         45 to 54 YEARS           35911.82   42100.20
> 7         25 to 34 YEARS           29973.91   39942.64
> 8   MALE UNDER 18 YEARS           33832.87   37700.70
> 9      65 YEARS AND OVER          36199.32   36722.61
> 10 FEMALE UNDER 18 YEARS          32367.59   36051.79
> ..                        ...               ...        ...
```

Merging the aggregate data back into the original data

Often, you will want to augment your original data with some of the calculated data as derived previously. In these cases, you can merge the data back into the original data using a common key. Again, we will use the `dplyr` package to take the results just obtained (`by.cat`) and join them back to the original data (`x`), using the common key `cat`.

We will be using a `left_join` just for an example; however, we could have used a right join to obtain the same results, since `by.cat` was completely derived from `x`. After joining the two dataframes, we will end up with a new dataframe named `x2`:

```
# Merge the summary measures back into the original data. Merge by cat.


x2 <- by.cat %>% left_join(x, by = "cat")
head(x2)
> Source: local data frame [6 x 9]
>
```

```
>          cat Avg.Total.Insured Avg.People      Year Year.1 Total.People
>        (fctr)              (dbl)      (dbl)   (fctr)  (int)        (dbl)
> 1 ALL AGES            251243    294700.5      2012   2012     311116.2
> 2 ALL AGES            251243    294700.5      2011   2011     308827.2
> 3 ALL AGES            251243    294700.5 2010 (10)   2010     306553.2
> 4 ALL AGES            251243    294700.5      2009   2009     304279.9
> 5 ALL AGES            251243    294700.5      2008   2008     301482.8
> 6 ALL AGES            251243    294700.5      2007   2007     299105.7
> Variables not shown: Total (dbl), Not.Covered (dbl), Not.Covered.Pct
(dbl)
```

Checking the time intervals

Earlier, we mentioned needing to have equally sized time intervals. Additionally, before we perform any time series analysis, we need to check for the number of non-missing time intervals. So, let's check the number of enrollment years for each category.

Using the `dplyr` package, we can use summarize (n ()) to count the number of entries for each category:

```
# -- summarize and sort by the number of years
yr.count <- x2 %>% group_by(cat) %>% summarise(n = n()) %>% arrange(n)

# - we can see that there are 14 years for all of the groups.  That is
good!
print(yr.count, 10)
> Source: local data frame [24 x 2]
>
>                     cat    n
>                  (fctr) (int)
> 1       18 to 24 YEARS    14
> 2       25 to 34 YEARS    14
> 3       35 to 44 YEARS    14
> 4       45 to 54 YEARS    14
> 5       55 to 64 YEARS    14
> 6     65 YEARS AND OVER    14
> 7             ALL AGES    14
> 8  FEMALE 18 to 24 YEARS  14
> 9  FEMALE 25 to 34 YEARS  14
> 10 FEMALE 35 to 44 YEARS  14
> ..                   ... ...
```

We can see from the above that every category has 14 years of data represented.

So, we don't have to worry about having a uniform time period for each subset. However, this is often not the case, and if you come across this, you may need to do the following:

- Impute data for years that are missing.
- Try to convert to equally spaced time series. Perhaps transform time period to a higher scale. For example for intermittent daily data, try to convert to weekly, monthly or quarterly.
- Use specialized time series techniques to account for unequally spaced time series.

Picking out the top groups in terms of average population size

In many instances, we will only want to look at the top categories, especially when there are many demographical categories that have been subsetted. In this example, there are only 24 categories but in other examples, there may be a much larger number of categories.

The dataframe x2 is already sorted by `Avg.People`. Since we know that there are 14 enrollment records for each category, we can get the top 10 categories based upon the highest base population by selecting the first 14*10 (or 140) rows. We will store this in a new dataframe, x3, and save this to disk.

Since we know each group has 14 years, extracting the top 10 groups is easy to calculate. After assigning x2, print the first 15 records and observe that the category break after the first 14 records:

```
x3 <- x2[1:(14 * 10), ]
head(x3,15)
   cat Avg.Total.Insured Avg.People Year Year.1 Total.People Total
Not.Covered
 <fctr> <dbl> <dbl> <fctr> <int> <dbl> <dbl> <dbl>
1 ALL AGES 251243.0 294700.5 2012 2012 311116.2 263165.5 47950.68
2 ALL AGES 251243.0 294700.5 2011 2011 308827.2 260213.8 48613.46
3 ALL AGES 251243.0 294700.5 2010 (10) 2010 306553.2 256602.7 49950.50
4 ALL AGES 251243.0 294700.5 2009 2009 304279.9 255295.1 48984.82
5 ALL AGES 251243.0 294700.5 2008 2008 301482.8 256702.4 44780.40
6 ALL AGES 251243.0 294700.5 2007 2007 299105.7 255017.5 44088.18
7 ALL AGES 251243.0 294700.5 2006 2006 296824.0 251609.6 45214.35
8 ALL AGES 251243.0 294700.5 2005 2005 293834.4 250799.4 43034.92
9 ALL AGES 251243.0 294700.5 2004 (4) 2004 291166.2 249413.9 41752.26
10 ALL AGES 251243.0 294700.5 2003 2003 288280.5 246331.7 41948.74
11 ALL AGES 251243.0 294700.5 2002 2002 285933.4 246157.5 39775.92
```

```
12 ALL AGES 251243.0 294700.5 2001 2001 282082.0 244058.6 38023.33
13 ALL AGES 251243.0 294700.5 2000 (3) 2000 279517.4 242931.5 36585.81
14 ALL AGES 251243.0 294700.5 1999 (2) 1999 276803.8 239102.0 37701.81
15 FEMALE ALL AGES 130200.9 150329.7 2012 2012 158780.9 136315.1 22465.78
#
  save(x3, file = "x3.RData")
```

Plotting the data using lattice

The lattice package is a useful package to learn, especially for analysts who like to work in formula notation (y~x).

In this example, we will run a lattice plot in order to plot Not.Covered.Pct on the *y*-axis, Year on the *x*-axis, and produce separate plots by category.

The main call is specified by the following:

```
xyplot(Not.Covered.Pct ~ Year | cat, data = x3)
```

Since we are plotting the top 10 groups, we can specify layout=c(5,2) to indicate we want to arrange the 10 plots in a 5*2 matrix. Not.Covered.Pct is to be arranged on the *y* axis (left side of the ~ sign), and Year is arranged along the *x-axis* (right side of ~ sign). The bar (|) indicates that the data is to be plotted separately by each category:

```
library(lattice)
x.tick.number <- 14
at <- seq(1, nrow(x3), length.out = x.tick.number)
labels <- round(seq(1999, 2012, length.out = x.tick.number))

p <- xyplot(Not.Covered.Pct ~ Year | cat, data = x3, type = "l", main =
list(label = "Enrollment by Categories",
     cex = 1), par.strip.text = list(cex = 0.5), scales = list(x =
list(labels = labels),
     cex = 0.4, rot = 45), layout = c(5, 2))

trellis.device()

print(p)
```

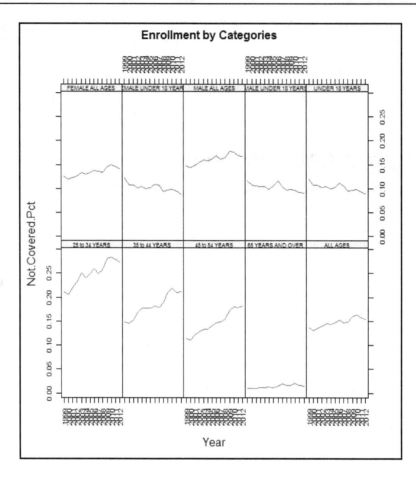

Plotting the data using ggplot

If you like using ggplot, a similar set of graphs can be rendered using facets:

```
require("ggplot2")

.df <- data.frame(x = x3$Year.1, y = x3$Not.Covered.Pct, z = x3$cat, s =
x3$cat)
.df <- .df[order(.df$x), ]
.plot <- ggplot(data = .df, aes(x = x, y = y, colour = z, shape = z))
+ geom_point()
+       geom_line(size = 1)
+ scale_shape_manual(values = seq(0, 15))
+ scale_y_continuous(expand = c(0.01, 0))
```

```
+ facet_wrap(~s)
+ xlab("Year.1")
+ ylab("Not.Covered.Pct")
+ labs(colour = "cat", shape = "cat")
+ theme(panel.margin = unit(0.3, "lines"), legend.position = "none")
 print(.plot)
```

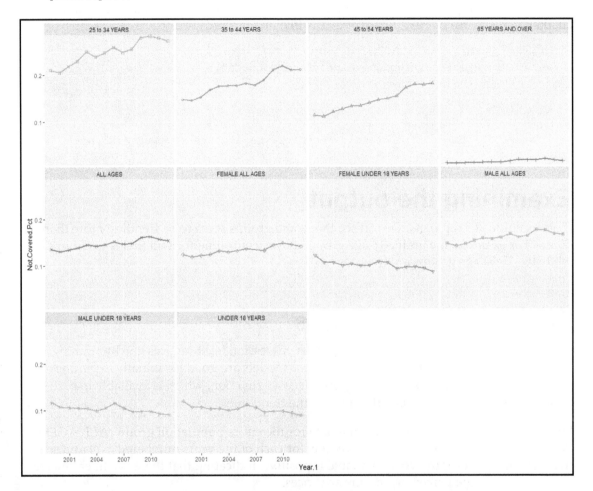

Sending output to an external file

One benefit of assigning plots to a plot object is that you can later send the plots to an external file, such as a PDF, view it externally, and even view it in your browser directly from R. For example, for the Lattice graphs example, you can use `trellis.device` and specify the output parameters, and then print the object. As we illustrated in an earlier chapter, you can use `browseURL` to open the PDF in your browser:

```
# send to pdf
setwd("C:/PracticalPredictiveAnalytics/Outputs")
trellis.device(pdf, file = "x3.pdf")
print(p)
dev.off()
#NOT run
#browseURL('file://c://PracticalPredictiveAnalytics//Outputs//x3.pdf')
```

Examining the output

If we examine our top plots, we can see that some groups seem to be trending more than others. For example, the under-18 age group shows a enrollment trend that is declining, while the 25-54 age groups are trending up.

Detecting linear trends

In a linear trend model, one constructs a linear regression least squares line by running an `lm()` regression through the data points. These models are good for initially exploring trends visually. We can take advantage of our `lm()` function, which is available in base R, in order to specifically calculate the slope of the trend line.

For example, the first 14 rows show the data for the entire population group (ALL AGES). We can run a regression on Not.Covered.Pct for each of the years numbered 1-14 and see that the coefficient for the Year.1 variable is positive, indicating that there is a linear increase in the non-coverage percentage as ime advances.

We can also the coeficient output by itself, by wrapping the lm() function within a coef() function.

After running the regression using the `lm()` function, we can subsequently use the `coef` function to specifically extract the slope and the intercept from the `lm` model.

Since this is a regression in which there is only one independent variable (Time), there will only be one coefficient:

```
lm(Not.Covered.Pct ~ Year.1, data = x2[1:14, ])
>
> Call:
> lm(formula = Not.Covered.Pct ~ Year.1, data = x2[1:14, ])
>
> Coefficients:
> (Intercept)        Year.1
>   -4.102621      0.002119
coef(lm(Not.Covered.Pct ~ Year.1, data = x2[1:14, ]))
>   (Intercept)        Year.1
> -4.102621443   0.002119058
```

Automating the regressions

Now that we have seen how we can run a single time series regression, we can move on to automating separate regressions and extracting the coefficients over all of the categories.

There are several ways to do this. One way is by using the do() function within the dplyr package. Here is the sequence of events:

- The data is first grouped by category.
- Then, a linear regression (lm() function) is run for each category, with Year as the independent variable, and Not.Covered as the dependent variable. This is all wrapped within a do() function.
- The coefficient is extracted from the model. The coefficient will act as a proxy for the direction and magnitude of the trend.
- Finally, a dataframe of lists is created (fitted.models), where the coefficients and intercepts are stored for each regression run on every category. The categories that have the highest positive coefficients exhibit the greatest increasing linear trend, while the declining trend is indicated by negative coefficients:

```
library(dplyr)
fitted_models = x2 %>%
group_by(cat) %>%
do(model = coef(lm(Not.Covered.Pct ~ Year.1, data = .)))
```

All of the generated models are now in the `fitted_models` object.

The `kable` function from `knitr` gives a simple output which displays the intercept as the first number and the coefficient in the model column. As a check, we can see that the coefficients in the `ALL AGES` model are identical to those derived in the previous section:

```
library(knitr)
kable(fitted_models)
```

Cat	Model
18 to 24 YEARS	-0.4061834427, 0.0003367988
25 to 34 YEARS	-11.375187597, 0.005796182
35 to 44 YEARS	-10.916822084, 0.005534037
45 to 54 YEARS	-11.544566448, 0.005829194
55 to 64 YEARS	-4.709612146, 0.002409908
65 YEARS AND OVER	-1.2562375095, 0.0006334125
ALL AGES	-4.102621443, 0.002119058
FEMALE 18 to 24 YEARS	-2.677300003, 0.001455388
FEMALE 25 to 34 YEARS	-9.990978769, 0.005088009
FEMALE 35 to 44 YEARS	-9.564724041, 0.004850188
FEMALE 45 to 54 YEARS	-10.36336551, 0.00523537
FEMALE 55 to 64 YEARS	-4.102774957, 0.002108343
FEMALE 65 YEARS AND OVER	-1.3674510779, 0.0006887743
FEMALE ALL AGES	-3.817483824, 0.001970059
FEMALE UNDER 18 YEARS	3.267593386, -0.001578328
MALE 18 to 24 YEARS	4.036127727, -0.001862991
MALE 25 to 34 YEARS	-9.715950286, 0.004983621
MALE 35 to 44 YEARS	-7.706624821, 0.003941543
MALE 45 to 54 YEARS	-10.975387917, 0.005549255
MALE 55 to 64 YEARS	-5.370380544, 0.002738269
MALE 65 YEARS AND OVER	-0.4834523450, 0.0002479691

MALE ALL AGES	-4.315036958, 0.002232003
MALE UNDER 18 YEARS	2.914343264, -0.001401998
UNDER 18 YEARS	3.086509947, -0.001487938

Ranking the coefficients

Now that we have the coefficients, we can begin to rank each of the categories by increasing trend. Since the results we have obtained so far are contained in embedded lists, which are a bit difficult to work with, we can perform some code manipulation to transform them into a regular data frame, with one row per category, consisting of the category name, coefficient, and coefficient rank:

```
library(dplyr)
# extract the coefficients part from the model list, and then transpose the
# data frame so that the coefficient appear one per row, rather than 1 per
# column.

xx <- as.data.frame(fitted_models$model)
xx2 <- as.data.frame(t(xx[2, ]))

# The output does not contain the category name, so we will merge it back
# from the original data frame.

xx4 <- cbind(xx2, as.data.frame(fitted_models))[, c(1, 2)]  #only keep the
first two columns

# rank the coefficients from lowest to highest. Force the format of the
rank
# as length 2, with leading zero's

tmp <- sprintf("%02d", rank(xx4[, 1]))

# Finally prepend the rank to the actual category
xx4$rankcat <- as.factor(paste(tmp, "-", as.character(xx4$cat)))

# name the columns
names(xx4) <- c("lm.coef", "cat", "coef.rank")
# and View the results
View(xx4)
```

As you can see, columns 2, 3, and 4 now contain a neatly arranged representation of the `coefficients`, `category`, and `coef.rank`, which was derived by ranking `lm.coef` from smallest to largest, and then pretending the rank order to the category:

	lm.coef	cat	coef.rank
structure.c..0.406183442737828..0.0003367987...	0.0003367988	18 to 24 YEARS	06 - 18 to 24 YEARS
structure.c..11.3751875969696..0.00579618220...	0.0057961822	25 to 34 YEARS	23 - 25 to 34 YEARS
structure.c..10.9168220838485..0.00553403690...	0.0055340369	35 to 44 YEARS	21 - 35 to 44 YEARS
structure.c..11.5445664482143..0.00582919407...	0.0058291941	45 to 54 YEARS	24 - 45 to 54 YEARS
structure.c..4.70961214602917..0.00240990753...	0.0024099075	55 to 64 YEARS	14 - 55 to 64 YEARS
structure.c..1.25623750951236..0.00063341249..	0.0006334125	65 YEARS AND OVER	07 - 65 YEARS AND OVER
structure.c..4.10262144273963..0.00211905813...	0.0021190581	ALL AGES	12 - ALL AGES
structure.c..2.67730000270634..0.00145538791...	0.0014553879	FEMALE 18 to 24 YEARS	09 - FEMALE 18 to 24 YEARS
structure.c..9.99097876897398..0.00508800858...	0.0050880086	FEMALE 25 to 34 YEARS	19 - FEMALE 25 to 34 YEARS
structure.c..9.5647240414497..0.004850187645...	0.0048501876	FEMALE 35 to 44 YEARS	17 - FEMALE 35 to 44 YEARS
structure.c..10.3633655124299..0.00523536960..	0.0052353696	FEMALE 45 to 54 YEARS	20 - FEMALE 45 to 54 YEARS
structure.c..4.10277495735534..0.00210834349..	0.0021083435	FEMALE 55 to 64 YEARS	11 - FEMALE 55 to 64 YEARS
structure.c..1.36745107793605..0.00068877425...	0.0006887743	FEMALE 65 YEARS AND OVER	08 - FEMALE 65 YEARS AND OVER
structure.c..3.81748382391257..0.00197005880...	0.0019700588	FEMALE ALL AGES	10 - FEMALE ALL AGES
structure.c.3.26759338613744...0.00157832779...	-0.0015783278	FEMALE UNDER 18 YEARS	02 - FEMALE UNDER 18 YEARS
structure.c.4.03612772673809...0.00186299125...	-0.0018629913	MALE 18 to 24 YEARS	01 - MALE 18 to 24 YEARS
structure.c..9.71595028579057..0.00498362081...	0.0049836208	MALE 25 to 34 YEARS	18 - MALE 25 to 34 YEARS
structure.c..7.70662482144783..0.00394154306...	0.0039415431	MALE 35 to 44 YEARS	16 - MALE 35 to 44 YEARS
structure.c..10.9753879171274..0.00554925524...	0.0055492552	MALE 45 to 54 YEARS	22 - MALE 45 to 54 YEARS
structure.c..5.37038054369785..0.00273826914...	0.0027382691	MALE 55 to 64 YEARS	15 - MALE 55 to 64 YEARS

Merging scores back into the original dataframe

We will augment the original `x2` dataframe with this new information by merging back by category, and then by sorting the dataframe by the rank of the coefficient. This will allow us to use this as a proxy for trend:

```
x2x <- x2 %>% left_join(xx4, by = "cat") %>% arrange(coef.rank, cat)


# exclude some columns so as to fit on one page
head(x2x[, c(-2, -3, -4, -8)])
> Source: local data frame [6 x 7]
>
```

```
>                      cat Year.1 Total.People     Total Not.Covered.Pct
>                   (fctr)  (int)        (dbl)     (dbl)           (dbl)
> 1 MALE 18 to 24 YEARS      2012     15142.04 11091.86        0.2674787
> 2 MALE 18 to 24 YEARS      2011     15159.87 11028.75        0.2725034
> 3 MALE 18 to 24 YEARS      2010     14986.02 10646.88        0.2895460
> 4 MALE 18 to 24 YEARS      2010     14837.14 10109.82        0.3186139
> 5 MALE 18 to 24 YEARS      2008     14508.04 10021.66        0.3092339
> 6 MALE 18 to 24 YEARS      2007     14391.92 10230.61        0.2891425
> Variables not shown: lm.coef (dbl), coef.rank (fctr)
```

Plotting the data with the trend lines

Now that we have the trend coefficients, we will use `ggplot` to first plot enrollment for all of the 24 categories, and then create a second set of plots which adds the trend line based upon the linear coefficients we have just calculated.

Code notes: `facet_wrap` will order the plots by the value of variable z, which was assigned to the coefficient rank. Thus, we can get to see the categories with declining enrollment first, ending with the categories having the highest trend in enrollment from the period 1999-2012.

I like to assign the variables that I will be changing to standard variable names, such as x, y, and z, so that I can remember their usage (for example, variable x is always the x variable, and y always the x variable). But you can supply the variable names directly in the call to `ggplot`, or set up your own function to do the same thing:

```
library(ggplot2)
.df <- data.frame(x = x2x$Year.1, y = x2x$Not.Covered.Pct, z =
x2x$coef.rank, slope = x2x$lm.coef)
#use ggplot to layer the different components of the visualization
.plot <- ggplot(data = .df, aes(x = x, y = y, colour = 1, shape = z))
+ geom_point()
+ scale_shape_manual(values = seq(0, 24))
+ scale_y_continuous(expand = c(0.1,0))
+ scale_x_continuous(expand = c(0.1, 1))
+ facet_wrap(~z) + xlab("Year.1")
+ ylab("Not.Covered.Pct")
+ labs(colour = "cat", shape = "cat")
+ theme(panel.margin = unit(0.3,"points"), legend.position = "none")
+ theme(strip.text.x = element_text(size = 6))
print(.plot)
```

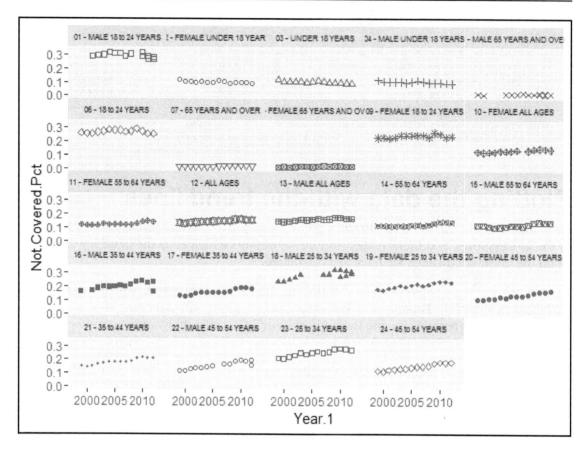

As you can see, for the `ALL AGES` category, the non-covered percentage is seen to be increasing over the time period, until 2010 (where the affordable care act was enacted), and then the percentage begins to decrease. However, for the same time period, the under 18 age group shows a decrease in the proportion of non-insured relative to the population size.

We can take a closer look at the top and bottom four categories, along with the `ALL AGES` category, to examine this more closely. This time, we will add our own trend line using the `geom_smooth` parameter, which will add a linear regression trend line:

```
# declining enrollment
.df2 <- rbind(head(.df,(4*14)), tail(.df,(4*14)), .df[.df$z == "12 - ALL
AGES", ])
.plot2 <- ggplot(data = .df2, aes(x = x, y = y, colour = 1, shape = z))
+ geom_point()
+ scale_shape_manual(values = seq(0, nrow(.df2)))
+ scale_y_continuous(expand = c(0.1,0))
+ scale_x_continuous(expand = c(0.1, 1))
```

```
+ facet_wrap(~z)
+ xlab("Year.1")
+ ylab("Not.Covered.Pct")
+ labs(colour = "cat", shape = "cat")
+ theme(panel.margin = unit(0.3,"points"),legend.position = "none")
+ geom_smooth(method = "lm", se = FALSE,colour = "red")
.plot2 <- ggplot(data = .df2, aes(x = x, y = y, colour = 1, shape = z))
+ geom_point()
+ scale_shape_manual(values = seq(0, nrow(.df2)))
+ scale_y_continuous(expand = c(0.1,0))
+ scale_x_continuous(expand = c(0.1, 1))
+ facet_wrap(~z)
+ xlab("Year.1")
+ ylab("Not.Covered.Pct")
+ labs(colour = "cat", shape = "cat")
+ theme(panel.margin = unit(0.3,"points"),legend.position = "none")
+ geom_smooth(method = "lm", se = FALSE,colour = "red")
print(.plot2)
```

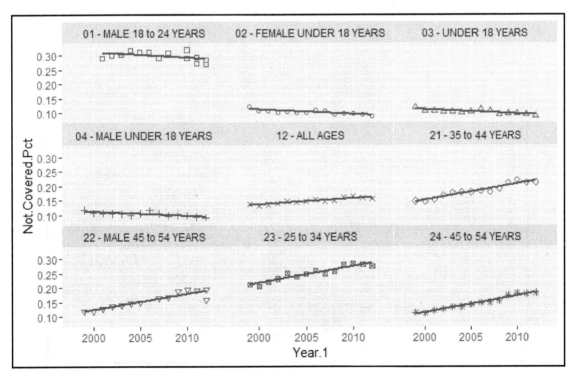

Plotting all the categories on one graph

Sometimes, it's nice to plot all of the lines on one graph rather having them as separate plots. To achieve this, we will alter the syntax a bit, so that the categories show up as stacked lines. Again, we can see the percentage of uninsured aligns across ages, with the under 18 group having the lowest uninsured rate, and the 25-54 group having the highest:

```
library(ggplot2)
### plot all on one graph

.df <- x3[order(x3$Year.1), ]
.plot <- ggplot(data = .df, aes(x = Year.1, y = Not.Covered.Pct, colour =
cat,shape = cat))
+ geom_point()
+ geom_line(size = 1)
+ scale_shape_manual(values = seq(0,15))
+ ylab("Not.Covered.Pct")
+ labs(colour = "cat", shape = "cat")
+ theme_bw(base_size = 14,base_family = "serif")
print(.plot)
```

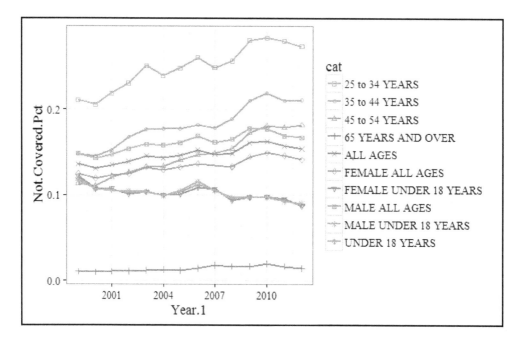

Adding labels

It can sometimes be a bit difficult to discern the differences between the categories based on the legend, especially as the number of categories increases, so we can use the directlables library to mark each line with the category name. Now we can see, for example, that ALL MALES has a higher uninsured rate than ALL FEMALES over all time periods:

```
#install.packages("directlabels")
library(directlabels)
direct.label(.plot, list(last.points, hjust = 0.75, cex = 0.75, vjust = 0))
```

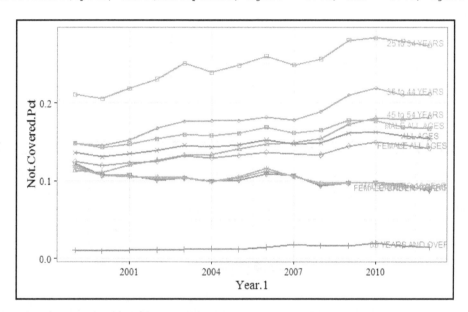

Performing some automated forecasting using the ets function

So far, we have looked at ways in which we can explore any linear trends which may be inherent in our data. That provided a solid foundation for the next step, prediction. Now we will begin to look at how we can perform some actual forecasting.

Converting the dataframe to a time series object

As a preparation step, we will use the ts function to convert our dataframe to a time series object. It is important that the time series be equally spaced before converting to a ts object. At a minimum, you supply the time series variable, and start and end dates as arguments to the ts function.

After creating a new object, x, run a str() function to verify that all of the 14 time series from 1999 to 2012 have been created:

```
# only extract the 'ALL' timeseries
x <- ts(x2$Not.Covered.Pct[1:14], start = c(1999), end = c(2012), frequency
= 1)

str(x)
>  Time-Series [1:14] from 1999 to 2012: 0.154 0.157 0.163 0c.161 0.149 ...
```

Smoothing the data using moving averages

One simple technique used to analyze time series involves simple and exponential moving averages. Both simple moving average and exponential moving average are ways in which we can smooth out the random noise in the series and observe cycles and trends.

Simple moving average

A simple moving average will simply take the sum of the time series variable for the last k periods and then will divide it by the number of periods. In this sense, it is identical to the calculation for the mean. However, what makes it different from a simple mean is the following:

- The average will shift for every additional time period. Moving averages are backward-looking, and every time a time period shifts, so will the average. That is why they are called moving. Moving averages are sometimes called rolling averages.
- The look backwards period can shift. That is the second characteristic of a moving average. A 10-period moving average will take the average of the last 10 data elements, while a 20-period moving average will take the sum of the last 20 data points, and then divide by 20.

Computing the SMA using a function

To compute a rolling five-period moving average for our data, we will use the simple moving average (SMA) function from the TTR package, and then display the first few rows:

```
#install.packages("TTR")
library(TTR)
 MA <- SMA(x, n = 5)
 cbind(head(x, 14), head(MA, 14))
>                [,1]        [,2]
>    [1,] 0.1541247          NA
>    [2,] 0.1574131          NA
>    [3,] 0.1629424          NA
>    [4,] 0.1609860          NA
>    [5,] 0.1485338 0.1568000
>    [6,] 0.1474000 0.1554551
>    [7,] 0.1523271 0.1544379
>    [8,] 0.1464598 0.1511414
>    [9,] 0.1433967 0.1476235
>   [10,] 0.1455136 0.1470194
>   [11,] 0.1391090 0.1453612
>   [12,] 0.1347953 0.1418549
>   [13,] 0.1308892 0.1387408
>   [14,] 0.1362041 0.1373023
```

There are many ways in which you can plot the moving average with the original data. Using base R, use the `ts.plot()` function to do this, which takes the original series and the moving average of the series as arguments:

```
ts.plot(x, MA, gpars = list(xlab = "year", ylab = "Percentage of Non-
Insured",
lty = c(1:2)))
title("Percentage of Non-Insured 1999-2012 - With SMA")
```

The following plot shows the original data as a solid line, and the computed moving average as a dotted line:

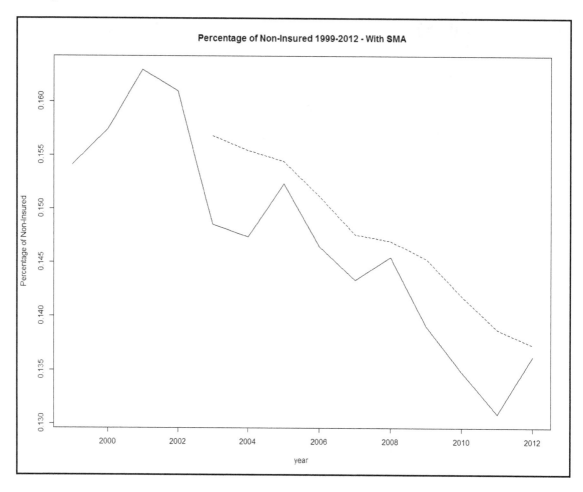

You can see how moving averages are helpful in showing the upward and downward movements of the data, and also help smooth the data to help eliminate some of the noise. Also notice that a moving average needs some starter data to begin calculations, so that is why the dotting moving average line is missing from the first four time periods of the graph. Only by the fifth period is it able to determine the calculation by summing up the values which correspond to the time period 1999-2003 and then dividing by five. The next point is derived by summing up the values corresponding to the time periods 2000-2004 and then again dividing by five.

Verifying the SMA calculation

It is always important to be able to verify calculation, to ensure that the values have been performed correctly, and to promote understanding.

In the case of the SMA function, we can switch to the console, and calculate the value of the SMA function for the last five data points.

First, we calculate the sum of the elements and then divide by the number of data points in the moving average (5):

```
sum(x[10:14])/5
> [1] 0.1373023
```

That matches exactly with the column given for the SMA for time period 14.

Exponential moving average

For a **simple moving average** (**SMA**), equal weight is given to all data points, regardless of how old they are or how recently they occurred. An **exponential moving average** (**EMA**) gives more weight to recent data, under the assumption that the future is more likely to look like the recent past, rather than the older past.

The EMA is actually a much simpler calculation. An EMA begins by calculating a simple moving average. When it reaches the specified number of lookback periods (n), it computes the current value by assigning different weights to the current value, and to the previous value.

This weighting is specified by the smoothing (or ratio) factor. When *ratio=1*, the predicted value is entirely based upon the last time value. For ratios *b=0*, the prediction is based upon the average of the entire lookback period. Therefore, the closer the smoothing factor is to 1, the more weight it will give to recent data. If you want to give additional weight to older data, decrease the smoothing factor toward 0.

Generally, the formula for an EMA is as follows:

{Current Data Point - EMA(previous)} x smoothing factor + EMA(previous day)

To compute the EMA, you can use the EMA() function (from the TTR package). You need to specify a smoothing constant (ratio), as well as a lookback period (n).

Computing the EMA using a function

The following code will compute an EMA with a ratio of .8, using a lookback period of 5. The ratio of .8 will give the most weight to the most recent period, whilel still allowing the past to influence the prediction.

Then we will use `cbind()` to display the data point, as well as the simple and exponential moving averages:

```
ExpMA <- EMA(x, n = 5, ratio = 0.8)
cbind(head(x, 15), head(MA, 15), head(ExpMA, 15))
>                  [,1]       [,2]       [,3]
>    [1,] 0.1541247       NA         NA
>    [2,] 0.1574131       NA         NA
>    [3,] 0.1629424       NA         NA
>    [4,] 0.1609860       NA         NA
>    [5,] 0.1485338 0.1568000 0.1568000
>    [6,] 0.1474000 0.1554551 0.1492800
>    [7,] 0.1523271 0.1544379 0.1517177
>    [8,] 0.1464598 0.1511414 0.1475114
>    [9,] 0.1433967 0.1476235 0.1442196
> [10,] 0.1455136 0.1470194 0.1452548
> [11,] 0.1391090 0.1453612 0.1403382
> [12,] 0.1347953 0.1418549 0.1359039
> [13,] 0.1308892 0.1387408 0.1318922
> [14,] 0.1362041 0.1373023 0.1353417
ts.plot(x, ExpMA, gpars = list(xlab = "year", ylab = "Percentage of Non-
Insured",
lty = c(1:2)))
title("Percentage of Non-Insured 1999-2012 - With EMA")
```

The following plot shows the data in graph form. You can see that each data point is closer to its EMA that to the SMA, which, as mentioned earlier, weights all previous data points equally within the lookback period. In this regard, EMAs react quicker to the recent data, while SMAs are slower moving and have less variability. Of course, both are affected by the parameters, especially the lookback period. Longer lookbacks will make for slower moving averages in both cases:

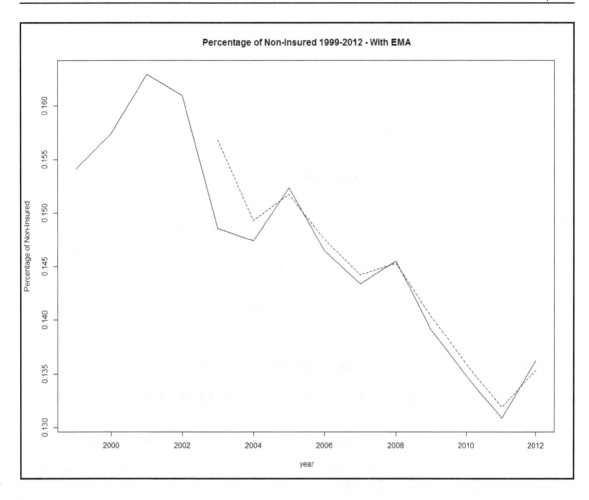

Selecting a smoothing factor

Sometimes selecting an appropriate smoothing factor is done via your own experience with the data, and let's you express your own view about how you expect the future to behave. For example if you thank that the data has recently changed to reflect new pattern, you might want to assume that the recent data is more important and use a smoothing factor close to 1. On the other hand, if you think that recent activity is just due to random fluctuations, you might want to choose a lower smoothing factor to give more weight to the past. A smoothing factor which treats the recent past with the distant past might be something like 0.5. The point is that it is not always necessary to automatically optimize the smoothing factor (as we will see next).

Using the ets function

While moving averages re extremely useful, they are only one component of what is known as an exponential smoothed state space model, which has many options to define the optimal smoothing factor, as well as enabling you to define the type of trend and seasonality via the parameters.

To implement this model we will use the ets() function from the forecast package to model the Not-Covered Percent variable for the "ALL AGES" category.

The ets() function is flexible in that it can also incorporate trend, as well as seasonality for its forecasts.

We will just be illustrating a simple exponentially smoothed model (ANN). However, for completeness, you should know that you specify three letters when calling the ets() function, and you should be aware of what each letter represents. Otherwise, it will model based upon the default parameters.

Here is the description as specified by the package author, Hydman:

- The first letter denotes the error type ("A", "M", or "Z")

- The second letter denotes the trend type ("N","A","M", or "Z")

- The third letter denotes the season type ("N","A","M", or "Z")

In all cases, N=none, A=additive, M=multiplicative, and Z=automatically selected.

So, for our example, if we want to model a simple, exponentially smoothed model, as we did in our manual calculations, we will specify model=ANN.

Forecasting using ALL AGES

The following code will perform the following steps:

1. First, it will filter the data so that it only includes the ALL AGES category.

2. Then, it creates a time series object.

3. Finally, it runs a simple exponential model, using the ets() function.

Note that we did not specify a smoothing factor. The `ets()` function calculates the optimal smoothing factor (alpha, shown via the `summary()` function (in bold below)), which in this case is .99, which means that model time series takes about 99% of the previous value to incorporate into the next time series prediction:

```
library(dplyr)
>
> Attaching package: 'dplyr'
> The following objects are masked from 'package:stats':
>
>       filter, lag
> The following objects are masked from 'package:base':
>
>       intersect, setdiff, setequal, union
library(forecast)
> Loading required package: zoo
>
> Attaching package: 'zoo'
> The following objects are masked from 'package:base':
>
>       as.Date, as.Date.numeric
> Loading required package: timeDate
> This is forecast 7.1
x4 <- x2[x2$cat == "ALL AGES", ]

# set up as a time series object
x <- ts(x4$Not.Covered.Pct, start = c(1999), end = c(2012), frequency = 1)

fit <- ets(x, model = "ANN")
summary(fit)
> ETS(A,N,N)
>
> Call:
>   ets(y = x, model = "ANN")
>
>    Smoothing parameters:
>      alpha = 0.9999
>
>    Initial states:
>      l = 0.1541
>
>    sigma:  0.0052
>
>         AIC        AICc        BIC
> -106.3560 -105.2651 -105.0779
>
> Training set error measures:
```

```
>                          ME        RMSE       MAE        MPE      MAPE
> Training set -0.001279923 0.005191075 0.00430566 -0.9445532 2.955436
>                          MASE        ACF1
> Training set 0.9286549 0.004655079
```

Plotting the predicted and actual values

Next, we can plot the predicted versus actual values. Notice that the predicted values are almost identical to the actual values; however, they are always one step ahead:

```
plot(x)
lines(fit$fitted, col = "red")
```

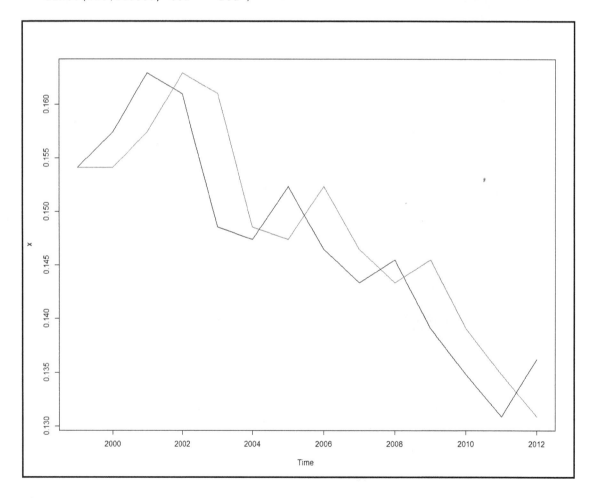

The forecast (fit) method

The `forecast` method contains many objects that you can display, such as the fitted value, original values, confidence intervals, and residuals. Use `str(forecast(fit))` to see which objects are available.

We will use `cbind` to print out the original data point, fitted data point, and model fitting method.

```
cbind(forecast(fit)$method,forecast(fit)$x,forecast(fit)$fitted,forecast(fi
t)$residuals)
Time Series:
Start = 1999
End = 2012
Frequency = 1
       forecast(fit)$method    forecast(fit)$x forecast(fit)$fitted
forecast(fit)$residuals
1999             ETS(A,N,N)  0.15412470117969    0.154120663632029
4.03754766081788e-06
2000             ETS(A,N,N) 0.157413125646824    0.154124700770241
0.00328842487658335
2001             ETS(A,N,N) 0.162942355969924    0.157412792166205
0.00552956380371911
2002             ETS(A,N,N) 0.160986044554207    0.162941795214416
-0.001955750660209
2003             ETS(A,N,N) 0.148533847659868    0.160986242887746
-0.0124523952278778
2004             ETS(A,N,N) 0.147400008880004    0.148535110462768
-0.00113510158276331
2005             ETS(A,N,N) 0.152327126236553    0.147400123991157
0.00492700224539561
2006             ETS(A,N,N) 0.146459794092561    0.152326626587079
-0.00586683249451758
2007             ETS(A,N,N)  0.14339666192983    0.146460389050636
-0.00306372712080566
2008             ETS(A,N,N) 0.145513631588618    0.143396972623751
0.00211665896486724
2009             ETS(A,N,N) 0.139109023459534    0.145513416937297
-0.00640439347776356
2010             ETS(A,N,N) 0.134795323545856    0.139109672931905
-0.00431434938604935
2011             ETS(A,N,N) 0.130889234985064    0.134795761065932
-0.00390652608086872
2012             ETS(A,N,N) 0.136204104247743    0.130889631147599
0.00531447310014455
```

We can also use `View` to show some of the `forecast` object in matrix form:

```
View(forecast(fit))
```

	Point Forecast	Lo 80	Hi 80	Lo 95	Hi 95
2013	0.1362036	0.1295509	0.1428562	0.1260292	0.1463779
2014	0.1362036	0.1267958	0.1456113	0.1218156	0.1505915
2015	0.1362036	0.1246817	0.1477255	0.1185823	0.1538248
2016	0.1362036	0.1228993	0.1495078	0.1158565	0.1565507
2017	0.1362036	0.1213290	0.1510781	0.1134549	0.1589522
2018	0.1362036	0.1199094	0.1524977	0.1112838	0.1611233
2019	0.1362036	0.1186039	0.1538032	0.1092872	0.1631199
2020	0.1362036	0.1173888	0.1550184	0.1074288	0.1649783
2021	0.1362036	0.1162475	0.1561597	0.1056834	0.1667238
2022	0.1362036	0.1151680	0.1572391	0.1040325	0.1683747

Plotting future values with confidence bands

Use the `plot` function to plot future predictions. Notice that the prediction for the last value encompasses upper and lower confidence bands surrounding a horizontal prediction line. But why a horizontal prediction line? This is saying that there is no trend or seasonality for the exponential model, and that the best prediction is based upon the last value of the smoothed average. However, we can see that there is significant variation to the prediction, based upon the confidence bands. The confidence bands will also increase in size as the forecast period increases, to reflect the uncertainty associated with the forecast:

```
plot(forecast(fit))
```

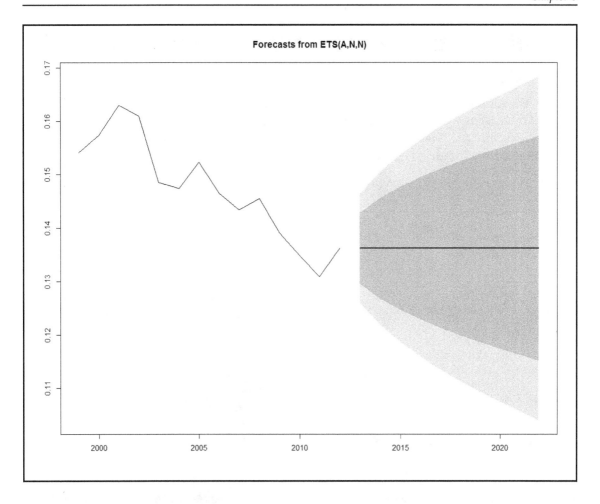

Forecasts from ETS(A,N,N)

Modifying the model to include a trend component

Earlier, we added a linear trend line to the data. If we wanted to incorporate a linear trend into the forecast as well, we can substitute A for the second parameter (trend parameter), which yields an "AAN" model (Holt's linear trend). This type of method allows exponential smoothing with a trend:

```
fit <- ets(x, model = "AAN")
summary(fit)
> ETS(A,A,N)
>
> Call:
> ets(y = x, model = "AAN")
>
> Smoothing parameters:
> alpha = 0.0312
> beta = 0.0312
>
> Initial states:
> l = 0.1641
> b = -0.0021
>
> sigma: 0.0042
>
> AIC AICc BIC
> -108.5711 -104.1267 -106.0149
>
> Training set error measures:
> ME RMSE MAE MPE MAPE
> Training set -0.000290753 0.004157744 0.003574276 -0.2632899 2.40212
> MASE ACF1
> Training set 0.7709083 0.05003007
```

Plotting the forecast yields the plot below:

```
plot(forecast(fit))
```

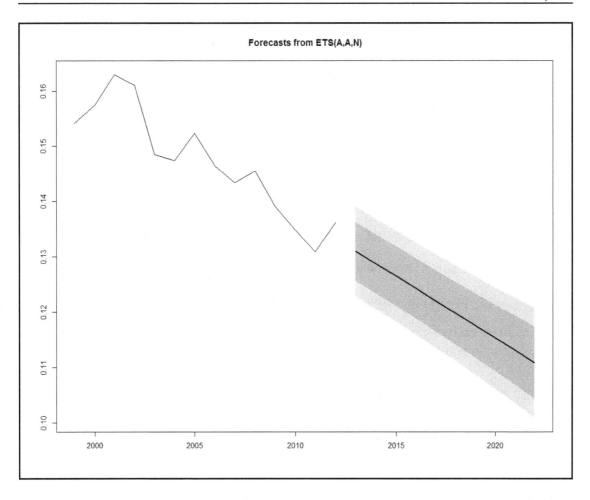

Running the ets function iteratively over all of the categories

Now that we have run an ets model on one category, we can construct some code to automate model construction over all of the categories.

In the process, we will also save some of the accuracy measures so that we can see how our models performed:

1. First, sort the dataframe by category, and then by year.

2. Then, initialize a new dataframe (`onestep.df`) that we will use to store the accuracy results for each moving window prediction of test and training data.

3. Then, process each of the groups, all of which have 14 time periods, as an iteration in a `for` loop.

4. For each iteration, extract a test and training dataframe.

5. Fit a simple exponential smoothed model for the training dataset.

6. Apply a model fit to the test dataset.

7. Apply the accuracy function in order to extract the validation statistics.

8. Store each of them in the `onestep.df` dataframe that was initialized in the previous step:

```
df <- x2 %>% arrange(cat, Year.1)

# create results data frame
onestep.df <- data.frame(cat = character(), rmse = numeric(), mae =
numeric(),
mape = numeric(), acf1 = numeric(), stringsAsFactors = FALSE)


#
#
library(forecast)
iterations <- 0
for (i in seq(from = 1, to = 999, by = 14)) {
j <- i + 13
# pull out the next category. It will always be 14 records.
x4 <- df[i:j, ]
x <- ts(x4$Not.Covered.Pct, start = c(1999), end = c(2012), frequency = 1)

# assign the first 10 records to the training data, and the next 4 to the
# test data.


trainingdata <- window(x, start = c(1999), end = c(2008))
testdata <- window(x, start = c(2009), end = c(2012))
```

```
par(mfrow = c(2, 2))

# first fit the training data, then the test data.
# Use simple exponential smoothing
fit <- ets(trainingdata, model = "ANN")
# summary(fit)
fit2 <- ets(testdata, model = fit)
onestep <- fitted(fit2)

iterations <- iterations + 1
onestep.df[iterations, 1] <- paste(x4$cat[1])
onestep.df[iterations, 2] <- accuracy(onestep, testdata)[, 2] #RMSE
onestep.df[iterations, 3] <- accuracy(onestep, testdata)[, 3] #MAE
onestep.df[iterations, 4] <- accuracy(onestep, testdata)[, 5] #MAPE
onestep.df[iterations, 5] <- accuracy(onestep, testdata)[, 7] #ACF1

if (iterations == 24)
break
}
```

Take a look at some of the rows from one of the categories extracted from the for loop. It is easy to look at the last group processed since since all intermediate object created in the loop are still intact.

First let's look at the actual data from the raw group:

```
tail(x4)
```

This shows a partial output of the last group UNDER 18 YEARS. NOTE: To see all of the years you need to run the command `tail(x4,14)` at the console instead:

```
> Source: local data frame [6 x 9]
>
> cat Avg.Total.Insured Avg.People Year Year.1
> (fctr) (dbl) (dbl) (fctr) (int)
> 1 UNDER 18 YEARS 66200.46 73752.5 2007 2007
> 2 UNDER 18 YEARS 66200.46 73752.5 2008 2008
> 3 UNDER 18 YEARS 66200.46 73752.5 2009 2009
> 4 UNDER 18 YEARS 66200.46 73752.5 2010 (10) 2010
> 5 UNDER 18 YEARS 66200.46 73752.5 2011 2011
> 6 UNDER 18 YEARS 66200.46 73752.5 2012 2012
> Variables not shown: Total.People (dbl), Total (dbl), Not.Covered (dbl),
> Not.Covered.Pct (dbl)
```

Accuracy measures produced by onestep

The `onestep.df` object produced from the for loop contains all of the accuracy measure for all of the groups. Take a look at the first 6. You can see that the accuracy measure `rmse`, `mae`, and `mape` are captured for each of the categories:

```
head(onestep.df)
>                 cat       rmse          mae      mape      acf1
> 1 18 to 24 YEARS     0.013772470 0.009869590 3.752381 1.0000552
> 2 25 to 34 YEARS     0.004036661 0.003380938 1.217612 1.0150588
> 3 35 to 44 YEARS     0.006441549 0.004790155 2.231886 0.9999469
> 4 45 to 54 YEARS     0.004261185 0.003129072 1.734022 0.9999750
> 5 55 to 64 YEARS     0.005160212 0.004988592 3.534093 0.7878765
> 6 65 YEARS AND OVER 0.002487451 0.002096323 12.156875 0.9999937
cbind(fit$x, fit$fitted, fit$residuals)
> Time Series:
> Start = 1999
> End = 2008
> Frequency = 1
>              fit$x fit$fitted fit$residuals
> 1999 0.11954420  0.1056241   0.0139200744
> 2000 0.10725759  0.1056255   0.0016320737
> 2001 0.10649619  0.1056257   0.0008705016
> 2002 0.10291788  0.1056258  -0.0027078918
> 2003 0.10393522  0.1056255  -0.0016902769
> 2004 0.09942592  0.1056253  -0.0061994140
> 2005 0.10320781  0.1056247  -0.0024169001
> 2006 0.11231138  0.1056245   0.0066869135
> 2007 0.10587369  0.1056251   0.0002485556
> 2008 0.09527547  0.1056252  -0.0103496921

mean(fit$residuals)
> [1] -6.056125e-07
```

Take a look at the residuals which resulted for the "UNDER 18 YEARS" category for the test dataset. The residuals seem to change for the year 2011, but the absolute value is still small across the board.

```
absresid <- abs(fit2$residuals)
plot(absresid)
```

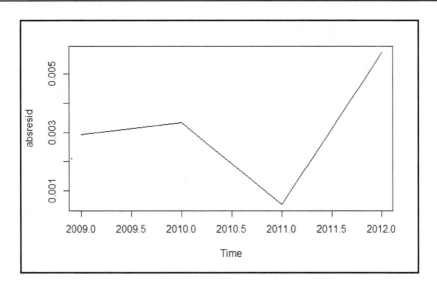

The `fit2` is test data, along with the fitted values from the model developed from the training data (`fit`):

```
cbind(fit2$x, fit2$fitted, fit2$residuals)
 > Time Series:
 > Start = 2009
 > End = 2012
 > Frequency = 1
 >            fit2$x fit2$fitted fit2$residuals
 > 2009 0.09745024  0.09451361   0.0029366252
 > 2010 0.09785322  0.09451391   0.0033393083
 > 2011 0.09397731  0.09451424  -0.0005369347
 > 2012 0.08877369  0.09451419  -0.0057404940

mean(fit2$residuals)
 > [1] -3.738216e-07
```

Comparing the Test and Training for the "UNDER 18 YEARS" group

We can also examine the plots for the training and test groups for this sub segment to see if anything is really going on:

```
par(mfrow = c(1, 2))
plot(forecast(fit))
plot(forecast(fit2))
```

From the following plots we can see that although there is a decline in the not-covered percentage for this group, there is probably not enough data to discern trend so that the projections are set at the mean values.

For the test data plot we can also see why the absolute residual plot dropped in xxx as it transitioned from a local peak in 2010 (when the Affordable Care Act was enacted) to the start of a decline in 2011:

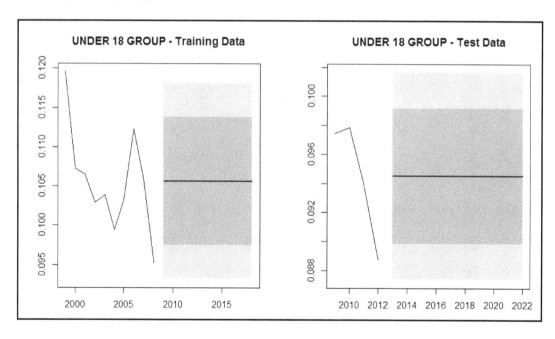

Accuracy measures

Using the residuals, we can measure the error from the predicted and actual values based upon three popular accuracy measures:

- **Mean absolute error** (**MAE**): This measure takes the mean of the absolute values of all of the errors (residuals)

- **Root-mean-squared error** (**RMSE**): The root mean square error measures the error by first taking the mean of all of the squared errors, and then takes the square root of the mean, in order to revert back to the original scale. This is a standard statistical method of measuring errors.

 Both MAE and RMSE are scale-dependent measures, which means that that they can be used to compare problems with similar scales. When comparing accuracy among models with different scales, other scale-independent measures such as MAPE should be used.

- **Mean percentage error** (**MAPE**): This is the absolute difference between the actual and forecasted value, expressed as a percentage of the actual value. This is intuitively easy to understand and is a very popular measure:

$$M = \frac{100}{n} \sum_{t=1}^{n} \left| \frac{A_t - F_t}{A_t} \right|,$$

where A_t is the actual value and F_t is the forecast value.

We can look at the worst-performing models, in terms of a metric such as MAPE, by simply sorting the `onestep.df` object by the MAPE columns:

```
onestep.df %>% arrange(., desc(mape)) %>% head()
>                             cat         rmse          mae        mape        acf1
> 1 MALE 65 YEARS AND OVER 0.002647903 0.002226841 17.440671 0.5781697
> 2 MALE 35 to 44 YEARS    0.039044319 0.024111701 14.218445 0.9999903
> 3 65 YEARS AND OVER      0.002487451 0.002096323 12.156875 0.9999937
> 4 MALE 25 to 34 YEARS    0.024195057 0.019901117  6.748294 0.9999310
> 5 MALE 45 to 54 YEARS    0.017711280 0.010388681  6.380865 0.9999900
> 6 FEMALE 55 to 64 YEARS  0.006749771 0.005610275  4.021224 0.5038707
```

Charting all of the MAPEs at once shows that the exponential model works better for the younger groups, and seems to degrade for older groups, especially for males:

```
lattice::barchart(cat ~ mape, data = onestep.df)
```

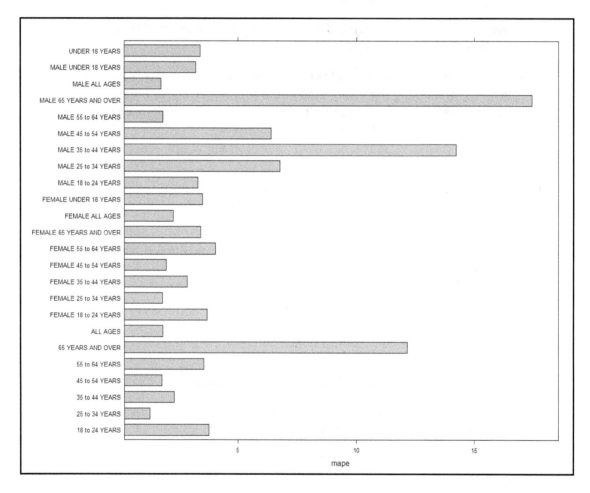

References

`http://www.census.gov/data/tables/time-series/demo/health-insurance/historic`
`al-series/hib.html`

Summary

This chapter introduced time series analysis by reading in and exploring Health Care Enrollment Data from the CMS website. Then we moved on to defining some basic Time Series concepts such as Simple and Exponential Moving Averages. Finally we worked with the R "forecast" package to work with some exponential smoothed state space models, and showed you one way to produce automated forecasts for your data. We also showed various plotting methods using the ggplot, lattice package, as well as native R graphics.

9
Introduction to Spark Using R

Data! Data! Data! I can't make bricks without clay!

- Sir Arthur Conan Doyle

So far, we have learned how to perform analytics on what can be referred to as "small data". However, as the amount of data increases, so does the size and the problem of how to analyze the vast amounts of data that is produced arises. When that occurs, we begin to approach "big data" and new approaches to solving problems develop and sometimes, new tools are needed as well.

To some extent, nothing changes. You still want high quality data. You still want to be able to examine the relationships and cast the problem within a predictive analytic framework.

What does change are the steps needed to achieve that end, bearing in mind that the data is more difficult to manage and as a result new tools have evolved to help you do that.

One of the tools that has evolved in recent years is Apache Spark.

In this chapter, we will cover some basics of Spark. We will start with a known small dataset, perform some data cleaning, and then transform this dataset into something much larger which we can use to bring into the Apache Spark environment. We will also learn how to adapt tools that we are familiar with, in order to work with Spark, and learn some new tools along the way.

About Spark

At the time of writing, Spark is probably the most popular very large dataset architecture for predictive analytics. Spark is a distributed architecture which helps you manage your large data and makes it easier to analyze. Spark is built upon Hadoop and they share the same filesystem.

However, Spark is not based upon the MapReduce paradigm, and uses the **resilient distributed dataset** (**RDD**) structure in order to implement in-memory analytics and manage the parallel processing cluster across all of the nodes of the environment. What that means for analysts is that queries can be very quick, since data is retrieved from memory, which offers much quicker retrieval than disk access. Quicker access means more time for analysis, and less time waiting for results.

Here are some advantages of Spark:

- Spark overcomes some of the limitations of memory-bound analytics, since it manages memory, and is able to optimize data access and querying.
- Spark has its own machine learning library known as MLlib, which implements several population predictive model techniques and optimizes computational speed for algorithms involving large datasets.
- Spark now includes the concepts of dataframes, which extends ease of use to analysts who use R or Python.
- Spark takes advantage of redundancy and fault-tolerant aspects of Hadoop. If one node fails for whatever reason, another node will take its place so that the analytics do not fail. This is very important when working in a production environment.
- Spark also supports other languages such as Java and Scala. Languages can be mixed within an analytics pipeline and analysts can share the same data. This can improve team collaboration and improve efficiency.

Spark environments

Spark runs in three different modes:

- Standalone
- YARN
- MESOS

For initial deployments (and for learning), it is best to start with standalone, which allocates clusters specifically for Spark use only. Furthermore, you can run standalone mode in local mode (your computer) or via cloud computing (an example would be using Amazon AWS).

Cluster computing

Cluster computing allows Spark to process and distribute data over many computers at once, in parallel. A **cluster manager** allocates resources for the cluster depending upon user requests. An important aspect of Spark is that it attempts to keep as much data in memory as needed, so that data is available for the various analyses as quickly as possible rather than having to wait to retrieve data from storage every time a query or model is specified.

Spark data is stored as RDDs, which allow different kinds of objects to be spread out over the cluster.

Parallel computing

Parallel computing refers to the ability to perform separate computing tasks at the same time. It does this by distributing the work load. For example if a dataframe needs to simply be sorted by last name, the cluster manager can pass the various names starting with 26 letters of the alphabet to 26 different nodes, have them each sort their own letter, and then ask for them all to be returned to one place where 1 final sort will be performed. This can be quicker than if only 1 machine performed the sort.

SparkR

Spark itself is written in a programming language called Scala and runs in a Java environment. However, you are not restricted to using Scala. Spark has several interfaces which are exposed through an API, which allows Spark programs to be written in these other languages:

- R
- Scala
- Java
- Python
- Clojure

We will be demonstrating some of the examples in this chapter using SparkR. SparkR is an R package that provides a frontend to use Apache Spark from R. This allows SparkR to allow data scientists to interactively run jobs from R on a cluster. One big advantage of using SparkR, for the traditional R programmer, is that it uses some of the techniques that they already know such as the concept of dataframes is also available within SparkR.

Dataframes

Spark RDDs can be a bit difficult to work with, so in recent versions of Spark, Dataframe abstractions have been built on top of RDDs, which allows analysts to view data in ways that they are used to looking at them, for example, being able to view them as tables and lists. This allows many high level languages (such as R and Python) to utilize syntax which is familiar to them and to be able to integrate optimized code, which is on par with native Scala or Spark SQL.

Databrick is a company founded by the creators of Apache Spark, which offers a free environment for running Spark programs in the cloud utilizing R, Java, Scala, or Python.

I will be using the Databricks environment for illustrating the necessary coding needed to run the chapter examples. These examples use the concept of Databricks notebooks. Databricks notebooks are similar to Jupyter or Zeppelin notebooks. The notebook metaphor allows you to display code and results all in one place.

Here is a simple example of a Databricks notebook which computes a histogram of an iris's sepal length and plots it using ggplot.

[Insert Databricks mockup 1 and databricks mockup 2 image]

As we shall see, the databricks notebook also allows you to mix different languages in one notebook; so, for example, you can construct one analysis using a combination of R, Python, and SQL code.

In order to get started:

1. Sign up for a free Databricks account at databricks.com.
2. Import the notebook used in this chapter.
3. Start up a cluster.
4. Start following along!

Building our first Spark dataframe

One of the challenges of working with Spark is finding analytic solutions when working with very large datasets. As a preparation step, in this chapter, we will build our very own large Spark dataframe.

Also note that the concept of large dataframe is obviously relative. Since the free databricks will limit the size of any dataframe created, we will end up building a 1-million-row dataframe of about 11 variables.

I will also show you how to build a similar dataset in base R, so that you can perform your own testing and be able to judge the performance benefits received from performing the analytics on Spark.

Simulation

We will end up building this Spark dataframe via simulation. This will take up a good chunk of this chapter. I feel this is a better way to go rather than importing an existing public dataset in which you cannot control the makeup of the data. With a simulated dataset, you are free to size it however you like (subject to account restrictions).

However, you are always free to import whatever dataset you would like and the analytic concepts that follow will be the same.

1. Preliminaries first, you will need to register and log on to your databricks account.
2. Next, create a cluster. Give it a name, such as MyCluster.
3. To conform with the examples in this chapter, make sure you choose Spark 2.1. This is very important. Since Spark is an Apache open source product, capabilities can evolve, so we want to make sure you can reproduce your code.
4. Select **Create Cluster**.

5. Allow some time for the cluster to be created. When it is completing, you will receive the **Running** status, as shown in the following screenshot:

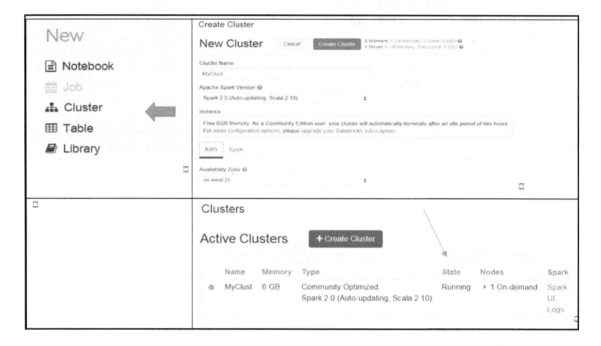

Importing the sample notebook

The best way to run the examples in this chapter is by importing the notebook from an external site. To do this:

1. Click on **Workspace**.
2. Right-click on **Training & Tutorials** (or an alternate folder) and select **Import**.
3. Drag the file downloaded from the publisher site into the drop area and click on **Import**.

See the following screenshot:

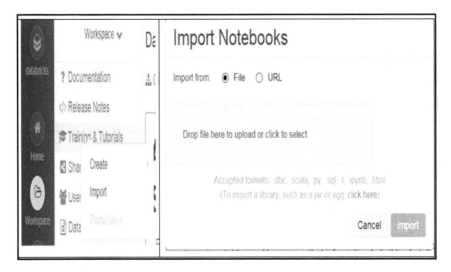

After you import your notebook, all of the code and output will appear and you will be free to follow along with the remaining code examples.

Notebook format

Databricks notebooks contain the written code in the cell in the upper pane, followed by any output in the lower cell, similar to the tutorial code for the 'diamonds' data which is displayed next.

To run the current cell, simply click on the triangle icon on the right.

- When the cell has run, you will be able to view your output below your code. That could be a plot or the output from the console. Always check for error messages and warnings, especially if the output is not what you expect.
- Also note that there are some situations where no output at all is produced. That may be okay, but be sure to check the timestamp on the output cell to make sure the cell was actually run:

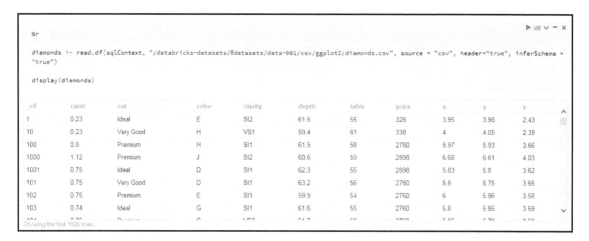

Creating a new notebook

As an alternative to importing a notebook, you can create a new notebook from the Databricks home screen and copy/paste the code in the chapter into the notebook cells. You might want to do this if you are using some of this chapter as a template and wish to add your own code.

You can use the keyboard shortcut sequence `<Ctrl> + <Alt> + N` to create a new notebook.

Becoming large by starting small

The strategy we will use in this chapter is to first retrieve a small existing publicly available dataset (Pima Indians diabetes). Then we will perform some basic exploratory analysis, compute some key statistical properties, and then use those properties to simulate a much larger dataset that we will use to input into Spark. The key characteristics that we will use to generate this 'big data' will be:

- **The means/standard deviations of the variables**: the goal will be to generate means and standard deviations for the large dataset, which are close to the equivalent means and standard deviations of the small dataset.
- **The correlations of the variables**: since statistical modeling and analysis is largely based upon the association among the variables, the goal of the simulation will be to preserve all of the 2-way correlation numbers for the large dataset which exist in the small dataset.
- **The underlying distribution of the variables**: we will assume normal distributions for all the variables, except for the outcome variables (Diabetes, versus NonDiabetes. However, we will simulate the outcomes to correspond with the proportion reflected in the sample dataset.

The Pima Indians diabetes dataset

To build the characteristics of the Spark dataframe, we will first take a small dataset, determine the basic statistical properties of this dataset, and then build a Spark dataframe based upon these properties.

The Pima Indians diabetes dataset contains the following attributes:

- Number of times pregnant
- Plasma glucose concentration with two hours in an oral glucose tolerance test
- Diastolic blood pressure (mm Hg)
- Triceps skin fold thickness (mm)
- 2-hour serum insulin (mu U/ml)
- Body mass index (weight in kg/(height in m)^2)
- Diabetes pedigree function
- Age (years)
- Developed diabetes (yes or no)

The data is a publicly available dataset. In fact, there are several versions of this dataset available. We will use the dataset contained within the `mlbench` package, which we will load into the R workspace.

Running the code

After loading the notebook, a series of code 'chunks' will appear. This particular notebook is an R type notebook, that is, by default, code lines can be R commands, SparkR commands, or special Databricks commands (such as display).

We will see later that we can have different cells for SQL commands (notebooks starting with %sql) or even intermix Python (%python) or scala code (%scala).

to run the contents of any particular code chunk you can use the folowingkeyboard sequence:

Alternatively, use can use the run cell icon (the first triangle icon):

Now that we now how to run individual code chunks, we will begin by running the initialization code which simply tests the Databricks system to see if it is operational and also sets some options.

Running the initialization code

The initialization code merely sets some options for later use and has no real output. We will just print "Hello World" to make sure that it is working:

```
options(digits=3)
options(repr.plot.width = 1000, repr.plot.height = 500, repr.plot.res =
144, repr.plot.pointsize = 5)
rep_times=1000
cat("Hello World")
```

The output cell prints **Hello World** and also gives you the time it took to run, the username, time and time, as well as the cluster it ran on. Pay close attention to the length of time that each code chunk ran. It will be useful for benchmarking code at a later date.

```
Hello World

Command took 0.00 seconds -- by r_winters at 2/27/2017, 6:20:39 PM on MyCluster
```

Extracting the Pima Indians diabetes dataset

After running the following code, we will have the `PimaIndiansDiabetes` R dataframe loaded and we will run the usual `str()` and `summary()` functions. Note that we need to first install the `mlbench` package to retrieve the data that is contained within the package.

At this point, no Spark directives are being introduced. Even though we are running in a databricks environment, the code is pure R, and you can replicate this code in your regular R environment as well.

```
# load the library
devtools::install_github("cran/mlbench")
library(mlbench)
data(PimaIndiansDiabetes)
str(PimaIndiansDiabetes)
summary(PimaIndiansDiabetes)
```

Examining the output

As usual, the `str()` and `summary()` functions will give you your first insights into the data. The outputs will appear in the console pane, which is typically right below the coding pane.

Note: not all output is shown.

Output from the str() function

- The `str()` function tells us that there are 768 observations and 9 variables. All of the variables have been loaded as numeric, except for the target variable diabetes, which has been coded as a factor with two levels.
- `neg` indicates the diabetic condition that is not present.
- `pos` indicates the diabetic condition that is present.

Again, the str() is a great way to quickly get insights. Always scan for 0's and NA's in the first few rows and start asking yourself if it is reasonable to expect those values.

Refer to the following figure:

```
'data.frame':    768 obs. of  9 variables:
 $ pregnant: num  6 1 8 1 0 5 3 10 2 8 ...
 $ glucose : num  148 85 183 89 137 116 78 115 197 125 ...
 $ pressure: num  72 66 64 66 40 74 50 0 70 96 ...
 $ triceps : num  35 29 0 23 35 0 32 0 45 0 ...
 $ insulin : num  0 0 0 94 168 0 88 0 543 0 ...
 $ mass    : num  33.6 26.6 23.3 28.1 43.1 25.6 31 35.3 30.5 0 ...
 $ pedigree: num  0.627 0.351 0.672 0.167 2.288 ...
 $ age     : num  50 31 32 21 33 30 26 29 53 54 ...
 $ diabetes: Factor w/ 2 levels "neg","pos": 2 1 2 1 2 1 2 1 2 2 ...
```

Output from the summary() function

The `summary()` function breaks out the diabetes variable into counts. Of 768 observations, there are 500 negative and 268 positive observations.

Note that the summary output has detected no missing values; however, if you look closely, you can see that there are zeros present for variables that should have a measurement (glucose, pressure, insulin, and mass). A zero for the number of times pregnant is acceptable.

We will address the zeros after we perform some plotting:

```
    pregnant          glucose          pressure          triceps
Min.   : 0.000    Min.   :  0.0    Min.   :  0.00    Min.   : 0.00
1st Qu.: 1.000    1st Qu.: 99.0    1st Qu.: 62.00    1st Qu.: 0.00
Median : 3.000    Median :117.0    Median : 72.00    Median :23.00
Mean   : 3.845    Mean   :120.9    Mean   : 69.11    Mean   :20.54
3rd Qu.: 6.000    3rd Qu.:140.2    3rd Qu.: 80.00    3rd Qu.:32.00
Max.   :17.000    Max.   :199.0    Max.   :122.00    Max.   :99.00
    insulin          mass            pedigree            age          diabetes
Min.   :  0.0    Min.   : 0.00    Min.   :0.0780    Min.   :21.00    neg:500
1st Qu.:  0.0    1st Qu.:27.30    1st Qu.:0.2437    1st Qu.:24.00    pos:268
Median : 30.5    Median :32.00    Median :0.3725    Median :29.00
Mean   : 79.8    Mean   :31.99    Mean   :0.4719    Mean   :33.24
3rd Qu.:127.2    3rd Qu.:36.60    3rd Qu.:0.6262    3rd Qu.:41.00
Max.   :846.0    Max.   :67.10    Max.   :2.4200    Max.   :81.00
```

Comparing outcomes

As mentioned in an earlier chapter, boxplots are a good way for comparing two numeric variables. We will compare Diabetes='neg' with Diabetes='pos'.

Position your cursor within the next cell and run the following code chunk. This code runs the boxplot() function for variables 1-7, and breaks it out by diabetes outcome:

```
#some basic exploratory analysis.  Box plots by outcome
par(mfrow=c(2,4))
for (i in 1:7) {
  boxplot(PimaIndiansDiabetes[,i] ~ PimaIndiansDiabetes$diabetes,
main=names(PimaIndiansDiabetes[i]), type="l")
}
```

After the run is complete (it should only take a second), the following boxplots will appear under the code that was just run:

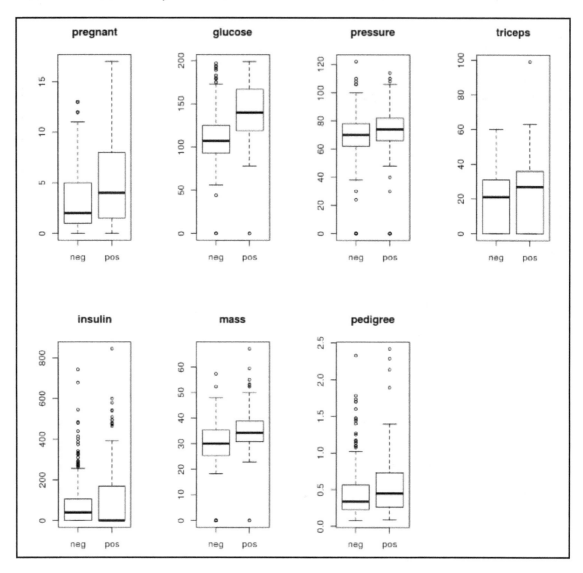

In the boxplots produced, you can see that the median values for all of the variables are always higher for the `Diabetes='pos'` class, except for the insulin variable, which is lower. This suggests that these variables may have some effect in predicting diabetes, but that there also may be some correlation among the predictors.

Checking for missing values

We can see from the prior summary that we have no missing values; however, we can see that there are quite a few variables with values of zero, which do not make any sense. For example, it is impossible to have a zero reading for blood pressure, but it is OK to have a 0 for the number of months pregnant. So, for most of these variables, we will assume that zero was recorded for NAs and we will map the data accordingly:

- First, we will copy the data to a new dataframe
- Then, we will change the zeros to NAs for the five variables listed in the code:

```
# we see that there are 0's which are really NA's
#some 0's are really NA's, we will change them in Spark
# keep pregnant = 0
PimaIndians <- PimaIndiansDiabetes
PimaIndians$glucose[PimaIndians$glucose ==0] <- NA
PimaIndians$pressure[PimaIndians$pressure ==0] <- NA
PimaIndians$triceps[PimaIndians$triceps ==0] <- NA
PimaIndians$insulin[PimaIndians$insulin ==0] <- NA
PimaIndians$mass[PimaIndians$mass ==0] <- NA
summary(PimaIndians)
```

Run another summary to ensure that the zeros have become missing values (NAs):

```
    pregnant           glucose          pressure           triceps
 Min.   : 0.000    Min.   : 44.0    Min.   : 24.00    Min.   : 7.00
 1st Qu.: 1.000    1st Qu.: 99.0    1st Qu.: 64.00    1st Qu.:22.00
 Median : 3.000    Median :117.0    Median : 72.00    Median :29.00
 Mean   : 3.845    Mean   :121.7    Mean   : 72.41    Mean   :29.15
 3rd Qu.: 6.000    3rd Qu.:141.0    3rd Qu.: 80.00    3rd Qu.:36.00
 Max.   :17.000    Max.   :199.0    Max.   :122.00    Max.   :99.00
                   NA's   :5        NA's   :35        NA's   :227

    insulin            mass            pedigree           age          diabetes
 Min.   : 14.00    Min.   :18.20    Min.   :0.0780    Min.   :21.00    neg:500
 1st Qu.: 76.25    1st Qu.:27.50    1st Qu.:0.2437    1st Qu.:24.00    pos:268
 Median :125.00    Median :32.30    Median :0.3725    Median :29.00
 Mean   :155.55    Mean   :32.46    Mean   :0.4719    Mean   :33.24
 3rd Qu.:190.00    3rd Qu.:36.60    3rd Qu.:0.6262    3rd Qu.:41.00
 Max.   :846.00    Max.   :67.10    Max.   :2.4200    Max.   :81.00
 NA's   :374       NA's   :11
```

Imputing the missing values

We will now perform a simple mean imputation. However, rather than substituting with a single mean number, we will replace the NAs with the mean values based upon membership of these four groups:

- Diabetes=pos/younger age range
- Diabetes=neg/younger age range
- Diabetes=neg/older age range
- Diabetes=pos/older age range

We already have the Diabetes=neg/pos category, so how do we categorize into the younger/older age group?

We will do that by automatically calculating a cut point. To determine the cut point, we will use the cut function on the Age variable so separate it into two levels. Then we will use dplyr to compute mean values for the five variables, depending upon how the age group was cut.

1. First, let's see how many observations fall into each of the four groups:

```
library(dplyr)
PimaIndians$agegrp <- as.numeric(cut(PimaIndians$age, breaks=2))
PimaIndians %>%
    group_by(diabetes,agegrp) %>% count()
```

2. The output is showing the four groups which were created, along with their counts.

```
Source: local data frame [4 x 3]
Groups: diabetes [?]

  diabetes agegrp    n
1      neg      1  460
2      neg      2   40
3      pos      1  235
4      pos      2   33
```

3. Next, we will substitute an imputed mean value for each of the four groups.

4. Note that only NA values are replaced. If they are not NA, we will keep the original value. This is something to always watch out for. You usually don't want to overwrite valid accepted values with imputed ones!

```
library(dplyr)
df <- PimaIndians %>%
    group_by(diabetes,agegrp) %>%
    mutate(
        insulin.imp = mean(insulin,na.rm=TRUE),
        glucose.imp = mean(glucose,na.rm=TRUE),
        pressure.imp = mean(pressure,na.rm=TRUE),
        triceps.imp = mean(triceps,na.rm=TRUE),
        mass.imp    =  mean(mass,na.rm=TRUE)
    )
df$insulin <- ifelse(is.na(df$insulin), df$insulin.imp, df$insulin)
df$glucose <- ifelse(is.na(df$glucose), df$glucose.imp, df$glucose)
df$pressure <- ifelse(is.na(df$pressure), df$pressure.imp,
df$pressure)
df$triceps <- ifelse(is.na(df$triceps), df$triceps.imp, df$triceps)
df$mass <- ifelse(is.na(df$mass), df$mass.imp, df$mass)
```

Checking the imputations (reader exercise)

After replacing the NAs, print the resulting dataframe and compare the assigned value with the imputed value. This is just a checkpoint to make sure that your imputation went smooth and that the results are reasonable. Always look for extreme values for imputations which can tell you if something is off.

```
print.data.frame(head(df[,c(
   "insulin", "insulin.imp",
   "glucose","glucose.imp",
   "pressure","pressure.imp",
   "triceps","triceps.imp",
   "mass","mass.imp")],10))
```

```
insulin insulin.imp glucose glucose.imp pressure pressure.imp triceps
    191         191     148         141     72.8         74.4    35.8
    129         129      85         189     66.8         78.4    29.8
    191         191     183         141     64.8         74.4    32.8
     94         129      89         189     66.8         78.4    23.8
    168         191     137         141     48.8         74.4    35.8
    129         129     116         189     74.8         78.4    27.2
     88         191      78         141     58.8         74.4    32.8
    129         129     115         189     78.4         78.4    27.2
    543         328     197         153     78.8         81.4    45.8
    328         328     125         153     96.8         81.4    34.3
triceps.imp mass mass.imp
       32.8 33.6    35.7
       27.2 26.6    31.8
       32.8 23.3    35.7
       27.2 28.1    31.8
       32.8 43.1    35.7
       27.2 25.6    31.8
       32.8 31.8    35.7
       27.2 35.3    31.8
       34.3 38.5    33.8
       34.3 33.8    33.8
```

Missing values complete!

When you are satisfied that the imputation has been performed correctly:

- Assign the temporary dataframe back into the PimaIndians dataframe
- Count the number of NAs in each row

The output of the head function shows NAs no longer exist. If there are still NAs, a row will be printed:

```
PimaIndians <- df
head(PimaIndians[rowSums(is.na(PimaIndians)) > 0, ])
```

```
Source: local data frame [8 x 15]
Groups: diabetes, agegrp [8]

# ... with 15 variables: pregnant , glucose , pressure ,
#    triceps , insulin , mass , pedigree , age ,
#    diabetes , agegrp , insulin.imp , glucose.imp ,
#    pressure.imp , triceps.imp , mass.imp
```

Calculating the correlation matrices

Now, we will calculate correlation and covariance matrices. This will give us a sense of how the predictor variables relate to each other. Later on, we will also use this information to construct our larger dataset:

```
# calculate correlation matrix and exclude NA's
correlationMatrix <- cor(PimaIndians[,1:8])

covarianceMatrix <- stats::cov(PimaIndians[,1:8])

# summarize the correlation matrix
print(correlationMatrix,digits=3)
```

The correlation matrix is laid out as an *n*n* table with the variables specified along the top and side of the matrix. To obtain the correlation of any variable with another, look up any pair of variables along the top and bottom of the matrix and refer to the number at the intersection. That is the computed correlation:

```
Correlation Matrix                                                              Covariance Matrix
                 pregnant  glucose   pressure  triceps   insulin    mass                          pregnant   glucose    pressure    triceps      insulin
pregnant  1.00000000 0.1281346  0.214178483 0.1002391 0.08217103 0.02171892    pregnant  11.35465632  13.947131    9.2145382  -4.3908410   -28.555231
glucose   0.12813455 1.0000000  0.223191778 0.2280432 0.58118621 0.23277051    glucose   13.94713066 1822.248314  94.4309556  29.2391827  1220.935799
pressure  0.21417848 0.2231918  1.000000000 0.2268391 0.09827230 0.28923034    pressure   9.21453818  94.430956  374.6472712  64.0293962   198.378412
triceps   0.10023907 0.2280432  0.226839067 1.0000000 0.18488442 0.64821394    triceps   -4.39004101  29.239183   64.0293962 254.4732453   802.979941
insulin   0.08217103 0.5811862  0.098272299 0.1848884 1.00000000 0.22805016    insulin  -28.55523074 1220.935799 198.3784122 802.9799408 13281.180078
mass      0.02171892 0.2327765  0.289230349 0.6482139 0.22805016 1.00000000    mass        8.46977418  55.726987   43.8046951  49.3738694   179.775172
pedigree -0.03352267 0.1372457 -0.002804527 0.1150164 0.13039587 0.15538175    pedigree  -0.03742597   1.454875    0.2646376   0.9721355     7.066681
age       0.54434123 0.2671356  0.330107425 0.1668158 0.22026068 0.02584146    age        21.57061977  99.082885   54.5234528 -21.3810232   -57.143298

                 pedigree       age                                                            mass      pedigree        age
pregnant -0.033522673 0.54434123                                              pregnant    0.4697742  -0.03742597  21.5706198
glucose   0.137245741 0.26713555                                              glucose    55.7269867   1.45487481  99.0828054
pressure -0.002804527 0.33010743                                              pressure   43.8046951   0.26463757  54.5234528
triceps   0.115016426 0.16681577                                              triceps    49.3738694  -0.97213555 -21.3810232
insulin   0.130395872 0.22026068                                              insulin   179.7751721   7.06668051 -57.1432983
mass      0.155361746 0.02584146                                              mass       62.1599840   0.36740469   3.3603299
pedigree  1.000000000 0.03356131                                              pedigree    0.3674047   0.10977664   0.1307717
age       0.033561312 1.00000000                                              age         3.3603299   0.13077169 138.3030459
```

For a small number of variables, it is easy enough to scan the matrix and pick out the significant correlations. For a larger number of variables, it would make more sense to pick out the larger correlations use code similar to this which picks out correlations > .5:

```
df <- as.data.frame(as.table(correlationMatrix))
subset(df, abs(Freq) > 0.5 & abs(Freq) <1)
```

We can see a high correlation among some of the variables-age, number of pregnancies, insulin, and glucose levels have the highest levels:

```
> subset(df, abs(Freq) > 0.5 & abs(Freq) <1)
        Var1     Var2       Freq
8        age pregnant 0.5443412
13   insulin  glucose 0.5811862
30      mass  triceps 0.6482139
34   glucose  insulin 0.5811862
44   triceps     mass 0.6482139
```

You can also create the scatterplots of these variables in a number of different ways.

Use the `pairs()` function to accomplish this using only base R:

```
pairs(PimaIndians[c(1,2,4,5,6,8)],pch=21)
```

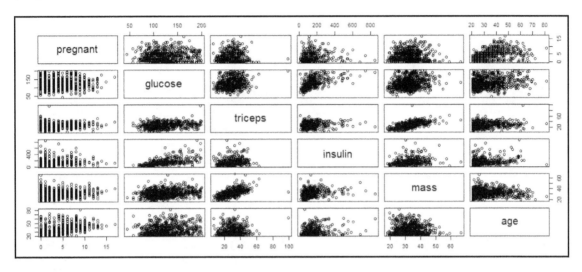

Calculating the column means

For the following simulation section, we will need to supply the column means via a vector, so let's calculate them now and display them as a horizontal barchart. We will calculate the column means first for the diabetes positive group and then for the diabetes negative group. Finally, we will calculate the means for the total, although we will not use them in the next section:

```
means.pos = colMeans(PimaIndians[PimaIndians$diabetes
=='pos',1:8],na.rm=TRUE)
means.neg = colMeans(PimaIndians[PimaIndians$diabetes
=='neg',1:8],na.rm=TRUE)
means.all = colMeans(PimaIndians[,1:8],na.rm=TRUE)
barplot(means.all[c(1,2,3,4,5,6,7,8)],cex.axis=.75,cex.names=.70,horiz=TRUE
,space=0)
```

The barplot below shows the calculated means for reference only. We are not comparing them since they all have different scale levels.

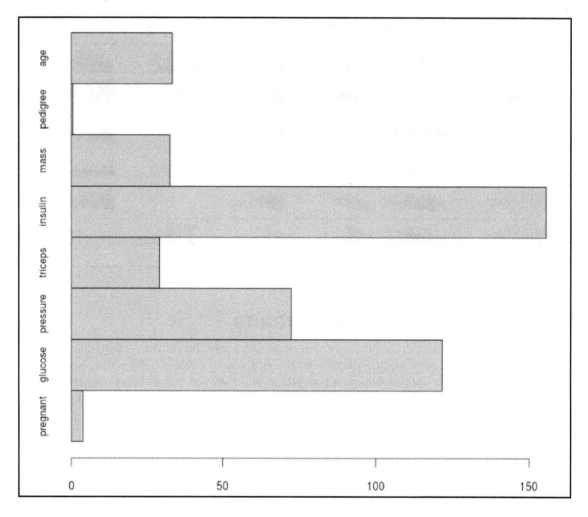

Simulating the data

Once we have calculated the mean values and covariance matrices for all of the columns, we are ready to simulate a big dataset for any number of observations we desire.

Which correlations to use?

For the covariance matrix, we can either use separate matrices for the two diabetes outcomes (1,0), or use a pooled covariance matrix, which shows the correlations among the variables regardless of the outcome.

We will use the separate correlation or covariance matrices since we have enough observations for each outcome (n=500 and n=268). If either of these classes were much smaller related to the other, we could use the pooled (or total) covariance matrix instead, since that would cover a larger set of observations.

Some notes on the code which follows:

- As a reminder, always start with a random seed prior to a simulation. That will ensure that you get the same random results <u>every time you run the code</u>.
- The `cor()` function will compute the correlation matrix among all of the variables, while the `cov()` function computes the covariance matrix. The major difference between a correlation and covariance matrix is that covariance is expressed in the same units as the variables, while correlation standardizes the relationship to a value between 0 and 1. However, they essentially measure the same thing.
- The `nbins` variable will divide the data into individual bins with 400 observations each. This will be handy to extract smaller samples of the data rather than performing analysis on the entire dataset. Again, this is another way of demonstrating that sampling is your friend.
- The datasets are generated using the `mvrnorm` function, which takes an input of mean values (of columns 1-8), along with the covariance matrix, which we just generated. Note: to get more information about this function, you can create a new cell anywhere in this notebook and run this command, which will invoke the R help system: help(mvrnorm, package="MASS")
- To increase the size of the dataframe, we generate the dataframe with `n1` observations and then repeat the dataframe a specified number of times, indicated by the `rep_times` variable. If you feel that the simulation is taking too long, you can reduce this variable to a lower number and the simulation will complete much faster.

- Finally, we need to distinguish between `data.frame` and `as.DataFrame` functions:
    - The `data.frame` is a normal R function which creates a dataframe from the arguments within the function.
    - The `as.DataFrame` is a SparkR function which converts the result to a Spark dataframe.
    - When in doubt, preface the function with either `base::` or `SparkR::` to specifically designate the package from which it is derived. Otherwise you may get an warning or error message which could be hard to debug.
- The last code line prints out the number of rows of the Spark dataframe using the `nrow()` function.

Run the next code chunk:

```
#generate spark dataframe
set.seed(123)
n1=268
n2=500
#data loaded into spark
#use separate correlation matrix for now. May want to use 1 pooled matrix.

correlationMatrix <- cor(PimaIndians[PimaIndians$diabetes =='pos',1:8])

covarianceMatrix <- stats::cov(PimaIndians[PimaIndians$diabetes
=='pos',1:8])

require(MASS)
nbins1=base::round(n1/400,0)
out_sd1 <- as.DataFrame(data.frame(data.frame(
sample.bin=base::sample(1:nbins1,n1,replace=TRUE)*(+1),
outcome=1,
mvrnorm(n1, mu = means.pos, Sigma = matrix(covarianceMatrix, ncol = 8),
empirical = TRUE)
))[rep(1:n1, times=2000), ])

nrow(out_sd1)

(1)Spark Jobs
Loading required package: MASS
Attaching package: 'MASS'
The following object is masked from 'package:SparkR':
    select
[1] 536000
```

```
Command took 2.88 minutes -- by r_winters at 2/13/2017, 3:15:24 PM on My
Cluster
```

Checking the object type

You can see that the resultant object is a Spark dataframe by issuing an `str()` function. The output will specifically say `SparkDataFrame`, followed by a description of the variables and data types. However, it will not list the number of rows:

```
str(out_sd1)
```

```
▶ (1) Spark Jobs

'SparkDataFrame': 10 variables:
$ sample_bin: num 78 212 110 237 253 13
$ outcome   : num 1 1 1 1 1 1
$ pregnant  : num 1.94252031814449 4.36423863864429 0.858675776495492 1.85534568833345 9.17100400066027 1.1186379328449
$ glucose   : num 157.123189654394 148.943347090497 172.842735207286 107.366227123907 105.302689867468 188.881198462925
$ pressure  : num 61.5029879083116 71.69507301027 74.4269535626088 74.3844944342854 78.1355932536701 61.8843444282885
$ triceps   : num 15.6917644265514 41.5591691064547 30.0192322177519 34.9364879662772 33.0035759583851 28.1923108753192
$ insulin   : num 129.597011349131 240.029631091656 379.471775333015 86.1971329956682 -67.8238532621351 181.68231106527
$ mass      : num 29.4401765315476 24.953572101178 32.846294404615 42.3403328136571 35.6341563357795 42.5202651318031
$ pedigree  : num 1.22263036150258 0.313509501680247 0.445328027648939 0.52963571807743 0.385501592130751 0.25120511045
$ age       : num 25.8341329573308 19.4383095827238 46.3093049981371 16.6689622302294 26.5530899692054 26.1512830183403
```

Simulating the negative cases

We just simulated the positive cases. Now, let's set up some similar code to simulate the non-diabetes patients (`outcome=0`).

For the negative cases, we will also multiply `sample.bin` by −1, so that in the future, we know that all the positive `sample.bin` instances correspond to positive cases and all the negative `sample.bin` instances correspond to negative ones:

```
set.seed(123)

nbins2=base::round(n2/400,0)
correlationMatrix <- cor(PimaIndians[PimaIndians$diabetes =='neg',1:8])

covarianceMatrix <- stats::cov(PimaIndians[PimaIndians$diabetes
=='neg',1:8])

out_sd2 <- as.DataFrame(data.frame(data.frame(
  sample.bin=base::sample(1:nbins2,n2,replace=TRUE)*(-1),
```

```
    outcome=0,
    mvrnorm(n2, mu = means.neg, Sigma = matrix(covarianceMatrix, ncol = 8),
    empirical = TRUE)
    ))[rep(1:n2, times=2000), ])

    nrow(out_sd2)
```

The output indicates that 500,000 rows were generated. Notice that it also indicates that two Spark jobs were run to obtain the result. For the curious, you can also click on the triangle icon to display detailed information about the Spark jobs from a processing standpoint, (although it contains no results output).

```
▶ (2) Spark Jobs

[1] 5e+05
```

Concatenating the positive and negative cases into a single Spark dataframe

We now have two separate Spark dataframes corresponding to positive and negative cases. For certain types of analysis, it would make sense to keep the outcomes separate; however, for illustration purposes, we will combine them into one single dataset using the `unionAll()` function.

```
    out_sd <- unionAll(out_sd1, out_sd2)
    nrow(out_sd)
```

The output from `nrow` indicates a total of 768,000 rows. This number represents our original 768 rows which has been multiplied by a factor of 1000:

```
▶ (1) Spark Jobs

[1]  768000
```

Running summary statistics

One of the first things I do upon creating a new data object, is to run summary statistics. There is a Spark-specific function of the R summary function known as describe(). You can the specific function summary(); however, if you do this instead of using describe(), I would preface it with SparkR:: in order to specify which version of summary you are using:

```
head(SparkR::summary(out_sd))
```

The output appears in a slightly different format than if you ran a summary on a native R dataframe, but contains the basic measures that you are looking for, count, mean, stddev, min, and max:

```
 ▶ (1) Spark Jobs

  summary          sample_bin              outcome              pregnant
1    count             768000               768000                768000
2     mean -113.67317708333333  0.3489583333333333    3.845052083332693
3   stddev  220.73245049349478 0.47664107119150484   3.3673858047181646
4      min             -500.0                  0.0  -5.267836632739748
5      max              267.0                  1.0  13.798168411407868
                glucose             pressure               triceps              insulin
1                768000               768000                768000               768000
2 121.68778671732643  72.40477794289117   29.24877013964472   159.46377333976378
3 30.441771824780293  12.09690590416991    8.923478186809195    91.29942740927545
4  39.06326135657574  35.40654724700748   0.7607894364323116  -148.15344457408253
5 219.71433564781285 112.13158466413095   58.23733534004559   456.09990684013997
                   mass              pedigree                  age
1                768000               768000               768000
2 32.442846279285206  0.47187630208324GG   33.24088541667883
3  6.874557449376662 0.33111303159707445   11.752580297416275
4  9.969765765918051 -0.5461478239604021   -1.469171542253246
5  54.28623709953233   1.687677997650607   73.95268273579066
```

We can also compare this summary with the summary of the original Pima Indians dataframe, and see that the simulation has done a pretty good job of estimating the means. The number of observations is approximately 1,000 times the original size and the ratio of diabetes to nondiabetes patients has been preserved:

```
#compare with original dataset
summary(PimaIndiansDiabetes[,])
```

```
    pregnant          glucose          pressure          triceps          insulin
Min.   : 0.00     Min.   :  0      Min.   :  0.0     Min.   : 0.0     Min.   :  0
1st Qu.: 1.00     1st Qu.: 99      1st Qu.: 62.0     1st Qu.: 0.0     1st Qu.:  0
Median : 3.00     Median :117      Median : 72.0     Median :23.0     Median : 30
Mean   : 3.85     Mean   :121      Mean   : 69.1     Mean   :20.5     Mean   : 80
3rd Qu.: 6.00     3rd Qu.:140      3rd Qu.: 80.0     3rd Qu.:32.0     3rd Qu.:127
Max.   :17.00     Max.   :199      Max.   :122.0     Max.   :99.0     Max.   :846
     mass            pedigree            age           diabetes
Min.   : 0.0      Min.   :0.078     Min.   :21.0     neg:500
1st Qu.:27.3      1st Qu.:0.244     1st Qu.:24.0     pos:268
Median :32.0      Median :0.372     Median :29.0
Mean   :32.0      Mean   :0.472     Mean   :33.2
3rd Qu.:36.6      3rd Qu.:0.626     3rd Qu.:41.0
Max.   :67.1      Max.   :2.420     Max.   :81.0
```

Saving your work

Now that we have produced our final Spark data frame, we can write it to disk. Then, from the next chapter onwards, we will read it back into the workspace rather than have to recreate it from scratch. If you are proceeding directly to the next chapter, you can skip this step for now:

- We will save in Parquet file format, which is a very efficient format for Spark and SQL. The %fs (file system) directive allows you to issue a directory (or file listing) command using the ls operating system command.
- Once the file is saved, you can validate the integrity of the file by reading it back in and assigning it to the out_sd dataframe (again).

- Use the `head` command to verify that the data was read back in:

```
saveAsParquetFile(out_sd, "/tmp/temp.parquet")
%fs ls
out_sd <- parquetFile(sqlContext, "/tmp/temp.parquet")
head(out_sd)
```

Summary

In this chapter, we have learned what Spark is and learned about some of its advantages. We began to write programs which load and save data into Spark Clusters. We learned a couple of ways how we can construct our own very large Spark dataframes based upon characteristics of small datasets.

We also learned how to write Spark programs in Databricks and how to run standard R analysis and install packages. We also reinforced our knowledge of missing value imputations by substituting some missing values in the original data.

In the next chapter, we will take what we have built and start to explore the data.

10

Exploring Large Datasets Using Spark

"I never guess. It is a capital mistake to theorize before one has data. Insensibly one begins to twist facts to suit theories, instead of theories to suit facts."

- Sir Arthur Conan Doyle

In this chapter, we will begin to perform some exploratory data analysis on the Spark dataframe we created in the previous chapter. We will learn about some specific Spark commands that will assist you in your analysis, and will discuss several ways to perform graphing and plotting.

As you go through these examples, remember that data that resides in Spark may be much larger than you are used to, and that it may be impractical to apply some quick analytic techniques without first considering how the data is organized, and how performance will be affecting using standard techniques.

If you are picking up where you left off in the previous chapter, you will have to load the saved Spark data frame before you begin. Recall that we saved the results of the diabetes data set as a parquet file, so we can use the parquetFile() function to read the data back into memory. Then filter out the positive diabetes cases since we will be explore them next:

```
out_sd <- parquetFile(sqlContext, "/tmp/temp.parquet")
out_sd1 = SparkR::filter(out_sd, out_sd$outcome == 1)
```

Performing some exploratory analysis on positives

Before we move on to exploring the entire Spark dataframe, we can look at some of the data already generated for positive cases. As you may recall from the prior chapter, this is stored in the Spark dataframe `out_sd1`.

We have generated some random sample bins specifically so that we can do some exploratory analysis.

We can use the `filter` command to extract random sample 1, and take the first 1,000 records:

- The `filter` is a SparkR command that allows you to subset a Spark dataframe
- The `display` command is a databricks command that is equivalent to the `View` command we have previously used and you can also use the `head` function as well to limit the number of rows that are displayed:

This code chunk extracts 1000 records from the positives and displays them:

```
small_pos <-
head(SparkR::filter(out_sd1,out_sd1$sample_bin==1),1000)
nrow(small_pos)

display(small_pos)
```

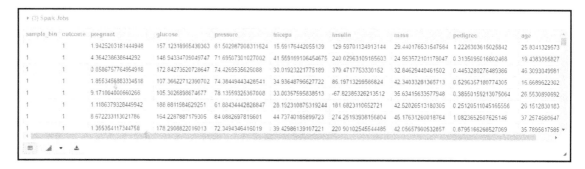

The data appears in tabular form, and you can scroll up/down, or left/right to look for missing values, extreme values, and so on.

The filter command serves two functions:

- Extracting a segment of interest for your analysis.
- Extracting a sample, which can be helpful for debugging your Spark data flow. This can help subsequent steps run quicker, and avoids unnecessarily running large jobs, especially if the sample reflects the makeup of the population.

Displaying the contents of a Spark dataframe

There are several ways of displaying subsets of your Spark dataframe. Some of the choices are as follows:

- `showDF`: This is a Spark command that displays the contents of a dataframe in a condensed manner.
- `head`: This is the normal R function that can be used on a Spark dataframe; it follows the same syntax as base R.
- `take`: This command also prints some rows, but collects the rows from the underlying RDD.
- `display`: This is a special databricks command that is roughly equivalent to the base R `View` command, but also allows you to plot a subset of the output via control icons below the horizontal scroll bar below the data. Using display also allows you to switch to graphing mode.

Graphing using native graph features

Click on the second icon:

You will be taken to a graph dialog, in which you can graph the various relationships among the variables. To graph these relationships, first drag a variable from the **All fields** column to the **Values** column:

- For example, the first plot displays a boxplot for insulin levels for diabetes=1
- Plot 2 shows a histogram of insulin levels with 20 bins defined

- Plot 3 shows a scatter plot between age and insulin levels
- Plot 4 shows the correlation matrix of age, insulin, and the number of months pregnant:

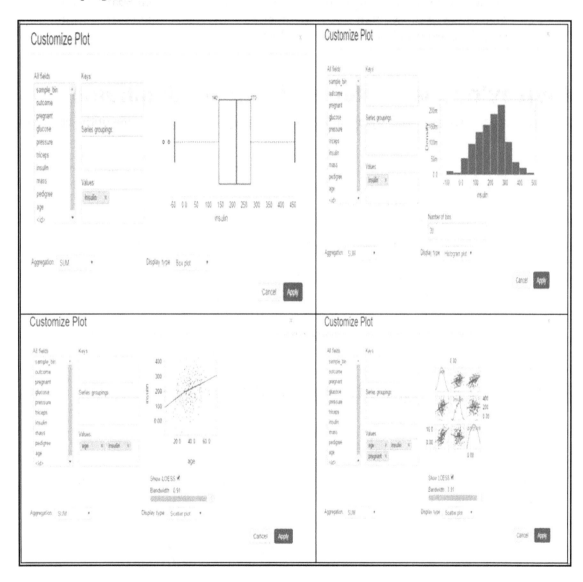

Running pairwise correlations directly on a Spark dataframe

Correlation and covariance functions are available which operate directly on Spark dataframes. The following example shows that, for patients with diabetes, there is an 11% correlation between age and glucose level:

```
corr <- corr(out_sd1, "glucose", "age", method = "pearson")
corr
```

> ▶ (1) Spark Jobs
>
> [1] 0.1130607

Cleaning up and caching the table in memory

Since Spark excels at processing in-memory data, we will first remove our intermediary data and then cache our out_sd dataframe, so that subsequent queries run much faster. Caching data in memory works best when similar types of queries are repeated. In that way, Spark is able to know how to juggle memory so that most of what you need resides in memory.

However, this is not foolproof. Good Spark query and table design will help with optimization, but out-of-the-box caching usually gives some benefit. Often, the first queries will not benefit from memory caching, but subsequent queries will run much faster.

Since we will no longer use the intermediary dataframes we created, we will remove them with the rm function, and then use the cache() function on the full dataframe:

```
#cleanup and cache df
rm(out_sd1)
rm(out_sd2)
cache(out_sd)
```

Some useful Spark functions to explore your data

Count and groupby

We can also use the `Count` and `groupby` functions to aggregate individual variables.

Here is an example of using this to tally the number of observations by outcome. Since the result is another dataframe, we can use the `head` function to write the results to the console.

 You might have to alter the number of rows returned by head if you change the query. It is always a good idea to filter results using a function such as `head`, to make sure that you are not printing hundreds of rows (or more).

However, you also need to ensure that you do not cut off all of your output. If you are unsure as to the number of rows, first assign the result to a dataframe and then check the number of rows (with `nrow`) first:

This code line count the number of rows by outcome. I know that there should be only 2 outcomes, but I place the count function within a head statement just to program defensively.

```
head(SparkR::count(groupBy(out_sd, "outcome")))
```

```
▶ (5) Spark Jobs

    outcome   count
1         0  500000
2         1  268000
```

Printing values from a Spark dataframe is very quick. Here are a few values from each outcome group. Note that the `sample.bin` is negative for `outcome == 0`, and positive for `outcome == 1`:

First print some of the negatives. We can see that some of the pregnant numbers are negative, showing that the simulation wasn't perfect.

```
head(SparkR::filter(out_sd,out_sd$outcome == 0),5)
```

> (2) Spark Jobs

	sample_bin	outcome	pregnant	glucose	pressure	triceps	insulin	mass	pedigree
1	-144	0	-1.481	73.4	66.6	19.8	104	23.9	0.112
2	-395	0	1.105	105.6	71.0	22.3	115	30.5	0.948
3	-205	0	-0.376	132.1	65.9	17.5	117	25.8	0.283
4	-442	0	0.853	149.1	68.0	18.4	164	25.7	-0.196
5	-471	0	3.480	115.2	58.5	32.2	239	31.6	0.754

	age
1	33.2
2	26.0
3	25.3
4	34.3
5	32.6

Now print some of the positives.

```
head(SparkR::filter(out_sd,out_sd$outcome == 1),5)
```

> (1) Spark Jobs

	sample_bin	outcome	pregnant	glucose	pressure	triceps	insulin	mass	pedigree
1	78	1	1.943	157	61.5	15.7	129.6	29.4	1.223
2	212	1	4.364	149	71.7	41.6	240.0	25.0	0.314
3	110	1	0.859	173	74.4	30.0	379.5	32.8	0.445
4	237	1	1.855	107	74.4	34.9	86.2	42.3	0.530
5	253	1	9.171	105	78.1	33.0	-67.8	35.6	0.386

	age
1	25.8
2	19.4
3	46.3
4	16.7
5	26.6

Covariance and correlation functions

Correlations and covariances can also be computed directly from a Spark dataframe. For our example, we can see that there is a larger correlation between age and glucose for non-diabetic patients:

First the diabetic outcomes. Correlation is .113 :

```
> corr(SparkR::filter(out_sd,out_sd$outcome==1), "glucose", "age", method = "pearson")

▸ (1) Spark Jobs

[1] 0.113
```

Now, the non-diabetic outcomes. Correlation is .22:

```
  corr(SparkR::filter(out_sd,out_sd$outcome==0), "glucose", "age", method = "pearson")

  ▸ (1) Spark Jobs

  [1] 0.22
```

For the entire population the correlation is 0.26:

```
  corr(out_sd, "glucose", "age", method = "pearson")

  ▾ (1) Spark Jobs
    ▸ Job 295   View (Stages: 1/1)

  [1] 0.269
```

Creating new columns

Usually it's necessary to create some new transformation based on existing variables which will improve a prediction. We have already seen that binning a variable is often done to create a nominal variable from a quantitative one.

Let's create a new column, called agecat, which divides age into two segments. To keep things simple, we will start off by rounding the age to the nearest integer.

```
filtered <- SparkR::filter(out_sd, "age > 0 AND insulin > 0")
filtered$age <- round(filtered$age,0)
filtered$agecat <- ifelse(filtered$age <= 35,"<= 35","35 Or Older")
SparkR::head(SparkR::select(filtered, "age","agecat"))
```

```
▶ (1) Spark Jobs

    age        agecat
1   26         <= 35
2   19         <= 35
3   46   35 Or Older
4   17         <= 35
5   26         <= 35
6   37   35 Or Older
```

In the code which you just ran, you may notice that some commands are prefaced by `SparkR::`.

This is done to let the program know which version of the function we wish to apply, and it is always good practice to preface commands in this way, in order to avoid syntax errors and misapplying identically named functions which occur between SparkR and normal R.

Constructing a cross-tab

Now that we have categorized age, we can run a cross-tab which counts outcomes by the age category.

Since there are only two outcomes and two age categories, this results in a four-cell crosstab:

1. First, display the results using the special Databricks `display` command.
2. After the results appear as shown in the table below, you can click the **plot** button (2nd icon on the bottom left) and the Customized Plot dialogue will appear, which will allow the results to be plotted as a bar chart. The plot show that diabetes occurs more frequently in the higher age group than in the lower age group, while the reverse is true for the non-diabetes group:

```
table <- crosstab(filtered, "outcome", "agecat")
display(as.data.frame(table))
```

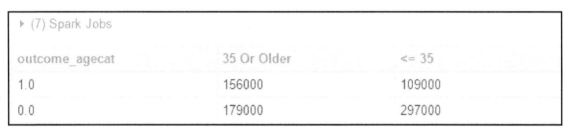

outcome_agecat	35 Or Older	<= 35
1.0	156000	109000
0.0	179000	297000

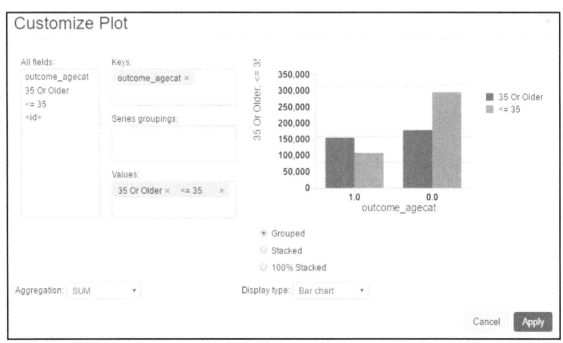

Contrasting histograms

Histograms are also a quick way to visually inspect and compare outcome variables.

Here is another example of using the Spark histogram function to contrast the mean values of body mass index for diabetic versus non-diabetic patients in the study. For the first bar chart, we can see a peak bar of about 38.9 BMI, versus a peak bar of 29.8 for non-diabetic patients. This suggests that BMI will be an important variable in any model we develop:

This code uses the SparkR histogram function to compute a histogram with 10 bins. The centroids gives the center value for each of the 10 bins. The most frequently occurring bar is the bar with a center value of 38.9 with a count of about 50,000. This type of histogram is useful for quickly getting a sense of the distribution of variables, but is somewhat lacking in labeling, and controlling various elements since as scales and ranges. If you wish to fine tune some of the elements you may want to start by using a collect() function to download a sample to your local R machine. We will discuss this capability later on.

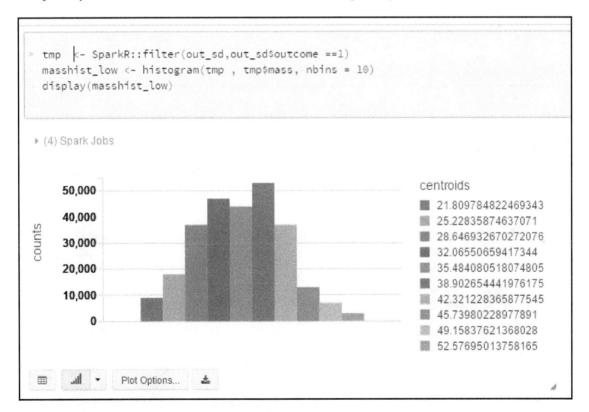

```
tmp     <- SparkR::filter(out_sd,out_sd$outcome ==0)
masshist_low <- histogram(tmp , tmp$mass, nbins = 10)
display(masshist_low)
```

▸ (4) Spark Jobs

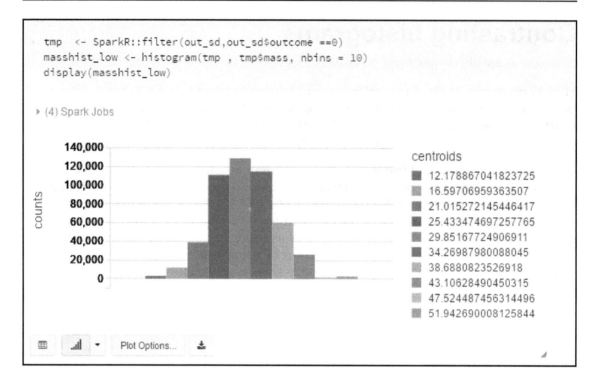

Plotting using ggplot

If you prefer to use `ggplot` to plot your results, load the `ggplot2` package to run your plots directly against the Spark dataframe. You will have more of an opportunity for further customization:

Here is a basic ggplot which corresponds to the histogram() functions illustrated above:

```
require(ggplot2)
plot <- ggplot(age_hist, aes(x = centroids, y = counts)) +
        geom_bar(stat = "identity") +
      xlab("mass") + ylab("Frequency")

plot
```

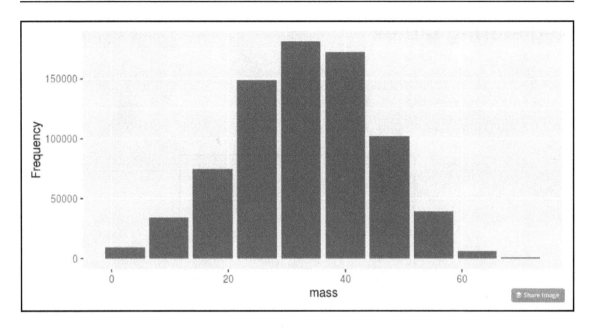

Spark SQL

Another way to explore data in Spark is by using Spark SQL. This allows analysts who may not be well-versed in language-specific APIs, such as SparkR, PySpark (for Python), and Scala, to explore Spark data.

I will describe two different ways of accessing Spark data via SQL:

- Issuing SQL commands through the R interface:

  > This has the advantage of returning the results as an R dataframe, where it can be further manipulated

- Issuing SQL queries via databricks SQL `magic`: directive

  > This method allows analysts to issue direct SQL commands, without regard to any specific language environment

Before processing an object as SQL, the object needs to be registered as a SQL table or view. Once it is registered, it can be accessed through the SQL interface of any language API.

Once registered, you can use the show tables SparkR command to get a list of registered tables for your session.

Registering tables

```
#register out_sd as a table

SparkR:::registerTempTable(out_sd,"out_tbl")
SparkR:::cacheTable(sqlContext,"out_tbl")

head(SparkR::sql(sqlContext, "SHOW tables"))
```

```
▶ (1) Spark Jobs

    database    tableName isTemporary
1   default           mc       FALSE
2   default    stopfrisk       FALSE
3                out_tbl        TRUE
4           spark_sample        TRUE
```

Issuing SQL through the R interface

Writing SQL this way consists of constructing a valid SQL string query via the `sql` function:

* The query must reference a registered table
* You can assign the results of the query to a dataframe:

Here is an example of getting a frequency count of the available samples from the registered object out_table. Note that the code begins with %r command which is a special Databricks directive that indicates that the code that follows applies to R. However, it is sometimes necessary to specify this (even in R notebooks), when a previous code chunks has used another language directive, such as %sql, or %python.

```
%r
rm(tmp)

tmp <- SparkR::sql(sqlContext, "SELECT sample_bin,   count(*) FROM
out_tbl group by sample_bin")
```

* Additionally in databricks, `sqlcontext` is preassigned, and so can be omitted in the code as follows.

```
tmp <- SparkR::sql("SELECT sample_bin , count(*) FROM out_tbl group
by sample_bin")
```

- Once you have extracted the data to a `tmp` dataframe, you can display the counts of each of the samples. In subsequent queries, you can select samples corresponding to the size and proportion of the outcome you are interested in:

```
head(tmp,1000)
```

	sample_bin	count(1)
1	-142	4000
2	184	1000
3	147	1000
4	170	1000
5	-305	1000
6	-492	2000
7	160	2000
8	169	2000
9	67	1000
10	70	1000
11	-335	3000
12	-500	1000
13	-282	1000
14	69	1000
15	-74	4000
16	-81	2000
17	-58	1000
18	-52	4000

Using SQL to examine potential outliers

Based upon the preceding `sample_bin` counts, we might decide to extract a sample based upon a sample of some negative and positive cases. We know that positive sample_bin represent an outcome of 1, and negative sample_bins represent an outcome of 0. We can also pick a cutoff value which will accomodate whatever sample size we would like. We will be looking to extract a 10,000 row sample, so we will set the bounds to +10 and -10.

```
bin_extract <- SparkR::sql("SELECT * from out_tbl where sample_bin >= -10
AND sample_bin <= 10")
nrow(bin_extract)
#nrow should be 10,000 in the output
```

Next, we will register bin_extract so that we can perform some SQL

```
SparkR:::registerTempTable(bin_extract,"bin_extract")
```

Creating some aggregates

If we were interested in comparing blood pressure values with the average age, we could then construct a query to calculate some mean and standard deviations on the larger Spark table (out_tbl), and then group the results by outcome. The output also indicates that diabetics are older:

```
bin_agg <- SparkR::sql("SELECT outcome,
mean(pressure) as mean_pressure,
std(pressure) as std_pressure,
mean(age) as mean_age,
std(age) as std_age
from out_tbl group by 1")
#register the table
SparkR:::registerTempTable(bin_agg,"bin_agg")
#print a few records
head(bin_agg)
```

> ▸ (5) Spark Jobs

	outcome	mean_pressure	std_pressure	mean_age	std_age
1	0	71.60760	7.454448	32.55031	9.274967
2	1	71.17571	9.905474	39.88985	2.276876

Picking out some potential outliers using a third query

Now we will construct a third query that will extract all records that may be considered outliers. For this example, we will define an outlier as any record that has age or pressure greater or less than 1.5 standard deviations below the mean for their outcome class. This is accomplished by joining our detail-level data with the aggregated means for age and pressure:

- We can also compute a new column, agediff, which is the difference between age and average age.

- We add limit=1000 as a protective filter, so that we retrieve more than the number of results. Placing limits on SQL queries tends to speed up result processing. In this case one record is returned:

```
anomolies <- SparkR::sql("select distinct
a.outcome,pressure,mean_pressure,age,b.mean_age,
(age-  b.mean_age) as agediff
from bin_extract a inner join bin_agg b
on a.outcome=b.outcome
AND
(a.pressure > mean_pressure + (1.5*std_pressure))
OR
(a.pressure < mean_pressure - (1.5*std_pressure))
OR
(a.age < b.mean_age - (1.5*std_age))
OR
(a.age > mean_age + (1.5*std_age))
order by agediff desc
limit 1000")
head(anomolies)
```

The output shows only one record with an age 1.5 standard deviations higher than the average. You can customize the cutoff standard deviation to increase or decrease the number of rows returned for the purposes of outlier inspection.

```
▶ (1) Spark Jobs

  outcome pressure mean_pressure     age mean_age  agediff
1       0 75.93101      70.87059 51.63939   31.19 20.44939
```

Changing to the SQL API

You can change to the SQL interface by coding %sql on the first line. That allows all subsequent code statements in that particular notebook cell to be interpreted as SQL only.

> If you wish to return to another language in a subsequent cell, enter %r, %python, %scala, and so on as the first line of the cell. If you do not enter one of these magic directives, it will be interpreted in the syntax of the default notebook type (in this case, R).

Here is the version of the count `sample_bin` query that we performed earlier in R, but now purely in the SQL interface. The results are shown as a pivot table. If you wish, you can manipulate the format by selecting the raw data icon (the first one on the left, below the data), or by selecting the Plot icon (the second one after that), and choosing a specific plot:

```
%sql
SELECT sample_bin , count(*) as k FROM out_tbl group by sample_bin order by
 k
```

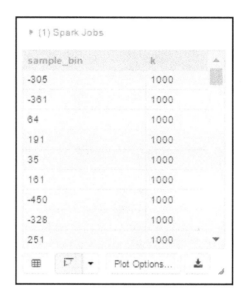

SQL – computing a new column using the Case statement

The SQL window allows us to utilize all of the benefits of standard SQL. That includes the ability to create new columns. In this example, we query the entire table and compute the average mass split by high mass (>30), and low mass (<-30).

In this way, we can see that the mean mass is higher at the upper end for diabetes patients than for the non-diabetes patients. The same seems to be true at the low end:

```
%sql
select case when mass > 30 then "BMI_HIGH" else "BMI_LOW" end as BMICAT,
outcome,avg(mass) from out_tbl
group by 1,2
```

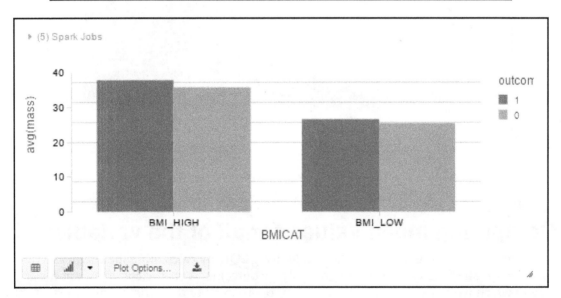

Evaluating outcomes based upon the Age segment

Splitting age at the 30 breakpoint also shows many more outcomes at the higher age range than at the lower:

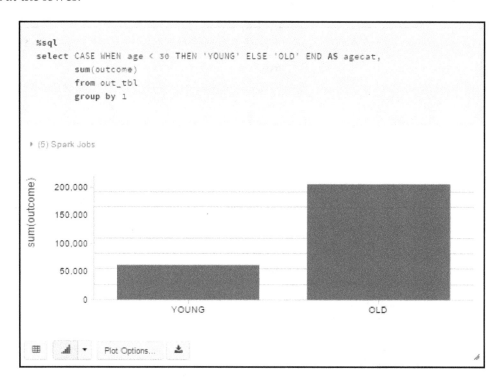

Computing mean values for all of the variables

Interesting comparisons can be made, purely using SQL, by calculating the coefficient of variation for all of the variables, and grouping by outcome. A coefficient of variation is a way in which we can standardize the means and variances of the variables and thus be able to disregard scale when making comparisons:

```
%sql
select outcome,
       mean(pregnant)/std(pregnant),
       mean(glucose)/std(glucose),
       mean(pressure)/std(pressure),
       mean(triceps)/std(triceps),
```

```
        mean(insulin)/std(insulin),
        mean(mass)/std(mass),
        mean(pedigree)/std(pedigree),
        mean(age)/std(age)
from out_tbl
group by 1
```

1. After the query is done, switch to the plot window, and change the plot type to line chart.

2. Then drag the outcome to the **Keys** pane.

3. Then drag all of the other variables to the **Values** pane.

A simple line graph will appear, which will allow you to compare the average values of these variables between both of the outcomes.

We can see that the mean values of the variables increase for diabetic patients, although the magnitude of changes is larger for some variables than for others:

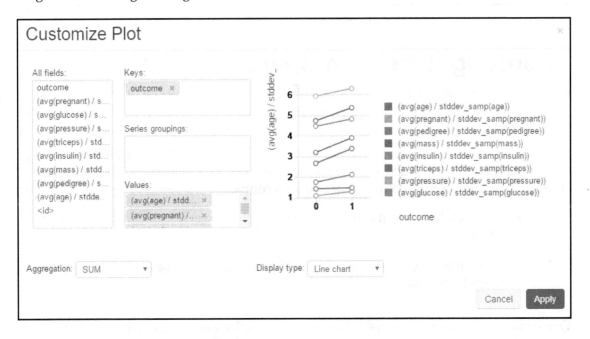

We can also demonstrate a query similar to the outlier query in the previous section. This time, we will be querying all records that have `age` or `pressure` records that fall above two standard deviations over the mean:

```
%sql
select distinct a.outcome,pressure,mean_pressure,age,mean_age from
bin_extract a inner join bin_agg b
on a.outcome=b.outcome
AND
(a.pressure > mean_pressure + (2*std_pressure))
OR
(a.age > mean_age + (2*std_age))
limit 100
```

▸ (5) Spark Jobs

outcome	pressure	mean_pressure	age	mean_age
0	75.93100817427452	71.60760161398534	51.63938860382109	32.55030965046543
0	75.93100817427452	71.17571330678416	51.63938860382109	39.889849391046326

Exporting data from Spark back into R

It will often be the case that some of the analysis you wish to perform will not be available within SparkR and you will need to extract some of the data from Spark objects, and return them to base R.

For example, we were able to run correlation and covariance functions earlier directly on a Spark dataframe, by specifying specific pairs of variables. However, we did not generate correlation matrices for the entire dataframe for a couple of reasons:

- The capability to do this may not be built into the version of Spark that you are currently running

- Even if it was available, these kinds of calculation could be very computationally expensive to perform

One strategy you may want to use is to use Spark functions to explore basic characteristics of the data, and/or utilize specialized packages written for Spark (such as `MLlib`) to perform this.

For other cases, in which you want to perform more in-depth analysis, simply extract a sample from the Spark dataframe, and perform the analysis using normal R dataframes. When doing this, it is good practice not to return the entire population, but only to return a sample or a subsegment. After all, if you extract the entire dataframe from Spark, you do not really need to use Spark in the first place, and might as well perform the whole analysis using local R!

We can use the `collect()` function to perform this, by first filtering by `sample_bin` and then returning the results to a local dataframe named `samp`. If you run a `str()` function on `samp`, you can see that the first line of the output indicates that the object is a normal R dataframe, and NOT a Spark dataframe:

```
#bring a sample back to R and visualize
samp <- SparkR::collect(SparkR::filter(out_sd, "sample_bin >= -50 and
sample_bin <= 50"))
str(samp)
```

```
▶ (1) Spark Jobs

'data.frame':    77000 obs. of  10 variables:
 $ sample_bin: num  13 28 12 40 7 39 41 38 13 33 ...
 $ outcome   : num  1 1 1 1 1 1 1 1 1 ...
 $ pregnant  : num  1.12 7.73 6.61 6.31 5.2 ...
 $ glucose   : num  189 143 146 167 189 ...
 $ pressure  : num  61.9 84.1 91.2 92.3 84.7 ...
 $ triceps   : num  28.2 57 29.4 58.2 41.5 ...
 $ insulin   : num  181.682 269.068 63.504 0.372 180.244 ...
 $ mass      : num  42.5 49.3 34.9 51.1 47.5 ...
 $ pedigree  : num  0.251 0.68 0.622 0.822 0.355 ...
 $ age       : num  26.2 41.8 31.6 37.8 37.5 ...
```

Running local R packages

Once you have extracted your sample, you can run normal R functions such as pairs to generate a correlation matrix, or use the `reshape2` package along with `ggplot` to generate a correlation plot.

Using the pairs function (available in the base package)

```
#this takes our "collect()" data frame which we exported from Spark, and
runs a basic correlation matrix

pairs(samp[,3:8], col=samp$outcome)
```

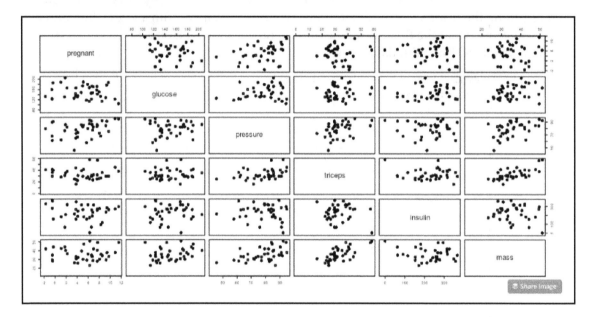

Generating a correlation plot

Here is a more sophisticated visualization which uses ggplot to illustrate how to generate a correlation matrix using shading to indicate the degree of correlation for each of the intersecting variables. Again, the point is to emphasis that you can perform analysis outside of Spark if your sample size is reasonable, and the exact functionality you need is not available in the version of Spark you are running.

```
require(ggplot2)
library(reshape2)
cormatrix <- round(cor(samp),2)
cormatrix_melt <- melt(cormatrix)
head(cormatrix_melt)
ggplot(data = cormatrix_melt, aes(x=Var1, y=Var2, fill=value)) +
geom_raster()
```

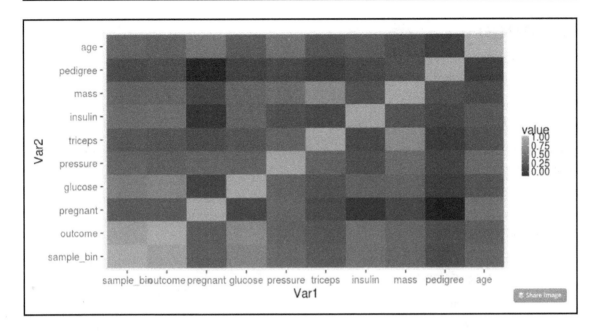

Some tips for using Spark

Take a look at the following tips:

- Sample when possible. Use the `sample_bin` methodology and filter command liberally. Sampling will speed up analysis both for the analysis phase and for the development/testing phase.

- Once testing has been completed on a smaller segment, it can be scaled up to a much larger population with confidence.

- Preprocess the data so that you can subselect potentially interesting sub segments.

- Cache analysis when it makes sense.

- If performance becomes a factor, try a larger number of partitions in your data.

- For larger number crunching, bring back a representative sample to local R.

Summary

In this chapter, we learned the basics of exploring Spark data, using some Spark-specific commands that allowed us to filter, group, and summarize our Spark data.

We also learned about the ability to visualize data directly in Spark, along with learning how to run R functions such as ggplot against data.

We learned about some strategies for working with Spark data, such as performing intelligent filtering and sampling.

Finally, we demonstrated that often we need to extract some Spark data back into local R if we want the flexibility to use some of our usual tools that may not be supplied natively in the Spark environment.

In the next chapter, we will delve into the various predictive models that you can use that are specific to large datasets.

11
Spark Machine Learning - Regression and Cluster Models

"The study of thinking machines teaches us more about the brain than we can learn by introspective methods. Western man is externalizing himself in the form of gadgets."

- William S. Burroughs (Naked Lunch)

About this chapter/what you will learn

In the previous chapters, we introduced Spark and SparkR, with the emphasis on exploring data using SQL. In this chapter, we will begin to look at the machine learning capabilities of Spark using MLlib, which is the native machine learning library which is packaged with Spark.

In this chapter we will cover logistic regression, and clustering algorithms. In the next chapter we will cover rule based algorithm, which include decision trees. Some of the material has already been discussed in prior chapters using PC versions of R. In this chapter, as well as the next, we will focus predominantly on how to prepare your data and apply these techniques using the MLLib algorihms which exist in Spark.

Reading the data

In the last chapter, we saved the out_sd to an external parquet file. In the real world, you will be faced with analyzing multiple data sources. Often, these data sources will have similar schemas but will differ by the time period that they were written.

For example, log files can be archived in different directories, categorized by date, and you as an analyst will need to read in multiple files and concatenate them together.

So although each individual file may be small, when aggregated together, they will yield a much larger file.

Let's pretend that we will be performing some machine learning on several files that have been written over the past two days. For illustration purposes, we will use the same file for the two inputs. However, in practice, you may be concatenating many days worth of transactions:

1. First, read the data back in. Recall that the files were saved in the previous chapter in parquet format:

   ```
   todays_file <- parquetFile(sqlContext,
   "/tmp/temp.parquet")
   yesterdays_file <- parquetFile(sqlContext,
   "/tmp/temp.parquet")
   ```

2. Concatenate the two days of data into one file using the Spark `unionAll()` function:

   ```
   out_sd <- unionAll(todays_file,yesterdays_file)
   ```

3. Once we read in the files, we can cache the `out_sd` file to allow it to be queried optimally for the rest of the session:

   ```
   cache(out_sd)
   ```

Next, use the SparkR `mean()` and `count()` functions to verify the integrity of the file. For example, we know from the original data that ~34% of the outcomes are positive, so we can use these functions as a calculator to determine that the files contain 536,000 positive cases. Why even do this? When dealing with large datasets, it is usually worth the effort verifying the contents of the file first before you start manipulating the records. Saving time by performing data prep is crucial:

```
head(SparkR::select(out_sd,
count(out_sd$outcome),mean(out_sd$outcome),mean(out_sd$outcome)*count(out_s
d$outcome)))
```

```
▸ (3) Spark Jobs

  count(outcome)  avg(outcome)  (avg(outcome) * count(outcome))
1       1536000     0.3489583                            536800
```

Running a summary of the dataframe and saving the object

Next, we will create a summary of the dataframe. However, instead of just printing the summary as we have done in the past, we will save the results of the summary to an object as well, since we will be using the aggregate information later in order to join it back to the original data. Again, if you will be manipulating large datasets, there is no need to run `summary()` functions more than once on the same data:

1. Set up some global options, such as thue number of significant digits, plot width and height, etc.

2. Assign the `summary` output to an dataframe.

3. Use the databricks `display()` function (or `head()` function) to print a portion of the file:

```
options(digits=3)
options(repr.plot.width = 1000, repr.plot.height =   500,
repr.plot.res = 144, repr.plot.pointsize = 5)
sumdf = summary(out_sd)
display(sumdf)
```

> (1) Spark Jobs

summary	sample_bin	outcome	pregnant	glucose	pressure	triceps	insulin	mass	pedigree
count	1536000	1536000	1536000	1536000	1536000	1536000	1536000	1536000	1536000
mean	-113.673177708333333	0.348958333333333	3.845052063332693	121.68778671732643	72.40477794289117	29.24877013964472	159.46377333976378	32.442846279285206	0.471876302083246
stddev	220.73237864042508	0.4766409160347798	3.3673847085630393	30.441761915341296	12.096901966371815	8.923475282028773	91.29939768938557	6.874555211563171	0.3311129238127968
min	-500.0	0.0	-5.267836632739748	39.06326135657574	35.40654724700748	0.7607894364323118	-148.15344457408253	9.989765765918051	-0.5461476239604021
max	267.0	1.0	13.798188411407868	219.71433564781285	112.13158466413095	58.23733534004559	456.09990684013997	54.28623709953233	1.687677997650607

Splitting the data into train and test datasets

Proceed to create our test and train datasets. The objective will be to sample 80% of the data for the training set and 20% of the data for the test data set.

To speed up sampling somewhat, we can sequentially sample the tails of the `sample_bin` range for the test dataset and then use the middle for the training data. This is still a random sample, since `sample_bin` was originally generated randomly and the sequence or range of the numbers have no bearing on the randomness.

Generating the training datasets

Since we want 80% of our data to be training data, first take all of the `sample_bin` numbers which lie between the high and low cutoff values. We can define the cutoff range as 20% of the difference between the highest and lowest value of `sample_bin`.

Set the low cutoff as the lowest value plus the cutoff range defined previously, and the high cutoff as the highest value minus the cutoff range:

```
#compute the minimum and maximum values of sample bin
set.seed(123)
sample_bin_min <- as.integer(collect(select(out_sd,
min(out_sd$sample_bin))))
sample_bin_max <- as.integer(collect(select(out_sd,
max(out_sd$sample_bin))))

Cutoff <- .20*(sample_bin_max - sample_bin_min)
Cutoff_low <- sample_bin_min + Cutoff
Cutoff_high <- sample_bin_max - Cutoff

rm(df)

#take 80% of the training samples.  These happens to be the ones that fall
in the middle.

df <- filter(out_sd, out_sd$sample_bin > Cutoff_low & out_sd$sample_bin <
Cutoff_high)
train_sumdf = summary(df)
```

Print some of the key fields using the Spark `select()` function within the databricks `display` command. Note that when printing the summary object in this way, there are always five rows (`count`, `mean`, `sdev`, `min`, and `mins`) along with one column for each variable:

```
display(select(train_sumdf,"summary","outcome","pregnant","age","mass","glu
cose","triceps"))
```

summary	outcome	pregnant	age	mass	glucose	triceps
count	1238000	1238000	1238000	1238000	1238000	1238000
mean	0.34733441103392569	3.8393078551561945	33.10107006771893	32.38097983343372	121.13880674688428	29.02635605075717
stddev	0.4761233042460107	3.4609137686182487	11.840237146096062	6.7386355088915995	30.58392015453745	8.83891870375425
min	0.0	-5.267836632739748	-1.4691715422253246	12.476112430010328	39.06326135657574	0.7607894364323116
max	1.0	13.798168411407868	73.95268273579068	54.15179128403151	219.71433564781285	58.23733534004559

Generating the test dataset

For generating the test data, we will select only the rows which fall beyond the cutoff points. That will yield the 20% sample. Note that the SparkR describe function is an alias for the `summary()` function. Use this when you want to avoid conflict of names between the Spark and base R functions.

```
#set the test data set to include the rest of the population
set.seed(123)
test <- filter(out_sd, out_sd$sample_bin <= Cutoff_low | out_sd$sample_bin
>= Cutoff_high)
test_sumdf = describe(test)

display(select(test_sumdf,"summary","outcome","pregnant","age","mass","gluc
ose","triceps"))
```

summary	outcome	pregnant	age	mass	glucose	triceps
count	298000	298000	298000	298000	298000	298000
mean	0.35570469798657717	3.8689156889824896	33.82172904758105	32.69986191673218	123.96844847374449	30.172758871343312
stddev	0.47872709853948375	2.9471078158413375	11.36279056675114	7.407060808651703	29.73566972935832	9.20917898210801
min	0.0	-2.7745181707450337	0.3325954626676797	9.969765765918051	49.71976008885286	5.837573292896575
max	1.0	11.726947624108954	55.30614098944598	54.28623709953233	194.24078367540534	51.93047275913541

A note on parallel processing

Spark will take advantage of parallel processing algorithms as much as possible. Extracting training and test data samples is a prime example of this, since extracting the training data set can be performed independently of the training data.

So, in Databricks, you will be able to visually see them run at the same time via a progress bar. In cases in which a block of code is dependent upon another block of code, you will see the execution begin, but it will be in wait state until the needed prior blocks have been completed.

The takeaway from this is that you should always try to develop your analytics code in a manner which utilizes this in order to take advantage of parallel processing.

Introducing errors into the test data set

Since both the test and training datasets have been generated by simulated random normal distributions, the data is almost too perfect. To compensate for this, and to make the data more realistic and help you develop more simulation skills, we can introduce some random error into the test data set. For example, we might want to add up to a plus/minus 10% variation into the test data variables.

To accomplish this, we will first generate an error distribution that we can apply to the original data. For simplicity's sake, we can derive four discrete error bins, each designating a different percentage adjustment to the data. Percentage errors between -10% and +10% are reasonable limits.

We will generate this by using the following `rnorm` function, and then set any value beyond +/- 10 percent to 0. This will become our own customized distribution for selecting a probability of error:

```
#set the random seed
set.seed(123)
#set the bins
x <- rnorm(n=25,mean=0,sd=4)/100
#assign errors conditionally
x <- ifelse(abs(x) > .10,0,x)
```

Generating a histogram of the distribution

Rather than simply plotting the distribution, let's plot a histogram of the distribution so that we can see what the approximate error bins will look like. In fact, let's generate two different histograms, one containing the actual counts and the other containing percentages:

```
par(mfrow=c(1,2))
h <- hist(x,freq=FALSE,right=FALSE,breaks=c(-.20, -.15,-.10,-.05, 0, .05,
.1, .15, .20))

print(h)

plot(h$mids,100*h$counts/sum(h$counts),type="h",lwd=25, lty=1,
main="Probability of Errors Introduced")
```

In the plots below, you can see from the histogram on the left that there are no values beyond the limits specified. In fact, since the distribution was generated with a mean=0, a good number of the test elements will have no errors added to them. This is by design.

The bar chart on the right has been generated simply to show the relative percentage of each bar (rather than the straight frequency). From this, we can see, for example, that the probability of an adjustment of 5-10% is about 12%:

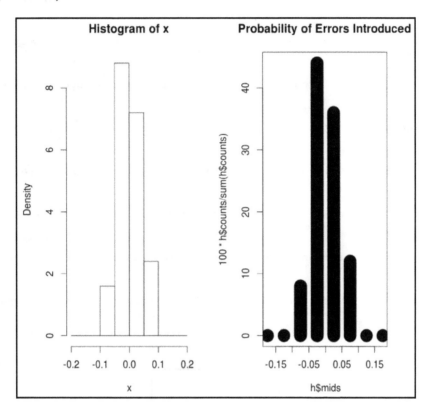

Generating the new test data with errors

Now we can introduce some variation into the dataset by adding a random percentage of each variable to itself. This is done by first sampling from the error distribution (x).

Note that we need to preface base: to the sample function, since the base sample function has a different syntax from the Spark sample function. If you do not do this, you will get an error:

```
# alter the test data set by sampling from the 'x' distribution and adding
or subtracting the introduced error adjustment.
```

```
test$age = test$age + test$age*base::sample(x, 1, replace = FALSE, prob =
NULL)

test$pregnant = test$pregnant + test$pregnant*base::sample(x, 1, replace =
FALSE, prob = NULL)

test$glucose = test$glucose + test$glucose*base::sample(x, 1, replace =
FALSE, prob = NULL)

test$pressure = test$pressure + test$pressure*base::sample(x, 1, replace =
FALSE, prob = NULL)

test$triceps = test$triceps + test$triceps*base::sample(x, 1, replace =
FALSE, prob = NULL)

test$insulin = test$insulin + test$insulin*base::sample(x, 1, replace =
FALSE, prob = NULL)

test$mass = test$mass + test$mass*base::sample(x, 1, replace = FALSE, prob
= NULL)

test$pedigree = test$pedigree + test$pedigree*base::sample(x, 1, replace =
FALSE, prob = NULL)

#calculation the number of rows again, to make sure they are the same as
before

nrow(test)
```

```
▶ (1) Spark Jobs

[1] 298000
```

Spark machine learning using logistic regression

Now that we have constructed our test and training datasets, we will begin by building a logistic regression model which will predict the outcome 1 or 0. As you will recall, 1 designates diabetes detected, while 0 designates diabetes not detected.

The syntax of a Spark `glm` is very similar to a normal glm. Specify the model using formula notation. Be sure to specify `family = "binomial"` to indicate that the outcome variable has only two outcomes:

```
# run glm model on Training dataset and assign it to object named "model"

model <- spark.glm(outcome ~ pregnant + glucose + pressure + triceps +
insulin + pedigree + age, family = "binomial", maxIter=100, data = df)
summary(model)
```

Examining the output:

You can observe the coefficients of the model in the Estimate column. You can also see that the residuals range from -2.54 to +2.40, which encompasses about 2.5 standard devations, and that the median value (not the mean) is supplied, which is -.326. Also note that p-values are not supplied in this version of `spark.glm`, since they are all displayed as 0.

The AIC for this model is listed at the bottom; however, it has no meaning unless it is compared with another model.

```
▶ (15) Spark Jobs

Deviance Residuals:
(Note: These are approximate quantiles with relative error <= 0.01)
      Min        1Q     Median        3Q       Max
  -2.54350  -0.68582  -0.32635   0.60581   2.39782


Coefficients:
                Estimate    Std. Error  t value  Pr(>|t|)
(Intercept)    -9.3308       0.021087   -442.49   0
pregnant        0.14879      0.00086434  172.15   0
glucose         0.0368       0.00010225  359.89   0
pressure        0.0098552    0.00021764   45.282  0
triceps         0.061359     0.0082994   204.94   0
insulin         0.0051072    3.0915e-05  165.2    0
pedigree        0.77574      0.0073594   105.41   0
age            -0.0085463    0.00026756  -31.942  0


(Dispersion parameter for binomial family taken to be 1)

    Null deviance: 1598954  on 1237999  degrees of freedom
Residual deviance: 1091651  on 1237992  degrees of freedom
AIC: 1091667
```

Regularization Models

Regularization models are an alternative to `spark.glm`; you can also run `spark.logit` and supply regularization parmeters to the independent variables.

By default, `spark.logit` will yield the same results as `spark.glm` without regularization parameters:

```
model2 <- spark.logit(df, outcome ~ pregnant + glucose + pressure + triceps
+ insulin + pedigree + age)
```

To verify this, run both `spark.logit` and `spark.glm` and verify that the results are identical.

Once you have verified this, you may add regularization parameters if you wish to smooth out the model by flattening the coefficients or set some of them to 0.

The model which has been run below only includes glucose, insulin, and pressure as predictors. Since the elasticnetparm (.8) is between 0 and 1, where 0 uses L2 and 1 will use L1, it will be using a combination of L1 and L2 regularization. Therefore, you will see some shrinkage of the coefficients to 0:

```
# Fit an binomial logistic regression model with spark.logit

model2 <- spark.logit(df, outcome ~ pregnant + glucose + pressure + triceps
+ insulin + pedigree + age, maxIter = 10, regParam = 0.1, elasticNetParam =
0.8)

summary(model2)
```

```
▶ (18) Spark Jobs

$coefficients
                Estimate
(Intercept)  -0.864
pregnant      0
glucose       0.00356
pressure     -0.00751
triceps       0
insulin       0.00216
pedigree      0
age           0
```

```
▶ (1) Spark Jobs

Deviance Residuals:
(Note: These are approximate quantiles with relative error <= 0.01)
     Min        1Q      Median       3Q        Max
  -2.19723   -0.78663  -0.46373   0.73562    2.11291

Coefficients:
               Estimate    Std. Error   t value   Pr(>|t|)
(Intercept)    -6.8738     0.01376      -499.54   0
pregnant        0.10571    0.00066769   158.32    0
glucose         0.027519   7.4042e-05   371.67    0
pressure        0.0061251  0.00017208   35.593    0
triceps         0.044508   0.00022808   195.14    0
insulin         0.0037124  2.4464e-05   151.75    0
pedigree        0.56068    0.0058485    95.868    0
age            -0.0048355  0.00021013   -23.012   0

(Dispersion parameter for binomial family taken to be 1)

    Null deviance: 1598954  on 1237999  degrees of freedom
Residual deviance: 1116432  on 1237992  degrees of freedom
AIC: 1116448

Number of Fisher Scoring iterations: 1
```

Predicting outcomes

SparkR does have a prediction method, aptly named `predict()`, so we can run predictions
on the training set:

- After running the following code, you will observe that the resulting object
  contains a new column named `prediction`
- We can also add a unary flag (1) to the results (grp) to indicate that the output is
  from the training data
- We will also append the total number of rows to each record, since we will need
  them later for calculations:

```
#look at the predictions vs. the training dataset
preds_train <- predict(model, df)
preds_train$grp <- 1
preds_train$totrows = nrow(preds_train)
```

The prediction variable is the probability that the outcome of the event (diabetes) will occur:

```
head(preds_train)
```

```
▶ (2) Spark Jobs

   sample_bin outcome pregnant glucose pressure triceps insulin mass pedigree
1        -144       0  -1.4808    73.4     66.6    19.8    104.1 23.9    0.112
2        -395       0   1.1046   105.6     71.0    22.3    114.7 30.5    0.948
3        -205       0  -0.3764   132.1     65.9    17.5    117.3 25.8    0.283
4         -23       0  -0.0204   111.9     64.6    34.0    106.4 44.0    0.520
5        -265       0   1.7489    83.4     48.4    15.1     55.3 29.1    0.298
6        -276       0   6.7640   157.6     82.2    15.4    187.0 29.9    0.582
     age label prediction grp totrows
1 33.20     0     0.0313    1 1238000
2 26.04     0     0.1690    1 1238000
3 25.33     0     0.1648    1 1238000
4  9.12     0     0.2240    1 1238000
5 16.81     0     0.0418    1 1238000
6 40.24     0     0.5483    1 1238000
```

Plotting the results

One way to plot this in Spark is to construct a histogram of the probabilities, using the midpoints of the binned range (centroids) for the *x* axis and the raw counts for each bin plotted on the *y* axis.

```
x=SparkR::histogram(preds_train,preds_train$prediction, nbins = 100)
x$centroids=round(x$centroids,2)
display(x)
```

After the `display` command has run, click on the Plot Icon (2nd Icon at the bottom left), and click on "Plot Options". The customize plot screen will then display:

1. Set **Display type** to **Grouped Bar Chart using a combination of the drop down selection and radio buttons**.
2. Drag **counts** from **All Fields** to **Values**.
3. Drag **Centroids** to **Keys**.

Centroids represent the <u>midpoints</u> of the bars. In the code above, we rounded them to two decimal places for readability on the generated plot. If the plot renders too small, you will need to open up **Customize Plot** again to see it again but larger.

The output shows a typical density for a logistic model, with most of the weight predicting a non-event. The higher probabilities, to the right, bin the frequencies for the probabilities which predict outcome=1.

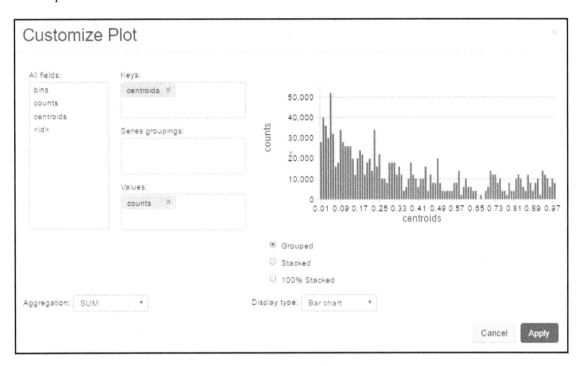

Running predictions for the test data

Next, we have similar code for the test data group. Set the `grp` flag to 0 to designate this is from the `test` group:

```
#run predictions on test dataset based on training model
preds_test <- predict(model, test)
preds_test$grp <- 0
preds_test$totrows = nrow(preds_test)
```

Print a few rows from the results using the SparkR `select` function to extract several key columns:

```
head(SparkR::select(preds_test,preds_test$outcome,preds_test$prediction,pre
ds_test$grp,preds_test$totrows))
```

```
▶ (2) Spark Jobs

  outcome prediction grp totrows
1       0     0.1685   0  298000
2       0     0.3754   0  298000
3       0     0.3441   0  298000
4       0     0.0729   0  298000
5       0     0.1767   0  298000
6       0     0.3189   0  298000
```

Combining the training and test dataset

Next, we will combine the training (`grp=1`) and testing (`grp=0`) datasets into one dataframe and manually calculate some accuracy statistics:

- `preds$error`: this is the absolute difference between the outcome (0,1) and the prediction. Recall that for a binary regression model, the prediction represents the probability that the event (diabetes) will occur.
- `preds$errorsqr`: this is the calculated squared error. This is done in order to remove the sign.
- `preds$correct`: in order to classify the probability into correct or not correct, we will compare the error to a `.5` cutoff. If the error was small (`<- .5`) we will call it correct, otherwise it will be considered not correct. This is a somewhat arbitrary cutoff, and it is used to determine which category to place the prediction in.

As a final step, we will once again separate the data back into test and training based upon the `grp` flag:

```
#classify 'correct' prediction if error is less than or equal to .5

preds <- rbind(preds_train,preds_test)
preds$error = abs(preds$prediction-preds$outcome)

#square the error to get the absolute squared error
```

```
preds$errorsqr = (preds$prediction-preds$outcome) ^ 2

#assign correct=Yes, or correct=No

preds$correct = ifelse(preds$error <= .5, "Y","N")
preds$errbin = round( (preds$error*10),0)

#separate the data again, including the new columns

preds_train = filter(preds, preds$grp==1)
preds_test  = filter(preds, preds$grp==0)
```

Next, print some of the results. You can see from the output that the first observation was classified as correct since the model probability was .03 and it is closer to the actual outcome (0). On the other hand, the sixth observation was (marginally) classified into predict outcome=1, but was wrong, therefore correct was set to N:

```
head(preds)
```

```
▶ (1) Spark Jobs

    sample_bin outcome pregnant glucose pressure triceps insulin mass pedigree
1         -144       0  -1.4808    73.4     66.6    19.8   104.1 23.9    0.112
2         -395       0   1.1046   105.6     71.0    22.3   114.7 30.5    0.948
3         -205       0  -0.3764   132.1     65.9    17.5   117.3 25.8    0.283
4          -23       0  -0.0204   111.9     64.6    34.0   106.4 44.0    0.520
5         -265       0   1.7489    83.4     48.4    15.1    55.3 29.1    0.298
5         -276       0   6.7640   157.6     82.2    15.4   187.0 29.9    0.582
      age label prediction grp totrows  error errorsqr correct errbin
1 33.20     0     0.0313    1 1238000 0.0313 0.000979       Y      0
2 26.04     0     0.1690    1 1238000 0.1690 0.028549       Y      2
3 25.33     0     0.1648    1 1238000 0.1648 0.027152       Y      2
4  9.12     0     0.2240    1 1238000 0.2240 0.050170       Y      2
5 16.81     0     0.0418    1 1238000 0.0418 0.001744       Y      0
5 40.24     0     0.5483    1 1238000 0.5483 0.300668       N      5
```

Exposing the three tables to SQL

We can now register our three key tables so that we can run some SQL code in order to obtain some additional diagnostics:

```
registerTempTable(preds, "preds_tbl")
registerTempTable(preds_train, "preds_train")
registerTempTable(preds_test, "preds_test")
```

Validating the regression results

Logistic regression in SparkR lacks some of the cross-validation and other features that you may be used to in base R. However, it is a starting point to enable you to start running large-scale models. If you need to employ some of the cross-validation techniques that have already been covered, you can certainly extract a sample of the data (via collect) and run the regression in base R.

However, there are some techniques that you can use to produce pseudo R-Squares and other diagnostics while continuing to work within Spark, which we will demonstrate.

Calculating goodness of fit measures

Confusion matrix

We can compute the confusion, or error, matrix in order to determine how our manual calculation performed, when we classified the prediction outcomes as correct or not:

```
#Confusion matrix
result <- sql("select outcome,correct, count(*) as k, avg(totrows) as
totrows from preds_tbl where grp=1 group by 1,2 order by 1,2")
result$classify_pct <- result$k/result$totrows

display(result)
```

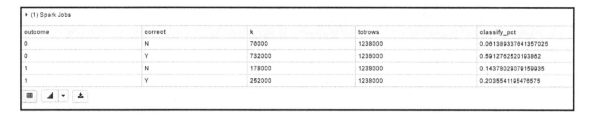

outcome	correct	k	totrows	classify_pct
0	N	76000	1238000	0.061389337641357025
0	Y	732000	1238000	0.5912762520193862
1	N	178000	1238000	0.14378029079159935
1	Y	252000	1238000	0.2035541195476575

To determine the grand total correct model prediction, sum the correct=Y columns previously:

Summary of correct predictions for training group:

Correctly predicted outcome=1	20%
Correctly predicted outcome=0	59%
Total Correct Percentage	79%

You can see that there is much more predictive power in predicting outcome=0 than there is outcome=1.

Confusion matrix for test group

The results for the test group are similar to those of the training group. Any discrepancies between test and training would warrant looking more closely at the model and observing how the data was sampled or split:

```
#Confusion matrix for TEST group
result <- sql("select outcome,correct, count(*) as k, avg(totrows) as
totrows from preds_tbl where grp=0 group by 1,2 order by 1,2")
result$classify_pct <- result$k/result$totrows
display(result)
```

outcome	correct	k	totrows	classify_pct
0	N	36000	298000	0.12080536912751678
0	Y	156000	298000	0.5234899328859061
1	N	40000	298000	0.1342281879194631
1	Y	66000	298000	0.2214765100671141

Add up the correct calculation is a similar way to the training group. The results are slightly less, which is normal when comparing test to training results :

Summary of Correct Predictions for Test Group:

Correctly predicted outcome=1	22%
Correctly predicted outcome=0	52%
Total Correct Percentage	74%

Distribution of average errors by group

Distribution of errors is another that you can look at how well a model has fit the data. In this analysis, we look at the distribution of errors for all four combinations of the following variables:

- Outcome
- Correct prediction flag
- Average error as grouped into categories via the `errbin` variable:

```
result2 <- sql("select outcome,correct,errbin, count(*) as k, avg(error) as
avgerr from preds_tbl group by 1,2,3 order by 1,2,3")
```

Plotting the data

Once the query has completed, issue a display command so that we can perform some visualizations.

```
display(result2)
```

1. Once the display has run, select the "Plot Options" icon (third icon bottom left), and select a **Stacked** bar chart plot from the plot menu.
2. Drag **k** (counts) to the **Values** box.
3. Drag **outcome** and **correct** to the **Series grouping** box.

4. Click **Apply** to update the visualization:

- As can be seen from the plot below, The lowest (and best) error for a predictor class was for the non-diabetic patients (bars 1-5, Outcome 0, Prediction N).
- The highest error can be seen for cases in which diabetes was predicted, but the patient was, in fact, nondiabetic (bars 6-11, Outcome 0, Prediction Y).
- A critical category, undetected diabetes (bars 12-16, outcome=1, prediction N) also had a relatively low error:

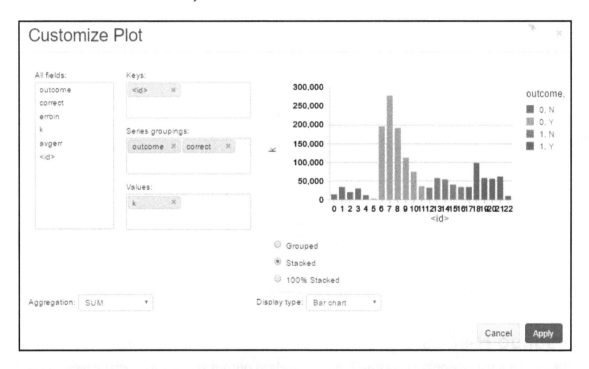

In this plot, we can look at the average error across both the test and training data and as well as outcome. Set up the "Series grouping" box to include both grp and outcome. We can see that the average error increases in the test data set for both outcome=1 and outcome=0.

A slight increase in error is to be expected when measured over the testing data:

```
#distribution of error bin
result2 <- sql("select outcome,grp,errbin, count(*) as k, avg(error) as
avgerr from preds_tbl group by 1,2,3 order by 1,2,3")
display(result2)
```

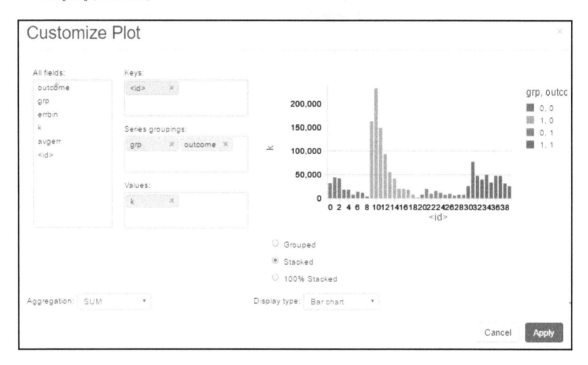

Pseudo R-square

Recall that a true R-square measure is not a standard output statistic for logistic regression but there are other goodness of fit measures we can use, such as the McFadden pseudo R-square.

We calculate this in code, by first obtaining both the residual deviance and the null deviance. The residual deviance measures the deviation in the model with all of the dependent variables included. The null deviation measures the residuals with only the intercepts included. You want the ratio of deviation/null.devation to be as small as possible for a good model. Subtract this value from 1 to obtain a pseudo R-square.

All of these measures are available via the `model_summary` object:

```
#mcfadden pseudo Rsquare

1-(model_summary$deviance/model_summary$null.deviance)
```

The calculation is automatically printed:

```
[1] 0.317
```

Root-mean-square error (RMSE)

We have already computed the squared error from the data, so to compute the root-mean-square error (RMSE), all we need to do is call SQL in order to take the average squared error for each outcome. We can see that there is much more variation in predicted outcome=1 (diabetes) than there is for predicting outcome=0:

```
result <- sql("select outcome,avg(errorsqr) from preds_tbl group by 1")
display(result)
```

Plotting outside of Spark

If you wish to use other tools to plot the data, you can first take a sample of the Spark data and plot it using another package such as `ggplot`. Note that some versions of Spark may now have ggplot integrated and available for use within Spark. However this example will show another example of extracting data which can be used by other packages.

Collecting a sample of the results

We will take a 2% sample of all of the predictions and then print some of the results. Note that the Spark sample function has a different syntax from the base R sample function we used earlier. You could also specify this as `SparkR::sample` to make sure you are invoking the correct function:

```
local = collect(sample(preds, F,.02))

head(local)
```

	sample_bin	outcome	pregnant	glucose	pressure	triceps	insulin	mass	pedigree
1	-265	0	1.75	83.4	48.4	15.1	55.3	29.1	0.298
2	-339	0	2.28	75.3	67.4	25.4	86.0	31.8	0.166
3	-367	0	4.21	87.6	72.2	31.6	73.8	33.3	0.701
4	-109	0	1.32	83.6	60.5	25.8	84.8	35.6	0.801
5	-239	0	2.08	110.9	60.4	33.6	269.4	39.9	0.459
6	-111	0	6.89	115.9	87.4	29.5	108.9	32.3	0.839

	age	label	prediction	grp	totrows	error	errorsqr	correct	errbin
1	16.8	0	0.0144	1	1238000	0.0144	0.000207	Y	0
2	36.5	0	0.0232	1	1238000	0.0232	0.000538	Y	0
3	26.9	0	0.1055	1	1238000	0.1055	0.011136	Y	1
4	21.3	0	0.0473	1	1238000	0.0473	0.002234	Y	0
5	36.0	0	0.2974	1	1238000	0.2974	0.088423	Y	3
6	38.8	0	0.3789	1	1238000	0.3789	0.143568	Y	4

Examining the distributions by outcome

Next, you can run `ggplot` to graphically display the errors grouped by outcome. The resulting boxplots show that the three quartiles for diabetes are above the non-diabetic patients. This demonstrates that the model's prediction error runs higher when predicting those patients who actually developed diabetes. This would certainly imply that the model needs to be improved:

```
library(ggplot2)
ggplot(local, aes(factor(outcome),error)) + geom_boxplot()
```

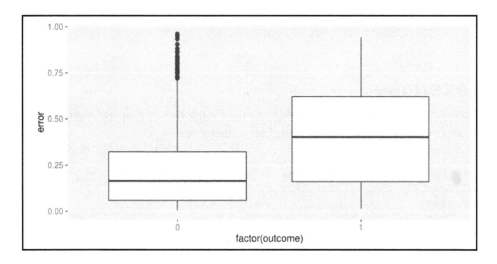

Registering some additional tables

We are now done with machine learning using logistic regression. For the next section (k-means), we will need to register some additional tables for dataframes that have already been produced:

```
registerTempTable(sumdf,"sumdf")
registerTempTable(out_sd,"out_sd")
registerTempTable(df,"df")
registerTempTable(test,"test")
```

Creating some global views

Creating global views will also allow us to pass data between different databricks notebooks. These views will be referenced in the next section. Use the %sql magic command as the first line in the databricks notebook to signify that these are SQL statements:

```
%sql
CREATE GLOBAL TEMPORARY VIEW df_view AS SELECT * FROM df

%sql
CREATE GLOBAL TEMPORARY VIEW test_view AS SELECT * FROM test

%sql
CREATE GLOBAL TEMPORARY VIEW out_sd_view AS SELECT * FROM out_sd
```

```
%sql
CREATE GLOBAL TEMPORARY VIEW sumdf_view AS SELECT * FROM sumdf
```

User exercise

After the views have been created, use SQL to read back the counts and verify the totals with the row counts produced for the original dataframes:

```
%sql
select count(*) from global_temp.df_view   union all
select count(*) from global_temp.test_view union all
select count(*) from global_temp.sumdf_view union all
select count(*) from global_temp.out_sd_view
```

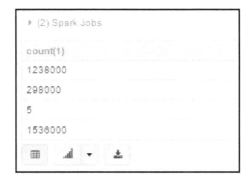

Cluster analysis

In this section, we will illustrate how to implement a cluster analysis directly in Spark using k-means. K-means is a form of unsupervised learning and is an excellent place to begin to explore big data, especially if your data is large and you have no clear definition of target variables.

Preparing the data for analysis

We will first perform some data preparation in order to normalize the data for k-means. Normalization is pretty much a requirement for k-means, since it forces each variable to be scale-independent so that measuring distances between the k-means clusters is also scale-independent.

Recall that one way to normalize a variable is to first obtain the mean of the variable and then divide by its standard deviation.

Reading the data from the global views

We saved the diabetes dataset as a table and a global view in the previous section, so we can now read it back using SQL. We will first read the training table (`temp.df_view`) and then follow by reading the test table (`test_view`). The resulting objects are both Spark dataframes.

After reading the table in, print the count of the rows. If you want to see the counts as one result, you can use a function such as cat() to print the results on one line:

```
df = sql("select age,
                  pregnant,
                  glucose,
                  pressure,
                  insulin,
                  pedigree,
                  triceps,
                  mass
from global_temp.df_view")

test = sql("select age ,
                    pregnant,
                    glucose,
                    pressure,
                    insulin,
                    pedigree,
                    triceps,
                    mass
from global_temp.test_view")

cat(count(df),count(test))
```

> ▶ (2) Spark Jobs
>
> 1238000 298000

Inputting the previously computed means and standard deviations

In order to normalize the data, we will need the means and standard deviations of each column. If you were doing this purely in base R, there would be many ways to do this using built-in functions and packages. However, using SparkR may limit how we would typically proceed, and force us to be more efficient and process the data in different ways.

Recall that we have already stored this data in a summary object (`sumdf_view` and so on), so in order to save some processing time, we will simply read the summary statistics back in and avoid having to recalculate the summary statistics.

First, we will read the means row in, followed by the `stddev` row:

```
means = sql("select age as age_mean,
                    pregnant as pregnant_mean,
                    glucose as glucose_mean,
                    pressure as pressure_mean,
                    insulin as insulin_mean,
                    pedigree as pedigree_mean,
                    triceps as triceps_mean,
                    mass as mass_mean
from global_temp.sumdf_view where summary='mean'")
stds = sql("select age as age_std,
                   pregnant as pregnant_std,
                   glucose as glucose_std,
                   pressure as pressure_std,
                   insulin as insulin_std,
                   pedigree as pedigree_std,
                   triceps as triceps_std,
                   mass as mass_std
from global_temp.sumdf_view where summary='stddev'")
```

Joining the means and standard deviations with the training data

Now we can join the aggregate means and standard deviations together using a `crossJoin`. No key is necessary since the tables have the same number of rows and they correspond 1 to 1.

Then join the summary data with the original data. The resulting object is another Spark dataframe (df_means) with the means and standard deviations of all of the variables joined to each row:

```
#join the means and standard deviations
both <- crossJoin(means,stds)
#join with the original data
df_means <- crossJoin(df,both)
nrow(df_means)
```

```
▶ (6) Spark Jobs

[1] 1238000
```

Print a portion of the resultant object. All of the original variables are displayed along with their corresponding means and standard deviations:

```
print(head(select(df_means,
"age","age_mean","age_std",
"mass","mass_mean","mass_std"
)))
```

```
▶ (3) Spark Jobs

          age          age_mean            age_std    mass            mass_mean
1 33.201751 33.24088541667883 11.75257647170343 23.91985 32.442846279285206
2 26.037762 33.24088541667883 11.75257647170343 30.46985 32.442846279285206
3 25.330797 33.24088541667883 11.75257647170343 25.78872 32.442846279285206
4  9.115341 33.24088541667883 11.75257647170343 44.01366 32.442846279285206
5 16.805305 33.24088541667883 11.75257647170343 29.11407 32.442846279285206
6 40.243232 33.24088541667883 11.75257647170343 29.93310 32.442846279285206
           mass_std
1 6.874555211563171
2 6.874555211563171
3 6.874555211563171
4 6.874555211563171
5 6.874555211563171
6 6.874555211563171
```

Joining the means and standard deviations with the test data

Similar to the preceding code, we join the means and standard deviations to the test data set separately.

Check the number of rows created. If you want to see the actual results, print a portion of the data as we did with the training data above:

```
test_means <- crossJoin(test,both)
nrow(test_means)
```

```
▶ (3) Spark Jobs

[1] 298000
```

Normalizing the data

We now have all the needed statistics to normalize the data. Recall that the formula for normalizing a variable x is as follows:

$$(x - mean(x)) / std(x)$$

In order to implement this, we will wrap the needed computations into a function and invoke it for both the training and test datasets:

- Use the SparkR `selectExpr` expression to calculate the normalized version of each variable using the formula above.
- Also, create a new variable with old appended to the name, which preserves the original value of the variable. After testing, you should remove these extra variables to save space, but it is good to retain them while debugging:

```
normalize_it <- function (x) {
selectExpr(x,
        "age as ageold","(age-age_mean)/ age_std as age",
        "mass as massold","(mass-mass_mean)/ mass_std as mass",
        "triceps as tricepsold",
        "(triceps-triceps_mean)/ triceps_std as     triceps",
        "pressure as pressureold",
```

```
                          "(pressure-pressure_mean)/ pressure_std as pressure",
                          "pedigree as pedigreeold",
                          "(pedigree-pedigree_mean)/ pedigree_std as pedigree",
                          "glucose as glucoseold",
                          "(glucose-glucose_mean)/ glucose_std as glucose",
                          "pregnant as pregnantold",
                          "(pregnant-pregnant_mean)/ pregnant_std as pregnant",
                          "insulin as insulinold",
                          "(insulin-insulin_mean)/ insulin_std as insulin"
             )
}
```

First, call the function for the `test` dataset:

```
test_normal <- normalize_it(test_means)
```

Next, normalize for the training dataset:

```
df_normal <- normalize_it(df_means)
```

Displaying the output

Print some of the output for the normalized training data.

```
head(df_normal)
```

Notice from the output below that the normalized values appear to range between -2 and +2 with a mean of 0. Any value close to these extremes falls near the extreme range for the variables.

For example, observation 4 shows a normalized age of less than -2, which corresponds to the original age of 9, while observation 4 also shows a normalized body mass of 1.68, which corresponds to the original body mass of 44.

This is at the upper range for a 9-year-old child, and we have been able to quickly identify some extreme values simply by looking at the relationship between some of the normalized values:

```
▸ (3) Spark Jobs

      ageold          age  massold         mass tricepsold      triceps pressureold
1 33.201751 -0.003329854 23.91985 -1.2397891    19.80557 -1.0582419    66.59577
2 26.037762 -0.612897400 30.46985 -0.2870003    22.31758 -0.7767366    70.97826
3 25.330797 -0.673051430 25.78872 -0.9679359    17.54818 -1.3112141    65.89486
4  9.115341 -2.052787712 44.01366  1.6831360    34.03530  0.5363971    64.62639
5 16.805305 -1.398466149 29.11407 -0.4842170    15.08383 -1.5873794    48.44238
6 40.243232  0.595813771 29.93310 -0.3650773    15.41831 -1.5498966    82.24149
     pressure pedigreeold    pedigree glucoseold     glucose pregnantold
1 -0.4802065   0.1122226 -1.0861966    73.38202 -1.5868256 -1.48080805
2 -0.1179241   0.9477453  1.4371804   105.55782 -0.5298630  1.10456706
3 -0.5381479   0.2829579 -0.5705558   132.05748  0.3406405 -0.37639825
4 -0.6430063   0.5199817  0.1452839   111.93177 -0.3204812 -0.02039326
5 -1.9808706   0.2984521 -0.5237616    83.44548 -1.2562449  1.74893121
6  0.8131598   0.5824100  0.3338248   157.58550  1.1792259  6.76401329
     pregnant insulinold     insulin
1 -1.5816013   104.09869 -0.6064124
2 -0.8138319   114.65470 -0.4907926
3 -1.2536288   117.33043 -0.4614855
4 -1.1479073   106.38615 -0.5813578
5 -0.6224774    55.32411 -1.1406391
6  0.8668333   186.98714  0.3014627
```

Running the k-means model

Now that the data is normalized, we can move on to model building.

SparkR contains a k-means model which is very similar in syntax to the base k-means model. There is an additional parameter, `InitMode`, in which you can specify that a random seed be generated for generating the starting cluster. As of this version of SparkR, you cannot manually set a seed. Therefore, be aware that the clusters generated may be slightly different each time the model is run.

Additionally, you can specify the outcome variable (glucose) as well as the variables to be clustered, so that you can evaluate the fit of the cluster model.

For illustration purposes, we will generate a model of five clusters.

Use `summary(model)` to display the coefficients needed to generate the prediction as well as the size of each of the clusters, as shown as follows.

```
model <- spark.kmeans(df_normal, glucose ~ age + mass + triceps + pregnant,
k = 5, initMode = "random")

summary(model)
```

You can see from the sizes that each of the clusters are approximately equal in `size`, except perhaps for cluster 1:

```
#here is the output from summary function

$k
[1] 5

$coefficients
    age          mass         triceps      pregnant
1 0.974506    0.871064     1.096543     0.9835401
2 -0.2056799 0.9210847    0.666911     -0.432624
3 0.7791526   -0.4984192  -0.2448071   0.8973491
4 -1.092614   -0.1553198  -0.1833185   -0.9076226
5 -0.2380403  -1.001556   -1.246133    -0.2903638

$size
$size[[1]]
[1] 170000

$size[[2]]
[1] 276000

$size[[3]]
[1] 298000

$size[[4]]
[1] 274000

$size[[5]]
[1] 220000
```

Fitting the model to the training data

Since you have the coefficients, you could actually predict the cluster membership manually via code. You would probably want to do this if you were implementing cluster assignment in a production environment. However, it is easier to use a `predict` method.

Let's fit the model first to the training data. We can print out some of the fitted values just to see what was generated. The last column indicates the cluster assignment for that observation:

```
fitted <- predict(model, df_normal)
SparkR:::registerTempTable(fitted,"fitted_tbl")
head(fitted)
```

```
▶ (3) Spark Jobs

      ageold          age massold        mass tricepsold      triceps pressureold
1 33.201751 -0.003329854 23.91985 -1.2397891    19.80557 -1.0582419     66.59577
2 26.037762 -0.612897400 30.46985 -0.2870003    22.31758 -0.7767366     70.97826
3 25.330797 -0.673051430 25.78872 -0.9679359    17.54818 -1.3112141     65.89486
4  9.115341 -2.052787712 44.01366  1.6831360    34.03530  0.5363971     64.62639
5 16.805305 -1.398466149 29.11407 -0.4842170    15.08363 -1.5873794     48.44238
6 40.243232  0.595813771 29.93310 -0.3650773    15.41831 -1.5498966     82.24149
   pressure pedigreeold    pedigree glucoseold    glucose pregnantold
1 -0.4802065   0.1122226 -1.0861966   73.38202 -1.5868256 -1.48080805
2 -0.1179241   0.9477453  1.4371804  105.55782 -0.5298630  1.10456706
3 -0.5381479   0.2829579 -0.5705558  132.05748  0.3406405 -0.37639825
4 -0.6430063   0.5199817  0.1452839  111.93177 -0.3204812 -0.02039326
5 -1.9808706   0.2984521 -0.5237616   83.44548 -1.2562449  1.74893121
6  0.8131598   0.3824100  0.3338248  157.58550  1.1792259  6.76401329
   pregnant insulinold    insulin      label prediction
1 -1.5816013  104.09869 -0.6064124 -1.5868256          4
2 -0.8138319  114.65470 -0.4907926 -0.5298630          3
3 -1.2536288  117.33043 -0.4614855  0.3406405          4
4 -1.1479073  106.38615 -0.5813578 -0.3204812          1
5 -0.6224774   55.32411 -1.1406391 -1.2562449          4
6  0.8668333  186.98714  0.3014627  1.1792259          2
```

Fitting the model to the test data

Fit the model on the test data and print out some of the results obtained for the test data:

```
fitted_test <- predict(model, test_normal)
SparkR:::registerTempTable(fitted_test,"fitted_tbl_test")
head(fitted_test)
```

```
       ageold         age  massold       mass tricepsold    triceps pressureold
1  33.96803  0.06187131 25.76803 -0.9709453   17.95158 -1.2660084    68.22192
2  32.27039 -0.08257709 31.69610 -0.1086242   31.44270  0.2458600    58.71235
3  36.56022  0.28243450 38.02934  0.8126340   35.80103  0.7342718    67.02700
4  47.25603  1.19251664 27.24542 -0.7560381   31.15899  0.2140669    82.06206
5  38.87426  0.47933086 26.24070 -0.9021892   34.23827  0.5591432    62.02162
6  38.18221  0.42044636 22.36163 -1.4664538   37.76050  0.9538583    66.80120
      pressure   pedigreeold    pedigree glucoseold     glucose pregnantold
1  -0.3457796 -0.201075157 -2.0323926  146.27194  0.80757994   0.8654326
2  -1.1318950  0.775602983  0.9172903  113.02193 -0.28467005   3.5297374
3  -0.4445586  0.048089812 -1.2798851  130.18584  0.27915780   1.1619962
4   0.7983271  0.155334447 -0.9559937   81.40550 -1.32325727   4.0704518
5  -0.8583318 -0.001603494 -1.4299647   96.97609 -0.81176945   4.1809552
6  -0.4632242  0.365889384 -0.3200930  120.42013 -0.04164209   3.2398957
      pregnant insulinold    insulin      label prediction
1  -0.88484678   175.2965  0.1734150  0.80757994           4
2  -0.09363786   255.2023  1.0486217 -0.28467005           1
3  -0.79677737   223.1728  0.6978036  0.27915780           1
4   0.06693614   146.7867 -0.1388513 -1.32325727           2
5   0.09975193   239.4030  0.8755728 -0.81176945           2
6  -0.17971108   142.0769 -0.1904382 -0.04164209           2
```

Graphically display cluster assignment

Bivariate cluster plots are often useful for seeing how the cluster assignments correlate with an *x-y* plot of two variables. Each cluster is plotted in a different color.

In Databricks, you can do this easily:

First, run the display command on some of the fitted data. In the code below, I have first extracted a 1,000-row sample. You want the sample to be small enough so that the points on the plot are not too dense.

```
tmp <- head(sample(fitted, F, .01),1000)
display(tmp)

#show cluster assignment by 2 variable matrix
```

Next, switch to the plot dialog box, Open the **Customize Plot** dialog. and perform the following graph setup:

1. Change the graph type to scatter plot.
2. Drag the prediction to the keys area.
3. Drag all the possible *x-y* plotting variables to the values area:
4. If you add a LOESS line to the plots, you will be able to pick out some of the clusters which are easily separable by a combination of two variables.

Click **Apply** to update the plot. In the following plot, the upward trending line at the intersection of age and pregnant shows distinct cluster separation as age and months pregnant varies:

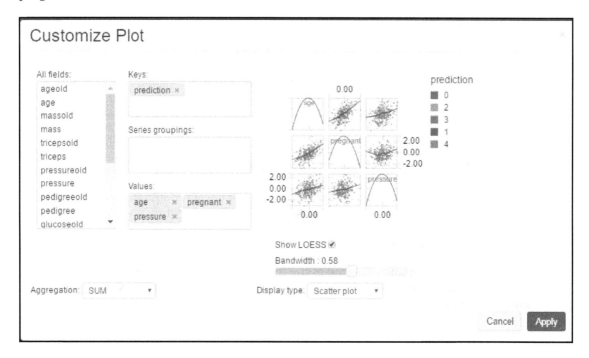

Plotting via the Pairs function

To get a larger and more detailed plot, you can also use the pairs function to produce a scatter matrix on your desired variables using color to outline the various clusters.

We can see that the clusters are separated from the rest in some cases, while in other cases there can be minor or major overlap:

```
pairs(tmp[c("age","mass","pressure","pregnant")],
  col=tmp$prediction)
```

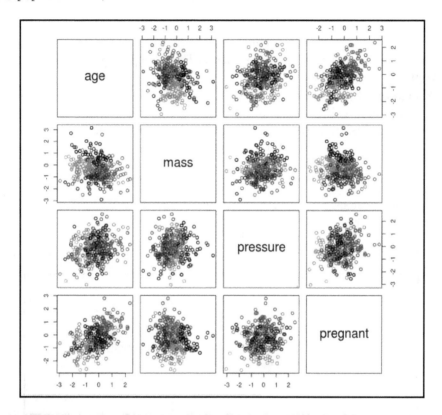

To start analyzing the components of the clusters, you can look at how the variables are plotted along each of the axes.

For example, the red cluster shows a relationship between older patients and number of months pregnant. This would seem to indicate a positive diabetes condition. To double-check, you can look at body mass, and also see that the higher values show up in the red cluster for all of the other variables as well.

On the other hand, the relationship between pressure and mass is not as clear, possibly due to the fact that other factors could be in play which are not apparent in a two-dimensional plot.

Characterizing the clusters by their mean values

Another way to look at the clusters is by looking directly at their mean values. We can do this directly by using SQL:

- First, look at any variables which have normalized values >1 or < -1, or high the highest absolute value for that variable. That will give you some clues on how to begin to classify the clusters.
- Also look at the magnitude and the signs of the coefficients. Coefficients with large absolute values can indicate an important influence of the variable on that particular cluster. Variables with opposite signs are important in terms of characterizing or naming the clusters.

```
tmp_agg <- SparkR::sql("SELECT prediction, mean(age),
mean(triceps),
mean(pregnant),mean(pressure),mean(insulin),
mean(glucose),
mean(pedigree) from fitted_tbl group by 1")
head(tmp_agg)
```

```
 ▶ (7) Spark Jobs

   prediction    avg(age)  avg(triceps)  avg(pregnant)  count(age)
 1          1 -0.2056799     0.6669110     -0.4326240      276000
 2          3 -1.0926137    -0.1833185     -0.9076226      274000
 3          4 -0.2453393    -1.2575343     -0.3066965      220000
 4          2  0.7708876    -0.2498310      0.8934643      298000
 5          0  0.9745060     1.0965432      0.9835401      170000
```

Scanning through the five clusters produced, you might categorize Cluster 2 as a group consisting of younger people with lower pregnancy rates since the mean values for both variables are near the negative -1 value. Remember that these are all standardize values so you can compare them, and use +1/-1 standard deviation levels as cutoffs. So, using that as a cutoff, you could also also hypothesize that Cluster 3 could be people with lower body mass since the triceps level is also near -1. Values close to 0 implies that the variable has a negligible influence on the cluster.

Calculating mean values for the test data

Results for this data set are similar to the training data:

```
tmp_agg <- SparkR::sql("SELECT prediction, mean(age), mean(triceps),
mean(pregnant),mean(pressure),mean(insulin),mean(glucose),mean(pedigree)
from fitted_tbl_test group by 1")
head(tmp_agg)
```

```
▶ (7) Spark Jobs

  prediction    avg(age)  avg(triceps)  avg(pregnant)  avg(pressure)  avg(insulin)
1          1  -0.1460594     0.7038619     -0.4245266      0.1764655     0.4348044
2          3  -1.2141664    -0.2855458     -0.8130297     -0.5550104    -0.2377346
3          4  -0.1562988    -1.2265138     -0.2037147     -0.3655402    -0.2354299
4          2   0.7498264    -0.2324546      0.5918927      0.2299495     0.3695036
5          0   0.6292312     1.0599987      0.8521112      0.2851198     0.5954573
  avg(glucose)  avg(pedigree)
1   0.10083870     0.29937091
2  -0.51709496     0.13754498
3  -0.16160085     0.19409315
4   0.09277286    -0.06523912
5   0.37704262     0.45119753
```

Summary

In this chapter we went beyond SQL, and started to explore the machine learning capabilities of Spark. We covered both regression and kmeans clustering using our diabetes dataset. We constructed our training and testing data sets, and learned how to introduce some variation into our data via simulation. A lot of Databricks visualization was covered, as well as some visualizations using the collect() function to export the data to base R so that we could use ggplot. We also learned how to perform some regression diagnostics manually using code. We then learned how to standardize a data set via code, and used the results to illustrate a kmeans example using Spark. Finally we looked at the resulting clusters and examined some simple interpretations.

12
Spark Models – Rule-Based Learning

In this section, we will learn how to implement some rule-based algorithms. The method in which these algorithms can be implemented depends upon the language interface you are using and the version of Spark which is running.

For Spark 2.0, the only languages which support rule-based decision trees are Scala and Python. So in order to demonstrate how decision rules can be constructed directly in Spark, we will illustrate an example that uses Python to determine the rules for being frisked.

For other languages, such as R, there is currently no facility to run a decision tree algorithm directly on a Spark dataframe; however, there are other methods that can be used which will yield accurate trees.

We will demonstrate how to first extract a sample from Spark, download it to base R, and run our usual tools, such as rpart. Big datasets will typically contain much more data than you might need for a decision tree, so it makes perfect sense to sample appropriately from your big data source, extract the data from Spark to R, and run your standard tools.

We will introduce the **One Rule (OneR)** package to see how each single variable is able to predict the outcome. The philosophy of OneR being less is more, we will demonstrate how OneR can optimally bin your numeric values and determine what your top predictors are using decision tree rules. You can also use the OneR package to perform feature selection.

Loading the stop and frisk dataset

We will be using the diabetes dataset which was constructed in the last chapter. For some of the other decision tree examples, we will need to load the stop and frisk dataset. You can obtain this dataset from the following URL: `http://www1.nyc.gov/site/nypd/stats/repo rts-analysis/stopfrisk.page`.

Select the 2015 CSV zip archive and download and extract the files to the projects directory, e.g C:/PracticalPredictiveAnalytics/Data, and name the file `2015_sqf_csv`

Importing the CSV file to databricks

Databricks contains a simple user interface which allows you to load a file to the Databricks HDFS filesystem. Alternatively, you can load the file directly to **Amazon Web Services** (**AWS**) and read the file directly from the Databricks API.

1. Switch to the Databricks application, select **Tables**, and then **Data Import**. Note that in some of the versions of Databricks this is embedded under the Data menu: Select "Tables", and then click the +.
2. **You may be prompted to create a new cluster. If so, first follow the instructions for creating a new cluster as we did in Chapter 9.**
3. Drag the file named `2015_sqf_csv` from the PracticalPredictiveAnalytics directory to the data import box, as shown next:

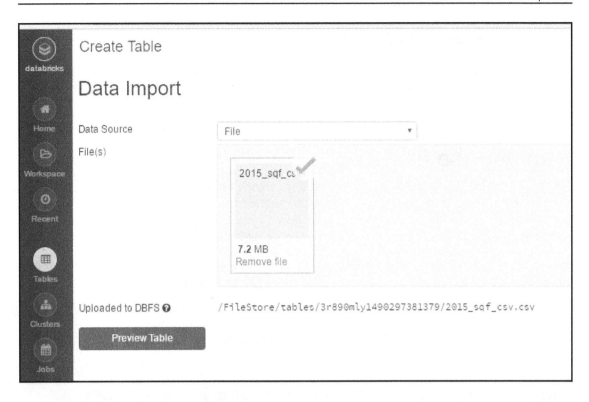

4. Click on **Preview Table**.

5. Enter **Table name** as stopfrisk.

6. Observe how the variables have been assigned (they are all assigned as character strings); however, do not change any of the attributes. Simply click on **Create Table** (the blue button on the left):

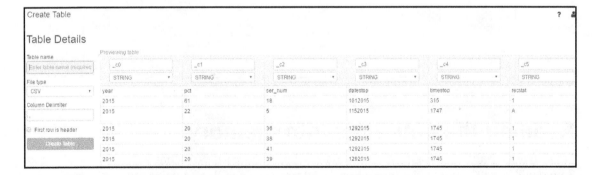

Reading the table

Once you have completed the preceding steps, the table you have just created will be registered in the databricks system and will remain persistent across sessions, i.e you will not need to reload the data every time you login.

Running the first cell

Begin by running the first cell (also referred to as a code chunk), which simply will get a count of the number of records by year. You can access the code in this chapter by downloading it from the book's site. Alternatively, you can copy each section of the following code into a new cell and create your own notebook that way.

Since stop frisk has been imported and has already been registered as a table, we can begin to use SQL to read it some of the counts in order to see how large the file is:

```
#embed all SQL within the sql() function

yr <- sql("SELECT year,frisked,count(*) as year_cnt FROM stopfrisk group by year,frisked")
display(yr)
```

After a few seconds, the output will appear as a simple formatted table. A simple calculation using the year_cat column shows that for 2015, 68% of those who where stopped, were also frisked:

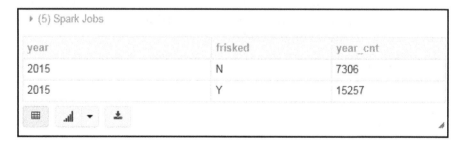

Reading the entire file into memory

Now that we have some aggregate counts, we have some idea of what we will be looking at. So we will read the entire file into a Spark dataframe via SQL and print the first record (you can print more if you like).

Just by looking at the first record(s), you can see that there are a mix of binary yes/no flags and some numeric variables:

```
df <- sql("SELECT * FROM stopfrisk")
head(df,1)
```

```
▶ (1) Spark Jobs

  year pct ser_num datestop timestop recstat inout trhsloc perobs crimsusp
1 2015  61      18  1012015      315       1     0       P   2.00   FELONY
  perstop typeofid explnstp othpers arstmade arstoffn sumissue sumoffen
1      10        V        Y       N        N                 N
  compyear comppct offunif officrid frisked searched contrabn adtlrept pistol
1        0       0        N                Y        N        N        N      N
  riflshot asltweap knifcuti machgun othrweap pf_hands pf_wall pf_grnd pf_drwep
1        N        N        N       N        N        N       N       N       N
  pf_ptwep pf_baton pf_hcuff pf_pepsp pf_other radio ac_rept ac_inves rf_vcrim
1        N        N        N        N        N     N       N        Y        N
  rf_othsw ac_proxm rf_attir cs_objcs cs_descr cs_casng cs_lkout rf_vcact
1        N        Y        N        N        Y        Y        N        N
  cs_cloth cs_drgtr ac_evasv ac_assoc cs_furtv rf_rfcmp ac_cgdir rf_verbl
1        N        N        N        N        N        Y        N        N
  cs_vcrim cs_bulge cs_other ac_incid ac_time rf_knowl ac_stsnd ac_other
1        N        N        N        Y        Y        N        N        N
  sb_hdobj sb_outln sb_admis sb_other repcmd revcmd rf_furt rf_bulg offverb
1        N        N        N        N     186    186       N       N       V
  offshld forceuse sex race dob age ht_feet ht_inch weight haircolr eyecolor
1       S        M   W      33   5      11     190       BR       BR
  build othfeatr addrtyp rescode premtype premname addrnum stname  stinter
1     M        L                         STREET                   AVENUE W
       crossst aptnum     city state zip addrpct sector beat post  xcoord
1 EAST 28 STREET        BROOKLYN               61      E    7       1000091
  ycoord dettypCM lineCM detailCM
1 156314       CM      1       14
```

Transforming some variables to integers

If you run an `str()` function on the variables in the dataframe, you will see that all of them are of type `chr` (character). We also saw that in the import file dialog:

```
str(df)
```

```
'SparkDataFrame': 112 variables:
 $ year    : chr "2015" "2015" "2015" "2015" "2015" "2015"
 $ pct     : chr "61" "22" "20" "20" "20" "20"
 $ ser_num : chr "18" "5" "36" "38" "41" "39"
 $ datestop: chr "1012015" "1152015" "1292015" "1292015" "1292015" "1292015"
 $ timestop: chr "315" "1747" "1745" "1745" "1745" "1745"
```

We will want some of these variables to be integers, so we can use the `cast()` function to change some of them. Also, clean up some of the leading and trailing spaces using the `trim()` function:

```
df$age <- cast(trim(df$age),'integer')
df$perstop <- cast(df$perstop,'integer')
df$perobs <- cast(df$perobs,'integer')
df$ser_num <- cast(df$ser_num,'integer')
df$datestop <- cast(df$datestop,'integer')
df$timestop <- cast(df$timestop,'integer')
df$repcmd <- cast(df$repcmd,'integer')
df$revcmd <- cast(df$revcmd,'integer')
df$compyear <- cast(df$compyear,'integer')
df$comppct <- cast(df$comppct,'integer')
df$ht_feet <- cast(df$ht_feet,'integer')
df$ht_inch <- cast(df$ht_inch,'integer')

df$height <- df$ht_feet*12+df$ht_inch
df$weight <- cast(df$weight,'integer')

str(df)
```

At the end of the code we run the `str()` function , in order to verify that these variables have been changed to integers. You will also see that one extra variable has been created (height) which has been calculated as `feet*12 + inches`. For our purposes, it is not necessary to keep separate variables for both height in feet and height in inches:

Here is the first page of the output of the str(). Note that ser_num,datestop, timestop,perobs, and perstop have been mapped to integer.

```
'SparkDataFrame': 113 variables:
 $ year     : chr "2015" "2015" "2015" "2015" "2015" "2015"
 $ pct      : chr "61" "22" "20" "20" "20" "20"
 $ ser_num  : int 18 5 36 38 41 39
 $ datestop : int 1012015 1152015 1292015 1292015 1292015 1292015
 $ timestop : int 315 1747 1745 1745 1745 1745
 $ recstat  : chr "1" "A" "1" "1" "1" "1"
 $ inout    : chr "O" "O" "O" "O" "O" "O"
 $ trhsloc  : chr "P" "P" "P" "P" "P" "P"
 $ perobs   : int 2 1 1 1 1 1
 $ crimsusp : chr "FELONY" "FELONY" "MISD" "MIDS" "MISD" "MISD"
 $ perstop  : int 10 4 16 16 16 16
```

Discovering the important features

We will now introduce the OneR package to discover some of the important features of the dataset. The OneR package will produce a single decision rule for each of the features and then rank them in terms of accuracy. **Accuracy** is defined as the probability of classifying the outcome correctly and can be expressed as a confusion or error matrix, which we have seen before in the previous chapters. The OneR package has some other nice features, such as the ability to bin integer variables optimally in order to yield the best predictor.

The OneR package does not run natively on Spark, so we first need to use the collect() and sample() functions to perform a 95% sample of the Spark dataframe and then move it to a local R dataframe via the collect() function.

Although this Spark dataframe is small enough to perform the example without the sampling, it is important to know how to sample from a dataframe, since if you are using Spark as intended, your dataframes will be too large to use the collect function to bring the entire dataframe into a local instance of R. For extremely large Spark tables, you may want to use a sampling percentage of 5-10% or so for an initial analysis. However, for our example we will use a sampling percentage of 95% to capture most of the data, since the 2015 stop and risk data is relatively small. However, if you were bringing in all of the years' data and concatenating it into one big Spark dataframe, you would consider bringing down the sampling percentage to a more reasonable number. Otherwise, you might end up with more rows than base R could handle.

Also note that the `OneR` package is not currently available as a default installed package. But you can use devtools to install the latest version from `cran`:

```
devtools::install_github("cran/OneR")
library(OneR)

#bring 95% of the rows from the Spark dataframe named "df" into a base R
dataframe named "local"

local = collect(sample(df, F,.95))
```

Eliminating some factors with a large number of levels

Since the dataset is very granular for some of the features such as zip code and GPS location variables, we will first perform a dimension reduction by only including features/variables with a maximum of 20 levels. That will help us formulate models later without worrying about overfitting due to some variables that having high dimensionality. However, the number 20 is not set in stone; you can change the default and always keep variables which you feel are needed in the model regardless of levels.

`OneR` has a function named maxlevels() which can accomplish this. Any variable which has a number of levels exceeding this is not included in the output.

After running the function, use the `str()` function to verify some variables have been eliminated. We originally started with 113 variables and now are down to 97. Some of the variables, such as the *x* and *y* coordinates, have been eliminated since GPS coordinates obviously have more than 20 levels:

```
frisked_df <- maxlevels(local, maxlevels = 20, na.omit = TRUE)
#check the output to see if the number of levels were reduced
str(frisked_df)
```

Observe the first 3 lines of the output showing that the number of variables has been reduced from 113 to 97:

```
'data.frame':   21359 obs. of  97 variables:
 $ year    : chr  "2015" "2015" "2015" "2015" ...
 $ ser_num : int  18 5 38 41 39 122 42 9 141 2 ...
```

Test and train datasets

Of course, we will want to partition the data into test and training datasets. We have covered many ways to separate into test and train. This next method of partitioning will take a 80%/20% training/test split by:

- first extracting the index numbers from the training dataset. We will use the `base::sample` function to accomplish this
- building the training dataset from these indices
- constructing the test dataset from the rows which are not contained in the index.

Once we obtain the train indices, we will use the `optbin` function from the OneR package, which will optimally split a numeric variable based upon its ability to predict a Yes or No outcome for frisked. We have already seen this kind of optimal splitting with Decision Trees. In the code below optbin is directed to find the best split point for all of the numerical variables as indicated by specifying frisked~.

```
set.seed(123)
train.index <- base::sample(1:base::nrow(frisked_df), 0.80 *
base::nrow(frisked_df))
train_data <- optbin(frisked_df[train.index,],frisked~.)
test_data <- optbin(  frisked_df[-train.index,],frisked~.)

#after partitioning, run a summary of the first 15 rows to see what the
output looks like

summary(train_data[1:15])
```

```
    year                 ser_num                        datestop
 2015:16034       (-0.523,265]  :10299    (1e+06,6.13e+06]    :8689
                  (265,1.53e+03]: 5735    (6.13e+06,1.23e+07]:7345


                    timestop      recstat    inout    trhsloc          perobs
 (-2.36,1.37e+03]    :6410        : 2043    I: 2955   H: 2387   (-0.36,2.74]:12670
 (1.37e+03,2.36e+03]:9624         1:10454   0:13079   P:13009   (2.74,360]  : 3364
                                  9:    8             T:  638
                                  A: 3529
            perstop        typeofid explnstp  othpers    arstmade   sumissue   compyear
 (0.911,8.1]:9942          0: 308   N:   20   N:11285    N:13211    N:15591    0:16034
 (8.1,90.1] :6092          P:9279   Y:16014   Y: 4749    Y: 2823    Y:  443
                           R: 454
                           V:5993
```

Examining the binned data

In the preceding output, observe that each numeric variable has been transformed into one of the two categorical bins. The two-binned categories are represented by starting and ending ranges separated by (,). They are easy to pick out since summary indicates them with a beginning (and an ending] :

Take a look at the train_dataset using the special Databricks display command.

```
display(train_data)
```

ear	ser_num	datestop	timestop	recstat	inout	trhsloc	perobs	perstop	typeofid	explnstp	othpers	arstmade
015	(-0.523,265]	(1e+06,6.13e+06]	(1.37e+03,2.36e+03]	A	O	P	(-0.36,2.74]	(0.911,8.1]	P	Y	N	N
015	(-0.523,265]	(6.13e+06,1.23e+07]	(1.37e+03,2.36e+03]	1	O	P	(-0.36,2.74]	(0.911,8.1]	V	Y	N	N
015	(265,1.53e+03]	(1e+06,6.13e+06]	(-2.36,1.37e+03]	1	O	P	(2.74,360]	(8.1,90.1]	P	Y	N	N
015	(-0.523,265]	(6.13e+06,1.23e+07]	(1.37e+03,2.36e+03]		O	P	(-0.36,2.74]	(0.911,8.1]	V	Y	N	Y
015	(-0.523,265]	(6.13e+06,1.23e+07]	(1.37e+03,2.36e+03]	1	I	H	(-0.36,2.74]	(8.1,90.1]	P	Y	N	N
015	(-0.523,265]	(1e+06,6.13e+06]	(-2.36,1.37e+03]	1	I	H	(-0.36,2.74]	(0.911,8.1]	P	Y	N	N
015	(-0.523,265]	(1e+06,6.13e+06]	(-2.36,1.37e+03]	1	I	P	(2.74,360]	(0.911,8.1]	P	Y	Y	N
015	(-0.523,265]	(6.13e+06,1.23e+07]	(-2.36,1.37e+03]	1	O	P	(2.74,360]	(8.1,90.1]	V	Y	Y	N

Showing the first 1000 rows

Running the OneR model

The syntax to the `OneR` model should be familiar. The outcome variable `frisked` is specified on the left side of the formula (~) and the features are specified on the right side. As you will recall, the metacharacter (.) designates that <u>all</u> features will be used as predictors:

```
model <- OneR(train_data, frisked ~ ., verbose = TRUE)
summary(model)
```

The (partial) summary output displays the accuracy based upon selecting only <u>one</u> variable as a predictor along with its classification rate. The significant variables are starred.

The attribute and the accuracy metrics for the first 7 variables are shown next. Notice that once accuracy reaches 67.61% it does not decrease:

```
    Attribute  Accuracy
1 * sex         68.56%
2   eyecolor    67.68%
3   haircolr    67.62%
4   year        67.61%
4   ser_num     67.61%
4   datestop    67.61%
4   timestop    67.61%
```

The call to the function is shown in the log, and the Decision Tree rules are displayed.

```
Call:
OneR(data = train_data, formula = frisked ~ ., verbose = TRUE)

Rules:
If sex = F then frisked = N
If sex = M then frisked = Y
If sex = Z then frisked = Y

Accuracy:
11728 of 17105 instances classified correctly (68.56%)

Contingency table:
        sex
frisked     F       M     Z    Sum
     N   * 668     4822    50   5540
     Y     505  * 10968  * 92  11565
    Sum  1173    15790   142  17105
---
Maximum in each column: '*'

Pearson's Chi-squared test:
X-squared = 348.29, df = 2, p-value < 2.2e-16
```

Interpreting the output

The output from the summary gives a good sense of the importance of each variable as an individual predictor. All of the accuracy measures range from 67.61% to 68.56%, so there is no obvious one single variable which can predict being frisked much better than the others.

However, the top ranked variable is sex with a 68.56% accuracy rate. The one simple rule that will classify the outcome into frisked or nonfrisked is:

If sex is male or unknown, then the outcome was predicted correctly 68.56% of the time.

This is reflected in the following two manually calculated contingency tables, in which an asterisk * signifies a correct classification (the following background is green). I added the second contingency table manually, which gives percentages instead of the raw counts supplied by the output.

The following is a confusion matrix with counts and percentages:

frisked	F	M	Z	Sum	Total Con
N	668	4,822	50	5,540	Classified
Y	505	10,968	92	11,565	11,728
Sum	1,173	15,790	142	17,105	

frisked	F	M	Z	Sum	
N	4%	28%	0%	32%	69%
Y	3%	64%	1%	68%	
Sum	7%	92%	1%	17,105	

- If sex=**M**, then being frisked was correctly predicted **64%** of the time.
- If sex=**F**, then not being frisked was correctly predicted **4%** of the time.

Although this is a small percentage, you can see that males, in general, are stopped much more than females. You can also derive some conditional probabilities from this, in that, if you are a female, there is a 3/7 or 43% chance that you will be frisked. However, if you are a male, there is a 64/92 or 70% chance that you will be frisked.

If sex=**Z** (unknown), being frisked was correctly predicted 1% of the time.

Constructing new variables

Even though OneR works by finding the single best predictor, we can also try to improve the predictions by constructing some new variables and tricking OneR into thinking it is one variable.

In the code below we are creating new variables by combining attributes of single variables such ass of build, eyecolor, and hair color. After running the OneR model again, you can see that it helps a bit in terms of prediction accuracy and one of the new variables (eye_hair_build) is now ranked second.

This is a simple example of how you can perform "feature engineering".

```
tmp <- train_data
tmp$eye_hair_build <-
paste(train_data$eyecolor,train_data$haircolr,train_data$build)
tmp$weapon <-
paste(train_data$knifcuti,train_data$riflshot,train_data$pistol,train_data$
machgun,train_data$othrweap)
model <- OneR(tmp, frisked ~ ., verbose = TRUE)
```

```
     Attribute       Accuracy
1 *  sex             68.56%
2    eye_hair_build  68.07%
3    eyecolor        67.68%
4    haircolr        67.62%
```

Running the prediction on the test sample

The `eval_model` function applies the rules of the prediction to the test data, and also produces the confusion matrix, for both absolute counts, and relative percentages, so there is no need to calculate the percentages manually, as we did above.

Applying the model results on the test sample shows the accuracy to be similar to the training sample, which somewhat validates the results.

The error rate is the percentages of wrong classifications, which is equivalent to 1 minus the accuracy rate:

```
prediction <- predict(model, test_data,type="class")
#Evaluate prediction statistics

eval_model(prediction, test_data)
```

```
Confusion matrix (absolute):
          actual
prediction    N    Y  Sum
         N   153  122  275
         Y  1269 2722 3991
         Sum 1422 2844 4266

Confusion matrix (relative):
          actual
prediction    N    Y  Sum
         N  0.04 0.03 0.06
         Y  0.30 0.64 0.94
         Sum 0.33 0.67 1.00


Accuracy:
0.6739 (2875/4266)

Error rate:
0.3261 (1391/4266)
```

Another OneR example

This example uses the much larger diabetes dataset. Since most of the variables in this dataset are numeric, OneR can bin all of them:

1. First, read the Spark diabetes table using SQL, which has already been registered in a previous chapter.
2. Collect a 15% random sample of the data and assign it to an R (not Spark!) dataframe named "local".
3. Bin all of the available variables based upon their ability to predict the outcome and assign it to an R dataframe named "data":

```
library(OneR)
df = sql("SELECT outcome, age, mass, triceps, pregnant,
glucose, pressure, insulin, pedigree
FROM global_temp.df_view")

local = collect(sample(df, F,.15))

data <- optbin(local,outcome~.)
summary(data)
```

```
▶ (1) Spark Jobs

            age                  mass                    triceps
(-1.54,37.1]:118790    (12.4,35]:121754    (0.703,32.8]:128435
(37.1,74]   : 67698    (35,54.2]: 64734    (32.8,58.3] : 58053
        pregnant               glucose                 pressure
(-5.29,4.91]:117506    (38.9,139]:139019    (35.3,75.6]:114164
(4.91,13.8] : 68982    (139,220] : 47469    (75.6,112] : 72324
         insulin               pedigree        outcome
(-149,205]:131628    (-0.548,0.529]:111914    0:121724
(205,447] : 54860    (0.529,1.69]  : 74574    1: 64764
```

4. Run the `OneR` model using all of the variables to predict the outcome. Recall that the outcome is an indication of whether or not diabetes is present:

```
model <- OneR(data, outcome~., verbose = TRUE)
summary(model)

prediction <- predict(model, data)
```

5. Evaluate the prediction statistics. Observe that Glucose and insulin have much better single variable accuracy results than do the other predictors:

```
eval_model(prediction, data)
```

```
    Attribute Accuracy
1 * glucose   76.54%
2   insulin   72.25%
3   triceps   65.73%
4   age       65.27%
4   mass      65.27%
4   pregnant  65.27%
4   pressure  65.27%
4   pedigree  65.27%
---

Chosen attribute due to accuracy
and ties method (if applicable): '*'
```

The rules section

Now that we know the important variables, it is time to examine how the OneR package outputs the decision rules. Since glucose was deemed the single best predictor, the decision rule for predicting diabetes is shown under the Rules: section, and the optimal cutoff point (139) for glucose is displayed in the contingency table as shown below.

```
Call:
OneR(data = data, formula = outcome ~ ., verbose = TRUE)

Rules:
If glucose = (38.9,139] then outcome = 0
If glucose = (139,220]  then outcome = 1

Accuracy:
142741 of 186488 instances classified correctly (76.54%)

Contingency table:
      glucose
outcome (38.9,139] (139,220]     Sum
    0     * 108498      13226 121724
    1         30521   * 34243  64764
    Sum       139019     47469 186488
---
Maximum in each column: '*'

Pearson's Chi-squared test:
X-squared = 39311, df = 1, p-value < 2.2e-16
```

Now, look at the confusion matrix contingency tables-one for the absolute counts and the other for the relative percentages.

For our example, a glucose level greater or equal to 139 predicts diabetes in 18% of the total cases. However, note that most of the predictive power comes from predicting the nonevent. That is to say that 56% of the correct prediction comes from glucose reading of less than 139, which predicts the absence of diabetes. This is valuable in that it may lead to determine the factors which prevent diabetes, however we may also want to be interested in the the accuracy of a model which is able to predict diabetes as well.

This would involve digging deeper into the interactions of the variables, and would require a more sophisticated algorithm. However, OneR does offer an interesting framework for variable selection.

```
Confusion matrix (absolute):
          actual
prediction       0       1     Sum
         0  108498   30521  139019
         1   13226   34243   47469
       Sum  121724   64764  186488

Confusion matrix (relative):
          actual
prediction    0    1   Sum
         0  0.58 0.16 0.75
         1  0.07 0.18 0.25
       Sum  0.65 0.35 1.00

Accuracy:
0.7654 (142741/186488)

Error rate:
0.2346 (43747/186488)
```

Constructing a decision tree using Rpart

While OneR is very good at determining simple classification rules, it is not able to construct full decision trees. However, we can extract a sample from Spark and route it to any R decision tree algorithm, such as rpart.

First collect the sample

To illustrate this, let's first take a 50% sample of the stop and frisk dataframe. We also want to make sure that the amount of data we extract can be processed easily by base R, which has a memory limitation that is dependent upon the CPU size.

- The code below will first extract a 50% sample from Spark and store it in a local R dataframe named `dflocal`.
- Then it will run an `str()` command to verify the rowcount and the metadata:

```
dflocal = collect(sample(df, F,.50,123))
str(dflocal)
```

The output indicates that there are 11,311 rows, which is roughly 50% of the 22,563 rows from the Stop and Frisk data.

```
'data.frame':   11311 obs. of  113 variables:
$ year    : chr  "2015" "2015" "2015" "2015" ...
$ pct     : chr  "20" "20" "67" "68" ...
$ ser_num : int  41 39 122 9 141 2 1 5 2 1 ...
$ datestop: int  1292015 1292015 2062015 2142015 3142015 1012015 1012015 1012015 1012015 1012015 ...
$ timestop: int  1745 1745 2155 200 15 10 50 115 229 230 ...
$ recstat : chr  "1" "1" "1" "A" ...
$ inout   : chr  "O" "O" "O" "O" ...
$ trhsloc : chr  "P" "P" "P" "P" ...
$ perobs  : int  1 1 2 1 1 1 2 5 1 1 ...
$ crimsusp: chr  "MISD" "MISD" "FEL" "FEONY" ...
$ perstop : int  16 16 5 10 15 5 5 45 1 5 ...
$ typeofid: chr  "V" "V" "R" "V" ...
$ explnstp: chr  "Y" "Y" "Y" "Y" ...
$ othpers : chr  "Y" "Y" "N" "Y" ...
$ arstmade: chr  "N" "N" "N" "N" ...
$ arstoffn: chr  " " " " " " " " ...
$ sumissue: chr  "N" "N" "N" "N" ...
$ sumoffen: chr  " " " " " " " " ...
```

Decision tree using Rpart

We will run our `rpart` algorithm as a regression tree. Recall that a regression tree is used when the output variable is in numerical form, rather than nominal form. Before we do that, we need to map our frisked=Y/N to frisked=1/0 and specify `method="anova"` in the call.

The last line of code (`fit`) will print out the decision rules to the console as text.

The `height`, `sex`, `age`, and `city` parameters appear as the primary splits:

```
set.seed(123)
library(rpart)
dflocal$frisked_bin <- ifelse(dflocal$frisked=="Y",1,0)
fit <- rpart(frisked_bin ~ sex + age + weight + height + perstop + city ,
method="anova", maxdepth=3, cp=.001, data=dflocal)
fit
```

```
 chr [1:11311] "N" "N" "Y" "N" "Y" "Y" "Y" "Y" "Y" "Y" ...
 n= 11311

node), split, n, deviance, yval
      * denotes terminal node

1) root 11311 2482.374000 0.6747414
  2) sex=F 753   185.620200 0.4409031
    4) height< 65.5 418    98.988040 0.3851675 *
    5) height>=65.5 335    83.713430 0.5104478 *
  3) sex=M,Z 10558 2252.643000 0.6914188
    6) city=BROOKLYN,MANHATTAN,QUEENS,STATEN IS 8339 1841.411000 0.6708238
      12) age>=28.5 2908   683.906500 0.6217331 *
      13) age< 28.5 5431 1146.745000 0.6971092 *
    7) city=BRONX 2219   394.402000 0.7688148
      14) age>=60.5 26     6.346154 0.4230769 *
      15) age< 60.5 2193   384.911100 0.7729138 *
```

Plot the tree

It is much easier to look at a visual representation of a tree. So you will need to install `rpart.plot` (if you haven't already) so that you are able to view it.

We can see that the first rule corresponds to the primary rule (splitting on Gender), which was generated by the `OneR` package earlier in this chapter.

```
devtools::install_github("cran/rpart.plot")
library(rpart.plot)
rpart.plot(fit,cex=.75)
```

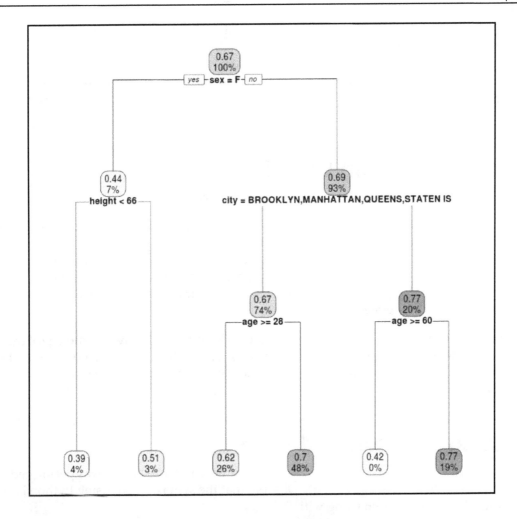

Running an alternative model in Python

In this example, we ran a decision tree in R by extracting a sample from the Spark dataframe and running the tree model using base R. While that is perfectly acceptable (since it forced you to think about sampling), in many instances it would be more efficient to run the models directly on the Spark dataframe using a `MLlib` package or equivalent.

For the version of Spark, you should be working with (2.1); decision tree algorithms are not available to be run under R. Fortunately, native Spark decision trees are already implemented in Python and Scala. We will illustrate the example using Python so that you can see that there are options available. If you will be following algorithm development in Spark you will find that often algorithms are written first in Scala, since that is the native Spark language.

Running a Python Decision Tree

Here are some notes on the Python decision tree code which appears below.

For the first code chunk, notice the "magic" directive in the first line of the code. The magic directive begins with '%' and specifies which language or API you will be using. Therefore, since we will be using Python instead or R, we need to specify `%python` as the first line. That is because the notebook was originally set up as an R notebook. When mixing languages, you need to specify the language used as the first line, unless you are writing in the default notebook language.

For those of you who are not familiar with Python, the import directives at the top of the code import the needed libraries and modules, which are to be used by Python, similar to how the library function is used in R. If you do not supply import directives, you will usually get errors.

Reading the Stop and Frisk table

The first code chunk will read the StopFrisk dataframe, similar to how it was performed earlier in this section using `spark.sql`. Observe that the syntax for sql using Python is very similar to what we have been using with R.

Within the SQL call, the outcome variable frisked is mapped to a binary variable using a CASE statement. The reason for doing this is that the `MLLib` algorithm handles integer data much better than character data. If using character data, it often needs to be mapped to an integer or a labeled point.

The resulting dataframe (df2) is then displayed using the show(5) function, which is the Python equivalent to the R head(df2,5) function:

```python
%python

from pyspark.mllib.tree import DecisionTree, DecisionTreeModel
from pyspark.mllib.util import MLUtils
import pyspark.mllib
import pyspark.mllib.regression
from pyspark.mllib.regression import LabeledPoint
from pyspark.sql.functions import *
from pyspark.ml.feature import StringIndexer

df2 = spark.sql("SELECT case when frisked='Y' THEN 1 else 0 END as
frisked2,case when sex='M' THEN 0 else 1 END as sex2, race, age, weight
FROM stopfrisk")

df2.show(5)
```

```
▶ (1) Spark Jobs

+--------+----+----+---+------+
|frisked2|sex2|race|age|weight|
+--------+----+----+---+------+
|       1|   0|   W| 33|   190|
|       1|   0|   B| 14|   140|
|       0|   0|   B| 14|   140|
|       0|   0|   B| 14|   180|
|       0|   0|   B| 13|   160|
+--------+----+----+---+------+
only showing top 5 rows
```

Indexing the classification features

Indexing is used to optimize data access and supply the parameters to specific machine learning algorithms in an acceptable format.

We will be incorporating the race variable into the decision tree model, so the first step is to determine what the different values of race are. We will do this by again using SQL to count the frequency by race. Notice we can say either "Group by Race" or "Group by 1" which is a shorthand reference to the first column specified in the select statement (which is race):

```
%python
dfx = spark.sql("SELECT race,count(*) FROM stopfrisk group by 1")
dfx.show()
```

Observe that there are eight values, **Q, B, U, Z, A, W, I,** and **P**:

```
▶ (5) Spark Jobs
+----+--------+
|race|count(1)|
+----+--------+
|   Q|    5090|
|   B|   11950|
|   U|     122|
|   Z|     298|
|   A|    1103|
|   W|    2514|
|   I|      77|
|   P|    1409|
+----+--------+
```

Next, use `indexer.fit(df2) transform`. This will map a string factor (`race`) to a numeric index (`race_indexed`):

```
%python
indexer = StringIndexer(inputCol="race", outputCol="race_indexed")
df3 = indexer.fit(df2).transform(df2)
df3.show(15)
#drop race for the final dataframe
df4 = df3.drop("race")
```

Look at the pairs of race and race_indexed to see how a number will be used in place of a character:

```
▶ (2) Spark Jobs

+--------+----+----+---+------+------------+
|frisked2|sex2|race|age|weight|race_indexed|
+--------+----+----+---+------+------------+
|       1|   0|   W| 33|   190|         2.0|
|       1|   0|   B| 14|   140|         0.0|
|       0|   0|   B| 14|   140|         0.0|
|       0|   0|   B| 14|   180|         0.0|
|       0|   0|   B| 13|   160|         0.0|
|       0|   0|   W| 13|   130|         2.0|
|       1|   0|   B| 25|   160|         0.0|
|       1|   0|   B| 15|   150|         0.0|
|       1|   0|   B| 23|   160|         0.0|
|       0|   0|   W| 16|   150|         2.0|
|       1|   0|   B| 30|   160|         0.0|
|       1|   0|   B| 18|   160|         0.0|
|       1|   0|   Q| 48|   160|         1.0|
|       1|   0|   B| 16|   160|         0.0|
|       1|   0|   B| 26|   155|         0.0|
+--------+----+----+---+------+------------+
only showing top 15 rows
```

We are looking at just a few records of the output. What we really want to see are all the values of race, along with their counts. We can use the CountDistinct clause in PySpark SQL to obtain that:

```python
%python
df3.registerTempTable("df3")

# Perform the same query as the DataFrame above and return ``explain``
countDistinctDF_sql = sqlContext.sql("SELECT race,race_indexed, count(race) FROM df3 GROUP BY race, race_indexed")
countDistinctDF_sql.show()
```

All of the values of race and its corresponding index are then displayed, along with the counts:

```
▶ (5) Spark Jobs

+----+------------+-----------+
|race|race_indexed|count(race)|
+----+------------+-----------+
|   W|         2.0|       2514|
|   B|         0.0|      11950|
|   P|         3.0|       1409|
|   Z|         5.0|        298|
|   Q|         1.0|       5090|
|   A|         4.0|       1103|
|   I|         7.0|         77|
|   U|         6.0|        122|
+----+------------+-----------+
```

We still need a codebook to decode the values of race, to make sure we understand what they designate.

```
race
        A               ASIAN/PACIFIC ISLANDER
        B               BLACK
        I                AMERICAN INDIAN/ALASKAN NATIVE
        P               BLACK-HISPANIC
        Q             WHITE-HISPANIC
        W           WHITE
        X               UNKNOWN
        Z               OTHER
```

Mapping to an RDD

The decision tree algorithm we will be using is from the standard Spark `MLlib` library. This implementation requires that the input be formatted in labeled point format. Labeled points assist in specifying which of the variables are target variables and which ones are features.

For this example, the target variable (frisked2) is the first variable listed (we will call the first variable column 0), so the target variable is designated as such within the LabeledPoint call as `line[0]`.

The independent variables, or features, are contained within the remaining columns and are specified as `line[1:]`. This is shorthand for column 1 and all the following columns until there are no more.

When referring to features, they are also numbered sequentially in the model, corresponding to the order in which they appear in the dataframe. For our model, they have the following nomenclature:

- Feature 0 - Sex
- Feature 1 - Age
- Feature 2 - Weight
- Feature 3 - Race

Since this is an RDD-based model, first map the dataframe to an RDD using labeled points, by first specifying the target variable, followed by the features:

```python
%python
rdd1 = df4.rdd.map(lambda line:LabeledPoint(line[0],[line[1:]]))
```

Print a portion of the resultant RDD. Debugging the output from an RDD can be difficult; however, you can see from the output that the first key pair of each labeled point is a 1 or 0. The second key pair (enclosed in brackets) is a vector of features, which you can match up to the predictors and scrutinize to make sure your labeled points are correct:

```
print rdd1.take(5)

(1) Spark Jobs
[LabeledPoint(1.0, [0.0,33.0,190.0,2.0]), LabeledPoint(1.0,
[0.0,14.0,140.0,0.0]), LabeledPoint(0.0, [0.0,14.0,140.0,0.0]),
LabeledPoint(0.0, [0.0,14.0,180.0,0.0]), LabeledPoint(0.0,
[0.0,13.0,160.0,0.0])]
```

Specifying the decision tree model

Remember we discussed the mapping of categorical features? Use the categorical features info parameter to specify which of the variables are truly categorical, that is, not just mapped to an index.

For our example, Frisked has two levels, so it is specified as 0:2 (the target variable with 2 levels) and Race has 8 levels, so it is specified as 3:8 (the third feature having 8 levels):

Set other parameters appropriate to the decision tree model:

- `numClasses`: This applies to the number of outcomes; in our case, it is 2.
- `maxDepth`: How deep would you like the decision tree to go? For illustrative purposes, we will set it to 2 levels deep, but for real-world problems, you should attempt to go a bit deeper. Remember, if you go too deep, the model will overfit.
- `maxBins`: In sparkR, you can go no more than 32 bins.

Now we are set and we can run our model. We will create a simple tree, no more than two levels deep:

```
%python

model_train =
DecisionTree.trainClassifier(rdd1,numClasses=2,maxDepth=2,maxBins=32,
categoricalFeaturesInfo={0:2,3:8}  )
```

After the model has completed, print it as a text file using the `DebugString()` function. That will give you your decision tree rules:

```
print(model_train.toDebugString())
```

```
▶ (6) Spark Jobs

DecisionTreeModel classifier of depth 2 with 7 nodes
  If (feature 0 in {1.0})
   If (feature 2 <= 154.0)
    Predict: 0.0
   Else (feature 2 > 154.0)
    Predict: 1.0
  Else (feature 0 not in {1.0})
   If (feature 3 in {5.0,6.0,2.0,7.0,3.0,4.0})
    Predict: 1.0
   Else (feature 3 not in {5.0,6.0,2.0,7.0,3.0,4.0})
    Predict: 1.0
```

In order to code what feature 0,1,2 and 3 mean, we will need to map the feature number to the feature names, and the resulting value of the features using the codebook and SQL code we ran earlier.

We can manually condense the output to simple English descriptions especially since the decision tree output sometimes gives nonsensical or redundant rules. See if you can spot it in the preceding code!

```
If sex is equal to 1 (Female)
   if weight <= 154 then subject was NOT frisked
```

```
    Else if weight > 154 then Subject WAS frisked
If sex is NOT equal to 1 (Male)
    BOTH race paths lead to Subject WAS frisked
```

Producing a larger tree

Sometimes with small trees, the decision rules can be too trivial or obvious. In this can, it often makes sense to increase the number of nodes in the tree. Here we will be generating a tree 15 levels deep:

```python
%python
rdd1 = df4.rdd.map(lambda line:LabeledPoint(line[0],[line[1:]]))
rdd1.take(15)
model_train =
DecisionTree.trainClassifier(rdd1,numClasses=2,maxDepth=15,maxBins=32,categ
oricalFeaturesInfo={0:2,3:8}  )
print(model_train.toDebugString())
```

Again, some of the rules look like they are redundant, so more work would be needed to transform this output to meaningful business rules.

```
▶ (20) Spark Jobs

DecisionTreeModel classifier of depth 15 with 4291 nodes
  If (feature 0 in {1.0})
   If (feature 2 <= 154.0)
    If (feature 1 <= 54.0)
     If (feature 2 <= 129.0)
      If (feature 1 <= 37.0)
       If (feature 3 in {5.0,1.0,6.0,2.0,3.0,4.0})
        If (feature 1 <= 23.0)
         If (feature 3 in {4.0})
          If (feature 1 <= 16.0)
           If (feature 1 <= 15.0)
            Predict: 0.0
           Else (feature 1 > 15.0)
            Predict: 1.0
          Else (feature 1 > 16.0)
           If (feature 1 <= 22.0)
            If (feature 1 <= 18.0)
             If (feature 1 <= 17.0)
              Predict: 0.0
             Else (feature 1 > 17.0)
              If (feature 2 <= 117.0)
```

Visual trees

Unless you are able to visualize the output, the decision tree rules can get difficult to interpret. Unless you implement the decision tree in the Scala language (which has a tree visualization method using the databricks Display command), some of your options are:

First parse the Spark output object to JSON format and then input using D3.js to visualize the tree. There are some prebuilt packages on Github, which can assist you in doing this.

Write the RDD you create to a file, input the RDD in Scala, and run DecisionTreeClassifier(). Then, fit the model and use the databricks display command on the model to display the tree.

Comparing train and test decision trees

There is no prediction method for decision trees. However, we can still generate trees from both test and training datasets and compare them for reasonableness.

Using our diabetes example, we can first run a Pyspark decision tree on the training data. Again, our outcome variable is the first column (#0), which is referenced in the LabeledPoint reference, and the features are designated by all the variables that follow (1:):

```python
%python

df = spark.sql("SELECT outcome, age, mass, triceps, pregnant, glucose,
pressure, insulin, pedigree FROM global_temp.df_view")

#sqlDF.show()

rdd1 = df.rdd.map(lambda line:LabeledPoint(line[0],[line[1:]]))

model_train =
DecisionTree.trainClassifier(rdd1,numClasses=2,maxDepth=2,maxBins=32,
categoricalFeaturesInfo={})

print(model_train.toDebugString())
```

The decision tree has identified features 4 (`glucose`) and 6 (`insulin`) as the two most important splitting variables. These two variables are a good choice since they both affect blood sugar levels:

```
 ▶ (6) Spark Jobs

DecisionTreeModel classifier of depth 2 with 7 nodes
  If (feature 4 <= 144.2881556590044)
   If (feature 6 <= 244.2896167908184)
    Predict: 0.0
   Else (feature 6 > 244.2896167908184)
    Predict: 1.0
  Else (feature 4 > 144.2881556590044)
   If (feature 6 <= 233.49668637807514)
    Predict: 1.0
   Else (feature 6 > 233.49668637807514)
    Predict: 1.0
```

Now, run the same code on the testing data. The results are similar; however, the tree reverses the order of features 6 and 4. In the real world that would be acceptable, but if we produced a completely different tree, we would need to look at why the two models differed and try to reconcile the different versions of the model. If you could not explain the differences, you might consider reworking or even abandoning the model if there were gross discrepancies:

```
%python

test = spark.sql("SELECT outcome, age, mass, triceps, pregnant, glucose,
pressure, insulin, pedigree FROM global_temp.test_view")

rdd2 = test.rdd.map(lambda line:LabeledPoint(line[0],[line[1:]]))

model_test =
DecisionTree.trainClassifier(rdd2,numClasses=2,maxDepth=2,maxBins=32,
categoricalFeaturesInfo={})

#model.save(spark, "/myDecisionTreeClassificationModel")

print(model_test.toDebugString())
```

```
▸ (6) Spark Jobs

DecisionTreeModel classifier of depth 2 with 7 nodes
  If (feature 6 <= 258.7717216438844)
   If (feature 4 <= 134.95577326132448)
    Predict: 0.0
   Else (feature 4 > 134.95577326132448)
    Predict: 1.0
  Else (feature 6 > 258.7717216438844)
   If (feature 6 <= 303.47523507134343)
    Predict: 1.0
   Else (feature 6 > 303.47523507134343)
    Predict: 1.0
```

Summary

This concludes this chapter, and this book. I started off by saying that this was a different kind of predictive analytics book, and I covered many different kinds of topics, from both a technical and conceptual viewpoint. I hope that you have learned a lot from this and that it has given you some new algorithms to use, and has taught you something about some 'older' tools, such as SQL, which are very capable of doing some of the heavy lifting that is sometimes needed. I also tried to emphasis 'small data', metadata, and sampling in the hopes that that will aid you in understand your data better, just by virtue of being able to look at individual pieces separately. I also hope that some of the material in the book will enable you to work collaboratively with different team members having different skill sets. That could be anything from someone who is an expert in optimizing code, or someone who is an expert in statistics, or even someone who has worked with all of the key people in your business and is able to communicate business needs and wants. Yes, it is great to be able to do it all, but Predictive Analytics is as much about listening, as it as about doing.

Much of what I discuss is applicable to any type of analytics projects you will be involved in, regardless of language or platform choice. That is why I wanted to include some cloud computing and SQL examples at the end, as well as a Python example, to demonstrate that Predictive Analytics practitioners can band together with different skill sets and integrate their work within the 6 steps that were discussed earlier in this book in order to implement a successful analytics methodology and framework.

Happy modeling!

Index

C

D

P

parallel computing 417
parallel processing 475
partitional clustering 212
physical transactions file
  creating 343
  reading 344
  rules subsets, creating 349
  rules, plotting 348
  text clustering 351
Pima Indians diabetes dataset
  about 423
  column means, calculating 435
  correlation matrices, calculating 433
  extracting 425
  imputations (reader exercise), verifying 431
  missing values complete 432
  missing values, inputing 430
  missing values, verifying 429
  outcomes, comparing 427
  output, examining 425
  output, from str() function 426
  output, from summary() function 426
plots
  interactive game 188
  Normal Q-Q 188
  residuals, versus leverage 188
  scale location 188
Poisson model 75
predictive analytics
  data analytics/research 17
  data engineering 17
  management 17
  reference link 9
  roles 13
  skills 13
  team data science 17
  terms 14
  used, in healthcare 11
  used, in marketing 11
  used, in other industries 11
predictive model
  about 31
  code description 33

script, saving 34
Principal Component Analysis (PCA)
  about 83, 148
  US Arrests, example 149
  using 149
probability functions
  churn dataframe, creating 243
  churner and non-churners, recombining 247
  no churn dataframe, creating 243
  simulated variables, creating 244
  simulated variables, verifying 244
  used, for generating data 241
projects
  setting up 22
  subfolders, setting up 22
pruning 198
pseudo R-square 490
Python
  decision tree, executing 529, 530
  Stop and Frisk table, reading 530

R

R Commander (Rcmdr) 23
R console 29
R interface
  Spark SQL, issuing through 458
R packages
  about 40
  correlation plot, generating 468
  executing 467
  pairs function, using 467
  stargazer package 40
  stargazer package, installing 41
  work, saving 43
R script
  about 34
  code description 36
  predict function 38
  prediction errors, examining 38
R
  about 19
  CRAN 19
  data, exporting from Spark 466
  exploring 20
  installation 20